Certain Lives

Certain Lives

The compelling story of the hope, tragedy and
triumph of three generations of women

Margaret Reeson

With best wishes,

Margaret Reeson.

AN ALBATROSS BOOK

© Margaret Reeson 1989

Published in Australia and New Zealand by
Albatross Books Pty Ltd
PO Box 320, Sutherland
NSW 2232, Australia
in the United States of America by
Albatross Books
PO Box 131, Claremont
CA 91711, USA
and in the United Kingdom by
Lion Publishing
Sandy Lane West, Littlemore
Oxford, England

First edition 1989
Reprinted 1990, 1992

National Library of Australia
Cataloguing-in-Publication data

Reeson, Margaret
Certain lives

ISBN 0 86760 086 1 (Albatross)
ISBN 0 7459 1297 4 (Lion)

1. Rootes, Anna. 2. Playford, Mary, 3. Higman,
Grace. 4. Women pioneers — New South Wales —
Biography. 5. Mothers and daughters — New South
Wales — Biography. 6. New South Wales — Social
conditions. 7. Pioneers — New South Wales —
Biography. 8. New South Wales — Biography.
I. Title.

994.4'009'92

Cover illustration: Arthur Boothroyd
Typeset by Leonard Communications, Sydney
Printed by Singapore National Printers, Singapore

Contents

Family Tree
Anna, Mary and Grace's family

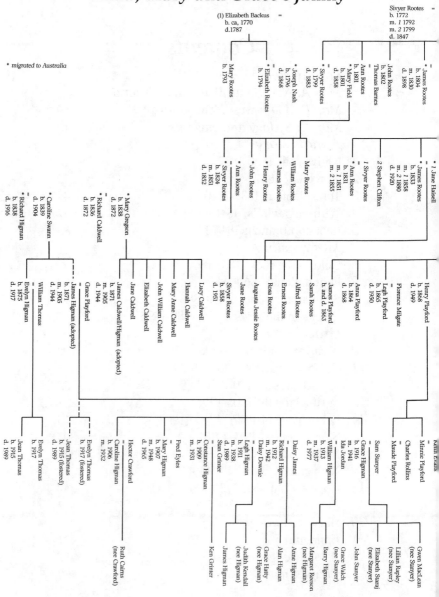

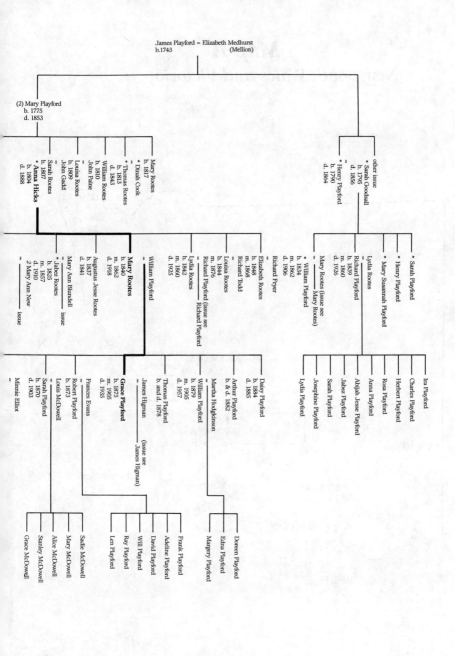

James Playford = Elizabeth Medhurst
b.1743   (Mellion)

(2) Mary Playford
b. 1775
d. 1853

other issue

* Sarah Goodsall
b. 1795
d. 1856

* Henry Playford
b. 1790
d. 1864

Lydia Rootes

* Richard Playford
b. 1839
m. 1860
d. 1926

* Mary Susannah Playford

* Henry Playford

* Sarah Playford

Jabez Playford

Abijah Jesse Playford

Anna Playford

Rosa Playford

Herbert Playford

Charles Playford

Ira Playford

Mary Rootes
b. 1817

* Thomas Rootes
b. 1813
d. 1843

* Dinah Cook

Louisa Rootes
b. 1809

John Gadd

William Rootes
b. 1810

John Paine

Sarah Rootes
b. 1807

* Anna Hicks
b. 1804
d. 1888

Mary Rootes (issue see
—————— Mary Rootes)

* William Playford
b. 1834
m. 1862
d. 1906

Richard Fryer

Elizabeth Rootes
b. 1848
m. 1868

Richard Todd

Louisa Rootes
b. 1844
m. 1876

Richard Playford (issue see
—————— Richard Playford)

Lydia Rootes
b. 1842
m. 1860
d. 1925

William Playford

Mary Rootes
b. 1840
m. 1862
d. 1918

* Jabez Rootes
b. 1825
m. 1857
d. 1910
2 Mary Ann New

=
issue

Mary Ann Blundell

* Jabez Rootes
b. 1825
issue

Augustus Jesse Rootes
b. 1837
d. 1841

Frances Evans

Grace Playford
b. 1875
m. 1905
d. 1935

James Higman
——————— (issue see
James Higman)

Thomas Playford
b. and d. 1878

William Playford
b. 1879
m. 1905
d. 1957

Martha Hodgkinson

Arthur Playford
b. & d. 1882

Daisy Playford
b. 1884
d. 1885

Minnie Elliot
=

Grace McDowell

Stanley McDowell
b. 1870
d. 1903

Sarah Playford
b. 1825
m. 1857
d. 1910

Louis McDowell

Alice McDowell

Mary McDowell

Sadie McDowell

Robert Playford
b. 1873

Len Playford

Ray Playford

Will Playford

David Playford

Adeline Playford

Frank Playford

Margery Playford

Edna Playford

Doreen Playford

Lydia Playford

Josephine Playford

Sarah Playford

Map A
New South Wales and Victoria

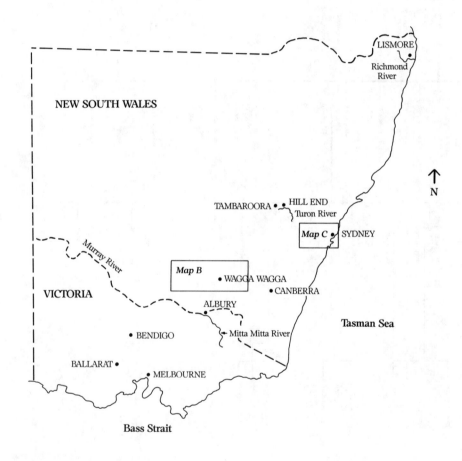

LISMORE

Richmond
River

NEW SOUTH WALES

N

TAMBAROORA • • HILL END
Turon River

Map C • SYDNEY

Murray River

Map B
• WAGGA WAGGA

• CANBERRA

VICTORIA

ALBURY

Tasman Sea

• BENDIGO
← Mitta Mitta River

BALLARAT •

• MELBOURNE

Bass Strait

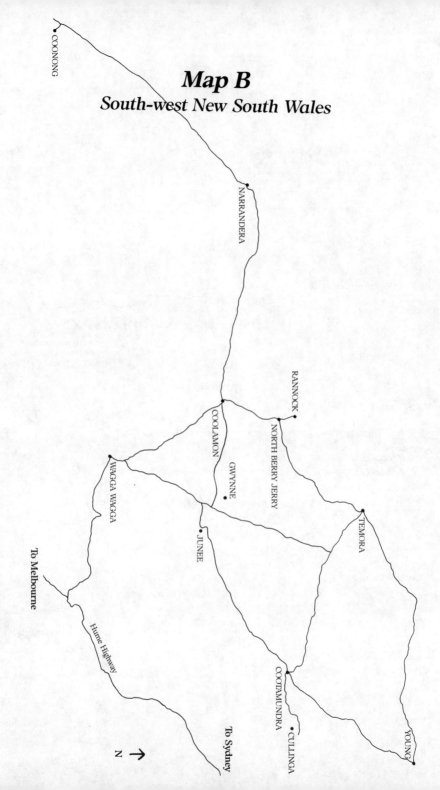

Map B
South-west New South Wales

COONONG

NARRANDERA

RANNOCK

COOLAMON

NORTH BERRY JERRY

GWYNNE

WAGGA WAGGA

TEMORA

JUNEE

To Melbourne

Hume Highway

COOTAMUNDRA

CULLINGA

YOUNG

To Sydney

N →

Map C
Sydney and environs

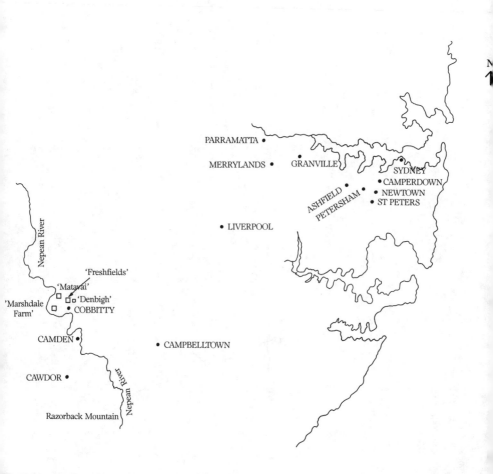

PARRAMATTA •

MERRYLANDS •   GRANVILLE •

SYDNEY
• CAMPERDOWN
ASHFIELD •   • NEWTOWN
PETERSHAM •   • ST PETERS

• LIVERPOOL

Nepean River

'Freshfields'
'Matavai' □
□□ 'Denbigh'
'Marshdale □   • COBBITTY
Farm'

CAMDEN •

• CAMPBELLTOWN

CAWDOR •

Nepean River

Razorback Mountain

Anna's story

1
Native soil
1830-1837

IF IT HAD NOT BEEN for the child's eager hand tugging her on, Anna would have turned and fled. Walking up the gangway, briefly poised over water between wharf and ship, between home and the unknown, her feet stumbled on the boards and she came close to falling. All the nightmares of many nights over the past months rose up to mock her. She wanted to shout, 'I'm not going! I won't. I want to go home!'

The little boy pulled her hand. 'Come on, Mamma. I want to see the ship. Come!'

Ahead of her was small Ann, her oldest child, struggling along with a bundle too large for her six-year-old arms. Behind pressed her husband James, balancing their trunk on broad shoulders, with other bundles festooned around him, looking harassed and a little impatient. Other passengers jostled behind him and beyond them again was the activity of the Portsmouth dockside.

'Keep moving along, Anna,' James urged.

There was no way of retreat. Choking on the words 'I can't', knowing that her husband could not hear her, knowing that the time to refuse to migrate to Australia had gone, Anna hitched her two-year-old higher on her hip and let small Jamie pull her across the last steps of the gangway onto the deck of the *Augusta Jessie*. It was June 1837.

If anyone had asked her what might upset her world, she would have said, 'The cholera... or maybe the burnings... or perhaps it could be my James without regular work this long time.' But nobody asked her the question and she did not ask it of herself. Why, indeed, should anything change? She knew that there had always been plagues, James was only one of many without work in the village and, even if the men rebelled from time to time, the rich always had their way in the end. A family struggled through.

Then James Rootes brought home the pamphlet. That night in the winter over a year ago, he sat crouched beside the hearth, straining his eyes to read in the flickering firelight. Anna paid no attention. Her man read every printed page he could get his hands on, proud that both of them had learned the art of reading at their East Sussex village school. She had no way of knowing that the innocent paper was to be an instrument which would change their world forever. Anna edged around her husband to reach the simmering pot of broth suspended over the fire. She poked discontentedly at the broth with her wooden spoon, dislodging a few lumps of potato and turnip and sinking them under the steaming fluid.

'There's not much for our soup again,' she muttered. 'Are you sure you couldn't trap a rabbit one night, just for the children?'

His voice was sharp, defensive. 'Do you want to see me transported for poaching, woman?'

She said no more. They both knew that poaching rabbits or game from the surrounding fields and woods was out of the question. It was not for want of game; rabbits often destroyed her vegetable garden. But bird, beast and fish were the property of the local peer and the squire up at the manor house, and were guarded zealously by gamekeepers. Anna knew what could happen to those who committed the double sin of being both poor and stealing game to feed their families; she had seen the agony of a family whose breadwinner was snatched from them and sent to the penal colony of Australia. Even if James had not his own strong moral resistance to what was viewed as stealing, the risks were too great.

Scooping the thin vegetable broth into the bowls, Anna gathered the little ones around the table and called James. After they had bowed their heads to thank God for their meal and the little ones were cheerfully crumbling their mother's good dark bread to sop up their broth, her husband spoke again.

'You know that poaching isn't the answer for us, don't you? — even if I wasn't caught . . . But they keep on taking everything away — our work, fair wages, the chance to own a little bit of land. God only knows where it will end. Will we have to give up in the end and admit we are paupers? Will we be forced to go to live in the workhouse?'

Anna watched the tightness of his square jaw, his bushy eyebrows meeting in an anxious frown. He was a strong man, a capable workman, reliable, intelligent, willing to work hard. Yet he was afraid. She wanted to put out her hand to touch him, to comfort him, but somehow she knew that it was her very presence and the presence of his three children that made him so afraid. In her mind she saw a brief picture of him trying to swim, but being dragged under by the weight of Ann and Jamie and baby Jabez, with her clinging more fiercely and demandingly than them all.

The bowls were empty and there was no more to offer for today. She stood up to begin gathering the bowls and preparing the children for bed. Tomorrow James would try again to find work; maybe he'd be successful but, after years of trying and failing more often than not, she hadn't much confidence. Surely there must be winter work somewhere for some of the men, even if the new machines had stolen much of it, she thought.

Anna was stooping over the narrow bed where the three children lay when James threw out one more statement. It was as if he couldn't say it to her face.

'I've been reading,' he said, and she heard the rustle of the pamphlet in his hand. 'There's a new scheme that might be the answer. We could emigrate. To Australia.'

Snow was drifting down onto the roofs and hedges as Anna hurried along the road which ran through the village of Northiam. The empty bucket swung from cold fingers as she dragged her shawl up over head and shoulders and lowered her head into the floating whiteness. Anna did not need to look up as she walked to fill her bucket at the parish pump. She had known every bend in the road since childhood: every cottage, every roadside tree, the school where the road forked and the Six Bells coaching inn opposite it, the village green and the very cobbles of the highway slicing through the village where travellers passed on their way from London to Rye. Beyond the village to the north, the River Rother wound slowly along its path through the marshlands dividing Northiam in Sussex from its neighbours in Kent. Now, in the bite of winter, the Rother marshes had flooded and were frozen over, and the chill of wind off ice blew up the slope to the village along the ridgetop, numbing Anna's fingers as she pumped water into her bucket.

Walking back, her cold hands awkward on the wooden bucket and, trying not to spill any splashes of water on her skirts or slip on the slush of the road, she observed her own house with fresh eyes. A layer of snow crusted the high curved ridge and had slipped off the steep pitch of the timber shingles to fall thickly under her windows. A faint glimmer of firelight shone through the diamond-paned glass, drawing her home.

The other houses of the street had been there all her life and throughout the lives of her parents and grandparents and many generations beyond that: thatch and shingle rooftops, half-timbered houses with dark wood patterning white walls, white-painted Sussex timber cottages tucked behind snowy hedges, the tiny Smugglers Cottage with its narrow one-up-one-down. Every house had its own story, stories retold to every new generation, stories which stretched back into time two hundred years, five hundred years, even fables reaching back a thousand years to Saxon times. Anna had been born in Northiam and so had James, and she had never dreamed they might ever leave. Yet even as she hurried home with her bucket, she passed the terrace of five cottages. This was the Workhouse, the unhappy place where the very old, the alone, the mad and the paupers of the village were given the thin charity of the parish. She shivered – and it was not only because of wind off icy marshes.

Behind her she heard a clatter of hooves and she stepped aside to let the coach pass by. A spray of muddy water flew up from the spinning wheels, damping her gown, and she looked up at the people huddled together on the roof of the coach, frozen from the long ride in bleak weather, thankful to be in sight of warmth and refuge at the Six Bells. The passing of the coach had never disturbed her before – she always knew that she had no need to travel on it – but now the sight of weary travellers climbing down into the stable yard of the Six Bells with their baggage had the power to upset her strangely.

Anna pushed quickly through her own door, shutting it to keep out the cold. The children had colds and the misty rain and frequent fogs made them miserable in the cold weather. James was gone for the day, to work with his brother at the cobbling trade, trying to earn a little money through the winter months when the landowners didn't hire many labourers. Little Ann was sniffling a little, but she had managed to rock baby Jabez off to sleep for her mother.

The mother threw more wood on the fire in the wide stone hearth and sat down at her spinning wheel. The wheel spun smoothly as her foot kept up its even movement on the treadle. Through her fingers flowed the fleece, twisting from the wrinkled texture of Southdown wool into the smooth thread of yarn, winding and winding, leaving her hands soft and oily. Her fingers knew their business well and she had no need to keep her mind on the work. Beyond the blurring wheel the fire crackled on the hearth and at last she allowed herself to think about the thing which James had said, the unthinkable thing which might jolt their lives out of the familiar path they had expected to follow.

Emigrate to Australia... Where was Australia? Anna tried to picture a distance which would take a person to the far side of the globe, but the old woman who had taught at their village school had known little more about the shape of the earth than her students, and Anna only knew that it was very far. London was far away, fifty-six miles so they said, and their neighbour the carrier set out with his wagon on Mondays and was on the road till he came home on Fridays. But she had never been there, nor had James. She had visited Rye on the coast and that too had meant staying for a night in a coaching inn – it seemed a very long way. She had watched vessels out of London plying up the Channel, travelling she knew not where. Beyond the Channel lay France, and the villagers knew well the stories of France from neighbours who had sailed to fight there in successive generations of battles between the French and the English, right back to the days when the Normans had fought the Saxons here in their own fields of Sussex and Kent. If they had not travelled to France to fight, they had gone secretly to smuggle contraband tobacco, wines, brandy or lace and to Anna the distance to France seemed far indeed. But Australia? People said that one was on board ship for months!

Leave Northiam – no, the idea was impossible. All their family was here and in neighbouring villages: elderly parents, all the brothers and sisters and their families, cousins and second cousins. All their friends were here: the neighbours of the village, the friends of the Methodist chapel and the Church of St Mary. Their ancestors' graves were here. Life was hard, but surely not so terrible that they should leave.

A stick on the fire shifted and dropped, suddenly sending a shower of sparks and flames flying up the chimney. With her fingers still guiding the fleece onto the spindle, the eye of her imagination saw that other fire the year they were married, and other fiery blazes since, and she began to feel the beginnings of understanding.

She remembered that time. The spring of 1830 was a beautiful one, and she remembered the time of their wedding as a rainbow of pink and lilac, blue and gold. She and James had known each other all their lives, born in the same village in the same December twenty-five years earlier. They learned to read and write at the same charity school, lived in the same village street, worshipped God in the same church and, when the little Methodist chapel was built during their growing-up years, they were part of that first Sunday School, too. They had wanted to be married for a long time, but James had been struggling to earn enough as sometime cobbler and farm labourer. Anna the bride was sure that her James could do anything, match anyone, and delighted in their tiny cottage and the joy of being man and wife at last.

At harvest time, she worked in the warm meadows with sleeves turned back and wide bonnet shading her face from the sun, tying up sheaves of oats, tilting each armful up against others to form standing stooks. Following the reapers across the fields, she was very aware of her own body aching from the hours of stooping and carrying, but young and healthy, strong and vital with energy and hope. Just ahead of her, his broad shoulders swinging with the sweep of his hook into the standing grain, was her James, her beloved, his workman's smock darkened across the shoulders with a stain of sweat and his face hidden under his hat. The whiskery beard of the grain tickled her face as she embraced another sheaf and she found herself laughing aloud at the delight of being alive and being in love with a good man. The days of harvest were long, the two of them rising before the first light of the sun and working till the late summer dusk finally gave way to night, but her pleasure overcame the deep ache of her limbs and the pink of sunburned cheeks. 'When the harvest is over,' she decided, 'I'll tell him – I'm nearly sure that I'm carrying his child.'

When the harvesters dropped down in the shade of a hedge in the heat of the day to share their bread and cheese, she sat near James, urging him to try her loaf, holding his broad hands in her own for a moment – 'to see if you are getting any blisters from the scythe', so she said.

It was while they were harvesting that the rumours began to run among the workmen.

'Have you heard?' they said, 'Have you heard about some workmen in Kent and what they did to the new machinery? One of the squires had put in one of those new machines, a great thing all metal which threshes the grain with hardly a man to work it. What about our winter work if we can't get work threshing?'

'What did they do, then?'

The slow voice went on. 'They broke it. Smashed the thing. That threshing machine won't be taking any men's work this winter. . .'

'They are paying us less and less, and prices are rising more and more. If they give machines the work that men should be doing, they won't need to pay us at all, and then what is to happen to us and our families?'

No-one knew the answer. Anxiety began to build among the men. Life for families of working people had been growing more and more difficult over the years since the Enclosures Act had put common land in the hands of the wealthy and come close to forcing the common people into slavery, unable to buy land. For years, as many as one man in three in the village was out of work and things were growing worse. More and more families had left the villages to search for work in factories and towns; the spectre of inhuman machines, whirling wheels, drumming metal, belching steam cast a shadow across the land, even across the party of harvesters, men and girls, eating their food under the hedge in Sussex.

When, at the end of harvest, the wealthy landowner called all the work people to the Harvest Home at Great Dixter, the great house beyond the village, Anna washed herself well and dressed in her Sunday-best striped muslin. She had scrubbed James' smock clean and laid it to dry over the springy grass near their cottage, and with her own hands had knotted the bright cloth at his neck. As they arrived at the festivities, she felt sure that her new husband was the finest man there. They skirted the vast house with its rich gardens and many glinting windows to find their way to the servants' hall. The tables were almost bending under the weight of beef and mutton, all the fruits of summer, vast plum puddings and pies, cider and ale. The lord and his lady walked among the working men and their families, congratulating them on the wonderful harvest now safely stored in the barns and hay ricks. Yet under the thin veil of prosperity and pleasantries, another layer lurked.

Even as the men were piling their plates with generous wedges of pie and potatoes, Anna overheard one mutter to another.

'Very fine meal, sir, yes, sir, a feast indeed, sir, a pain in the belly from overeating tonight, sir, then see my children starve through the winter. . .'

'Why can't they just pay us a fair wage? That's what I want to know.

Those full barns and ricks of hay are there through our sweat. And look at this house – you could fit the whole village inside it, I reckon. They can afford it.'

It was not only the lord and the question of fair wages that angered the workers. As the rector of the village church walked among the people, men dutifully pulled their forelock in deference to him and women bobbed a curtsey but, after he had passed by, a murmur of dissatisfaction trailed at a distance behind him. The appearance of the parson's titheman at the feast was greeted with ill-concealed dislike.

'Out looking for his tithes any day now,' said one.

'What does he do with all our gifts? Just fills up the Tithe Barn and leaves our families short.'

'It wouldn't be so bad, maybe, if his own parishioners were the only one who had to pay the tithes. But we aren't even Church of England,' James complained. 'We're Methodists and Baptists, too. But we still have to pay – a tenth of our firewood, a tenth of our hay for the cow, the tenth piglet. It's not right!'

'Hush,' Anna whispered. 'Don't let anyone hear you. They'd just say you were not a truly religious man if you weren't willing to pay your tithe to the church.'

'But you know that's not so – it's not my religion, it's plain justice!' James began to argue, till Anna tugged at his sleeve and pulled him off to have another plate full of food. It seemed a pity to waste such a feast.

When the first of the fires lit the sky over Kent one night in August, James was shocked. A hay-rick had been set ablaze and a farmer's threshing machine had been destroyed. 'Not violence – we mustn't turn to violence,' he insisted. 'The farmers must see for themselves that we need fairer wages. . .'

Then came the night when Anna woke to see a strange light flickering against the tiny window. She pushed the window open and saw the glow of fire at a distance. James came to stand beside her, wrapping a blanket around their shivering shoulders to enclose them together from the cold night air.

'It's another hay-rick going up. The troubles are getting closer to home every day.'

Inside the blanket, Anna leaned against the warmth of her husband, thankful for the protection of his arms around her and their unborn child.

'Will it come here, to Northiam?' Her voice was small and anxious.

'We have our share of hotheads here – and hungry young families in plenty. But surely some of us can talk sense with the farmers. They are not fools.'

Through November, angry labourers broke other equipment and set fire to more hay-ricks. Hated tithemen with their demands were turned into objects of ridicule, being trundled out of the parish with legs dangling from a wheelbarrow to the jeering laughter of the villagers. Northiam and the neighbouring villages of Beckley, Ewhurst, Peasmarsh and Brede were at the centre of the circle of discontent, which began to spread beyond the county.

Men of the Methodist chapel like James Rootes and his friends found themselves meeting for serious talks. James and his brother Sivyer Rootes were both more skilled than some of their neighbours in reading and writing, so James came home from chapel with some friends and they sat till late at Anna's table composing a written statement to the farmers, politely demanding that labourers' wages should rise from fourteen pence a day in summer to a living wage of two shillings and threepence. Anna watched from her corner by the fire as they wrestled with the most careful choice of words and the scribe sharpened his quill for the task. A small deputation of men was chosen to visit the farmers to present their case and did their best to speak with reason and dignity of the human needs they represented.

Yet by the time Anna's first child was born several months later, the gains of the initial negotiations had been lost. The anger of the labouring classes had spread much more widely across England than its small beginnings in Sussex and Kent and the governing classes began to retaliate with harsh punishments. A few were condemned to death and hundreds of others imprisoned or transported to Australia. Instead of finding their lives made easier with work to do and fair wages, workmen found that an amendment to the Poor Law Act gave the Act sharper and more cruel teeth than ever before. No able-bodied man could receive public assistance in times of poverty unless he were willing to be incarcerated in the local workhouse, to work at stone-breaking or other toil for no pay. However, the meagre food and accommodation of that place was designed to be less than the poorest labourer could afford. It meant separation of a man from his family and the loss of all hope of escape to a better life. Men like James Rootes fought such a fate with every ounce of strength in their bodies.

Before baby Ann was walking, the spectre of another horror, even more frightening than having little work and less money, cast long shadows across the countryside. The first time a neighbour called for Anna to come to a cottage to help a sick woman, she had expected to find something which her herbal remedies and good sense could help. But within a day the poor woman was dead and people started to whisper to each other, 'It's the cholera!'

Rumours had reached the village of an epidemic of cholera, a terrible new ill carried from somewhere in the East by traders, spreading from community to community by some means which remained the deepest mystery. While it remained a rumour from London, the people could bear it, but when the people of Northiam saw the sudden and cruel illness striking down their wives, their old people, their babies, the fear became very real. Anna had learned from her mother the uses of good herbs and poultices, and was becoming skilled in caring for women in childbirth. Despite her small frame, she was strong and full of energy, and her compassion was seasoned with commonsense. But cholera was something beyond her experience and far beyond her skill.

James pleaded with her. 'Must you go to that house again? What about little Ann — she might be infected.'

'Somebody must go — I never take baby with me. But those poor, poor people — at least I can try to help, and wash them, and — and lay them out . . .'

House after house saw a sad procession leaving its door, the fewest possible number of people carrying the body hastily away, wrapped in cotton saturated in pitch. There seemed to be no time to weep for one before another was ill. Villagers tried to stay away from the houses where cholera had struck, following advice to get plenty of fresh air away from the village, and faithfully wearing flannel next to the skin and avoiding raw vegetables. There was great scrubbing of floors and walls, lime-washing, fumigating with fuming sulphuric acid, salt and black oxide of manganese, and entire stocks of bed linen were boiled and laid out to dry. Fires in those days of plague blazed to destroy the personal things of those who had died.

'Perhaps it is a judgment on us all,' some said.

'God is punishing us for our unfaithfulness — we have ignored church and chapel for years now. Perhaps God saw us laughing at religious things down at the ale house.'

James and Anna spent many hours praying desperately for protection and healing, Anna often murmuring her prayers while her hands were occupied with cleansing a body soiled by the effects of the disease. In the middle of the stench of illness and the pain of a dying friend, she found herself clinging to phrases from the hymns she sang in chapel. Over and over in her mind she repeated parts of one of Mr Wesley's hymns – 'Give to the winds thy fears, Hope and be undismayed. . . God shall lift up thy head. . . Through waves and clouds and storms he gently clears thy way; Wait thou his time. . .' Sometimes it seemed to make little sense, yet the words kept singing themselves in her mind, and she worked on.

When the worst of the epidemic had passed and fresh grave mounds lay in the village graveyard in place of those friends who had been among the living, James and Anna found that they had passed through the fire unscathed. Even little Ann had survived, and Anna's new pregnancy seemed unaffected.

When the cholera epidemic was at its height, a young man arrived in the area. James and Anna Rootes first met him at the Methodist chapel. The little chapel had been a special place for Anna ever since she had first discovered for herself as a fifteen-year-old that God loved her and wanted her to be his child. As the Rootes family sat in their place, they stared curiously at the new young man dressed in the sombre garments of a Methodist preacher.

'My name is Thomas Collins and I come as your new minister here in Sandhurst Circuit.' He looked across the sparsely populated chapel and it seemed to Anna that he was summing them up even as they were examining him. He looked very young, younger than James' twenty-eight years, and very much alive. Anna settled little Ann on her lap and prepared to listen.

It was soon clear that Thomas Collins had not come to soothe and comfort, to lull his people into a little gentle sleep on a Sunday morning or evening. He was enthusiastic, vivid in his preaching – and very noisy in his methods. He was determined the people of the villages should hear his message clearly and come to a choice about what they heard. The Methodist singing had always been sweet, but Thomas encouraged singing of a strength and power that they had not known before. When he read from the Bible, the words sprang to life, and when he prayed the people felt the passion of the man and were moved by it. Villagers who had begun to think seriously of their spiritual welfare under the threat of cholera listened to the young preacher with minds that were ready to consider that his words might be true.

At first, some people of the area viewed his ways with suspicion. 'A man who is so loud can't be properly religious,' they decided. 'He is wanting in dignity.'

Yet the people of the villages came to hear him and his words struck a deep chord for many of them who had been looking for a clear word about themselves and God. Anna found herself sitting in her place in chapel night after night, praying silently for her neighbours, hearing the young minister trumpeting a call of hope and new beginning for people who were often without hope. She watched young girls kneeling to pray for forgiveness before the congregation and older women, with the honour of many children, prepared to humble themselves before God. She saw men who had never entered a Methodist chapel enter with hesitation and leave with a new approach to a difficult life. Thomas Collins preached with fire in his words, and Anna recognised young men who were close neighbours and friends responding to the invitation he gave to them all to return to a forgiving Christ. Even James' friend Silas Gill, a young giant of a man better known as a boxer at county fairs or a smuggler than as a man of religion, was one of those who walked forward to kneel for prayer.

Someone said to Thomas Collins one night, 'Wasn't there rather a lot of wild fire at your service?' And the story came back to the people that Collins said, 'Better to have some wild fire than no fire at all! God has given us all different gifts. Some men have the gift of slowly and quietly polishing perfect pillars for God's temple — my work is more like blasting in the quarry, and raising rough stones for God's work can be noisy!'

During the three years that Thomas Collins worked in their area, the membership of the Methodist congregations grew nearly three times what it had been, their chapel debt was paid off and the chapel stewards held a good sum on their behalf. For James Rootes, Thomas Collins became a beloved brother. James was not one of those who experienced a dramatic conversion to religion at that time; his Christian faith had begun more quietly at the age of twenty and had become gradually more and more real to him. But Thomas encouraged James to try preaching and took him with others when he went to preach in other villages. James began to grow in confidence till he was able to prepare and preach a service of worship without help. During the week he would be Rootes, often unemployed labourer, or Rootes, part-time cobbler with his brother Sivyer, but on Sundays he was Mr James Rootes, lay preacher. Anna was very proud of him.

Even so, lay preaching did not bring in money to put food on the table and the years continued to be difficult. Poaching was illegal, smuggling was illegal and very dangerous, cobbling paid very poorly and farm work became more and more hard to find as greater numbers of machines were established on farms. For every farm machine that was smashed, three more seemed to appear. James could have chosen to join a gang of labourers travelling as permanent migrants under a gang-master and moving from farm to farm, but it would have almost certainly meant receiving wages that cheated the workers, and he would have been forced to abandon Anna and the little ones, three of them now, to struggle for themselves.

Tinkers travelling through country roads with their wares and jugglers and clowns passing from one village fair to another brought news from beyond the county.

'Have you heard about those Dorset men? Transported they were. Off to Australia, in chains more than like, because they spoke about wages.'

'Just six ordinary workmen from the village of Tolpuddle, good honest Methodists, too — all they did was agree together to form a cooperative union and all promised to refuse to work for less than ten shillings a week.'

'And why shouldn't they, indeed? They've already done something about conditions and pay for the woolcombers and tailors — why not the farm labourers?'

'They've frightened the landowners, that's the trouble. They think that if men start plotting unions like that, the next thing will be we'll have a terrible revolution like France — trying to overturn the proper order of things, that's what they think!'

Anna heard the stories with fear. People described the leader of the banished men of Tolpuddle as a Methodist lay preacher, a mature labourer who had educated himself, a man who cared deeply for justice and the needs of families living under oppression, a man who studied the scriptures and interpreted them in action. She heard the stories and watched her James anxiously; the descriptions of George Loveless of Tolpuddle were a little too close to describing James Rootes. It did little to comfort her to learn that many people felt that the sentencing of the men of Tolpuddle had been totally unjust and that after a year or so they had been pardoned and returned to England.

'Poor men, they'll never feel safe or at home here again,' she said.

On a fine autumn day, the first day of September, the travelling fair came as always to Northiam. The village green blossomed overnight with the tents and stalls of the stallholders, vivid with colour and movement. Anna walked among the stalls with baby Jabez on one hip and Ann and Jamie skipping delightedly around her skirts. The little girl gazed longingly at a wooden doll on a stick and the small boy stared open-mouthed at a man with a trained monkey on his shoulder. The shouts of salesmen hawking their wares competed for attention with the antics of jugglers. A cluster of pretty girls in their brightest gowns giggled under an ancient oak where, according to village legend, a long-ago Queen Elizabeth had once rested.

Anna pulled her children along, drawing them away from the things they coveted, knowing that there was no money in the purse to spend on trinkets this year. There had been very little money for a long time. She remembered when she and James were young, how the two of them used to visit the fairs at Northiam and the neighbouring villages. Things had been hard even then, but James always saved a little money to buy her a fairing. She remembered standing with him at a stall in the days when she was a slim little thing, long before there were any hints of lines on her face, and choosing a bright ribbon for her bonnet. James had been proud of her then and she had run the satin smoothness of the ribbon through her fingers, cherishing the softness.

Now she knew that lines of anxiety were beginning to etch themselves into her face, drawing her mouth down a little at the corners. Her fingers were always too rough to appreciate the touch of new ribbon, and the pink bonnet ribbon was now frayed and faded, only a dim reminder of what once had been. There could be no little fairing for the children today. The best she could hope was that James would sell some of his vegetables.

Around the bend in the line of tents she found a cluster of women, friends from chapel, heads together in conversation.

They looked up as she approached and one asked, 'Well, Anna, is your man talking about migrating too?'

'He just said. . .' Anna was afraid to go on. She had thought — had hoped — that when James had spoken of Australia or Canada he was only dreaming strange dreams, without real intention of action. But if other men were talking about it too. . .

'We always thought that the fare would be too much, but now. . .'

'There's this new scheme, with landowners in Australia getting a bounty for workpeople they help migrate. . .'

'And the church wardens and parish overseers are starting to talk about giving assistance to families wanting to migrate. Maybe that will save them the worry of the workhouse overflowing with people who can't find work!'

'They say there is plenty of work in the colony for good men. Who knows?'

The women looked at each other. Each one understood the pain that her husband was living: the pain of being without work much of the time, of seeing children hungry, of sometimes feeling a failure as husband and father. Each had seen her husband make his own choices about smuggling and gang labour, poaching or sabotaging modern farm machinery, fighting to retain the jobs that remained or coming very close to giving up and resorting to the workhouse. Their men were good men, honest, strong – and despairing.

'I suppose,' Mercy Gill said slowly, 'if Australia has work. . .'

'If we'd be allowed to buy a little bit of land there one day. . .'

'So long as someone else paid for our passage. . . Our family couldn't afford to pay to travel on the back of a cart as far as Brighton!'

Anna turned away from her friends abruptly. Her mouth had crumpled suddenly and she didn't want them to see her weep.

When the decision was made at last, everything fell into place more quickly than Anna had dreamed. The strange doctor came visiting their villages along the Rother, talking to men of the border area between Sussex and Kent. Dr Galloway came in early April when the trees were still bare against blue-grey skies. By the time the bluebells were displaying their delicate hue in the woods near the village the Rootes family was committed to migrate to Australia.

Dr Galloway came to old St Mary's church on the hill in Northiam one evening, and Anna sat rigidly beside James with the children drowsing around her while she heard the story of the Bounty Scheme. The doctor told them of the problems of major landowners far away in the colony of New South Wales, where convict labour had always been used because it was a penal settlement.

'The landowners want to employ more good free men as well as the convict labour. As things stand, most of the convicts only stay till their sentence expires and some of them will only work if they are flogged. Many of the convicts are better highwaymen or pickpockets than they are shepherds or farmers – a great many of them came from our English cities and had never worked on the land in their lives. So the men with land are looking for good honest men, men who know the soil. It is a great opportunity for the right men and their families!'

The doctor's voice went on, talking about the bounty of thirty pounds that prospective employers would be paid for each married couple they brought out to the colony, with extra for children. He assured them that they must be healthy and industrious and would need testimonials from their clergyman and important people in the community.

Anna's eyes flickered around the church, watching the faces of her friends intent on the surgeon's words. In the dim light of the lamps she saw James' brothers and their wives, Sivyer and Mary, Thomas and Dinah. His older half-sister Elizabeth Nash was there with her husband and some Playford cousins, and their aging parents sat slumped in the shadows, listening and fearing. Among the families were people who had been her friends since she was a tiny child, people who had been to the charity school with her, women who had once danced with her around the maypole in the days when they were girls together, women whose babies she had delivered. She watched their faces, and tried to imagine their tightly-bound community ripped apart and scattered. It did not seem possible.

The stranger among them finished his talk. Many men crowded around him, asking eager questions, and James Rootes was among them. Later he talked to Anna, his face alight with an enthusiasm she had not seen for a long time.

She clutched at a straw. 'But we are too old! Didn't he say that all the migrants must be under thirty years of age? We're thirty-two — we can't go to Australia!'

'I think he might still accept us. We're strong and healthy, and the children are strong — Anna, it could be the answer to all my problems.'

She let him go. Silently she prayed, 'Lord, help him make the right choice. If you want us to leave home, please stay with us. And please, Lord, help me to bear it!'

Within weeks, the ferment within the villages of the border began to resolve. Many families had presented themselves to Dr Galloway, armed with their letters of recommendation. The parish overseers drew on the Poor Rate to offer coach fares to Portsmouth and needed clothing and equipment. In the next year, some thirty people were to migrate to Canada and thirty-one to Australia. When the first party to go gathered to talk excitedly about the prospects of sailing in June from Portsmouth on the ship *Augusta Jessie*, James and Anna Rootes were among them.

Held very carefully in cupped hands, Anna carried an uprooted clump of primrose plants, earthy roots trickling through her fingers. In the woods she had walked through the dappled shade, touching for the last time the ancient oaks of childhood. She climbed to the high point at Mill Corner and stood, panting a little, staring out over the generous curves of the South Downs to the flat marsh country in the distance. There were the golden-greens and blues of the landscape, with rain clouds building on the horizon and patchwork fields of ripening rye and barley cross-stitched with the hedgerows below. Among distant hop gardens, oast houses pointed to the sky, and she thought back to days of hop-picking. The village lay below on each side of the road which ran from London to Rye. Along that road would come the coach and find them waiting at the Six Bells Inn, familiar and comforting with its steeply pitched rooftops, its dormer windows and dark timber patterning and white walls. They would stand at the inn door with their things and all the family would be there to say goodbye. On another hill she could see the old church of St Mary's, the place where many of her ancestors had worshipped and where she and James had been married. In her mind's eye she saw the dim interior with its tapestry, some ancient stones still remembering the worshippers of the twelfth century. Almost hidden was the little Methodist chapel with its rich associations for her, its memories of her growing up and the beginning of faith. Thomas Collins had gone now, moved by the Methodist Conference to the faraway Orkney Isles, but the afterglow of his years with them still lingered and lit up the lives of the villagers.

Anna stood quietly, clutching her earthy bundle and breathing in the winds of the hilltop. It was good to be away for a little from the cottage down in the village. Down there her mother was minding the children and perhaps weeping amid the chaos of strapped bundles, their few sticks of furniture seeming somehow pathetic in the stripped room. James was there, probably being irritable and grumpy, trying to be sure he had forgotten nothing for their journey across the world, trying to hide his own uncertainties behind bluster. His old parents were hovering around the house, prophets of doom, pointing out every possible hazard that might lie in their path. She had escaped just for a short time, feeling that she had to be free for an hour from the crowded grief of the house.

The climb through the woods had tired her. Her body felt heavy and awkward with the weight of another baby; she tried not to remember that unless their ship were delayed for several months the child must be born at sea. Anna lowered herself onto the grass. Laying the primrose plants on the grass, she unknotted the corner of her shawl and spread it open, revealing the daffodil bulbs she had collected. She fingered the bulbs, the roundness, the tiny roots, the potential within them.

'Will you live? Will you have flowers in New South Wales?' she muttered.

She rolled them over in her hands. A small determined line set around her mouth. There will probably be arguments over the plants, she thought. 'James will say, ''What on earth are you doing with bulbs and primrose plants? You can't be thinking of taking them with you, surely!''' she said aloud. 'And I'll say, ''Of course I am. And some violets, too, these growing by my door – you'll see. They'll live. . .'''

The rain cloud was misting steadily closer and Anna saw that she must move soon or be wet. She pulled her bonnet back on over her dark hair and tied the ribbons firmly. The wide wings of the bonnet shut out the view on either side, hiding the village and much of the downs. Gathering her bulbs and primrose plants again into her shawl, she turned to go down to the village. Tomorrow they would all be on the coach to Portsmouth, perched outside on the cheapest seats, leaving behind most of their family and everything that was known. She would still have James and the children, and the cow and her plants. From within the narrowed vision of her deep bonnet, she brushed aside a tear. All she could do was look directly ahead.

And now, at last, Anna stood on the deck of the *Augusta Jessie*. Around her jostled other families, all struggling with their baggage and their anxieties, calling children, dragging cages of chickens, milling about in the narrow spaces: friends and strangers, crew and emigrants. Behind were the streets of Portsmouth, frightening in their activity and crowds. She had seen a chained gang of prisoners, working at the docks, and the prison hulks strung forbiddingly across the harbour, and James had whispered, 'You'd better get used to it – you'll be seeing convicts all the time in Australia.'

Behind, far behind in the village, was her mother and James' parents, and all their family.

'Anna, you must come below now.' James spread a protective arm around her shoulders.

She looked back over her shoulder once more, then turned away and followed her husband.

2
Uprooted
1837

STUMBLING DOWN INTO THE SHIP, clinging to James' arm, it was
the noise which first threatened to engulf her. Voices – shrill,
upraised, anxious, commanding – filled the gloomy space of
steerage. As Anna descended, feeling for the next step with her foot,
the moving mass of humanity below shifted and stirred, anonymous
women hidden within bonnets, men obscured behind bundles and
boxes: a dense confusion of strangers.

'Anna! Anna Rootes!'

An upturned face caught the light and she saw Mercy Gill with
little Dinah.

'Come this way – our family has kept a space for you all near us.'

Clutching small Jabez to her side and herding Ann and Jamie
before her, Anna thankfully pushed her way through the crowd to
her friend. Silas Gill, his smile wreathed in whiskers, towered over
the crowd.

'This way for the women and little ones,' he shouted, and Anna
thankfully lowered Jabez onto an empty lower berth. 'One berth
for you two and one for the little ones.' She saw, in the confusion
of migrant families, that a long table with benches bisected the length
of the lower deck and on either side the walls were lined with banks
of berths, little more than narrow wooden shelves ranked one above
the other.

James and Silas disappeared into the crowd with boxes to be
stowed in the hold for the voyage. Anna and Mercy sat side by side
with their children scrambling around and over them in the berth.
Among the moving crowds surging past their narrow haven, the
women caught sight of familiar faces from their home district – the
Glassons, the Shoesmiths, James Noakes, young George Drury

travelling alone to the new land, the Glovers. Other friends must be there too, but in the flood of people it was hard to be sure.

Small Jamie scrambled over her lap, treading on Jabez and pushing Ann aside. There was little space for the children, and Mercy's children stood close, holding onto their bundles of bedding while little Dinah wrapped her arms tightly around her mother's neck. Anna leaned back to look over her head at the layers of berths immediately above.

'We will be packed as close as plates on a shelf,' she said. 'A dish of butter on the top shelf, some bread in the middle and turnips at the bottom!'

'You'd best be a turnip then,' said Mercy. 'At eight months you can't go climbing shelves. Come, children, help us.'

Mercy Gill began laying bedding bundles in place and lifting small boxes. Anna struggled to her feet and did her best to supervise her own things, but she did not feel well. Her back ached and the awkwardness of her swollen body made lifting and stretching over the berths a burden. All she wanted to do was lie down and shut her eyes. Even so, when James and Silas returned to the women in their section of the steerage compartment, James found Anna with her area neatly organised and a little box, lined with mossy Sussex soil and filled with primroses and violets, set at the foot of her berth.

When the uproar on deck warned the passengers that the *Augusta Jessie* was casting off, Anna didn't want to look.

'I'll just sit down here,' she said firmly. 'We'll only be in the way of the sailors.'

James took the older children on deck to see the excitement — the sailors in the rigging, ropes being dragged on board and coiled, the gangway pulled in. Anna sat very still, staring blindly ahead of her. She had already said her farewells at Northiam, and Portsmouth had no special associations. It was the last glimpse of her mother's face and the tears of old Mr and Mrs Rootes that stayed with her.

'Never again in this life,' she thought, 'will I hold my mother. I won't be there when she is old and weak. I won't be there to see her laid to rest . . .'

Some of the younger family members spoke of following them to Australia one day, if it turned out to be as good a place as it was painted. Elizabeth Nash, James' older half-sister with grown-up children said, 'We'll probably come next year, or the year after —

write and tell us what you think.' His brothers Sivyer and Thomas with their wives promised to come, and the Playford cousins, Henry and Thomas with their wives and little ones, had all promised, 'We'll see you in Australia!' Perhaps that was true. Anna wasn't sure, but she clung to the thought that she would see them again. But not her mother. Staring into space, she faced the truth that she would never see her beloved mother who had taught her everything she knew of caring for a family, and the skills of a midwife and herbalist. Her mother had never forgotten that long ago day when an aged John Wesley had preached in their village and the spirit of a young Lizzie Fayes had caught fire; her mother's faith and her love for her Methodist group had always been part of Anna's world.

Some time later, when the motion of the vessel had settled into a deep roll and the shouting of the sailors had subsided, she climbed up to the deck and stood at the rail. They were out in the Channel with sails spread and the deep green of the water surging beneath them. Portsmouth had vanished, as had the sad string of decrepit convict hulks with their cargo of misery. Behind them stood the white cliffs and beyond rolled the emerald of the Downs. Somewhere, she wasn't even sure of the direction, lay Northiam, and Rye, and the River Rother.

When her family called her to come to a meal she had no hunger for, they found her standing at the rail, still staring back to England.

The first week or so of the voyage passed in a blur. The children were seasick and so was Anna, dreadfully, exhaustingly. The narrow space of her berth closed in around her, the wooden slats over her head pressing down, the berth beneath her lunging and swaying. James leaned over her to ask if she would like a little oatmeal or some ship's biscuit, but she turned away. She was not alone; the ranks of shelves around her groaned with their burden of seasick travellers. People spoke of the terrors of the Bay of Biscay and the Atlantic stretching away before them, but Anna dared not think of the months of travel ahead. She lay with her head buried in the pillow she had stuffed with down from Northiam geese, and it even seemed to her distressed mind that she could hear the geese and ducks and hens, and even the lowing of a cow, but she dismissed the sounds as nothing but a tantalising dream.

A week after the *Augusta Jessie* sailed, King William IV died and the young Victoria came to the throne, but even if Anna could have heard that news she would not have cared. King William or Queen

Victoria, what did it matter? She was disorientated with seasickness, fearful for her little ones, always conscious of her heavy body. The excitement and enthusiasm of James only irritated her and when someone said in her hearing, 'Oh, nearly half of the babies born at sea survive,' she had not been comforted.

Anna woke one morning and the motion of the ship no longer troubled her. A cup of tea and hard biscuit was palatable for the first time since sailing and, when she climbed slowly to the deck, the sun was shining and the air was unexpectedly warm. The sea spread dark blue to the horizon and England had vanished. Around the deck, women were spreading their bedding, fluffing up feather mattresses, sunning their blankets; cheerful voices floated up from below as steerage passengers swept and scrubbed their living area. As she walked tentatively around the deck, she discovered that whaleboats had been roofed over to protect pens of chickens, ducks and geese and when a sailor walked by with a brimming bucket of milk she suddenly knew that the farmyard sounds of her dreams had been real enough. In a protected corner, a young schoolmaster sat with a group of children chanting their alphabet, and further around she met a little group of Sussex wives sitting together with their sewing spread across their laps.

'Feeling better this morning, dear? Come and sit in the sun with us, then.'

Sitting quietly with her hands idle in her lap, she found herself relaxing. The great venture to Australia would still not be easy or comfortable or without anxiety, but perhaps, after all, it would not be impossible.

The Union Jack was spread over the rail of the poop deck and Dr Galloway, Prayer Book in hand, was transformed into the ship's chaplain. The crew stood to attention in clean white uniform and the officers had honoured the Sabbath Day with their best dark jackets. Anna watched her three children from the corner of her eye, Jamie fidgeting a little and Jabez stretching up his arms to be carried. With the rest of the passengers and crew, the Rootes family waited in their tidiest clothes for the doctor to read the service of Morning Prayer.

She observed the doctor closely as he read carefully through the prayers and scriptures for the day and opened a book of sermons to read to the emigrants. He was a good, honest man, she decided, and was doing his best to keep them all healthy. They said that he had refused to take more emigrants on board than could be sensibly accommodated, and certainly she had heard stories of other ships where there had been dangerous overcrowding so that the poor people in steerage had little space or air or light. Anyway, two hundred and thirty-two people was more than enough for the *Augusta Jessie*. Dr Galloway was very particular about the travellers having their lime juice and eating wisely, and even visited their quarters to be sure that everyone was obeying his instructions about airing their bedding and sweeping under berths.

He read on solemnly, even a little ponderously, the profound words skimming over the heads of many of his hearers, creating an aura of Sunday sanctity and putting some in mind of the Sunday dinner they would enjoy that afternoon, with good salt pork and potatoes, maybe a sago pudding, and hot chocolate to drink. Anna listened carefully. Her James would like it; he loved the challenge of thinking and relished a good, strong sermon. For herself, she liked something with simplicity, a message that spoke plainly and spoke to her heart. She caught Mercy's eye and thought she saw a faint twinkle there. Sunday on the *Augusta Jessie* was clearly to be kept with dignity and devotion, but in the disciplined order of the service there was little in common with the energy and fervour of their little Methodist meetings at home. If someone were to suddenly cry, 'Glory! Praise the Lord!' everyone would turn in shock and hiss 'Hush'. It seemed unlikely that anyone would burst into tears of penitence, or start to speak before their fellow travellers of the things that God was doing in their hearts as they tore themselves away from their homeland.

'Still,' she thought, 'our group can get together later to sing and pray for each other. I know I'll be glad for somebody to pray specially for me!'

The first pangs clutched her body one afternoon in July. More and fiercer pains came later as Anna sat very still at the long table where the emigrant passengers sat for their meals, her fingers whitening as they gripped a spoon. Around her, other passengers paid no attention, chewing noisily on their small ration of dried beef, dipping into their bowl of lentils, complaining about the lack of cheese. Her children sat beside her, Jamie with a milky moustache and Jabez with the remains of his bread and milk trickling down his chin. The pain passed and she wiped her children's faces with a hand that trembled just a little. The time had come. She had known all along that one day the dull ache which had been part of her lower back for weeks now would become an intense pain, that it would come in waves, that there would be no escape from it. Now was the time.

'Children, come!' Her voice was sharper than usual, its edge startling the children. As she slid awkwardly along the backless bench, they followed, and when they were free of the table she added urgently, 'You must go to your father, now.'

Her eyes searched for James and found him. Dragging the children with her, she thrust them at him and said, 'It's now. Take them. I think I'll go to my bed.'

As she turned to go, another pain gripped her, halting her momentarily and sending all her concentration to her woman's body preparing itself to be delivered of a child. When she could speak again she said, 'Tell Mercy. . . please.'

Lying on her narrow berth, hiding behind the inadequate drapes of blankets Mercy had hung around for privacy, Anna felt the tossing of the *Augusta Jessie*, up and down, side to side. Beyond the sheltering walls of the ship flowed the waves, deepest blue of the Atlantic, rolling on and on with no land in sight. Outside, the sky darkened into a warm night and inside the little cave of her berth, Anna laboured by the light of a little lamp which swung over her head. She watched the rhythm of its swing, tossing dark shadows from side to side against the lowering berth overhead and the coarse blankets curtaining her. Mercy was there, gently talking to her, encouraging her to be brave, asking 'Well, a boy or a girl this time?', her sure hands at work in a way Anna dimly recognised as the tasks she herself had often done for others. If she had been home in Northiam, her mother would have been there.

Once Anna whispered, 'I don't even know where we are. . . but it feels a very long way from home. . .'

In her mind over and over the words repeated themselves, '. . . half the babies will live', and she silently cried, 'Lord have mercy.' She heard, somewhere beyond the curtain, James asking, 'Should I fetch Dr Galloway now?'

'Your Anna is a strong girl. Any minute now this baby will come and we won't need to trouble the doctor.'

Anna heard a rending cry and did not know that it was her own voice. But she knew that the child was born.

He was a little boy, a fine and healthy child. They named him Augustus Jesse.

The first time Anna noticed the harsh coughing of an emigrant's child, she was sitting on deck in the sunshine with her baby sleeping beside her and her hands full of sewing. Beyond the ship's rail spread the sunlit ocean, dancing and sparkling, but the child nearby was gasping, struggling for breath. Anna twisted in her seat, peering along the line of passengers. Somewhere among the people, heads bent over their net-mending or stitching of garments, a child was very ill. Anna recognised the sound; she had heard before the rattling gasp of whooping cough.

Few of the other passengers paid much attention. Conversations went on uninterrupted, some voices whining a little with boredom, some argumentative, fashioning disputes out of nothing. It was another day like many other days, with more than two hundred people trapped in a confined space for months with no escape from each other. Captain Edenborough was a skilful ship's captain and Dr Galloway was caring for his party of chosen emigrants with wisdom, but they were all growing very weary of the journey. The excitement of watching schools of dolphin performing their ballet beside the ship, or flights of flying fish, had paled and the occasional passing whale no longer brought people running to the rail to exclaim. The worst days were those spent wallowing, becalmed, with sails dangling limply and the knowledge that at day's end they were no nearer their destination. Then tempers flared and passengers complained bitterly about everything. Dr Galloway had insisted that there should be good order and productive activity. The people were kept busy with the discipline of shipboard hygiene, cleansing their sleeping quarters, deck scrubbing, useful handwork, lessons for the children and the rhythm of weekday responsibilities and Sunday worship and rest. Even so, they all knew that the journey would take four or five months; they were barely half-way and were already very weary of it.

The child coughed again, a spasm of coughing. Anna put aside her sewing and stood up. She moved along the line till she found a woman with her little child limply held against her shoulder shuddering with coughing.

'Has the doctor seen this little one?' Anna asked briskly.

The woman shook her head.

'It is only a little cough – he'll be better soon.'

'Perhaps...'

Anna walked on to watch her children, Ann and Jamie, bent earnestly over their slates with the other children under the care of the schoolmasters. They looked well, cheeks bright with sea air and sunshine, less troubled by the confinements of the voyage than their parents. (James was so pleased that his children had a chance to begin to learn to read and write on board ship. 'We don't know if there will be a school for them when we arrive – four months of good teaching will be a great start!' he said.) Her children had not been coughing – yet – but who knew whether they might catch something? She walked back to her place by the sleeping baby and little Jabez and picked up her sewing, stabbing her needle in and out without thought for what she was doing.

The sick child was coughing again and the mother got up to carry him down to his bed. As the sounds of distress faded into the distance, Anna was weaving a prayer into her sewing.

'Dear Lord, protect my children.'

The day of the funeral was fine, with the ship flying before a good wind. It was Wednesday, emigrants' washing day and, when a group of passengers came on deck to stand silently with heads bowed to farewell the little boy who had died of whooping cough after weeks of illness, the deck looked unfitting: indecently colourful, with the rigging vivid with flags of damp washing streaming before the wind.

Anna stood close to James, feeling the comfort of his elbow pressing against hers, her own children around her feet and the baby in her arms. Captain Edenborough and Dr Galloway stood with the parents and their friends. Resting on a plank laid across the rail of the bulwarks, something lay hidden under a Union Jack. Anna couldn't blot from her mind the memory of the previous evening when she had helped the sobbing mother to stitch the body of her child into a canvas bag, and the sailor who had passed by and commented, 'Don't forget that you'll need sand or some stones to make it sink . . .'

Dr Galloway read the words of the funeral service quietly. The ship's bell stopped tolling.

'We commit this body to the deep.'

A sailor tilted the plank and the hidden bundle slid away from under the flag and plunged into the depths with a small splash. The only sounds were the cry of the gulls, the flapping of washing and sobs of the mother. Anna turned away and pressed her face into the cloth of James' shoulder. The ship was flying on and the place where the child's body had fallen had vanished forever.

The *Augusta Jessie* sailed on, passing south through the Atlantic. The weather grew warmer in the tropics and in the airless heat of steerage, Anna and the children found it hard to sleep. At the long mess table where the emigrants ate, rumours of what might happen when they crossed the Line, the mystical Equator, passed up and down with the salt pork and rice.

'They say King Neptune will board us!'

The children came from their classes with tales told by their teachers, and sailors winked and hinted. Some passengers came to table with stories of paying a sailor for a look through a telescope — 'and I saw the Line, as clear as day, a black line right across the sea!'

'Then you were tricked out of your money. We saw the sailor fix a hair across the telescope.'

One evening with the tropical sun falling towards the sea in streaming banners of scarlet, gold and salmon, there was a shout of command. It seemed to come from the water under the bow. Anna was swept along in the rush of passengers running forward. Being small, she missed the first sight of King Neptune clambering from the bowsprit to the deck, but she heard the shouts of the people around her. An unexpected shower of water broke over them and she found herself damp and laughing at the sight of a noble Neptune astride the deck, trident in hand and grinning from behind a mockery of false whiskers and royal crown. His assistants were tossing buckets of water into the crowd, sprinkling or soaking the emigrants.

Anna backed away, shaking water from her bonnet and hair, and clutched her little ones around her as they giggled. A thinly disguised assistant of King Neptune flourished a monster shaving brush afoam with soap under the nose of Jamie.

'Do you need a shave, my lad? No? Ah, you, sir!' A protesting passenger was pinned down and smothered in lather. More water flew as other passengers were captured and ducked without ceremony into a tub of water.

James Rootes had escaped the attentions of Neptune's crew, but Anna found her heart lifting at the sight of his face crinkled with laughter, not creased with anxiety. He was looking well, rested, relaxed. Her James was looking foward with hope and great confidence that God was with them in this great adventure.

There had been many times when she was almost angry at his confidence; she resented the way in which he brushed aside her litany of a hundred disasters that could cripple them, as if unwilling to look squarely at the hard truth of things. But now his hopefulness touched her anxiety and she felt herself being lifted up in her spirit.

The sun sank at last into the warm sea and the stars began to prick holes of light through the curtain of darkening blue. Anna stood for a few moments of quiet against the rail of the ship, baby Augustus against her shoulder. The revelling on deck was over and King Neptune and his men had vanished as mysteriously as they had come. Below, the sounds of a fiddle and dancing feet drifted up to her; the passengers were dancing and enjoying an unusual issue of ale to celebrate the occasion of passing into the Southern Hemisphere. Anna and the other Methodists would not join in the dancing, it being seen as a worldly activity not suitable for those with a longing for the spiritual. But she did not feel deprived of joy. Soon she would tuck the sleeping Augustus and the other children into their bed. Then she would join her friends, the little group from Northiam and Beckley and neighbouring villages, who were growing closer and closer in friendship. They would laugh together over the sight of Silas being ducked and others having lather scraped from their faces. They would sing, joyfully perhaps or gently, and they'd pray together as they often did.

And then, even if the North Star of home had at last disappeared over the horizon and new stars shone in strange, unknown constellations, perhaps she'd feel safe.

With the endless repetition of the waves rolling under the *Augusta Jessie*, the days passed. July, August and September came and went. If they had been at home, they would have been helping with the harvest. The children were well, brown and happy, proud of their new learning. Other women had lost their babies, but Anna's Augustus was fat and dimpled, smiling toothlessly at his mother. James spent long hours talking with the other men about the future, the hopes of employment on the land and questions about the ones who might employ them. They even talked about the dream that one day they might be able to own land of their own.

There were jewel days of aquamarine and jade, turquoise and sapphire, when the sun gleamed from leaping dolphins and the high arcs of flying fish. On the days when the sun made rainbows through translucent veils of seasprays, and the spreading black and white wings of the albatross circled over the ship, Anna felt at peace. Surely God was with them.

Yet as the ship passed south of the Cape of Good Hope and the weather grew colder, Anna's moods swung from high to low and back again. Pulling her shawl around her and dressing her children in warmer clothes, she found the sharper edge of the air reminded her of home, of sitting by the fire with her mother, of the end of harvest and the colours of autumn. As the *Augustus Jessie* sailed south of the Great South Land, Australia, they began to be buffeted by wild storms. The children were sometimes frightened, clinging together on her berth, feet tucked up under them and trying not to slide when the ship heeled deeper and deeper till they felt they must capsize, then lurching back again. For days Anna chose to crouch on the floor beside the mess table to feed the little ones; that way their bowls were less likely to be smashed over the edge of the table. James came to sit with them as much as he could, doing his best to calm their fears, but it was not easy for any of them to be brave.

'None of us can go up on deck for our daily exercise till the storm eases,' James said. 'The decks are awash up there.'

'We don't *want* to go on deck, I'm sure,' Anna said. 'I hate it enough down here.'

'We'll be safe, though, so long as we keep well enough out to sea. They say that the southern coast is a wild and rocky shore. . .' James stopped. He had seen the look on Anna's face and wished he had not spoken.

As the storm went on, even though she had assured James that she had no desire to go on deck, Anna found the atmosphere in steerage more and more bruising. It was not only the crowding but the noise and the smells. The constant bang and thud of sliding furniture in the cabins and the discordant clanging and scraping of household objects which steerage passengers had hung about their berths made Anna's head ache. The children, her own and others, were irritable, whining and whimpering in the crowded half-light of the avenues of berths. The atmosphere below deck was redolent of unwashed bodies and chamber pots, garments stained by seasickness, ill-prepared food in the galley. Since the storm had begun, it had been impossible to wash or dry baby Augustus's linen, and the pungent smell hung around the berth. Jabez was coughing, and every time he coughed she was terrified that she might hear the beginning of whooping cough which was afflicting other families. Every sound and smell was magnified and at last she could bear it no longer.

When at last it was possible to go on deck, she said, 'Mercy, can you watch the children for a minute? I need some fresh air – I'll just stand near the top of the steps – I promise I'm not going right out on deck!'

Clinging to the railing at the top of the companionway, she breathed in great gulps of clean air. In the darkness, the rain had stopped and the ropes and spars shone eerily with phosphorescence. The stars had all disappeared. The cacophony of rattling metal and the wind still tearing at the tatters of a torn sail beat upon her, but out in the wild darkness at least she could breathe. The ship rolled under her, tossing her hard against the side of the hatchway, and she almost lost her footing. The wind flailed the wings of her bonnet around her face and she felt the loose ribbons under her chin slipping. A gust snatched the bonnet from her head and sent it on birdwing off over the dark sea, trailing its ribbons like a tail. Anna clung in frustration to the rail with no hands to snatch at her fleeing bonnet.

She found herself shouting into the night. 'How dare you take my bonnet! How dare you take. . .'

She couldn't go on. She nearly said 'my home, my family, nearly everything that is important to me.' She had nearly shouted at God for snatching away her home, leaving her in the dark, afraid. But she had not the courage to blame God. So she turned and clambered back down into the thick and odorous atmosphere of steerage to turn on her husband and say accusingly, 'And now I've lost my bonnet!'

When at last the winds eased and shipboard life settled to its regular pattern, Anna remembered her little box of plants. During the storm she had forgotten about it and some of the plants had been wilting even before that. Now she stared at the contents of the box. The daffodil bulbs were showing no sign under the soil. Perhaps they would flower again in foreign soil, perhaps not. The violet leaves looked limp and pale, dying for water or dying for homesickness. The primrose plants were quite dead.

A ship came within signalling distance and Anna watched the language of flags passing between the *Augusta Jessie* and the other. Sailors interpreted and the message was passed among the passengers.

'It's the *Charles Kerr* out of Falmouth carrying a full load of convicts.'

'Bound for Sydney, then.'

'Well, of course. Or perhaps Van Dieman's Land. These new settlements at Port Phillip Bay and Adelaide have decided that they are too good to be penal colonies.'

They were too far away to see the people on the other deck clearly, but Anna gazed at the indistinct shapes and featureless human beings on the distant deck. Convicts. Were they fiends who had run amok with an axe, wickedly poisoned their master or robbed a coach on an English highway? Or were they frightened lads who had not been quick enough one night, out poaching game? Or perhaps men like James, wounded beyond measure by the terror of unemployment, who had been convicted and transported for smashing farm machinery?

'Do you think they are chained?' she whispered to James.

'I don't know. Perhaps, if they are violent. They can hardly run away...'

'It would be awful to be a convict. Under guard like that and not knowing if you'd ever be able to go home again. We could go home again if we wanted, couldn't we, James? James?'

But James said nothing.

When at last the *Augusta Jessie* sailed along the eastern coast and they knew that soon they would find the entrance to Sydney Harbour, Anna decided that she wasn't ready to leave the ship. She watched the passing coastline rippling by, heaped-up rocky headlands guarding curves of beaches, dark olive-green bush hiding any signs that human beings might be there. The ship had become a haven, a small space where she had marked out the safe limits of 'our berth', 'Ann and Jamie's bed', 'our place at table'. It was crowded, it was inconvenient, it was confining, but somehow safer than the vast wilderness of the land beyond the harbour with its strange and unnatural greens.

'Tomorrow we'll berth, and then a day or so later we'll be free to leave the ship,' James promised. 'We'll all be glad to get off and to dry land.'

'I hope they don't push us off in too much of a hurry.' Anna's voice was uncertain. 'What will happen now? What if nobody wants to employ you after all? What if we all hate it here?'

Then she clutched at a straw to put off the moment of losing her place on the familiar ground of a British ship.

'Well, I can't possibly go ashore till I have a bonnet to cover me.

I'm not arriving in Sydney as a bareheaded hussy, thank you. Whatever would someone think of me, if they were looking for a family to work for them? No, I'll stay here till you get one for me.'

James sighed. He'd thought she'd be pleased to arrive. You never knew with women, he thought, and went to stare over the rail at the land he hoped to make his own.

Anna stared, too. She had come to please him, but he couldn't make her like it if it was too awful. Discontented lines settled on her face, but behind the mask of her face her feelings were not so much discontent as fear of what she did not know. Beyond the ship the opalescent sheen of the Pacific smashed in boiling foam against the foot of the sandstone layers of Sydney Heads. The sun lit up the bushland and the long waves of blue silk and white lace floating filmy veils of spray behind them.

Anna watched with downturned mouth. 'Not so pretty by half as the white cliffs of Beachy Head at home,' said Anna.

3
Transplanted
1837-1840

WITH A NEW BONNET triumphantly in hand, James came back on board the *Augusta Jessie* after his first foray into the streets of Sydney.

'Here, you can be decent again. I found a shop full of clothes — all sorts of materials for dresses, umbrellas, boots, even stays and such — run by a Mrs Hordern,' he said, and grinned as Anna turned the bonnet in her hands and lifted it over her dark hair. She was still tying the wide ribbons under her chin when he began gathering the children.

'Come then, are you ready? Are you all tidy and clean? We'd best try to make a good impression or no-one will want us.'

Anna scrubbed Jamie's hands one more time; she had been trying to keep him clean all the morning while James had been out exploring the town. Mercy and Silas were ready, too, and the others, to go ashore and present themselves to prospective employers. For a week their families would be able to continue to sleep on board the ship, but if at the end of the week they were still without an employer, they would have to move into emigrant barracks. Though they tried not to show it, each family was nervous.

The families clustered together on deck, almost hesitant to move ashore. The men were jubilant, excited. It was a beautiful October day with the harbour full of craft, rowing boats moving around beneath the height of sailing ships, the dockside busy with barrels and boxes as whalers and merchant ships unloaded their cargo. The convict ship, the *Charles Kerr*, lay at anchor and they were near enough to see more clearly the faces of some of the men.

The ship's boat came towards them across the water, bringing Dr Galloway and a strange gentleman, and ready to take some of the migrants off to the shore. As the gentlemen climbed the rope ladder onto the deck, Anna heard the stranger's words.

'Only one adult death during the whole voyage? That is magnificent, my dear Galloway.' The stranger cast an appraising eye over the families as they waited. 'And a mere eight infants – a trifling number compared to the record of most of the emigrant ships. From what I've seen so far you've done splendidly. It is not always so – not everyone responsible for these bounty or government migrants takes so much care with his party. Well done! Perhaps we are beginning to break from our ghastly history of hell ships coming to New South Wales.'

They passed on and someone whispered, 'That was Governor Bourke.'

Following the others, Anna reluctantly climbed down the rope ladder into the ship's boat, clinging anxiously to the rope and praying that the wind wouldn't whip her long skirts into the air. At last she stood on the wharf with the unfamiliar feel of stable ground under her feet. They had arrived. They were safely past the dangers of the sea and had been protected from a much worse passage in ways she had not realised at the time. As their group began to move again to face selection by employers, she found herself silently thanking God for his goodness.

Sitting rigidly on a bench in the barracks near the wharf, Anna followed the groups of settlers with her eyes. Some were clearly rich men, looking for people to work on their large properties. Others seemed to be agents of others, seeking out suitable farmers and mechanics for their masters. James stood beside her. Earlier that day, before they left the ship, James had been hopeful and told his friend Silas Gill that any of their Sussex and Kent families would be a bargain for an employer, even without the bounty of thirty pounds. Now it seemed to Anna that his confidence was trickling away, leaving him clutching his papers of recommendation in clammy palms. The children were sitting unusually still, feeling the importance of the occasion.

Fragments of conversation floated by as men walked along the rows of new migrants, inspecting, asking questions, examining papers.

'There's a lot of feeling about this news that they are talking about cutting off transportation of convicts – people are signing petitions to keep it on . . .'

'. . .the cost of paying free workers will hurt a lot.'

'. . . it's getting harder and harder to get enough convicts assigned for farm labour these days. I wrote a formal request months ago for another nineteen assigned workers and all they sent me was one. One!'

'. . .at least these free labourers are coming in families – that should begin to even up the balance of men and women. I don't know about your place, but we have plenty of problems with too many men without women.'

'. . .at least some of these children should grow up to be a new work force for us. Some of the bigger ones can start work straight away.'

'. . .but paying for all this migrant labour, even with the inducement of a bounty – they'll still have to be paid wages and that will be much more costly to us than rations and clothes for the convicts. It'll bankrupt us before long!'

'The latest idea of importing coolies from India or Mauritius – what do you think?'

'Smacks of slave labour to me. If Britain has just gone to immense trouble to rid the country of slavery, why should we follow America and begin the practice here?'

Anna listened with only part of her mind. The problems of landowners in finding labour did not interest her. She was watching the faces of the men, looking for signs of response to her James. Would they find a good master? Would they have to travel to a wild and primitive place? Was this adventure going to be a success or a disaster?

A man was talking to James. The crumpled letters of recommendatioan were changing hands. The man looked intently across at Anna and the children and she found herself flushing under his stare. Was he looking to see if she had strong arms or would be likely to bear more healthy children, or might make a good field worker or dairyhand? I'm not a slave, she thought angrily, to be stared at like that, or a cow you are thinking of buying. She felt an urge to stand up and announce, 'I'm a good healthy woman, an honest Christian. I can read and write which is more than you can say for most. I'm clever with sickness and childbirth and I've always had enough energy to work three other women into the ground. Now then, what am I offered?' But that was insane. She dropped her eyes to the floor and waited.

When James came to her, his eyes were alight with enthusiasm.

'We've been taken on. A wealthy landowner up-country at Cobbitty needs more workers and his agent has hired us. We are to leave in a few days with some other families who have been hired to work in the same district. The Gills won't be far away. God has his hand in this, I'm sure.'

He tugged her to her feet and took Jabez up on his shoulder. 'Come and see the town. Who knows when you'll have a chance to come back to Sydney again?'

The dray lurched violently over some rocks and Anna braced herself against the row of sugar bags behind her. The baby in her arms had at last dozed off to sleep after hours of restlessness and she fastened the front of her gown where she had been comforting him. Jabez was snuggled beside her tucked under one arm, nearly asleep from the monotonous swaying of the bullock dray. Anna's arms ached from holding the two little ones and she longed to stretch, to move from the small space among the cargo where she had been sitting. Ann and Jamie were sitting at her feet wearied with the journey, almost too tired to keep up the childish arguments which had occupied them for what seemed like hours.

Ahead, she could just see the team of bullocks straining against the harness, dragging behind them the weight of months of provisions for the landowner and their own boxes. Their things looked small and inadequate now and Anna wished, as she swayed with the motion, that she had been able to bring more things from home. In among the smaller things stowed around her was her little box of plants, the leaves of the violets looking bedraggled and pathetic and nothing but a patch of lifeless roots to show where the primroses had been. James had stopped saying 'I told you they'd die.' Perhaps he was right, she thought, but I had to try to bring something like this from home.

The day before, they had left the *Augusta Jessie* for the last time. All their fellow-travellers had found employment and they were dispersing, spreading out in several directions. They had become very tired of each other's company, but the farewells were sincere enough. Their things had been loaded onto a river boat and they had travelled for some fourteen or fifteen miles along the Parramatta River to the town of Parramatta. From there they had been loaded onto the bullock dray with the other cargo and set off along a lonely track through scrub. When it was nearly dark, they had stopped at a wayside shanty and spent the night, glad to be still for a little while. Now they travelled on.

It would still be some hours, James told her, before the dray had made its way over the twenty-five miles of rough road from Parramatta to the south-west country. Although she was tired and very stiff, Anna felt the stirrings of new hope for the future. James was always the one who looked forward with optimism while she saw the real or imagined dangers on the way. But this morning they rode through a scented land to the sound of birds. Over her head was a sky of blue without a smudge of cloud. Under the unfamiliar eucalyptus trees were shrubs and grasses – and flowers! Not the well-loved flowers of home, but flowers nonetheless and she longed to be walking beside the dray, stooping to breathe the perfume, picking a spray here, a single bloom there.

'Look, James, flowers!'

'Well, it *is* spring, you know.'

'Spring? In October? How peculiar. . .'

James was not looking at roadside wildflowers. His farmer's eye watched for signs of cleared land and country under wheat or oats, or sheep grazing beyond the road. The bullock driver had been telling him of fine land out where they were going, land that yielded quantities of wheat beyond his dreams, where cattle and sheep flourished.

'You are onto a good thing, going to Mr James Hassall,' the bullock driver told him. 'You'll need to work hard – he expects a lot of his people – but he is a good master. Most of us working on his places have been assigned to him over the years – serving our time, you know. But those who do the right thing have been given their ticket-of-leave sooner than they might, and most of us reckon we'll stay on in Australia and find work. Maybe get a little place of our own one day.'

'What is this Mr Hassall like? Is he gentry or from the nobility at home?'

'Nobility? Not him, though for New South Wales I suppose he counts as gentry. They say that his father arrived in New South Wales before Mr James was born with barely a penny to his name, a weaver turned missionary. About the only thing he had in his favour was that he was not a convict and that he was honest and hardworking. That's about forty years ago. But men in those days were being given grants of good land and his father got a lot. Specially down this way in the Cowpastures – lovely country, rich, on the Nepean River. They say the old man left his properties to his children – four sons and four daughters. The oldest of the Hassalls lives in these parts, too; he's the Reverend Thomas Hassall, landowner and Church of England rector. Then there were Mr Samuel and Mr Jonathan, both dead now, and the two older daughters, Mary and Eliza. Those daughters both married Methodist ministers, Walter Lawry and William Walker, but the women have died, too. That leaves your new boss James Hassall and the two younger sisters and their husbands with all the family lands. Mr James Hassall has 'Matavai' and 'Freshfield' down this way at Cobbitty and at least two or three other properties on the Hawkesbury River or well up country to the south. So, not quite gentry, not like you mean from England, but rich. You should do well, working for that family.'

They drove on, the bullock driver flourishing his whip from time to time when the bullocks hesitated. At a sharp bend where the road was being cut into a hillside, the dray slowed and the driver shouted a greeting to a couple of troopers leaning on their rifles. Rounding the bend, they saw a gang of men who had been working on the road straighten up and step back off the road to the sound of a horrid jangling.

'Mamma, those men are chained togeth...'

'Hush!'

The children leaned over the edge of the dray, staring frankly at the prisoners, but Anna edged backwards. It was hard to meet the eyes of the men of the chained gang – resentful, angry, despairing eyes. The bullocks drew them slowly past and she suddenly saw herself through the eyes of the convicts, a whole family with little children and their luggage, travelling free while they stood, tools in hardened hands, linked together by their chains. A man twisted away and turned his back, not willing to look at the rich man's drayload or the free man's family. His bare back was ridged with scarring from the lash and Anna gasped to see it. Was this to be part of her new world?

The country grew more undulating and in the distance to the south and the west they could see fringes of purple-blue hills. Fields of oats and maize stood by the road and they passed cattle and sheep spread in large numbers across the land.

'It's good country, you know. Work hard, know a bit about farming, get some land for yourself one day and you'll be right. They need men who know about land – most of the men who were assigned as convict labourers were London thieves or highwaymen on the moors and care nothing about the land. Men like that chain gang back there just take up highway robbery again, once they are free. They call them bushrangers in these parts. . .'

'Bushrangers?'

'Why do you think I'm giving these beasts a hurry-up through the scrub? If any of the gangs of local bushrangers knew that we were coming through with this big load of cargo, we'd find ourselves with a pistol pointing at our hats and anything worth having disappearing off the dray into the bush. I don't mind telling you that I'm always glad to get safely back to Matavai.'

Anna listened with horror. Just when she was beginning to feel happy and hopeful, they threatened her with bushrangers. It wasn't fair.

They jolted on, struggling over hills and moving slowly and carefully when the road edged around steep hillsides. Despite the alarming stories of the driver, she found herself drowsing, nodding and jerking awake, seeing what seemed to be the same trees passing her over and over. The creak and rattle of the dray lulled her and so it was almost a surprise when James called back to her.

'We're here. This is Matavai.'

Anna blinked and stared around her. The dray had stopped on a ridge of high ground above the surrounding countryside. She had a confused impression of buildings, some of sandstone blocks and others of sheets of bark or rammed earth, a two-storeyed house of brick, a sweeping carriageway, shrubs and flowerbeds and staring faces watching the dray. A tall man emerged from the house of brick and the bullock driver muttered, 'That's your boss.' Others came forward to help lift down the children – men in working clothes, ordinary men and, though she knew that most of them must be convicts or former convicts, somehow there didn't seem to be anything frightening about them.

James jumped to the ground and lifted the baby from her arms. It was hard to stand up after sitting still so long and she swayed a little as she put a tentative foot out onto the wheel and jumped down.

'This is my family, sir,' James was saying. 'My wife Anna, and Ann, young Jamie, Jabez and Augustus.'

James Hassall nodded and Anna liked the warmth of his smile.

'Welcome to Matavai. My wife will be pleased to have another woman on the place and some children.'

It was only then that Anna realised that all those standing within sight of the dray were men. She had heard that there were few women up-country, but she had not given it much thought. As they were being directed across the thick grass to a small cottage among the trees, she saw for the first time a woman standing in the doorway of the big house. Anna's midwife's eye saw that the woman in the door was very soon to have a child. And that Mrs James Hassall seemed very young indeed.

In the first days at Matavai, after she had settled their things into their little cottage and laid all their freshly washed clothes out on the grass and over bushes to dry, Anna and the children explored the farm community. Like a great ship sailing through the rich river flats below, the community stood on a broad ridgetop. Matavai House was the ship's bridge and, though small when she thought of Great Dixter at Northiam, it stood high above the other farm buildings and looked out over the surrounding farm to the river and far beyond to the Blue Mountains to the west and the hills of the 'new country' to the south. Behind the big house stood workmen's huts. The long block of convict quarters lay just below the top of the ridge on a wide ledge, like a long boat suspended beside a sailing ship. At the foot of the ridge swept waves of new green and the last of the blossom in an orchard with all the fruit trees she had known at home.

When they had been travelling to New South Wales, she had imagined living in a lonely place, perhaps a shepherd's hut or a cottage cut off from any neighbours, and the thought had frightened her. But it was not like that; here was a busy community with its stone barn and the groom at work among the fine horses in the stables, the blacksmith's shop ringing with the sounds of metal on metal, the dairy, the bakery, a stonemason at work, even men making bricks for new buildings. Everywhere she turned there was wealth and industry, work to do and a prosperous place to do it. It was even beautiful in a way she had not dreamed that a strange land could be.

James laughed at her when she had dug a little patch near the cottage door to plant her poor violets.

'It's too late for them. Even if they live, they won't flower for another year!'

'I'll still put them into the ground anyway. I didn't bring them all this way for nothing,' Anna replied.

He left her tucking daffodil bulbs into the soil, patting them down gently, and when she looked up she caught a glimpse of a face in the window of the big house. The shy young wife was watching her. The ringing of the bell divided their days into pieces, the first clanging breaking into their sleep at dawn. Anna pushed open their shutters to watch the convicts coming sleepily up from their quarters to begin work – the cook to the big house kitchen, the dairyman to the milking, the gardener with his spade over his shoulder. She had somehow expected to see men in chains every day, but only their drab issue clothing distinguished the men from any other workmen. By the time she had lit their own fire and prepared their family breakfast, the bell had rung again to call the men from their work for their own breakfast. Bells for work, bells for rest; the days flowed on with their rhythm.

James took a letter to Mr Hassall. It was the letter written by the Methodist minister back home at Northiam who had addressed his letter of transfer to 'The Methodist Missionary in NSW or elsewhere'.

'A Methodist church near Matavai? No, nothing between here and Parramatta. I'm sorry.'

'We'd like to go to church somewhere.'

'Then join us at our little chapel for the services of the Church of England.'

Anna was disappointed that there was no Methodist minister or local services. She liked the Wesleyan Methodist way of doing things and was sceptical about a clergyman of the Church of England preaching in a way she would find satisfying.

'We'll go, certainly,' James said. 'The Rev. Thomas Hassall may not be so bad, after all.'

On their first Sunday they walked with others from Matavai to the Heber Chapel at Cobbitty. Carriage folk were arriving with well-dressed women being handed down from their seats by gentlemen in tall hats. A young woman with a cascade of ringlets springing from below the frame of her bonnet climbed from her carriage carefully, arranging the folds of a wide shawl across the front of her dress. She looked across at Anna with a small smile of recognition; Anna had not seen Mrs Catherine Hassall so closely before. Parties of convicts arrived with their overseers and were led to seats at the back. Anna was amazed by the numbers of people congregating outside the building; somehow she had expected very few people to live in the district. As they entered the crowded building, she saw the familiar bonnet of Mercy Gill and the bearded head of Silas. She had not dared to hope that the Gills' new place would be near enough for them to meet sometimes. Anna nudged James and saw James' face light up.

The rector entered the pulpit. At home in Sussex they had sometimes been very disappointed with the rituals and flabby platitudes they associated with the local church and Anna steeled herself to face life without the comfort of her own way of understanding Christian faith. She eyed their new rector critically. The Rev. Thomas Hassall was a man in middle life with a strong face who looked at his congregation with warmth and love.

'My text,' he said, 'is from Luke chapter 15 and is the story of the one lost sheep. Jesus said, "Joy shall be in heaven over one sinner that repents. . ."' As he began to speak of the things of God with simplicity and clarity, Anna found herself disarmed and she heard James beside her trying to suppress his affirming 'Amen!' to a mumble.

'My friends,' he said as he came to his final prayers, 'we are outgrowing our chapel. It is good to see so many of our old friends here today and we welcome several new families just migrated to these parts. But if our numbers grow any more, we'll be forced to sit outside under a tree. Should we knock out a wall of the chapel and make it larger, or keep the chapel for our Sunday School and subscribe to a new church building?'

As they moved out through the crush of people at the end of the service, Anna went to hug Mercy and give little Dinah a kiss.

'Where is your place? Is it far?'

'We're at "Camperdown" on the other side of the river. The owner generally lives in Sydney so there is a manager and overseer in charge. And you?'

Anna began to talk and, arm in arm, the women walked through the trees around the chapel, sharing the events of their first week in their new life. Their children had clustered into a group and were eyeing the other groups of boys and girls in the church yard, some from among the carriage folk and others the children of working people. There were some women there, but many more men.

They followed their husbands towards the road and smiled at each other as they overheard their conversation. James and Silas were giving their verdict on the preaching and Anna heard James pronounce, 'And he even preached the gospel!'

James was happy. On the property of Matavai there was plenty of work: shepherding, work with cattle, work in the paddocks, fencing.

Mr Hassall already had nearly thirty convicts working for him and at least one tenant farmer just on Matavai and there were other properties nearby where more workers would be needed. When Mr Hassall talked to him about his wages, James was delighted. He was to receive better wages than he had ever done and was being encouraged to use Matavai land to prepare his own vegetable gardens and keep some poultry.

'Anna, we've done the right thing. This is beautiful farming country. We're both workers, you and I, and this is surely our new beginning. Thank God.'

It was then that they wrote their first letters home with news of their new place: the welcome, the good season, the fine farming land and the opportunities open to others of their family who might join them. As she wrote, Anna pictured her beloved family at home and if her written words painted the picture of New South Wales in colours more inviting than the reality, if she unwittingly held up their new world to the view of brothers and sisters and cousins as a hawker displays his wares, who could blame her?

They would regret those letters, but by then it would be too late.

The doctor's gig stood in the carriageway outside the big house. He had been there for several hours. Anna stood silently in the doorway of her cottage watching the house, waiting for a sign. She felt helpless; all she could do was to pray for the safety of the girl struggling in childbirth in the house on the ridge. It wasn't her place to offer her help. Mrs Hassall had some of her women relatives with her. Anna's friends and neighbours could ask her to come and be with them as a skilful midwife, but the quality was not going to call in the wife of a labourer when they could have the services of a doctor. Anna had her own opinions of doctors; she had heard stories of many who were careless, dirty or rough, and she hoped that the man with young Mrs Hassall was a good man.

Little by little, she had been learning more about the Hassalls. James and Catherine Hassall had only been married a year, Catherine a girl of nineteen and her adoring husband fifteen years her senior. Mr James Hassall was a man who enjoyed life to the full. He was a lively uncle to his many nieces and nephews, involved in farming and politics, hunting and exploring new country, public life and grand parties. On the death of his brother Jonathan, he had inherited Matavai to add to the properties he already owned. His flocks and herds were considerable. Now he looked for an heir.

There was movement at the big house. At last the doctor emerged and drove away and the news went around the community that Mr Hassall had a son.

'Perhaps they'll ask me to do the baby's washing,' thought Anna.

As Christmas approached, the first bright shining of their new home began to dull. On a hot Sunday in December, Mercy and the children did not appear at the Heber chapel. Silas came for Anna.

'Mercy says can you come? Our children are very ill and she needs your help.'

With her own baby tied to her back in his shawl, Anna left her other children with James and set off for 'Camperdown' with Silas. The brilliant sunshine which had seemed so delightful in their early days in the district had been growing hotter and hotter, scorching the land around and making her long skirts and petticoats uncomfortable as she walked. At first she had taken pleasure in the bright days, but now, trudging through thick dust, she knew that she had hardly seen rain since they arrived at Matavai two months earlier. When they came to the crossing over the Nepean, it was not hard to balance on the dry stepping stones, well above the flow of the water.

As they climbed Brownlow Hill, Silas talked about the epidemic which was attacking children on their side of the river. A number were very ill and already several children had died among the neighbours' families.

'We've not been sleeping these past days – one or the other has been ill at night. Now little Dinah, our pretty little thing, is so sick. We've prayed and prayed, but . . .'

The cluster of buildings of a farm came in sight and they quickened their steps. A figure outside a hut started to run towards them: it was young George, the eldest son.

'Ma says hurry!'

Grasping Augustus with one arm, Anna rushed forward, not knowing what she could do or whether there was hope, but wanting desperately to reach her friend. Even as she came to the door of the slab hut she heard a shriek. Mercy was crouched over Dinah's still body. It was too late.

Silas dropped to his knees beside the bed and she heard his harsh question: 'Lord, did we do wrong to come here?'

Christmas was not Christmas at all that year, or so it seemed to

Anna. To celebrate Christmas in the heat of summer was a mockery and to celebrate the birth of Jesus in the middle of grief was hard indeed.

On Christmas Eve, the Sunday congregation gathered by the chapel, standing in subdued groups under the shade of the trees. For seven families, new mounds of earth in the churchyard marked the place where one of their children had been laid in the past two months. Anna stood beside Mercy, her arm around her friend's shoulders, as they silently looked down at a tiny grave. There were no words.

Inside the chapel, the summer heat was intense and the congregation felt the oppression of it. The Rev. Thomas Hassall, slightly red-faced in his clerical robes, spoke gently to his people. It was not the time to preach of joy and angel choirs.

He announced his text. 'I want to speak about the fifteenth chapter of 1 Corinthians: "O grave, where is thy victory?" The events of the past few weeks have touched us all. Children we loved have been dying and we weep together.'

Anna clung tightly to her husband's hand. Her own children were near and well, but tears were streaming down her face for Mercy and Silas and those other grieving neighbours.

The rector went on. 'At Christmas, we remember that Christ came into this world knowing that he, too, was going to die. He died, yet we believe that he is alive forever. And if he is alive, then we have hope. If Christ defeated death, then we too can believe that death is not the end. We believe that those beloved children are safe, alive with God. In the end, even in our grief, we believe that death has not won, but through Christ God gives the final victory to us!'

To the mother sitting with her family in the hot summer atmosphere of the chapel with tear-stained cheeks, it was a strange, unnatural Christmas Eve indeed.

Christmas Day was Anna's birthday. For a Sussex working family there had never been a giving of costly gifts, but she had always had the greetings and love of parents and family with a strong sense of security and home. On this first Christmas Day in Australia, her Northiam family was a world away and she clung to James and her children fiercely, her lifeline against a rising tide of homesickness. It was with a stab of jealousy that she watched carriages arrive at the big house and saw James Hassall with his wife and new baby greeting his brother Thomas. Mrs Ann Hassall and eight young Hassalls spilled out onto the carriageway and disappeared into the house. That evening, other carriages joined them and women alighted, clusters of curls and ringlets falling to smooth bare shoulders and rich gowns, elegantly dressed men dismissing their coachmen and ushering their children into the house. Matavai House was full of light from many candles and lamps and the sound of Christmas songs and laughter wafted across through the warm dusk. Anna sat with James outside their cottage after the children were in bed and watched the shadows passing across the lighted windows of the big house. 'Those Hassalls have everything,' she murmured fretfully to James. 'They're rich, and they have all their friends and family around them. Nothing can touch them. Not like us. . .' There was no way she could know that within the month, the Rev. Thomas Hassall would have to conduct more funerals of children, or that one would be his own youngest daughter.

Summer came and went and the cooler winds of autumn, but no rain came to soften the soil. Across the river flats, farm workers followed their bullock teams dragging ploughs through hard ground. Dust hung in the air but, with no rain for many months, the earth could not be sown. A few farmers planted a little wheat or maize, but as the winter frosts lay over the paddocks there was little sign of growth. The little creek running below the ridge at Matavai dried up to a few waterholes and the water barrels which caught rainwater for drinking were empty. A new daily task for the convicts was water-carrying from the muddy, often polluted river. James Hassall watched the unrelenting blue of the sky and muttered to his workers about the prospect of shortages.

On a day when the frost chilled her feet and the sky was a rich cobalt blue, Anna carried the armful of linen and baby things from the big house and laid them carefully on the table of scrubbed poles which James had built for her near their little hut. Her water kettle was steaming over the fire she had built within a circle of stones and she poured hot water into the big tub. The water looked rather muddy and maybe Mrs Hassall would be disappointed if her linens started to turn brown, but Anna plunged the fabric into the water and began to scrub. Her older children were at school at the Heber chapel with their teachers Mr and Mrs Horne. Jabez was collecting twigs for her fire and Augustus crawled around her feet, clawing his way up her skirt till he stood upright on stout one-year-old legs.

She looked out from her high vantage point across the country. Never had she seen at home in Sussex anything like what was happening to the land. At home, rain was natural, a drifting in from the sea, misting over the Downs, moist air softening the light, turning grasses to many shades of green. Here there was nothing which to her eyes was truly green, only the drab dullness of olive and grey-green. Even where fields of vivid young wheat should have stood, there were only patches of an uncertain crop. All that was left was the hint of a long-ago colour, like the tired folds of an old green skirt which has been scrubbed and bleached and faded in the sun till nothing is left but a faint undertone in memory of what once was. Sheep and cattle were dying for want of water and feed and, if rain didn't come soon, hundreds more would surely die. Was this the fine country where they had encouraged their family to join them?

She heard footsteps and turned, half-expecting to see the man from the dairy passing by or the convict baker with loaves for the big house. It was her husband, looking wretched and moving on unsteady feet into their cottage.

Anna dropped the soapy fabric into the water, scooped the baby away from the fire and hurried after him.

'Are you worse?'

He lay twisted into a knot on their bed, clutching arms across his body.

'All morning. . . I had to come home. . . My insides are being ripped out.'

She crouched beside him, feeling his trembling. All night he had been restless, leaving her side to disappear into the dark and later coming back emptied and in pain. When the workbell had rung that morning, he had brushed off her demands that he stay at home.

'I have to go, I'll be all right — I'm no worse than the others with the dysentery. The boss needs us to cut branches of leaves for sheep feed — they are dying fast enough as it is.'

Now her hands were tender, though her voice was sharp. 'I *told* you not to go. It was so cold this morning, too. It serves you right if you are worse. I'll make you a cup of tea.'

As she swung the kettle over the fire, she looked suspiciously at the water. It really was a funny colour.

James Rootes lay ill and Anna let her other tasks wait while she cared for him. She watched him growing weaker. Other people — children and adults — had been dying of the exhaustion of dysentery and she saw him wasting each day. Some of her children were not well, but her husband was the weakest of all.

To him she said very little, yet within her raged anger — and fear.

Her eyes were screaming, 'James, how *dare* you bring us to the far side of the earth and then go and die! How could you think of doing it? Dear God, what will happen to us if he dies. . .'

To James she whispered, trying not to let the children hear her, 'Don't die, don't leave us, don't leave me alone here – please.'

Beyond the cottage door, the country lay dry and empty. Her heart cried out for the long winding village street of Northiam with its riches of family and friends. Here she felt alone, isolated, bereft of the loving people of her life. She sat immobilised, her face hidden in her hands.

An arm embraced her shoulders and she sat up, startled. Mercy stood there. Beyond she saw other migrant women lifting her little ones into their arms, carrying pots of food.

'We've come to be with you, dear,' Mercy said. 'God knows how often you have come to help us and our families. Don't worry about the little ones or cooking meals. And Mr Hassall asked me to tell you that he has sent for the doctor to see your James. He's really sorry that he's so sick.'

A week later when the danger of death had passed and James Rootes was slowly regaining his strength, Anna walked again through her parched garden. The countryside was as dry and forbidding as ever, but it was no longer empty. Within the community of Matavai and on the farms beyond, she knew it was peopled with friends.

When the letter arrived saying that two of James' brothers, his half-sister Elizabeth Nash and two Playford cousins with all their families were soon to leave Northiam and Beckley for Australia, her feelings were mixed. She longed to see them, yet feared that perhaps it was a mistake for them to come. And she was learning that she and James had a new family, their neighbours at Cobbitty.

The day the ship *Palmyra* came into Sydney Harbour, with the first three families of their relatives and other friends from Sussex, had been proclaimed a Day of Humiliation and Prayer across the colony. The effect of the drought had not eased and now, well into spring in September 1838, the spring rains had not come.

In the Heber chapel, landowners and labourers knelt together pleading with God for the blessing of rain. Somewhere, somehow, they felt that the many evils of the colony – greed, brutality, crime, selfishness – had caused God to withhold the rain as a punishment. In chapels and churches across the colony, men and women begged for mercy. Outside the places of prayer the grass was gone, gnawed to the ground, and the spring day shone in all its devastating brightness on dying sheep and cattle.

The day came when a loaded bullock dray creaked into the yard at Matavai and Anna ran across the open ground from her hut with skirts flying and arms spread to welcome the tired people perched among rice bags and tins of tea.

'Sivyer! Mary, my dear! Dinah, Thomas, all you poor dear little ones – here, pass me the baby. . .' She was almost incoherent with excitement as one after the other James' brothers and their wives and children scrambled down out of the dray into her arms.

'And you are going to work with us here, Sivyer, for Mr Hassall, here on Matavai! And Thomas will be close in Camden – oh, let me look at you. . .'

Later, when the first excitment eased and they had time to talk quietly, Anna and James heard the story of the *Palmyra*. Only days after sailing, the first case of scarlet fever was diagnosed on board. Through the months of travel, the disease had stalked among them, selecting victims. There had been no escape. Anna realised now that Dinah's arms were empty; her only child was gone. Cousin Thomas Playford, the shoemaker, had lost a child, too, as had many families. The *Palmyra* had been quarantined on arrival and there had been an outcry over the standards of hygiene and general health care, but that was too late for the many families who had lost parents or children.

At such cost they had come to the new land. They stared through the open door at the barren land beyond, not wanting to believe that this was the land of promise.

'You are here and we're so glad to see you. It must rain some time and things will get better,' James said, reaching for his Bible and opening it. 'Let's have family prayers together and thank God that you are here.'

Anna added more water, drop by drop, to the dough she was mixing. The water was precious she knew, because she had dragged her bucket up the hill from the river. The flour was very precious, too. Mr Hassall had given out a meagre ration of flour to his labourers and convicts, with strict instructions not to waste it. Outside the door of her hut were the remnants of their struggling vegetable garden, withering pumpkin leaves and a few potatoes. James had worked so hard on that garden, carrying water from the river, and she always emptied the tin dish in which she washed the children onto the vegetables, with sometimes the last drops being poured onto her violets.

Two years had gone by since they first arrived at Matavai. Augustus was running everywhere now and the other children grew taller. She didn't enjoy carrying water these days: a fifth child was due in the new year and she often felt tired.

She turned the moist dough in her hands, flattening a portion into a circle. Among the stones of her fire there was a glow of coals and she poked a place for the bread damper beneath the hot ash. James would be home from the fields before long. A pot of mutton had been cooking slowly and smelled savoury, but she knew that it was mostly bones with little good meat. As the drought had gone on, Mr Hassall had been killing his sheep for meat for rations for his staff, but the animals were so thin that they did not make good eating. Bit by bit, the convict rations had been cut and, if it had not been for their own vegetables, the Rootes would have gone hungry many times. People said that, if you had any wheat on your place, you could get twenty shillings a bushel for it, but after three poor or failed harvests, few people had any wheat to sell.

It wasn't so bad, she decided, for people like themselves. Mr Hassall was a fair man and, though their rations had been cut back and weevilly rice had been substituted for good flour, people on the land survived better than many of the new migrants just arriving in Sydney like cousin Henry Playford. Letters from friends who had just landed in Sydney spoke of a decent loaf costing more than five times the usual price and vegetables at any price could not be found. The government had to feed them all, as it was getting harder and harder to get work. Even so, the convicts on Matavai were grumbling more and more loudly.

A group of workmen walked past her little fire as they made their way back through the dusk to their quarters. Odds and ends of conversation drifted past her; resentful, angry words about hunger, about shortage of food, about the unfairness of the system.

'I reckon that man has a store full of food, all locked up to keep us out — rice, tea, sugar, even flour. He's just too mean to give us decent rations...'

'It's always the same — the rich and the poor. A man ought to take what is his right.'

Late that night, Anna woke to the sound of dogs. Dogs were in full cry, snarling, barking, chasing an unseen person through the dark. She sat up, her heart thumping, and clung to James.

'What's happening? Is it bushrangers? Is it the Aborigines?'

Slivers of light flickered through the cracks in the slab door and James opened it just a little. Shouts of rage were added to the baying of the hounds, then the crack of a pistol. Anna cowered behind James, both peering through the gap in the door. The convict overseer stood silhouetted against the light of a lantern, pistol in hand. A man stood at bay, a sack of food fallen at his feet, defiance fading in his eyes. They recognised one of the men from their own convict quarters.

James whispered, 'He'll be up before the magistrate next week and in irons till then. He should pray he comes before the Rev. Thomas Hassall — they say he never has a man flogged.'

Anna shuddered. The men on Matavai were all known to her. Sometimes in the evenings she would go in search of Jamie or Jabez and find them squatting by the fire in the convicts' huts, listening to the stories of the men, tales of their life before imprisonment, ghoulish stories of life on a convict ship or dreams of what they would do when they were free. The little boys would be entranced by the colour of their stories and the men would be gentle with them or tease them, according to their nature, and share scraps of their own food simmering over the fire. Some were there for burglary or political activism, others for machine-breaking or being cattle thieves. One had made a fraudulent trade of writing begging-letters.

Sometimes she would hear them singing sad songs from home, or rolling home drunk from a visit to the local grog shanty. Some were looking forward to an early release, while others talked bitterly of miscarriage of justice and their hatred for all authority. They were human beings who had become part of her world. Anna crept back to her bed and lay sleepless, picturing the fate of the man who had stolen from his master.

The creak of the cart warned her the day they brought the convict back from the Quarter Sessions at Campbelltown where he had been tried. When the cart stopped in the middle of the yard, the blacksmith ran across from his smithy and the gardener dropped his spade to help drag a limp figure from the back of the cart. Anna shut her eyes to hide the sight of the man half-dragged, half-carried between two men, to disappear down the path to the men's quarters. She didn't want to look at the wounds on his back. When the blacksmith came to her door, she was already gathering clean boiled water and salt with some homemade salve and a towel.

'Can you come, Mrs Rootes? He's bad.'

They had come for her before, at other times like this, and she followed him with a set face, down the little path over the bank to the rough huts below. Down in the huts, the grace and elegance of the big house was a world away. Outside the sun was blazing, but inside the hut was shadowy, odorous and hot. At first she could not see, but she heard a shuddering sigh from the corner and, as her eyes adjusted to the shade, she saw a figure lying on his face on a bench.

Anna knelt in the dust beside him. She had a brief glimpse of a young face she knew, pale and exhausted, and a streak of tears on his dusty cheek before he rolled his head away, hiding his face in his arm. Very gently she washed his back, cleansing the skin of dried blood and dirt, dipping her cloth into the warm salty water. The marks of the lash crisscrossed from shoulder to waist: thick weals, broken flesh. Flies buzzed around her head, trying to settle on the wounded back, and she waved them off.

The blacksmith still stood behind her, watching, and he asked curiously, 'How many, mate?'

'Fifty.'

She couldn't bear to think about it. She had seen the terrible triangle in the public square, where men were tied, 'kissing the three sisters'. She had once seen a man flogged, a thick and brawny man swinging the cat-o'-nine-tails, and she could still hear in memory the grunt as the scourger swung and the gasp or the scream as the nine thongs descended. That man had stopped from time to time to untangle the twisted thongs so that the punishment should not be diminished. With her softest touch she spread salve over the wounds.

'Let me wash your face, lad.'

The man slowly turned his head and she sponged away the dusty sweat and the streaks of tears. His eyes had been closed but, as she laid her hand briefly on his tangled hair, he opened them and looked at her. The hurt and the anger was still there, but they were not directed at her. She stood up awkwardly and collected her things. As she turned to go back into the glare of the sun, she felt his hand grasp her skirt.

A husky voice whispered, 'I thank you.'

'God protect you, lad.'

She walked away. Perhaps she was one of the few women who ever came near their hut. Had he been remembering his mother, home in England? Or a sister, who would have wept for him? There were so very few women in the lives of the convict men. Would it be different for them all in the colony if there were more wives and mothers? Perhaps.

When at last the rains came, they came with such force that the river flooded, sweeping away fences and soil and uprooting trees along the river flats. Yet when the waters subsided, leaving muddy highwater marks well up tree trunks, the community along the Nepean was full of hope. After the disasters of the previous years, with the long drought, there was promise of a great harvest. The grasses sprang up, vividly green, and the wildflowers bloomed again.

More and more migrant families had been arriving from England and little cottages sprang up on all the farms of the district. Landowners still worried about the threat of the end of transportation of convicts with the loss of cheap labour, but things on the land were looking more promising and there was a degree of new optimism as more free settlers changed the balance of felon and free. The overcrowded congregation at the Heber chapel opened a subscription list to build a larger church of stone, complete with tower, and James Rootes added his gift to the list of contributors. As more Methodist families arrived in the area, the Rootes family joined others for regular Methodist meetings on the verandahs of Matavai House or Thomas Hassall's Denbigh. Small schools across the district were filled with the children of migrant families and the new numbers of married women were filling the cradles of the colony.

Anna's fifth baby was born safely at Matavai early in 1840, her first little Australian, a fine fat baby girl they called Mary. At the Heber chapel in March, with the congregation crowding to the doors, James and Anna stood before the people for the baptism of Mary. The little child, well-fed and contented, lay placidly in the arms of the Rev. Thomas Hassall as the water of baptism touched her head. Anna watched with a knot of emotion as Mr Hassall prayed a blessing for her and gently placed her back in Anna's arms.

Surely, she thought, our worst times are over now.

4
Withering winds
1840-1844

WITH BABY MARY ON HER HIP and the other children walking beside her, Anna followed James up the slope away from Matavai, climbing away from the farm and on over the hill. It was early spring and the wattles were in flower, the grey-green bush rich with gold. She pulled a sprig of it, fat yellow puffballs nodding in clusters among green needles, and poked it into the ribbon on her bonnet where it danced joyfully in rhythm with her step. Augustus was starting to lag behind, his short legs refusing to keep up, and James lifted the child onto broad shoulders.

She started to sing a breathy fragment of a hymn of praise, but the hill was too steep for singing. Even so, the tune ran on in her head, a song she loved: 'On Christ the solid rock I stand, All other ground is sinking sand. . .' Ahead of her James strode, her strong, trustworthy man who had just been promoted to overseer on Matavai. James had never known quite how terrified she had been when he was so ill. For so long she had been the one to keep on worrying about everything that could go wrong for them, or that made life difficult — the seeming hopelessness of the long drought, the shortages of food, the companionship of convicts, the doubts whether they could ever earn enough to begin to buy some land for themselves. James had always been confident that things would turn out well eventually and now she was beginning to believe him. The rains had come and transformed the grey land into a place of lush pastures and growing crops. The sheep had plenty to eat and her own vegetable plot was full of spring greens and good things for the family pot. Even her violets had flowered this spring and the slips of other flowers offered by her friend Mrs Hassall from the terraced gardens were thrusting out vigorous growth.

She was growing daily more tolerant of their convict neighbours – and in any case, the Governor had just announced the end of transportation to New South Wales, so newly convicted criminals were not going to enter her world again, she hoped. As to land of their own, land prices were increasing almost monthly, first doubling then quadrupling for the rich lands to the south, and their dream of a little farm of their own seemed to be fading. Yet James was not anxious about it. 'With the end of transportation,' James told her, 'men like Hassall are going to need free workmen like me more than ever – he'll be in deep trouble for want of labour as it is. My job is very safe, and he'll probably have to pay me more to keep me – not like back home! *Later* we'll have plenty to buy our land.'

Today, she was happy. The sun was shining, the children were well, James was free of work for the day, and they were all on their way to a camp meeting in Bill Brown's paddock. Back in their cottage the never-ending work of making a home waited for her, but today was delightfully Sunday, and she was free.

The miles passed under their feet, the paddocks with their springtime crops and the bush with green and gold overhead and purple of creeping vine underfoot. Others joined them, families of other Methodists also carrying their food for the day and their Bibles. There were the Gills and the Browns, Starrs and Nashs, Vidlers and Towners, Fosters and Wheatleys, Dousts and Shoesmiths and others. They met and greeted each other in Bill Brown's paddock, embracing and exclaiming over young babies, laughing, whispering news, sharing the ups and downs of previous weeks.

Mercy ran up to Anna with news. 'Mr James Hassall is taking on Silas! We're coming to live on Matavai.'

'On Matavai? Oh, Mercy!' Anna hugged her friend with tears in her eyes. 'There'll be us, and Sivyer and Mary, and the Fryers and Unicombs and Platts, and William Bottom, and *you*! We'll be a whole village of old friends, almost.'

Nearby, the little slab chapel stood empty. Often, the people of that part of the district met there for worship, praying and singing with sheets of overlapping bark for a roof and round timber poles set upright in the earth for walls. But today, for the camp meeting, there were far too many people to crush into the tiny building. Instead of logs for seats, Anna settled her children around her on the thick grass with its new gold of dandelions and daisies; for the roof she had the spreading branches of a bush-apple, and beyond that the sky.

Far away in Sussex and Kent were the ancient church buildings where their ancestors had prayed for generations and the newer Methodist chapels with their special memories. Here in the Cowpastures, Anna found herself detached from her past; here were no castles, no ancient churches, no Methodist ministers. For her and the other migrants there was no common memory linked with this land, no long-established roots. She looked up through the branches of the bush apple and away to the encroaching bush from which Bill Brown had wrested an open paddock. Beside her, the children sat beheading dandelions or threading daisy chains, and small Augustus lay on his front watching a beetle in the sweetness of bruised grass. Baby Mary was sound asleep. Was this their new beginning?

Silas stood up, towering over the people.

'Let's sing!' he said, and in his deep and powerful voice he began to sing, drawing the other voices with him.

Others took their turns to lead their friends. Another big man, one Tom Brown, rose to pray, his voice echoing back from the stony ridge behind them. They said that Tom had been a prize-fighter and had been brought back to God at the height of a thunderstorm; the energy and power he had once used to knock men down was now channelled into his desire to serve God. Listening to the volume of his prayer, it crossed Anna's mind to be glad they were not having their meeting on the Matavai House verandah this time — it would rattle the walls and wake up Mrs Catherine's babies!

They'd asked James to preach: 'You're a lay preacher, you do it — some of us have a bit of trouble with reading, anyway!' Anna watched her husband standing in front of the crowd on the grass, Bible in hand and painstakingly prepared notes in his pocket. He didn't take this lightly. She'd watched him work on his sermon night after night by the light of the slush lamp, and she knew that he wanted to draw the people to God. She'd heard his sighs and watched him strike out whole paragraphs with a dissatisfied pen, but now he was on his feet, doing the best he could.

They stayed in Bill Brown's paddock all day, until the sun began to fall towards the distant Blue Mountains. The gathering of migrants sang till they were hoarse, shared their lunches, prayed till they felt God standing right beside them, his feet among the daisies. One after another scrambled to their feet to tell the story of their own spiritual journey, of the stresses of settling in a strange land, of loneliness and deprivation. They confessed to things which had been making them feel cut off from God and encouraged each other. There were tears of penitence and shouts of laughter and praise. Silas and Tom outdid each other with the power of their songs and prayer, the sound climbing up the rocky wall behind them and flowing out over the bush below.

With the bush darkening around them, they walked home, each family carrying exhausted little ones to their huts and cottages, the long miles passing under their feet as they talked of the day. They would meet again for a camp meeting, perhaps next year, and in the meantime they had plans for regular Methodist services as usual. From time to time the ministers from Parramatta, Rev. John McKenny or the young John Watsford, would travel to lead them, and they would continue to take advantage of the ministry in the district of the rector, Thomas Hassall. A plan which pleased Anna very much was the decision to divide the people of the widely scattered settlements into three groups for class meetings. More than fifty adults had committed themselves to meet regularly for mutual spiritual support.

Perhaps this as well as their beautiful children was to be their new beginning. Surely nothing could go badly wrong for them now?

She had always thought that while she and James and their children would probably suffer hardships and pain from time to time, people like the Hassalls were protected from trouble. James Hassall could have what he perceived as trouble, when his staff didn't please him or when something went wrong with one of his precious horses, or when some public decision such as the issue of transportation went against his judgment, but even so, he and Mrs Catherine Hassall lived in a safe and privileged position. Their large brick house stood proudly on its ridgetop, the sun warming the handmade bricks, shrubs and vines entwining the verandah pillars, terraced gardens falling away down the slope.

Anna stood at an upstairs window, bucket and rags in hand as she washed the small square window panes. Behind her the Hassalls' bedroom was rich with brocades draping the vast fourposter bed. Mrs Catherine's lovely gowns were hidden inside the cedar wardrobe, but some of her dainty things were laid on the dressing table, elegant, expensive. The mirrors and the paintings, the china ewer and bowl on marble-topped washstand, the jewel box and thick rug on the floor were for Anna things of dreams and her hands did not hurry as they wrung out the cloth and washed another window pane. Through the window, she looked down on the terraced gardens and the wide paddocks beyond. A shout of laughter floated up to her and she saw her Augustus' little friend John Hassall jump out from among the flowering bushes to surprise his mother. Mrs Catherine pretended to be astonished, leaping back and then chasing the little boy along the path among the flowers and catching him up in her arms. As they disappeared again on a lower path, the young mother was dropping big kisses on her child's head.

Anna picked up her bucket and moved off to wash the windows in the little boys' bedroom full of everything a proud father could buy for his sons. From these windows she looked down on the rooftops of the dairy and bakery, carriage house and saddlery, with the convict quarters beyond. Walls of great sandstone blocks and shingled roof sheltered the barn and stables, with the blacksmith's shop at the end of the row. She could see some men leaning on the door of the blacksmith's shop, watching and talking, while a man stooped over the hoof of one of James Hassall's many fine horses. Her own little house was there with its roof of split shingles. A man was polishing the carriage in the driveway and her Augustus was down there beside him, dancing around his feet and probably asking more of his three-year-old's questions. As the damp cloth in Anna's hand poked into corners of the panes, washing away the last of the summer dust, she elbowed aside the heavy curtains, the fabric brought from England to decorate a rich man's home. Her own house had no such curtains, but she had curtained off a corner with flourbags to protect their clothes. One day, she dreamed, they would have a larger house – and better furniture – and curtains. . .

Yes, the Hassalls really did seem to have everything.

The knock on her door was sharp, repeated.

'Mrs Rootes! Mrs Rootes, can you come?' The voice was that of one of their neighbours, calling her urgently.

Anna opened the door. The man's face was anxious and he was breathing heavily as if he had been running.

'One of our lads is really ill and the baby has a bad fever – my wife asked me to fetch you.'

Anna called her Ann to stay home from school to mind the little ones and went with the neighbour. The rich river farmlands along the Nepean were becoming the home for a growing number of free families, nearly all of them living in small communities and scattered cottages on the land of their masters, the landed gentry. Most of them worked very hard, man and wife and any able children, all with the dream of one day being able to leave the employment of their bosses to take up land of their own.

As they strode along the track, Anna asked, 'Do you know if your boy has a pain in his head? Or his stomach? Or a rash?'

But the father wasn't sure. All he knew was this: his children were ill, and his wife trusted Mrs Rootes to be able to offer help. Anna hurried on, her forehead puckering as she tried to imagine what she might face. Childbirth was one thing – with that she knew what she was doing, and it was her belief that more mothers and babies survived under her care than when the women went to the town hospital. Simple childhood ills she could treat, or wounds, and she was gradually adding more medicinal herbs to her little garden at Matavai – but some diseases were far too hard. Even the skilled doctors were mystified by many of the diseases which cut their way through the population.

Dogs began barking in greeting as they approached the workman's cottage, and a woman's face appeared in the doorway, a face lined with worry. Anna stopped at the bedside to look at the children who lay there. As she asked the mother about their illness, she turned back the blanket and saw the fierce red rash spreading from their necks down over their bodies.

As the mother was whispering, 'I'm so glad you've come. I thought you might know what we could do. . .', Anna was shaking her head. She saw all the signs of scarlet fever. They all knew about scarlet fever. It had swept through migrant ships, taking a dreadful toll of lives and had been moving from community to community ever since, even though the authorities had done their best to quarantine incoming ships with the disease. There was little she or anyone else could do.

It was some weeks later when Augustus climbed onto her lap one evening complaining of a headache. At first she thought that he had been playing in the sun too long. He laid his head against her shoulder and she cuddled him to her, stroking his face. It was then that she realised that his skin was burning and he was trembling.

'Mamma, I don't feel well.' The child's voice was shaky and tearful. 'My throat hurts.'

'Mamma's little lad . . . there now, lie back and sleep while I hold you.'

She held him, but he didn't sleep. His shivering increased even though she wrapped a blanket around him, and cool water on his face did not reduce the fever.

'Jamie, run straight for Mrs Gill. Tell her I need her.'

Even as Anna lifted the little boy onto the bed, he began to retch and by the time Mercy came hurrying in, the mother's imagination had leapt forward. If it was the disease she feared there would soon be a sign.

'Mercy, can you look after the other children? Just for tonight? I'm afraid. What if it's. . .'

'Scarlet fever?'

'Yes.'

She stooped over the little boy, cleaning his face, crooning softly to him and behind her she was faintly aware of Mercy gathering the other children and taking them into the other room. With James beside her, she watched beside her child, and when the red rash began to break out on his neck, she saw it growing while she whispered harshly, rejecting what she saw, 'God, no. No!'

'Can you do anything, do you think?' James' voice was husky.

'Only keep him cool and try to get him to drink some water – and pray. . .'

The night was very long. James lay down to try to get a little sleep for part of the night, but Anna stayed by Augustus Jesse, ready with the basin, gentle with cool cloths. The red rash spread, down his chest and over his body, and the little boy with the enquiring mind asked her, 'Mamma, why does my throat hurt? Why is my tummy so red? Why, Mamma?' There was no answer.

In the morning she left the child for a few minutes to hurry up to the big house to say that she could not come to do housework for Mrs Hassall today. She knocked on the door, but waited for what seemed a very long time before the door opened.

A tousled young woman stood in the doorway, ringlets limp and uncombed and dark shadows under her eyes.

'Oh, Mrs Rootes. Something terrible has happened. I don't know what to do – little John's ill. He was crying in the night a lot, with headache he said, and vomiting, and now he has an awful red rash all down his neck and chest.'

In big house and in cottage, mothers stayed with their three-year-old sons. The doctor was brought to see John Hassall, but Anna knew that John – and Augustus – would live or die as God willed, and there was little the doctor could do about it. News passed around the district of other families where scarlet fever had struck. Baby Mary Rootes was ill, too, but not so ill as Augustus. The people who had become a closeknit group of friends in the Rootes' regular class meeting met for prayer together, gathering very early in the mornings before work, or late after dark, praying for the lives of the little boys and the others who were ill. Each family knew that perhaps the disease would touch their own homes, and each cared very deeply about the pain of their friends. Women came to the cottage door to leave a fresh loaf, or a pot of broth, and men put a hand on James Rootes' shoulder in silent sympathy. Anna was only vaguely aware of the concern of her friends. She slept little and then only when Mercy came to stay beside Augustus, watching and praying yet feeling a deep hopelessness. There was no tonic that she knew of for scarlet fever, and her child's fever continued to burn. Sometimes in the night she looked up from her window and saw a light burning upstairs in the big house; another family was walking the same path.

Through the window a steady clanging sounded. Her mind knew that it was only the blacksmith beating out redhot metal on his anvil in the smithy just behind her house. But her child was dying and she cried to James, 'Tell him to stop!' The ringing of the metal had been going on and on, and it sounded like the tolling of the death knell.

That evening at the end of April 1841, Augustus Jesse, her baby of the voyage, died. From the moment she had first seen the rash she had feared it, and now it was true. 'Was there something more I could have done?' she wondered. Had she given up when perhaps some other herbal remedy, some other care might have saved him? She didn't know.

Within the week, baby Mary was recovering, but the other three-year-old, the heir of their master Mr Hassall, was gone as well. Anna went quietly to see Catherine Hassall. The young woman sat slumped in her elegant chaise longue, haggard and pale, her eyes swollen and red with weeping. The two women sat in silence for some time, thinking, remembering, understanding. They spoke a little of their sons, little boys who had played together in the gardens of Matavai.

As Anna walked back to her own cottage, she understood that, after all, the rich were not wholly protected from this world's pain.

She had no way of knowing that the death of their son was only the first rent in the firm fabric of their lives for the Hassalls; the weave of their established world was beginning to unravel.

It was April once more and the autumn rains were soaking the district. Last year in April they had followed the little coffin of Augustus Jesse to a grave in the grounds of the church at Cobbitty. Then they had walked past hewn blocks of sandstone ready to rise as walls for the new church. Today the church stood complete, slender gothic windows echoing the lines of the steeple, and carriage folk, working people and the last of the convicts gathered to see the Bishop of Australia, Bishop Broughton, declare the new St Paul's Church at Cobbitty open. 'I helped to pay for that!' James whispered with pride.

As the Bishop and his party came in procession to open the door, Anna realised that a significant figure was not there.

'Where's the rector, Mr Hassall?' she murmured to a neighbour.

'They say he's ill and can't come.'

'Not come? After all the work he's done? After calling us all to help build this for at least five years? The poor good man...'

James shook his head in disappointment. Though he loved his Methodist meetings, the preaching and leadership of Thomas Hassall had become very important to him and he had come to value the rector as a man of God. To Anna he was a good Christian man who comforted her in sorrow and baptised her babies.

The people followed the Bishop through the arched doorway into the new house of God. Anna hesitated, waiting for others to go before her. She looked back for a moment at the Heber chapel, now to be simply a schoolhouse. With its simple bricks and plain square windows and doors, it looked a little old-fashioned beside the handsome new church with its arches and tower. In St Paul's there would be pews at the front owned by the gentry, properly paid for and with their own little gates, and pews at the back marked for convicts and strangers. Somewhere in between she hoped there would be a place for her and her family. As she drew the children with her along the aisle, the violins in the gallery overhead began the opening bars of a hymn of praise. Long ribbons of sunlight fell across the people from the clear glass of the high windows, lighting the Bishop in the three-tiered pulpit. She bowed her head. In this building, she prayed, many people would have their hearts turned to God.

After the service of worship, as the people moved out again into the late afternoon sun, knots of parishioners spoke together. Silas Gill was muttering to James Rootes that he felt more at home up in the slab-and-bark chapel out on the stony ridge. Others talked together of farms and prices, of shortages of labour, of politics.

'What's happening to our wool market overseas?' said one. 'Wool prices are falling every week – don't they want our good wool any more?'

'It's not just wool – wheat is down, too. And livestock.'

'And have you heard of those Sydney merchants? Bankrupt! Something is going badly wrong in the colony these days. . .' and the men wandered off together, shaking their heads, trying to decide who to blame.

Anna had not heard them. She had gone to stand once more near the grave of her little boy. Another child was growing within her now, but she did not forget.

James Hassall rode into Matavai one afternoon and Anna saw his face as he went by. His shout for the groom was abrupt and sent the man running to take the reins and lead away the horse as his master strode into Matavai House.

'What's the matter with the boss?' Anna murmured to Mercy. The two women sat outside Anna's cottage door, Anna's new baby Lydia and Mercy's new son sleeping in their baskets nearby and their laps full of chicken feathers as they plucked chickens for dinner at the big house.

'Who knows? He looks very upset about something.'

'His temper is getting shorter every day. James says it is something about land, and not having enough men to work for him. He is a worried man, I think. But I don't understand what is going on, really.'

'Are you working at Matavai House tonight,' Mercy asked, 'to help with their dinner party? Well, then, you might hear some news then.'

In the dining room at Matavai that night, the candles shone from the candelabra and wall sconce onto the long table with its silver and glass, flowers and fruits, heaped plates of beef and chicken with vegetables from the Matavai gardens. Anna stood at the kitchen table, helping the cook to prepare the plates for the rich plum pudding which was to be sent to the table soon, and as the door opened and shut she caught brief glimpses of the guests at table. She could see the back of the head of the Rev. Thomas Hassall and

Mrs Hassall, with the familiar faces of James and William Macarthur and their ladies of 'Camden Park', the Charles Cowpers of 'Wivenhoe' and the Oxleys of 'Kirkham'. Mrs Catherine was looking very pretty this evening, with the candlelight lighting up her glossy curls and the glint of jewellery against the curve of her shoulders in the lowcut gown, but Anna noticed the slightly anxious expression she sometimes wore when she was hostess of a party of older and respected neighbours.

The talk seemed to be about politics and plans for the new Legislative Council to be elected in June next year, in 1843. James Macarthur was planning to stand, it seemed, and there was a question of whether or not Charles Cowper also intended to stand for the electoral district of Camden. The conversation was becoming heated, slipping into remarks on candidates' religion and morals, and attitudes to former convicts who were now wealthy citizens. Twenty-four men were to represent all the districts of New South Wales, including Port Phillip, town and country, and the men at the table, all substantial landowners, were gratified to know that the weight of the 'country interest' would far outstrip the representation from town dwellers. Even so, they had cause for pessimism. Voices were raised and the cook glanced at Anna with raised eyebrows.

'Not having it all their own way for once,' he whispered as he stirred the custard.

Fragments of conversation drifted through the door, but Anna did not understand much of it and, when she did, it seemed to have little link with her own life.

'How in heaven's name do they propose that we run our properties? Sheep-walks of thousands of acres with no shepherds, no cattlemen, no boundary riders — we might as well abandon the hundreds of thousands of sheep out there and let the Aborigines have the place after all!'

'They've stopped transportation so we've lost all our assigned labourers. Now the first flood of free migrants has slowed to a mere trickle and I for one can't afford to pay enough free men to work on my properties.'

Anna heard them speak of labour, and was glad that at least James, Sivyer, Silas and the rest ran no risk of losing their jobs while labour was in such short supply.

'I've always contended that coolie labour from India is the next best — at least they are never likely to want to rise above their station like some of these upstart British migrants who seem to think that Jack is as good as his master. . .'

'Well perhaps, but personally I'd rather get our labour from the Irish Catholic, even though the Bishop fears we'll be overrun by Popery. At least they are British. . .'

'This clamour for the vote from some of these men with absolutely no claim to it, no property to speak of at all – the thing is ridiculous. The men to lead and the men to vote must surely be those of the landed gentry and substantial merchants and such, otherwise we will be reduced to the lowest possible standards. . .'

'But prices on all our stock are falling so badly. A year ago prices weren't so very bad, but now! Several years of drought, then a flood, and now the bottom is falling out of the market for everything we produce. . .'

'I'd planned to sell some flocks of sheep to ease my worries out on my Burruwa estate and right out along the Murrumbidgee, but no-one wants to take them, even as a gift! And the price of wool has halved. . .'

'It's not only us – the merchants are in trouble, the businessmen, and the money men. Too much speculation in land, everyone trying to build their kingdoms on paper with unwise borrowing and lending, subdividing farms nearer to Sydney into imaginary suburbs with imaginary buyers for the land, easy credit and harsh interest rates. . .'

'And talk about insolvencies! In the newspaper every week some other man we know – pastoralist, merchant, businessman – is being called to a meeting of his creditors, and faced with bankruptcy. None of us is safe.'

'Did you hear someone say that this year, 1842, there have been close on 600 insolvencies? The whole system is crumbling. . .'

The last dishes were returned to the kitchen, the gentlemen sat over their port and the ladies retired to visit briefly Mrs Catherine's little James who was safely in his bed upstairs. Anna stood at the scullery bench, hands deep in a dish of water washing the delicate china plates and cups. Each piece was beautiful, fragile, and she handled them with care. The guests had dined well, in grace and comfort, which made their conversation on financial fears not only hard to understand, but also quite unbelievable.

Anna replaced the lovely china on the kitchen dresser and dismissed the conversation she had heard from her mind.

The first rumours began when James Hassall put 300 acres of his Matavai land on the market.

'*Selling* bits of Matavai?' people said. 'Men like Hassall are always buying more. What is going on?'

Workmen were sent off to one of the newer pieces of land far south on the Murrumbidgee to work with sheep, but the stories drifted back that perhaps Hassall had overstretched himself, that no-one wanted to buy the sheep he wanted to sell, that the prices for his wool were so bad that it was scarcely worth shearing if it was money he was after.

'Maybe the poor man has just lost interest in all his farms just now,' Anna suggested. 'Now that his second little son has died, he has no heirs to build up his lands for.'

One day Anna stood at the kitchen table in Matavai House, cutting up the last of the summer peaches and apricots for preserves, and her master's wife wandered aimlessly into the room. The younger woman walked idly around the room, touching things which she was not seeing, living in a small, sad world of her own.

'A lovely crop of fruit in the orchard this year, Mrs Hassall,' offered Anna.

'Oh. Yes. I suppose it was.' The young woman turned her back on the workers at the kitchen table, staring blindly from the window onto her summer garden, and Anna remembered that when the orchard down by the creek had been awash with blossom, this woman had often walked under the trees with her little two-year-old son, the child named for his father. Now the ripe fruit had all been picked and the child was dead.

The fruit was heaped into the big pot, sugared and set to cook for jam. The aroma of cooking began to fill the kitchen and the master's wife turned to go.

'I can't bear the smell of cooking,' she said softly to Anna as she went. 'It makes me feel sick . . . Oh, what good is it? Any child I have will only die.'

They had heard the stories many times over the past year or so; gloomy tales of rich merchants who had lost their wealth or pastoralists who were being forced to sell. Anna listened with only part of her mind when the stories were being told. She was not specially interested in the doings of people she didn't know in parts of New South Wales where she had never been, nor did she understand much of what people were saying about insolvencies and business failures, speculation in land and problems with overseas markets.

'It's nothing to do with me,' she insisted, and went on her way with the established rhythm of feeding baby Lydia, caring for small Mary and the three older children, cooking, washing, helping in the big house when she was needed, enjoying meeting her friends in her Methodist class meeting. Rich men might have their worries, but it did not touch her family directly so it did not touch her. James Rootes sometimes had a chance to read the *Sydney Gazette* or the *Australian*, and the tales of calamity and failure filled the pages. The price of sheep had fallen to three or four shillings, but a flock-master had discovered the possibilities of slaughtering, skinning, cutting up and boiling down surplus sheep in great iron vats, then selling the extracted fat as tallow for greatly improved prices. The newspapers gave instructions on the best methods for boiling down; and the stench of boiling carcasses drifted across the countryside. Even so, Rootes felt secure in his position with James Hassall; though other men were unemployed and tramping the roads of New South Wales searching in vain for work, Hassall was a good master and needed men like himself, his brother Sivyer and Silas Gill.

But the talk continued. Waiting for James after church one Sunday, Anna listened to her neighbours in anxious conversation outside St Paul's Church. Men stood in tight groups with knitted brows and solemn voices.

'The rector holds major shares with the Bank of Australia, so I'm told, and men like the Macarthurs and Oxleys.'

'And James Hassall will be hard hit, I believe — he's a big shareholder, too.'

The Hassall carriage rolled to a halt near the church and James and Catherine Hassall climbed into their seats with heads held high, nodding polite farewells to others who had been at church with them that morning. The master wore a strangely set expression for one who was usually so good-humoured, Anna thought. Though she did not understand what the neighbours were talking about, she felt that Mr Hassall was a very troubled man, and she knew that Mrs Hassall was paler and sometimes red-eyed. The workman's wife had thought that this was because her mistress was still a very sad person, and was suffering the ills of early pregnancy, but perhaps there was more to it than that.

By the time Catherine Hassall had been delivered of a baby daughter, late in 1843, it was clear that her husband was a very worried man. From time to time he sold a few horses, but he and his wife no longer held great parties at Matavai House. It became clear that James Hassall was in financial straits, caught with enormous holdings of land and insufficient labour, his shares in the failed Bank of Australia less than worthless with his unlimited liability and having thousands of sheep which he could neither sell nor earn on their wool. Then Governor Gipps announced new laws which meant that no man could 'squat' on vast tracts of land beyond the limits of location for a mere licence fee of ten pounds; properties were to be leased in smaller and limited acreages, each with a licence of ten pounds. The Governor was trying to break the power of squatters to control the whole of New South Wales which was then more than half the entire eastern side of Australia, but opposition was intense as landowners claimed their 'right' to possess land which they considered to be waste land, and which they had filled with sheep.

The master's horse was often saddled early through the next months and Hassall rode off to meetings of landowners, men striving to hold what they had built up. His affable nature became more and more tense and short-tempered, and Anna tried to keep out of his way. She felt sorry for his wife. Anna herself was contented. Her vegetable garden was flourishing, her children were strong and healthy, her little cottage near the blacksmith's shop was homelike, and her flower beds were well-established, with Northiam violets and daffodils blooming in the spring around her doorstep.

James Rootes went one day in May to a meeting of the Pastoral Movement. That evening he sat at their family table, surrounded by his five children and their mother. The food on the table was ample and the children looked well.

'It was a lively one there today,' he said at length, when the last morsel had been eaten. 'About a hundred of us in the yard at the Camden Inn, all yelling at once. Some say that the Governor's plan is to cripple the whole wool industry by making it hard for sheep farmers to run their big places way out in the back blocks. It is hard enough to get working families to go way out there anyway, and they reckon they can't afford to make all the improvements the government demands if they only have a lease and no certainty about whether they'll still have the land in a year's time. Others say that the Governor just wants to protect the ordinary people – or we'll end up like serfs in Russia and never have a chance to have a place of our own, if all the land is grabbed by the first rich men to get there.'

James reached for his worn Bible for their evening prayers as a family. He added, 'Mr Hassall was one of the men chosen to be on a committee of squatters from these parts to work for the Pastoral Association. But everyone says that he and his brother the rector are in a lot of financial trouble.'

Anna wiped sticky hands and faces of her children as they prepared to listen to their father read from the Bible and pray with them at the end of the day.

'Do you think Mr Hassall might have to sell their lovely carriage, or some more of his horses then?' asked Anna.

James sighed. It seemed to him that his wife had not been listening. 'It will be worse than that, I guess.'

In the winter in 1844, there was a small notice in the newspapers announcing that the estate of Mr James Hassall had been sequestrated. Even then Anna did not see what it might mean for her family. She was carrying her seventh baby and was absorbed in the inward-looking thoughts of the child to come.

'My dear woman,' James said impatiently, 'don't you understand? This means that Mr Hassall can't pay his creditors. He'll be applying for a certificate of insolvency soon enough, like so many other landowners and businessmen over the past few years. The government is taking charge of his land till he can pay — and he can't pay, I don't think.'

'But — can't he sell something? One of his little farms on the Hawkesbury? Or a lot of his sheep?'

'And who'd buy a sheep in these times? Sheep are only good for boiling down, and the way they are doing that, New South Wales will soon be left empty of sheep. No, he's broke, finished. He won't be selling bits of land or a few horses. They'll take it out of his hands and he'll come close to losing the lot.'

Anna stood very still. Instinctively her hands were cupped protectively around the swell in her apron, the new life still to be born into an uncertain world.

'Not — not Matavai, too?'

'Even Matavai.'

5
Root and branch
1845-1851

ANNA'S SEVENTH CHILD was born on a hot December day in the summer of 1844. As she lay exhausted, damp with the sweat of summer and the sweat and blood of the birth struggle, the cry of her new-born daughter mingled with the sound of men shouting and the jingle and beat of passing horses. Her sister-in-law Mary Rootes and Mercy Gill had been with her through the long hours and now Mary said, 'Another healthy child, Anna, thank God. Now let me clean you and you can sleep.'

Mercy Gill pushed open the window shutter a little, letting in a gust of warm wind as she watched the passing parade.

'There go most of Mr Hassall's horses. Off to the sale. The stables will soon be nearly empty – and they say they may even have to sell the carriage.' Mercy's voice was wistful.

Anna listened vaguely to the voices of the women. She was so very tired. She submitted gratefully to her sister-in-law as the cool water was sponged over her soiled and weary body, cleansing, refreshing. If she had still been home in Northiam, she thought, her mother would have been there, too. Mercy washed the baby, murmuring gently as the tiny girl wailed. She herself was expecting another child in a month and the two women had been sharing their weariness. With Mary supporting her, Anna stood briefly on the cool stone floor while the stained sheets were stripped from her bed and replaced with clean linen. At last she lay back, clean, tired, with baby Louisa at her breast.

'A pity about those lovely horses,' one of the women remarked, 'and he won't get much for them – they say that horses bought for fifty pounds are only selling for about seven pounds these days.'

Mercy gathered up her dish and tossed the water away through the door, sprinkling Anna's garden. She sniffed, wrinkling her nose in disgust. The wind was bringing a hint of the stench of the distant boiling-down of sheep. 'What a stink! We can be glad we don't live any closer to the boiling-down works.'

'Sivyer reckons that they'll be sorry one day – some quick money now, but hundreds of flocks gone forever. You can shear a sheep again next year, Sivyer says, but this boiling down . . .!'

'My Silas says that it won't be long before there will have to be a big sale of everything – not just Mr Hassall's horses, but the sheep and cattle and the farms, too.'

'And this place? Matavai?'

'Who knows?' Mercy sat down heavily. 'Since the Bank of Australia fell, poor Mr Hassall and a lot of his friends are in bad trouble. He won't be able to pay us all, and he mightn't even have a farm for us to work on in a few months. Silas thinks that maybe if Matavai goes, we might leave and go north to join his brother on the Hunter River.'

Anna lay back wearily, the baby cradled in her arms and the talk of the women flowing over her. The tiny one had dropped off to sleep against the curve of her breast. Anna traced the outline of the baby's head with a gentle finger, a tiny vulnerable creature, dependent on her parents. A slow tear trickled down Anna's cheek and slid onto the downy head.

'Poor little thing,' she whispered. 'What a time to bring you into the world.'

Before Mercy Gill had been delivered of her ninth child a month later, the news was in the newspapers for all the world to see. James Hassall had been declared insolvent and the *Sydney Morning Herald* announced that 'his Matavai estate, Cook's Vale estate and Burruwa estate will sold at auction when the survey is complete.'

'But what are we going to do?' Anna demanded.

She sat on the stool by the bed, baby Louisa propped against her shoulder smelling of milk and urine. With one hand she supported the baby and with the other folded a clean cloth for the child. James lay on the bed, the bedclothes thrown back against the summer heat, and tried to pretend he was asleep.

'James! You aren't listening!' Her voice was sharp, anxious. 'What about us? He's selling Matavai – or they are auctioning it out from under him. Where do we go now? We left Northiam because you had no work. Are you going to end up like all these other men we see on the road — all those new migrants with no jobs, all those ex-convicts with no-one to take them on?'

James rolled over and watched her, his busy little wife, always at work, always off helping one neighbour or another, always quicker to see the problems of every situation than the solutions. The light of the candle flickered against her face as she stooped over the baby, darkening the worried shadows around her eyes and her mouth. His happy little Anna was still somewhere under there, hidden under the facade of a worn and fading woman.

Her voice was going on and on. 'And James, we've just had our birthdays and we're both forty. What if we're out on the road with a new baby and five other children?'

'Woman, come here!' His voice was very gentle and he spread his strong arms out to receive her as she climbed onto the bed beside him. 'You're worrying again. When are you going to trust God with our lives and not try to carry it all by yourself?'

He pulled out the long pins which bound her hair tightly to her head for the day and released her long hair.

'See? Hardly any grey hairs yet. We are only at the beginning of what is going to happen to us in Australia. God often works out very hard things for our good. And Mr Hassall said today that he'll still have "Freshfield" left in this district, and he'll be needing some good men to help him rescue what is left after all the auctions. He's been a good boss and things are pretty tough for him, too, these days. Things will work out — I'm sure God hasn't brought us so far just to abandon us.'

Anna turned her head into the shelter of his shoulder and tried to smooth the frown from her brow, to reverse the droop of her mouth. But even as James began to pray aloud for themselves and their little ones, she wondered whether God was listening.

The day the drays and wagons dragged their loads out of the gates of Matavai, Anna went back to the little cottage with the rammed earth walls and sandstone floor where they had lived as part of the community for their eight years in New South Wales. The auctioneer had come and gone, his hammer pounding the death knell of Matavai with its close community, its parties, its horses and its gardens, its industry and sense of purpose. Now almost all the Rootes household things had gone and the older children had set off to walk ahead across the paddocks to Freshfield. Anna crouched by her garden, tool in hand, digging under her thick bed of violets.

It was autumn and there were no flowers, but these plants had travelled from Northiam and they would travel on.

At the big house, workmen were removing the last of the furniture and she saw Mrs Catherine Hassall come to the open door and stand staring down across the terraced gardens and the orchard to the green river flats beyond. The younger woman stepped from the verandah and walked to stand beside Anna. She nodded towards Anna's earthy hands.

'You are taking some of your plants with you? So am I.' There was an edge of bitterness in her voice. 'At least we can start new gardens, can't we?'

She turned her back on Anna, gazing back to the lovely house she was losing in the bad times that were dislocating so much of her world.

'I'm glad that you and Rootes are coming with us to Freshfield. It won't seem so strange if some of the familiar people are there. I suppose I should be very glad about it – the Freshfield place is smaller, but it is closer to St Paul's Church and much closer to Denbigh and all the Thomas Hassalls. . .' Her voice trailed away and she added very softly, 'But I came here as a bride and had my first two little boys in that house.'

The eyes of the two women met briefly, mistress and worker.

'Oh, you know,' Catherine Hassall said, and fled.

The lantern hung down from a long hook in the ceiling, dropping a circle of light on the people in the room. The cottage kitchen was crowded: the weekly Methodist class meeting drew labourers and shepherds, blacksmiths and stonemasons, older women and young mothers. Their Bibles were open at the passage they had been studying and the sound of their singing sifted up through the sheets of bark on the roof and floated on out into the quiet night.

Anna looked from face to face. These were her dear friends, many of them people she had first met at Wesleyan Methodist meetings years ago at home in Sussex, people who had shared the experiences of migrating to a new country. All of them had begun in New South Wales as farm labourers or workmen for one of the landowners, working long hours with the help of wives and older children, gradually gathering a nest-egg of funds to buy their own farm. They all had a dream of one day having a place of their own. It was nearly ten years since the first of them had arrived in the district and changes were coming.

A big bearded man was speaking. 'It's not easy, out in the new country,' Thomas Southwell said. 'If you can get it, it is easier to keep your work here where the farms are settled and you know the river will run. It's hard on the women, out in the new country – my wife is home by herself with the children on our place down on the Limestone Plains while I'm here driving the bullock wagon load to Sydney. She'll be alone for weeks while I'm on the road – and there are some rough characters out there. But they are changing the laws about buying land and if you have the money and the strength and a good family of children to help you, now is the time to try to get hold of new land.'

'Are there any churches out there? Or class meetings?'

Southwell laughed. 'If we want churches out in that country, we'll have to build them ourselves! Most of the settlers and shepherds out in the bush are a godless lot – but you can't blame them. All they have out there is great empty bush and the only comfort is the grog shanty.'

He looked around at his friends. He, too, had come from the south of England and lived in the Cowpastures with them for a short time before he took his family south. This man had set a pattern and he looked around at other strong healthy families who could face the work of pioneering new country.

'You could do it,' he assured them. 'This is going to be good country, and at the moment most of the people who are trying to live there are as wild as the bush animals – bushrangers, drunkards, pagans. Some blokes go crazy with the loneliness of it. But if we go out in families, a few families near each other, and go out like old Abraham and his people, going off to a new place God is going to show us, and we work hard, and help each other, and teach our children to have faith in God – why, we could change things!'

Anna looked at James. The idea of setting off into another unknown, to try to conquer a little patch of virgin bush, to start all over again, terrified her. Other women were eyeing their husbands. Many of them had recently had to look for new work because their masters had lost property and there had been a loosening of the ties they had begun to establish. If they were to begin something new, now was the time. Her eyes circled the room, gazing at the faces in the ring of lantern light. Without recognising what she was doing, she was memorising the faces of her friends for the time when they would spread far across the country and she would see them no more.

Silas and Mercy were among the first to go. Anna clung to Mercy till her friend climbed up among the cargo on the back of the dray with her children. She watched as the dray creaked slowly away to follow the Great North Road. James Hassall had offered Silas an increase in wages to encourage him to stay, but the Gills had decided to travel north to join his brother at Maitland on the Hunter River.

Other families followed over the years, each household farewelled with prayers and tears and a deep sense of loss for those who stayed. Tom Brown with his brother Bill and their families, as well as the Starrs and Wheatleys, set off to the south to settle in the Goulburn area. Vidlers went south-east to the Illawarra, the Nash boys crossed the Blue Mountains to the west, the other Starrs, Unicombs, Fosters and Shoesmiths moved off to the north and the Towners to Sydney and then north.

Every time another household left, Anna watched them go with anxiety.

'James, do you want to go, too?'

'No, I'd rather stay. This is a very good district round here. I'm hoping that with all the changes — people selling up and leaving — that maybe I can buy property for us here in the Cowpastures.'

Another season came and went and another child was born to Anna and James Rootes, Elizabeth. The year was dry and hard and farms where many workmen's families had once lived were studded with empty cottages, the cold ashes of old fires dead in the grates. Their oldest child Ann was seventeen and walked across the paddocks between Freshfield and Denbigh daily to work in the house of Thomas Hassall's family; she brought home stories of the disappointment of the Rev. Thomas Hassall as he saw his congregations dwindling away, with his own gardens dying and financial worries of his own. Freshfield was a good farm, but it wasn't Matavai, and James Rootes was unsettled. Anna was very thankful when at last James came home with a fresh lift in his stride.

'There is a farm for us! No, not a week's drive from here. Someone is selling up his small place here on the Nepean River, with a river frontage and land sloping back up to higher ground so we can put our house above any of the floods. When we were at Matavai we were looking straight down to it — it borders that land. We'll let others go off to explore the wilds. You and I are staying here!'

The day that Anna and James Rootes moved their things onto their own land, into their own little cottage, was the beginning of a new life for them all. James took Anna's arm and they walked a little way down the slope past their house to look at the cows. Though he could not see the wide river running along the foot of his land, James knew it was there, and that the land was rich. He knew that there would be droughts and floods, almost certainly diseases and loss of stock, but for the first time in his life he was not a labourer. He was a farmer, and the land was his.

'What will we name this place?' he asked.

'I still think about home. I imagine walking again over the Downs and down to the marshland along the Rother. What about "Marshdale Farm"?'

They walked back, past their chickens and their pig, back to the slab cottage with its little verandah for shelter from the sun and the newly dug garden beds for Anna's flowers. She was already talking about planting a furze hedge, honeysuckle and a cherry tree. They could hear the sound of their children's voices, seven healthy children from the eight she had borne: few women could claim as much. Not all their old friends had gone. Sivyer and Mary were still there, and sister Elizabeth Nash and her Joseph, with the Dousts and the Wards and the Whitemans and others. The Methodist class meetings were smaller and had lost some of their sparkle with the absence of men like the Browns and Silases, but they were still very important to those who remained.

'At last I think things are settling down and we'll be able to make a good life here,' James said, and Anna looked at her new house and smiled.

'Your Playford cousins want to come here for Christmas! Henry and Sarah and their children.' Anna waved the letter under James' nose as he stooped to drag off his workboots at the end of the day. 'In our own home, too! If they are coming all the way from Sydney we must invite your brother Sivyer and his family for the day – and dear sister Elizabeth and hers – there will be all our children and theirs – think of all the food we'll have to bake – and where in the world will they all sleep? We'll never fit around the table!'

James almost made the mistake of telling his wife to send a return letter telling his cousins that a visit would be too difficult to manage, but saw Anna's face in time. She was glowing. Already she was picturing the crowd of faces around her table, the brothers and sisters, children, nieces and nephews, cousins. Long ago they had all been neighbours and dear friends, sharing Christmas worship and Christmas dinner around James' parents' table in Northiam. James' mother had been a Playford, and there had always been Playford aunts and uncles and cousins coming through Christmas snow to sing carols with them at midnight. She remembered her birthday, celebrated delightfully on Christmas Day with all the ranks of family to greet her. What did it matter if here at Marshdale Farm they lived in a slab cottage with a barrel for a chimney? Who cared if most of the children would be sleeping on the floor – it was high summer and there would be no need to share the blankets! What if she had to cook for a week to be ready? As to space around the table, they would just have to sit close, and put the children on stools at their feet, or even put the table outdoors under the trees in the shade. Even though she could already see long lists of things which could go wrong, she didn't care. At last they could have a great family Christmas together.

On Christmas morning, Anna was up and wrapped in her apron in the cool of the early summer dawn. The house was quiet except for the gentle snoring of some of the visitors and she tiptoed past her little girls who had chosen to sleep on the kitchen floor. As she lit the fire and hung the kettle to boil, she opened the shutters to let in the pink-streaked and pearly dawn light. In the trees by the house there was a carolling of birds, notes cascading joyfully; there had been no carol singers in shawls and scarves singing outside her window in the snow, but with the birdsong in her ears she began to hum 'Peace on earth and mercy mild, God and sinners reconciled . . . Glory to the newborn King!'

The day was poured full to overflowing with people, excitement, conversations, children, food, Christmas church service. Everyone seemed to be talking at once and her kitchen was crowded with sisters and cousins and daughters, all underfoot. Food was borne in by each successive family to arrive: kingly turkeys, vast boiled puddings in their cloths, baskets of homebaked loaves, buckets of apricots and peaches fresh-picked from family trees. Anna moved anxiously among the multitude, trying to find spaces to put all this bounty. James and her children came to her with birthday kisses. 'Happy Christmas and Happy Birthday, Mamma!': the soft cheeks of her little girls and the proud young whiskers of her teenage sons.

Anna felt that she had not paused since the early quietness of the morning till at last the tribes of relatives sat at peace along the verandah and on the nearby grass in the gentle twilight. Everyone had dined overwell and some of the men looked ready to doze off to sleep . The teenage cousins and second cousins were together on the grass, tangled closely together like a litter of puppies, with some of the younger cousins on their laps. Anna watched her oldest daughter with an astute eye; her cousin Sivyer had not left her side all day. Her boys James and Jabez had been wrestling with their Playford cousins William and Richard and the whole assortment of little girls had watched and giggled.

The parents talked quietly together of past years, of Northiam and Beckley far away on the other side of the world, of Henry Playford's work for a brickworks in Newtown and the Rootes' farms, of skills in nursing of both Sarah Playford and Anna herself. Little by little the talk turned to the old stories of their voyages to Australia, each family on a different ship and all arriving in New South Wales between October 1837 and early 1839. Some had borne children on board ship, others had lost children and relatives, some had suffered from epidemic diseases during the voyage. None had forgotten anything of that crossing of the bridge from the old world to the new.

'I'm still amazed that our family ever arrived in the colony at all!' Cousin Henry Playford leaned back against a verandah post and began a story he had told many times.

'We came by the *Juliana*, sailing out of Gravesend in October 1838. The storms started before we were even past the Isle of Wight, and all of us were very sick and very sorry we had come. The Captain didn't put in at Plymouth as he'd first thought – he could see that a lot of us would have escaped there and then. We fought our way on through bad weather, trying to sail through the Bay of Biscay, but when we were nearly through we were driven back and had seven days of storm. With the ship tossing and pitching so terribly, I was sure we'd go straight to the bottom at any moment.'

Anna nodded. She remembered her own fear of storms.

'Most nights we didn't sleep because of water washing across our sleeping deck. Then one morning at daybreak we found that we were almost on rocks off the coast of Spain. We were nearly wrecked, but thank God we survived that time. The next terror was illness – so many were ill, and a number died, including some of our old friends from Northiam and Beckley. I was wishing we'd never thought of leaving home.'

'But that was not all,' Sarah went on. 'As we sailed south through the Atlantic, some of the sailors started to complain about the rations. Lots of people spent all their time complaining! Anyway, a number of sailors were angry with the Captain. Then one wild afternoon I couldn't find little William. He was only four, and always wandering off, getting into little adventures, and someone said that he might have gone up on deck. So I went up searching – and there he was, all eyes, watching a mutiny!'

The young ones in the deepening shadows on the grass had stopped talking among themselves and were listening to every word.

'The rain was pouring down in torrents, and little Will was soaked to the skin. Every flash of lightning lit up the swords and cutlasses and pistols, all shining, and the angry faces, and the dreadful language, enough to singe your very ears. You may be sure I grabbed young William by the collar and dragged him back down below deck so fast he didn't know what was going on, poor lad. He thought it was all so interesting, bless him, but I was terrified!'

Anna was awed. Their own voyage seemed very dull by comparison. 'But what happened to the Captain and the sailors?'

'The Captain had enough loyal men with him to arrest the mutineers and clap them in irons till we reached Capetown in South Africa. But even then that wasn't the end of our adventures. We were sailing close to the coast, just off Capetown, looking at the fine houses and gardens, when there was an awful crash and we'd run aground on rocks! The *Juliana* rocked horribly and we all started screaming and crying. I was sure that we'd sink any moment and I was hugging my children to me and praying and sobbing. . .'

'We were as loud and emotional as a Methodist meeting!' interrupted Henry. 'We were a mile off the coast, but boats came out, and there were the ship's own boats. After we'd all been elbowing each other in our fright to get our turn with our children on the boats, all of us came safely off. Even our boxes were saved later, though everything was very wet with salt water. We were kindly cared for in Capetown. They offered us work there but we chose to come on to New South Wales a month later on the *Morayshire*.'

'Do you remember any of that time, William?' one of the cousins asked.

'I just remember the sailors with the cutlasses really shiny and sharp – I think I wanted one like them!'

His mother murmured, 'That boy hasn't changed – still always curious and always wanting to be in places where he could be in danger. Sometimes I worry about that boy. . .'

The memories flowed on, a fugal conversation with each adding to the theme of migration and resettling.

'I still miss Sussex. Sometimes I dream of walking again along the road from Beckley to Northiam between the hedges, looking at the Downs and the marshes, and I dream of meeting my old parents again and all our friends. . .'

'I do, too. And it is always green and soft there.'

Sarah told of how, only months before they arrived in New South Wales, a portion of the large estate of one Solomon Levy near the town of Sydney had been subdivided into blocks of five and ten acres, and gentlemen had bought blocks at this new town to build fine mansions and villas with good orchards and parklands where once wheat had been grown. Others had bought land for market gardens and nurseries, or built modest cottages for workmen. In the area was plenty of good timber as well as an abundance of brick-earth, and Henry Playford had found work with a brickmaker by the name of Bucknall, earning ten shillings and sixpence for every thousand bricks. They now had their own cottage with its outside kitchen, stable, wells, and acres of back paddock for their cows and chickens.

'We are quite content there at Newtown now,' Sarah added. 'We have arranged for our William to be apprenticed to cousin John Playford as a bootmaker – he is growing into a strong lad, but he has a mind of his own and needs some strong guidance.'

It was nearly dark. The young ones had gone for a walk together. The women gathered up the last of the empty baskets and dishes, while the men of the local families put the horses into the shafts of their carts for the drive home. A sickle of moon shone over the paddocks and the new orchard as they listened to the laughter of returning boys and girls.

Anna held tightly to James' arm. Through all their many ups and downs, he had always been a solid rock, immovable, a boulder thrusting firmly upward as the river of living swirled fiercely around him. She was glad that he was there to cling to.

'James!' she whispered, 'I'm glad, after all, that we migrated.'

The ribbon of the seasons unwound year by year, colour merging into colour; mother-of-pearl of winter sky, green of spring crops, yellow-gold of wattle, pink and white of fruit blossom, ecru of dry summer grasses, gilt of harvest, mud-brown of flood waters. The paddocks of Marshdale Farm saw their share of drought and flood, disease and fine crops, but James was his own man and as his children grew they worked beside him. His family was his great pride: Ann a fine young woman happily planning her marriage to her cousin Sivyer Rootes, his boys James and Jabez strong youths, his four little girls Mary, Lydia, Louisa and Elizabeth steps and stairs around their mother's skirts. His sons had left the school at Heber chapel to work with him on the farm, and as the four little girls grew they helped with cows, poultry and pigs.

Although so many of the families of their Methodist friends had moved away to other parts of New South Wales, new familes had come and, after a few barren years when Anna sorrowed over the diminishing of their fellowship, new links were being cemented. A group of friends who loved to worship God in the Wesleyan Methodist way began to meet in a cottage at Cawdor, south of Cobbitty, just where the southern road began its daunting climb up the steepness of Mount Razorback, and the Rootes family often joined them. Anna was prepared to take the long walk, and when James felt the time had come when he could afford a pony and trap, her Sunday excursions became pure pleasure. She privately added her opinion to the discussions about whether they should build both a school house and chapel on the land James Macarthur offered the group, and whether it should be of timber or brick, though people thought that it was the voice of her husband they were hearing. As the new church building began to rise on the fertile land skirted by the deep folds of Razorback, Anna felt even more at home in this district.

One day in May in the autumn of 1851, the Rootes family gathered at St Paul's Church, Cobbitty, for the first family wedding in Australia. Anna's oldest child Anne was to marry her cousin, Sivyer. As Anna entered the church, rows of smiling guests welcomed her, Methodists from the farms, relatives from town, Anglican friends from St Paul's. The Rev. Thomas Hassall waited with the young groom for the bride to appear. He had been a friend and pastor to the family for years now and, though the Rootes enjoyed all their Methodist links, they held a strong respect and affection for the Anglican rector and often worshipped at St Paul's. Their daughter had worked at Denbigh since she was fifteen, waiting at the Hassall table and being part of that large and lively family, seeing the picnics and hunting parties, horse-riding and dressmaking, gardening and dinner parties, grand visitors, courtships and weddings. It seemed very right that Thomas Hassall should celebrate their family wedding. He had been a very real part of their world.

Heads turned towards the door and with a sudden choking of te
Anna saw her daughter, in the loveliness of her bridal day, clinging
to her father's arm. 'Once,' she thought, 'I was like that, going to
meet my James, but that's more than twenty years gone and now
I'm wrinkled and getting more toothless by the year.' The ancient
words of scripture came to her mind – 'To everything there is a
season, and a time for every purpose under heaven . . . He hath
made everything beautiful in his time. . .'

Hands were clasped, vows made to love and to cherish till death
parted them and shy kisses were exchanged. Anna watched with
eyes brimming as her eldest child passed into a new family.

After the wedding service, family and guests moved out of the soft
dimness of the church into sunshine and set off to walk back to the
wedding feast at Marshdale Farm. The Playford families walked
with their Rootes cousins, seventeen-year-olds James Rootes and
William Playford joking and teasing with their younger brothers
Jabez and Richard, and the four little girls following them down
the road, four sizes of legs twinkling along in four sizes of lace
pantalettes. A group of men of the family and friends strolled along,
more interested in the elusive hints that were floating around the
colony about some shepherds finding gold dust in creekbeds out
past Bathurst than in talking about weddings – 'Some people are
saying that it might turn into another California. . .' 'Not likely. . .'
'There won't be enough gold there to make it worth leaving home
for, that's my opinion!'

As Anna hurried back to the house, it seemed to her that her world
had settled into a satisfying and secure pattern and that her old
longing for Northiam had almost faded away. At a curve in the road
before her was their own farm, hers and James'. Her garden was
growing up around the house: the apple and cherry trees, the
peaches, a flowering hedge and the Northiam violets in a shaded
corner. Inside the house, waiting on the broad hearthstone, was the
Dutch oven full of food. There were shelves of cakes made with her
own butter and eggs and preserved fruits, and there was a pig they
had been fattening now dropping slow sizzling juices from the spit
into the hot coals below. They might well face more hard times of
drought or flood, but she no longer feared the workhouse for herself
or her little ones. Most satisfying of all, her family was with her,
all surviving early childhood except little Augustus Jesse – not
many women could claim such a blessing. Her house was now in

sight and her feet speeded up till she was almost running to put more wood on the fire and to be ready to welcome the wedding party home.

Three days after Ann and Sivyer's wedding, the *Sydney Morning Herald* of 15 May 1851 announced that an extensive goldfield had been discovered in the Wellington district of New South Wales and the whole colony suddenly seemed to go mad. Within weeks of the announcement, Anna received a letter from cousin Sarah Playford: young William had run away from the bootmaker's shop to join the gold rush.

Mary's story

6
Gold in the rock
1851-1860

IT WAS A VERY COLD, wet winter in 1851. As she dipped chilled fingers into the dish of grain and flung it in a wide arc for the fowls, the child shivered. Hens which had huddled, fluffed-feathered, under the hedge, came running for the grain and, as young Mary Rootes tossed another sweep across the gleaming wetness of the house yard, seed rained on their bobbing heads. She hurried to collect the eggs. Her footprints left their trail across the mud, tracking across the starlike prints of the fowls, puddled wheel ruts, deep curves of horseshoes and marks of cattle. Mary cradled the eggs in the corner of her shawl and slipped and slithered back toward the house. Her father and brothers came from the barn, moving with her towards the comfort of the slab cottage of Marshdale Farm with the slush lamp already alight in the window and smoke curling up into the damp air.

'That wind must be coming off snow on the Blue Mountains,' her father said. 'It's freezing the nose off my face.'

The light and the fire were in the outside kitchen, and Mary stooped under the string of moist washing festooned across the room to find a place near the hearth. Her mother ladled rich mutton broth into their bowls, the steam rising in lazy curls, white in the lamplight. The savoury aroma was pleasing and she felt hungry, but as she moved to the table her mind was on other things. She was imagining cousin William. To her twelve-year-old mind, he was almost grown-up at seventeen, and she remembered his powerful arms pinning her brother James to the ground when they were playing at wrestling together. He was big enough to go off looking for gold if he wanted to, she supposed, but what if he didn't have a warm blanket or possumskin rug? And what would he eat, if his mother wasn't there to cook for him? She eyed her brother across the table. He was cheerfully spooning broth into his mouth and talking to Father about their lambs in the bleak winter weather — would *he* want to leave home and go after gold? The talk of gold was on the lips of everyone, and every week another man left his forge, or his master, or his sheep, or his workbench, to disappear over the roads crossing the mountains, travelling towards the teasing will o' the wisp of gold. Who knew what James might do?

'Father,' she said later, when the bowls were empty and the last of the potatoes and mutton had been eaten,'Could we pray for cousin William tonight? I think his mother must be worried about him.'

'Of course. Mind you, it would take a grand lump of gold to tempt *me* from my own fireside in weather like this! He'll go home soon enough.'

The boy in the tent shivered and pulled his blanket closer round his shoulders. He could never remember being so bitterly cold in his whole life. All night the stars had blazed from a clear sky; he had lain awake staring up through the narrow opening of his little tent, too cold to sleep, sometimes adding more sticks to the fire. He ached in every limb. Since that day weeks before when he had stood in front of a digger's outfitters in George Street, Sydney, and paid his earnings as a cobbler to buy a blanket and red serge shirt, a big hat, a pick, a pan for the gold and a frying pan, he had walked more miles than he could count. He had followed the tracks of wheels of buggies and drays, the hoofprints of many horses, all climbing up and up through high bush, across narrow bridges over mountain streams, under the shadow of towering walls of sandstone and granite, through the spray of waterfalls. The track was alive with travellers, like a purposeful line of ants following on each other's heels in a steady stream. For the first time since he had been a tiny child back in Sussex, he saw snow falling, up there in the high country, and beyond the mountains he followed the stream of people down onto rich plains spreading out to the west. In wayside shanty or sitting on a log with a fellow traveller, sharing a billy of tea, the story was the same: 'Don't worry about Orphir where they found the first gold — the place to go is the Turon — they say there is gold to be had for the washing there along the river.'

So he had come to the Turon, and now William Playford lay shivering and aching in every muscle. In his bag was a little gold dust, laboriously washed from the gravel and silt of the river, while he stood at the river's edge swirling the muddy water in the pan. Sometimes a speck of gold twinkled at him from the last dregs and sometimes not. He had swung his new pick till his hands blistered, hacking into the river bed, levering up great rocks, but the river rushed down and filled the holes as he dug down to the hopeful washdirt. The boy had worked hard, with some success, but around him in other tents and humpies along the green banks of the Turon were many men who were already close to giving up. Not all those who had hurried west to the gold had the strength they needed to dig and shovel, not all were discovering a fortune among the rocks or were prepared to risk losing the security of their old trades, professions or farms. For the many who were screaming with glee at nuggets and gold dust, many others were toiling very hard and finding nothing.

The sky was lightening as William rolled out of his blanket and stood up. Beyond the tent, puddles were frozen over and frost lay crisply on heaps of gravel. Today was Sunday and the miners would all take a holiday: it would be a day for drinking and quarrelling, with the sly-grog shanties doing a roaring trade and miners arguing about their gold. The boy rubbed his hand across his face. The sharp bristles of his new beard prickled his palm and he knew that his face was probably dirty. He tightened his belt about his waist and thrust the curved bowie knife into it. There was no mirror to see himself, but William had a strange feeling that even his own mother might not recognise him this morning. At home his family would be walking in their best clothes to church, clean and brushed, Bibles in hand. There would be no church here among the eruptions of gravel and earth, though a few miners sometimes gathered on a fallen log with a Methodist preacher. William found that he did not really mind so much. By choice, he avoided the tents selling liquor, preferring to keep his wits about him and hold onto the money he was winning from his gold. His mother would probably hope that he was in church somewhere today, but any kind of church seemed very remote from the crowded intensity of the Turon. In fact, everything from the past seemed very remote – his home in Newtown, his relatives, the bootmaker's bench.

With his wide hat jammed down over his ears, the youth wandered off along the river bank, another small object being swirled along in the flood of gold-seekers.

The young girl stood impatiently, held captive on a stool while her mother ripped stitches from the hem of her dress. The mother pulled and tugged, trying to draw the skirt further down to cover the girl's long legs decently.

'You are growing so quickly, child,' muttered the woman, and she made it sound almost a sin as she looked grimly at the strip of unfaded cloth bordering the lower edge of the skirt. 'Only fourteen years old and taller than me already.'

Mary Rootes plucked at the fabric which strained around her body. She knew already that last year's summer dress would be hopeless, even if Mother fussed with the hem for the whole afternoon, and on the far side of the room she could see the book she was reading, beyond her reach, tantalising.

'But Mamma, it's too tight in the bodice. I can hardly move in it. Look!'

'Oh dear.' Anna Rootes looked at the new shapeliness of her growing daughter and admitted defeat. 'Maybe we'll have to pass it on to Lydia and sew you another dress. Take it off then.'

Mary unhooked the long line of buttons and wriggled gratefully from the dress. Lydia was pulling a face. Her expression said, 'Why should Mary always get the new dress and me the old one?' After Lydia's turn, Louisa and Elizabeth would wear it, if it still survived.

'Go fetch the cows then, child — your old smock will do well enough for the cows. Pa has put them down in the river paddock today.'

Mary pulled the loose smock over her head and tried to slide her book into the pocket without her mother seeing. If Mamma noticed she would say, 'As bad as your father — always with your nose in a book!'

Her mother's voice followed her across the yard. 'And don't come back late, like sometimes! Your father won't half be cross if you don't bring the cows back till it is nearly too dark to see to do the milking.'

The girl moved quickly away down the slope from the cottage, following the post-and-rail fence as it flowed down the hill towards the river. She felt more at ease without the strictures of the outgrown dress and her feet knew their way across the paddock. The book came out of her pocket and she walked along reading phrases aloud, the words of poetry falling oddly among the wild wheat along the track, fragments of Milton's *Paradise Lost* being echoed by song of currawong. It would not be long before the teachers at the school at Heber chapel would farewell the tall girl, too old for school and, anyway, what did a farmer's daughter need with more education?

Mary turned the pages carefully, her back leaning against a gum tree, memorising the lines, not caring when the sense of what she read was unclear to her. She understood enough, and the very sound of the rich phrases on her tongue gave her pleasure. Her father had taught her to love books. In the evenings he would sit, absorbed, then his bristling brows would arch and he'd say, 'Listen to this!' and he'd read out yet another passage which stirred him. He read the newspaper for news of explorations and adventures and filled the minds of his children with stories of his Methodist friend the Rev. John Watsford among the cannibals of Fiji, or the arguments against the slave trade in faraway America. Nor were her father and teachers the only ones who were giving Mary her love for the written word: the Rev. Thomas Hassall always kept a collection of little books in his saddlebag, and Mary had been among the many young people to whom he distributed them.

Mary thrust the book back in her pocket and ran on. A cool wind had risen and streaks of sunset clouds coloured the distant mountains as she walked behind the cows. She realised that time had passed quickly and she was going to be late home. It wasn't only Pa who would be angry if she brought the cows in late; if Mamma caught her with a book in her pocket, she'd be in trouble for wasting time when there was work to be done. Mamma was a practical person, always busy, always just a little anxious about everything, showing her love for her family in action.

'I'm going to be late – I'll take the cows up the short way. It's not quite dark. Mamma won't know, and anyway, I'm not scared like her. . .'

Mamma had told her more than once to walk around by the track from river to house. 'Don't go straight up through that strip of bush after dusk – long ago a convict died there, so they say, and people say that his ghost still visits the place.'

Following the cows among the trees, she was full of the imagery of poetry layered over the earthiness of cowpats on dry grass and the beasts with heavily swinging udders. Deep shadows fell over the track, dimming the clear lines of trees and rocks, adding mystery to tangles of undergrowth. 'No ghosts here,' she thought, 'and anyway, I don't believe in them – I think.' But as she walked through deepening dusk, some of the images from school verse mingled in her mind with the whispered tales of mystery. Quiet sounds in the grass ceased to be simple. The cows plodded placidly forward, but Mary's feet slowed. Ahead was something pale and flickering, suspended above the earth, dancing eerily to silent music. . .

Aloud she said, 'It's nothing – it's nothing – Jesus, help me keep walking – it's Mamma who is always afraid of things, not me – just keep walking and it'll disappear. . .'

Running a little to walk beside the last of the cows, she laid a hand on the warm hide and moved forward, nearer to the dangling thing under the tall eucalypt – and saw it solidify into long twisting strips of eucalypt bark, dangling freely from the trunk with the last light of evening reflecting from the pearly pale inner surface. The girl laughed with relief and clapped the cow briskly on the rump. She felt suddenly strong and confident, almost a grown woman who could look after herself. The lights of the house were being lit as she brought the cows into their yard for milking.

'It's good that it wasn't poor Mamma bringing in the cows just then – she'd have been so scared!' thought the girl.

The tide of purpose which had swept gold-seekers to the Turon in 1851 swirled on, carrying William Playford along with it to Tambaroora and Hill End the next year and then on with the others south into Victoria to the new fields opening up. He was caught up in eddies of men, carrying their swags and their pans or riding with Cobb and Co, circling around briefly at Castlemaine and Bendigo and finding themselves in the muddy ditches of Ballarat in 1854. William was taller now, broader in shoulder, muscular from heavy work with pick and shovel, his beard thick and dark. When other miners moved on, he moved with them, packing up tents and leaving a ravaged landscape behind them, torn earth and fallen trees among the antbeds of mounded soil with rabbit warrens of mines just beneath the surface. Sometimes they had been lucky, sometimes not.

Ballarat was different. The gold was there, they all knew it, but no longer could men pan for gold among river stones or find it within the rocks of an open paddock. Easy nuggets were rare and, though a few men found them, for many more the gold was elusive. When Will came to Ballarat he found many working among the hills, but men said, 'The only way to get it out is to go down – way down deep.' Villages sprang up overnight: there were grog shanties and the lemonade tent, tents for commissioners and diggers and the somewhat more substantial homes for family men who built rammed earth walls waist high with canvas roofs to keep off the rain. Among the hills of mineshafts, a town of solid stone and brick was beginning to spring up.

Will Playford and his mates spent their days working together on their narrow lease of earth, taking turns to go down the shaft with a pick, hacking into the rock face deep under the surface, or standing above, winding up the buckets full of rock and earth on the simple windlass. The deeper they drove, the higher the water level rose in the bottom of the shaft and the more they were forced to bail muddy water. William with the thousands on the Ballarat fields worked constantly in wet conditions, clinging to the hope that one day they would strike it rich.

In the evenings and in the quietness of Sundays, when few men worked in the diggings, William strolled with his friends along the rows of tents and buildings which purported to be a main street, sniffing the aroma of the bakery and curiously observing the josshouse for the Chinese miners. They would pass the gold office and the bank where they rarely had the pleasure of doing business and yarn with the man shoeing horses. They were aware of the establishments where women offered to take in miners' washing and other women offered other things. The young man from the cobbler's shop in Sydney had become an experienced miner and home ties seemed far away. Sometimes on a Sunday when he had no taste for drinking in one of the hotels and there was little else to do, he joined others in the tent where the Methodists met for worship, but the rows of backless forms wedged into the ground were punishingly uncomfortable and the young minister, the Rev. Theophilus Taylor, tended to preach sermons which were excellent but interminable.

As spring warmed into the summer of 1854, William was feeling discouraged. During the winter there had been a general spirit of optimism on the Ballarat fields as many men were doing well, but it was becoming harder and harder, and the problems of deep-sinking mines meant that the ordinary miner, even more than the man working for a major company in one of the large mines, could work extremely hard for very little. Ripples of anger had been running among the thousands of miners in the area for some months; there was talk of injustice and corruption among the authorities, men were angered at having no vote and being unable to buy land locally and, perhaps most of all, they were rebellious about the payment of licence fees and the repeated efforts of the authorities to hunt down any men without their licence.

'So, what are we going to do?' William sat on a slag heap at the top of their hole in the ground and raised an eyebrow at his mates. A hot wind was blowing, but his trousers were wet from working in the water at the foot of the shaft and it cooled him a little. In his shirt pocket was his precious licence, somewhat limp and dog-eared from being carried in rough conditions, but the licence hunters could appear at any moment and had recently been coming twice a week.

'There's not a lot we *can* do. Without paying for a licence we can't dig for gold. Without gold we'll have no money to buy better equipment for deep-sinking – and a pick and a bucket are useless the deeper we go. And if we can't buy heavy equipment we'll have to lose our independence and work for a company. Anyway, we'll soon have to choose between buying our next licences and buying bread.'

'You'd better have another wager with the flour miller, Playford!' The man laughed. Some months earlier, William had had an argument with the miller over his strength. The miller had taunted the young man that he would not be able to carry a full 150 pound flour bag across the street. William declared that he would carry it a mile. 'Carry the bag a mile and keep the flour!' With a grunt, the young man had hoisted the bag across his shoulders and set off, followed by a tail of admirers. He had never admitted that it was hard work, but he had kept that bag of flour.

'I'm going to the meeting about the licence fee at any rate,' William said as he prepared to descend yet again into the watery depths of their hole. 'Why should I be taxed for working when I'm not winning gold?'

Christmas was less than a month away and the weather was getting very hot. Angry meetings of miners had produced no results, when one evening the miners were given the news that troops had been sent to Ballarat by the Victorian Governor and had entered the area with bayonets fixed. Some hothead had stoned the soldiers and there had been a skirmish with some bloodshed.

The next afternoon, William Playford stood shoulder to shoulder with hundreds of men listening to speakers, some moderate and speaking of 'moral force', and some fiery. The flag of the Southern Cross floated above their heads as a motion was put that they should all burn their licences. Around him a storm of voices shouted 'Aye!' and Will's fingers tightened around the paper in his pocket. A few held their papers high overhead and saw them ignite, blaze and blacken. Against his hand over his own paper, Will felt the thud of his heart. To fight? To protest against injustice? To keep silent and go on with his work? To risk the loss of his licence? To risk days chained to a log for speaking against some of the corruption he knew existed? He heard his own voice saying, 'Aye', but the sound was uncertain, unconvincing.

A hot north wind whipped dust into the air the following day as William Playford hauled another bucket of rock to the surface. Across the hills of the Ballarat goldfields miners were at work. Some spoke among themselves of the tensions of recent weeks, some spoke of their licences, burnt or salvaged, but most had put aside politics and public issues to spend the day hard at work. William stood at the head of their narrow claim, wide hat pulled hard over his ears to give a little shade and his sweaty arms straining to turn the handle on their windlass.

There was a yell of warning. 'Look out, men! It's another filthy licence hunt!'

He lifted his head. Up the slope rode a party of police and commissioners riding fast, scattering among the humps and hillocks of the diggings with rifles held high. William watched, open-mouthed. What had the diggers done, for heaven's sake? Just hard at work on a hot day. . .

Through a gritty curtain of dust he watched a bitter play being acted out on the wide stage of the hills. Diggers shouted earthy abuse, a chorus of cursing. Stones flew. An enraged commissioner roared, 'We'll stand no more of this nonsense about licences,' and read the Riot Act. His words were punctuated by obscenities from his hearers. The hail of stones was answered by a volley of shot over the head of the crowd. William clutched his only weapons, his shovel and a battered bucket, and dropped to the ground. In his pocket, tattered and precious, was his licence, but he was sure that his mate had not taken his down into the mine where it would disintegrate in wet trousers.

'Stay down there, mate.' His face was pressed against the roughness of the pit top slag as he called down the hole. 'Things are going crazy up here — licence hunt!' Across the diggings he saw other men being rounded up, handcuffed, dragged along behind police horses to be chained in the sun in the churned and upheaved soil of the goldfields. William saw them go, and joined his voice to the babel of voices — Irish, American, French, Swedish, German, English, Italian, Chinese — which spoke with rage and resentment of injustices.

Swept up in the common anger, William Playford followed the

crowds who converged on Bakery Hill that afternoon. From among the murmuring men, for the moment without leadership, a tall man leaped onto a stump and shouted 'Liberty!' Hundreds of diggers fell on their knees, dragging hats from their heads, as they answered Peter Lalor's call to volunteer to defend their rights and liberties. William knelt in the dust, elbow to elbow with friend and stranger alike, unsure what was happening, confused, excited, only certain that a lot of things on the goldfields were not fair.

Before he had time to consider, he found himself carried deeper into the whirlpool. A stockade was being built on Eureka, the hill where many Irish had their workings, a hasty piling up of pit-slabs into a breastwork. William and his friends joined the thousand and more men at the heart of the flood of anger. Round and round swirled the waters of resentment, reaction, fear, panic, ill-advised heroics. Leaderless men argued over the few weapons and miners play-acted at being military at drill. Men worked to produce handmade pikes, knowing even as they worked that no pike could stand against a soldier's firearm. A brass band played martial music while every man seemed to be giving orders which no man obeyed. William began to feel that he was being swept away, out of control, in danger of drowning in the high tide of excitement.

Leaders came to the stockade to plead for calm. They begged the men to disperse, to forget confrontation, not because the cause was not just, but because this way could only end in tragedy. A Catholic priest implored his Irish Catholic people to lay down their arms and attend Mass with him next day, Sunday. Men began to waver. It was Saturday evening and the crowded stockade started to thin as men began to drift away.

'My own tent and hearthstone is pretty rough, but I'm going to sleep there tonight,' said some. 'Or someone will take off with my tools while I'm gone.'

'What is Saturday night without some grog?' asked others. 'No supplies in the stockade — I'll be back in the morning.'

'Tomorrow is Sunday — nothing is going to happen on a Sunday. If there is going to be a good fight, it'll keep till Monday, so I'll be off.'

'Fight or no fight,' said William, 'I can't see how we can win. Can you? Am I supposed to fight with my shovel? And I'm no soldier. I'm good enough in a hand-to-hand brawl with another man, fists and muscles, but I wager a policeman would shoot me down before I could get him pinned to the ground.'

They stood leaning against the slabs of the stockade wall. Within the wall there was confusion, lack of direction. Beyond the dry hills lay their goldmine, exhausting work at the best and heartbreaking work often, but something they understood.

'I'm off,' said William abruptly. 'Why be stone dead at twenty-one for a principle – or a bit of paper?'

As they walked away, the silhouette of Eureka stockade stood black against the night sky on its hilltop. Pinpricks of light shone through the cracks from the campfires of those who remained. Fragments of conversation hung suspended in the warm air; talk of gold, or ideals, the wish to be free to work, of women, or of licence fees. Somewhere a man was playing his flute, a thin thread of melody.

William walked away, thinking that perhaps he might chance one of Theophilus Taylor's marathon sermons in the morning – if nothing else, it might have a calming effect. But by morning William had other things on his mind.

'Father, what is it?' Mary saw the look on her father's face, but could not read what it meant. His newspaper was in his hand.

'Cousin Henry Playford's boy, young William, off after gold. Where was he when last we heard?'

Her mother looked up from the bread dough she was kneading. 'Bendigo, was it? Or Ballarat? In Victoria, at any rate, but that boy never seems to stay anywhere for long.'

'There has been trouble on the goldfields at Ballarat. Serious trouble, men killed. An uprising.'

He read fragments aloud; of the march of 400 armed troops and police on the sleeping stockade at four in the morning in the quiet of Sunday 3 December 1854, of the handful of rebels still within the stockade – a mere 150 or so – having little warning of the attack, of the charge, the hand-to-hand fighting being all over in ten minutes, the Southern Cross flag torn down, the tents ablaze, men shot, men bayonetted, men arrested, mad firing by the victors at anything and anyone, even far from the stockade itself...

'Madness!'

'How – how horrible!' Her mother's face was very pale. 'But where was William? Was he there? Oh, poor Sarah – that boy was always an adventurer – his poor dear mother! Shot in a riot!'

James Rootes sat quietly, folding his newspaper. 'Be calm, Anna. We'll wait and see what has happened to that boy before we consign him to his funeral. The paper says that about thirty miners were killed and some five soldiers, and some hundred prisoners taken to the government camp, but out of thousands of miners around Ballarat our William would have to be very foolhardy or unlucky to be in the middle of it.'

Mary listened in silence and when her father had gone she picked up the newspaper for herself. She tried to picture her second cousin, a boy like her big brother James, somehow part of a violent battle, facing death. She could not. All she could see was a lighthearted lad as she had last seen him three-and-a-half years earlier, not even well-remembered, talking about sheep with her brothers.

Cousin Sarah Playford lay very ill in her house in Newtown near Sydney. Though her mother did not describe the disease in detail, she had whispered to Mary and Lydia, 'It's cancer, so there is nothing anyone can do.'

Mother had announced, 'I'm going to see her, and look after her for a while if I'm able – we were friends long ago in Northiam when I was Anna Hicks and she was Sarah Goodsall. The two big girls can come with me.'

Now Mary sat in the coach, her wide skirts crushing against Lydia's and her mother's, and stared from the window as they sped along. The green paddocks of the Cowpastures and the familiar landmarks of the Nepean River and Campbelltown were far behind and the scatterings of villages lay to right and left of the dusty road. Liverpool Road ran into Parramatta Road at the 'Speed the Plough Inn' at Ashfield and settlement grew closer and closer. She had never been to Sydney before. Once or twice her parents had travelled to visit their relatives there, and they had told her of great stone buildings, and many shops, but Mary longed to see the sea, and the wonderful new railway. They said that the railway line ran all the way from Sydney for fourteen miles to Parramatta, just like one heard about in England.

The coach lurched through potholes and laboured up hills. Patches of bush alternated with clusters of houses. The house paddocks gradually became smaller till some houses only had space for an orchard, a well, a stable and room for a few horses, chickens and the family cow. The silver line of the railway ran beside the road as they neared Newtown and Mary stared at it, hoping in vain for a sight of the steam train which ran each day. Great chimneystacks smoked overhead from the brickworks of Newtown: she had never seen anything like them and was awed. With Lydia, Mary gazed and chattered, the limits of the known world of the farms of Cobbitty and Camden exploding around them.

When cousin Sarah Playford opened the door to them at her house near the brickworks, Mary was shocked at what she saw. When cousin Sarah had come to Ann's wedding five years before, she was a cheerful, brisk woman. The woman at the door was pale, her skin like thin parchment stretched over bones, and when Mary leaned forward for a kiss of greeting she was aware of her fragility. Mary and Lydia hung back in the corner of the room, anxious and a little afraid of what they were seeing, but their mother was confident and assured, ready with practical help. When things were looking at their worst, Mamma was at her best, encouraging others with her strong faith.

'There is no hope, of course,' cousin Sarah murmured. They were sitting in her little parlour and the sick woman lay back in her chair. 'No doctor can offer any answers, and I refuse to go to a hospital – dreadful, dirty places they are. So I'll just wait till God calls me.'

She was silent for a while, her eyes closed, gathering her strength.

'Some days, like today, I feel well enough to get up and dress. Other days I wonder if I'll see another sunrise. I just want to live till William can come home. He's been away from home for five years, and I love him. I pray for him every day. I'd so much like to know that he is safe – and that he has found faith in God for himself. . .'

Days passed. The girls helped cousin Mary Susannah in the kitchen, scrubbed invalid washing, swept and dusted, milked the cow, working and talking in an undertone, always conscious of the sick woman in the house. Their mother prepared special meals and when cousin Sarah lay ill in the big four-poster bed, spent hours with her friend quietly talking and praying while her careful hands cared for the fragile body.

There was an abrupt knocking on the door one morning and Mary went to open it. On the doorstep stood a tall man, broad of shoulder, fearsome of whiskers, battered hat shadowing his face. Mary saw in that first moment a traveller's swag over the shoulder, thick red dust on the heavy work trousers and broken boots. She hesitated, hand on the door, almost ready to shut it in the face of the vagrant.

'I've come home to see my mother.' The voice was deep, very weary – and familiar.

'It's – it's William!'

She flung the door open and he came in, almost staggering with tiredness.

'Am I too late?'

Mary found herself almost babbling with relief and delight. Cousin Sarah's special prayer had been answered and William had come. She ran for her mother, snatched the rolled swag from his shoulder, made him tea, then watched the door close behind him as he went to be with his mother.

Later that evening, Mary brought a tin dish of warm water and a towel for William. He sat by the kitchen fire with his trouser legs rolled high and his blistered feet soaking.

'Your feet, cousin! Where have you been?'

'A very long way. The message came to me that my mother was dying, passed from man to man on the road and among the diggings. I was back in New South Wales, on my way between diggings. After the troubles at Ballarat I'd been mining at Bendigo, but I was heading north. When the message about Mother reached me I was 250 miles from Sydney, and I had no horse.' He waved at his boots, caked with dirt and with the soles peeling back. 'That's why my boots are nearly done for — and my feet. It took me a week of walking. The nearer I got to Sydney, the more worried I was — I kept thinking that I'd left it too late and I wouldn't see Mother ever again. The last 150 miles took me three days.'

He dried his feet. 'I think I'll go and say goodnight to my mother and then get some sleep.'

'Wait. Let me put some of my mother's ointment on the blisters.'

Mary crouched on the floor beside this almost-stranger who was her relation, and smeared ointment thickly on the horny and blistered feet. As she worked she brooded on the bonding between mother and son which drew a young man so far and with such urgency. She nearly spoke to him about it, meaning to tell him that she thought he had done a fine thing, but as she glanced up at the big young man slumped in the chair, she knew he was asleep already.

It was another ordinary Sunday, just like so many other Sundays for as long as Mary could remember. Several years had passed since the brief excitement of the visit to Sydney when cousin Sarah was ill. Now cousin Sarah was dead and life had settled into an uninterrupted rhythm. Mamma had filled the camp oven with food prepared for the day, boots were cleaned, frills ironed and the buggy prepared on Saturday, and on Sunday morning Papa, Mamma and a buggyful of sons and befrilled daughters drove to the little Methodist church at Cawdor. The church stood alone in the paddocks, the green slopes of Mount Razorback rising beyond it and a sprinkling of farm cottages visible through trees across the undulating land. Mary picked her way past piles of bricks and building material to the door. There were so many families in the area now that the building was being extended. Everything was as usual; large families filing into their pews, duty-bound to be present, some men prepared to doze through the sermon as always, some women with their minds on other things, girls watching the boys, the boys wishing they were somewhere else. Mary knew that Mamma sometimes talked of the old days, when crowds of friends had met for whole days of prayer and sharing from the Bible, when it sounded almost exciting to be a Christian. Going to church was not like that for her. It was comfortable, an undemanding duty, more likely to be a place to learn the latest gossip or hear a list of complaints about their building debt.

Her father stood to lead the first hymn. They had no harmonium or violin and James Rootes' firm voice pitched a note. At a stamp of his foot they began to sing, following his direction into an old hymn of faith. Mary sang, but her singing was half-hearted.

Then the minister began to speak and, at first unwillingly, she listened.

'There is rust on your shields,' said the Rev. C.W. Rigg. 'Rust — and cobwebs — and a coat of dust on your shield of faith. When did you last pick it up? When did you last hold your shield against the darts of fire which the Enemy is aiming at you? Look at your spiritual armour — your helmet of salvation, the sword of the Spirit, the shoes of peace, the breastplate of righteousness. Are you wearing it? Have you forgotten that daily you are under attack? In the days when it was a struggle to survive, many of you kept your spiritual armour bright, in good repair, because you knew how desperately you needed it. Now that things are more comfortable, it is easier to do without the discipline of armour, and a shield can be a heavy weight. Beware — you are exposed to the Evil One.'

He looked at the younger people. Mary felt that he was staring straight at her.

'And some of you have never owned a shield of faith. You have sometimes hidden behind your parents' shield, but that is not enough. Where is your own faith? Do you, yourself, trust in Jesus Christ to save and protect you? Or are you open, vulnerable to every fear, every bitterness, every destroying thought?'

Mary sat very still, pleating and repleating the ends of her bonnet ribbon till it began to fray in her fingers. It was not that she did not know the scriptures or had never heard the claims of Christ: she could never remember a time when these things were not part of her world. But she knew now that she had never made her parents' faith her own, that she was indeed without her own shield of faith. The preacher was inviting people to be part of a new group to learn more of the things of the spirit. 'I'll be one of them,' she thought.

The missionary box was her father's idea. He found the suggestion in a copy of the *Christian Advocate* and passed it on to Mary.

'You girls have time to go out collecting,' he announced. 'You need something useful to do after you've finished helping your mother in the house. And if you get a collecting box, I'll put in the first donation.'

Mary was pleased with the idea for several reasons. For one thing, she was growing more and more close to her father; the two of them would often talk about ideas and books and Pa's latest enthusiasms were the the plight of Negro slaves in America and news of conversions among the cannibals of Fiji. For another, she had heard her parents' old friend John Watsford, a former minister of their district who had gone to Fiji in 1844, speak with passion of the needs in the Pacific. She had listened with awe; against the plain backdrop of Cawdor Methodist Church on a Sunday morning, Watsford had painted word pictures of giants of men with great knobbed warclubs, island women defying their husbands to become Christians, missionary women dying a world away from home, Watsford's family stumbling through a night of cyclone winds with their home destroyed and their only protection the strong arms of Tongan Christians. This they did, he said, in the name of Christ, to bring the people of the islands the good news that God loved them, and the tall girl in the pew felt her heart reaching out in response.

There was another reason, too, why Mary Rootes liked to visit her neighbours, collecting for missions. Now that Pa's farm was going well, and James and Jabez had married and moved off to their own farms, there were limits to the ways a young lady of nineteen could fill her days. There was house and yard work, of course, but her parents were now able to employ some workers to help. She could sew, and was becoming a skilled needlewoman, and she could garden, or cook, or read. Yet she knew that she would never have the freedom to choose to travel, or work as a missionary, or anything else with a challenge.

A recent issue of their church paper quoted a sermon on the role of women. It began by explaining that a modern woman would never be involved in the male world of business, trade, manufacture or leadership, not like the more primitive women of the Old Testament. It went on: 'Women are not to be men, in character, ambition, pursuit or achievement; but they are to be more; they are to be the makers of man; they are to affect for all that is good and great those with whom they are linked in life. . . they may be the regulating power, the animating and inspiring force, the soothing and resuscitating influence, by which the mighty engine of masculine life may be aided in its actions, its order and its results.' It had sounded noble, but to a single girl living with three younger sisters it offered little, except to hope one day for marriage.

So Mary tied her bonnet strings firmly under her chin, put the horse in the gig and with her missionary box in hand and Lydia for company she set off to persuade the neighbours to give to the missionary cause. Knocking on farmhouse doors was a far cry from confronting the powers of darkness in a violent Fiji, yet it gave Mary a sense of purpose. Some householders were friendly and generous while others had their own opinions.

'I don't hold with interfering with the heathen — let them be, that's what I say.'

'How can you come asking for money for something like that, so far away, when we have such a big debt on our new church building?'

'I'd like to help, but we've had a bad year.'

'Oh, do you have a missionary box too? We are busy filling ours — come and see my missionary duck.' And they were taken into the yards of the Dousts, and young Sarah Cox, the Whitemans and the Secoldes, to see missionary hens and a missionary duck and even some missionary rabbits in their cages; creatures who did not know that they were being fattened so that one day they would be sold, to die for the missionary cause.

Lydia chattered as they drove home, listing the events of the next months.

'And after the big missionary weekend when we'll all open up our missionary boxes there'll be Easter, and after that the big picnic. I just can't wait for the picnic! There's never been anything like it round here. All those people coming from Newtown Methodist Sunday School *on the train*!' She giggled. 'Seeing it is all the Sunday schools of Newtown circuit, and all the teachers and that, I was just wondering – well, wondering if *he* might come!'

'Who, pray tell, might *he* be, sister?' Mary looked at her sister with eyebrows raised.

'When we went to see poor cousin Sarah Playford before she died, I liked talking to cousin Richard – he was such a nice boy – such nice eyes – I just thought maybe he'd come to the picnic, seeing he lives at Newtown and all – it doesn't matter really. . .' She broke off, confused.

Mary drove on in silence. She knew cousin Richard, not much older than herself. They had always known the Playfords, visiting and being visited at intervals over the years. She had never taken a great deal of notice of Richard. More vividly in her memory, though even that was rather vague, was Richard's older brother William. Someone had said that William had left the goldfields and had been working on the railways, one of thousands of men labouring to build the beginnings of a network of railway tracks leading out from Melbourne and Sydney. Perhaps he was still in Victoria on the line from Melbourne to Ballarat. Maybe he was working on the new line just completed which ran from Sydney to Campbelltown. It was his younger brother Richard who was making Lydia giggle and turn red. If Richard came to the picnic, she decided that she ought to keep a sisterly eye on Lydia.

They turned into their own gate and she scrambled out of the gig. Lydia ran in to show their mother the heavy collection box while Mary unhitched the horse. Just before she dismissed the thought of Playfords from her mind, she had a sudden memory of a pair of calloused and blistered feet.

'It'll rain – I know it will rain,' Lydia fretted. 'Every year the Methodist Sunday schools in Newtown make big plans for their picnic and then it pours, and they end up eating their sandwiches in rows in the Sunday School room, all crowded up with umbrellas dripping in every corner. I've heard all about it. . .' she hesitated, then went on, almost defiantly, 'in letters from Richard Playford.'

Mary laughed at her. 'Rain? Nonsense! Look at the sky this evening.'

It had been a beautiful day, Easter Day 1859, with the crisp edge of autumn in the air. Mary was happy. Easter had never been more wonderful. It wasn't that the preaching had been more inspiring or the singing more emotional, but this year it had become real for her. She felt that she, too, had been there, there with the mindless crowds, there with the frightened disciples, there with those who turned their back on Jesus. She had looked at his face. She knew that he was dying for the sins of the whole world – and for her. With a sense of awe and recognition, as if she was seeing clearly for the first time a thing which had long been there just beyond the corner of her eye, she said with the Roman soldier, 'Truly this is the Son of God!' This morning, as they sang of Christ alive and among them, she had felt a great joy. She believed it. She really and truly believed that this Jesus Christ was her Lord, alive and with her, not because her parents said so, but because she knew it. All day she had felt a smile on her face, refusing to go away. Lydia's gloomy predictions about rain on a picnic hardly counted, yet she felt a great love and warmth towards her pretty sister that was all bound up in the same package as her new-found assurance that she too had a 'shield of faith'.

The smile was still on her face next morning. The sun was shining. Lydia sat up in bed unwinding the curling rags from the fat ringlets which sprang around her cheeks, pink with pleasure. An aroma of fresh-baked buns wafted in from the kitchen and there was the clatter of their mother up with the birds to fill baskets with picnic foods. Mary climbed out of bed, singing happily as she dressed. Louisa and Elizabeth were already up, giggling as they pulled and tugged on the laces of their older sisters' stays.

'Let Lydia have the tiny little waist – she's the one who is hoping to meet a young man today!' Mary said, laughing at her sisters. 'I'd rather be able to breathe, and enjoy the picnic lunch.'

Layers of pretty petticoats over the circle of crinoline hoops were dropped over their heads, and when their mother came in to inspect them, their wide sweeping dresses were in place, filling the room.

'When I was a girl, we were never so extravagant with fabric. We couldn't afford it and as for this modern fashion of great hooped skirts, I think it is downright foolishness. You all just mind that you don't get your hoops caught in a buggy wheel!' Her words were sharp, but Mary knew her mother well. Behind the severity, the older woman was delighted with her four teenage daughters.

James Rootes' buggy spun down the road with its cargo of laughing girls, picnic baskets and parents. With a thunder of hooves, a six-horse wagon went by, a freight of children cheering from their nests on hay bales. Other buggies and gigs, wagons and carriages sent up their dust plumes along the roads through the farms, all heading to Campbelltown railway station. It was only months before that the stretch of line between Liverpool and Campbelltown had been opened, and the crowds of country children from the Wesleyan Sunday schools of Campbelltown, Camden and Cawdor waited in the station yard, straining for their first sight of the train.

Lydia fidgeted with her bonnet strings, twirled ringlets round agitated fingers, and Mary caught her pinching colour into her cheeks.

'What if he comes?' she whispered to Mary. 'Do I look tidy? What if he doesn't want to talk to me?'

The dark smoke cloud of the train appeared, then they heard its thunder as it charged along the tracks at a speed like a galloping horse. Children, parents and teachers backed away, then cheered as the open carriages of the train, almost overflowing with four hundred waving guests, came to a halt. Gentlemen in top hats consulted and commanded and the mass of excited humanity ordered itself into a procession of Sunday schools, bright banners on poles at the head of each group. They passed through Campbelltown and climbed the hill to where Mr Chippendalls' paddock spread in the sunshine.

'Look where you are going, girl!' Mary said, tugging at Lydia's arm. The girl had nearly tripped because she had been trying to look over her shoulder as she walked.

'Richard Playford came! But he's way back there, ever so far back with all the Newtown people.'

On the wide hilltop in the brightness of the autumn day, the children sat in a great circle on the grass. Singing floated into the air and a prayer of thanksgiving. The minister from Newtown circuit, Stephen Rabone, stood to speak. Mary eyed him with some interest. She knew of Stephen Rabone as a respected man who had given many years as a missionary to Tonga in the days when the Tongan church had exploded into life. Part of her mind was busily observing as she listened, looking at the faces around the circle, almost seven hundred of them, town children impressed by the wide countryside falling away below them and country children excited by their first sight of a steam train. Lydia was nudging her and nodding across the circle. Richard Playford was there among the crowd. Mary thought she saw another familiar face, but wasn't sure.

The picnic baskets were laid out — sandwiches and cakes, buns and fruit. Stephen Rabone said, 'Let's give thanks to God!' and, after the prayer, the crowd fell upon the mountains of food. After the meal, the crowd moved to where swings had been set up and there was a maypole, races, games and sports. Mary caught her younger sisters wickedly laughing at Lydia. Lydia was seated on a swing with second cousin Richard pushing her up into the air and back again in a foam of crinoline petticoats. The older girl could not hear their conversation, but snatches of their laughter drifted across.

A deep voice spoke beside her. 'I think my brother is enjoying himself, don't you?'

She turned. A big young man smiled at her. 'I've just been talking to cousin Anna and cousin James,' he said. 'If they hadn't told me, I don't think I'd have recognised Lydia — she's grown up. But I remember you.'

They talked a little, remembering his mother, speaking of his father and sister. 'I've been working as a labourer on the new railways, on the line that's going to run from Melbourne to Bendigo,' he said. 'Hard work, but no worse than goldmining. Don't know yet, but maybe I'll go mining again — try my luck on one of the new fields. Or I might travel — go with one of the expeditions of exploration. I'm always good for a bit of adventure — something new.'

She listened with awe. Her own life seemed limited to such a small radius. Although she loved to travel with her mind, to read and think, she knew that for a girl there could never be any choices such as cousin William could make. She couldn't choose to be a miner or a railway fettler, she certainly couldn't choose to set out with any expedition to the most remote places in Australia. A little sigh escaped her.

Men were shouting for boys and men to join in a great tug-of-war, the last of the sports before the children ate the rest of the cakes and set off for home. William tipped his hat to her in polite farewell and wandered off, and when last she saw him he was heaving at the rope in the tug-of-war, wide shoulders straining and a triumphant grin on his face.

The floods which swept through the farmlands along the Nepean early in 1860 were for many families a time of dreadful disaster. Lives were lost, stock was drowned, farm buildings washed away and the work of years destroyed. Yet even as the skies still hung dark over paddocks where the debris left by floodwaters hung from the branches of trees, and men ankle-deep in stinking mud struggled to dispose of the carcasses of drowned beasts, the Rootes girls were excited. In a strange way the flood had done them a service.

'We are going to Sydney for a few weeks! To stay with the Playford cousins in Newtown till the floods are all gone down and everything is back to normal again!' Lydia was ecstatic. She had her things half-packed while the others were still wondering if they should go.

'You just want to see that Richard Playford again – we know,' teased Louisa, and Mary went to talk to her mother again.

'No, child, I want you girls away for a while.' Anna Rootes was firm. 'We've been through bad floods before and this is a very bad one. Some people are already ill with influenza – you know your father isn't well – and I don't want all of you ill as well. Our servant girls can help me clean up.' Her voice was a little wistful as she added, 'Some people are saying the floods are a judgment on us all for losing our first love for God – saying that there has been a lot of rottenness in our community.'

Mary was brisk. 'So it may be, but I think it is more likely that our sin has been to build our houses too near the river. And you know quite well our little church is overflowing at the moment, with thirty-two of us preparing for membership. No, I don't think God is sending floods to strike us down. But, if you like, we girls will have a lovely visit to Sydney.'

So they went to Sydney, four girls thrilled to travel all the way in the latest technology of a steam train. Their widowed cousin Henry was good to them, and cousin Mary Susannah, but they all knew that for Lydia the visit centred around Richard. Richard worked as a sugar boiler at the sugar refinery in Liverpool Street and every evening he took Lydia out walking.

There was no sign of Cousin William. 'Who knows where he is?' his sister remarked when Mary asked the question. 'That one is always off on his own affairs. He writes to us from time to time – on the railways in Victoria till recently, then off again after gold. There is a new rush just started to a place called Kiandra in the Snowy Mountains, so Will might go there. He'll come home when he's ready.'

Lydia Rootes and Richard Playford were married on the day after Christmas, 1860. The home at Marshdale Farm, Cobbitty, had never looked better, with the summer garden a blaze of colour. James Rootes had added more rooms to the house and, as he had become more prosperous, they had bought more and better furniture. Anna Rootes had the curtains and bed drapes that she had dreamed of and a stone bread oven had been added to the open fireplace. Christmas that year was very exciting, with the three married family members coming home with their babies and spouses for Christmas dinner, Mamma's birthday and the wedding. Mary stood in the crowded parlour watching the backs of the heads of the bridal party. Lydia had chosen sister Louisa and a Rootes cousin as bridesmaids, and the broad back of William Playford stood beside Richard. The Methodist minister William Clark was solemnly reading the marriage service. 'Do you Lydia, take Richard. . .' but Mary was only partly listening. Lydia was there, her little sister, getting married, and she'd be leaving tonight to travel all the way to Sydney to live. She was going to miss her so much.

'You came,' she said later, when she carried her tray of good food to the guests on the verandah. William Playford was there, leaning against a verandah post and eating cake.

'Of course. Richard wanted me to be here, and I only have one brother. If it hadn't been for the wedding, I'd probably be off somewhere in the centre of Australia by now. I thought it would be good to go out with the Victorian expedition with Burke and Wills to cross the continent from south to north and back. They needed a few good practical bushmen, so they said. Too late now, they've already gone. A bit disappointing really. . .' He took a hearty bite of tart and went on. 'So, after I decided to forget about the expedition, I went off to Hill End, in NSW, after gold again. Didn't do too badly either. I'm beginning to put something away in the bank for the day when I'll settle somewhere. Have a look at these — hold out your hand!'

Mary lowered her tray and held open her palm. William pulled out a little pouch from its hiding place and tipped into her hand several small and glowing nuggets of gold.

7
Foundations
1860-1872

MARY ROOTES CLUTCHED her travelling basket on her lap and watched the fluid lines of open countryside turn into the tighter geometry of the town. From time to time the train paused at a platform with a great hissing and puffing, then heaved itself onward with a showering of cinders. Beside her sat a family of neighbours who had offered to chaperone her on her journey – 'Our Mary is going to visit her married sister in Sydney – she'll be met at Newtown,' Mamma had explained. With nervous fingers Mary smoothed her hair under her little flat hat. In church at Cawdor the hat was the newest style and her hair was bound in a dark, glossy bundle in a fashionable woven net, but suddenly she felt sure that a big, black smudge of soot must be on her nose, or her hat awry – 'I just want to be *neat*,' she said sternly to herself.

Lydia's letter had said, 'One of us will meet you at Newtown and bring you home. It might be William, because he'll be here for a visit.'

The train slowed, then shuddered to a stop at a platform. An attendant shouted, 'Newtown!' Mary leaned quickly through the open window.

'Someone has come, thank you,' she said to her travelling companions as she struggled to open the carriage door, lift her basket and force the awkward bulk of her crinoline hoops through the narrow doorway.

'Is it any easier sideways? Quick, give me the basket.'

Scarlet to the ears, she yanked the skirts free and tumbled onto the platform. The broad young man beside her had a wicked grin on his face.

'And how are you, cousin Mary? Very charming gown indeed –

but it would never do on the goldfields!'

Mary did her best to look dignified and walked home to Lydia's house on the arm of her cousin William.

There was a magical quality about the next few weeks. Lydia and Richard Playford's little cottage was at Shepherd's Paddock, between the highway and the railway line at Newtown, and every stick of furniture, every stitch of house linen, every pot and pan had been gathered with delight by the newly married pair. Lydia led her sister through the house, showing off every tiny detail. With Lydia clinging to Richard's arm, they walked around the house yard and paddock, demanding that Mary admire their cow, their ducks and chickens, their pig. 'We'll have a horse, too, and a carriage one day – you wait and see. Look, there's even the horse trough and a little stable waiting.'

Mary's sister was wrapped in an aura of utter contentment, somehow set apart from her in a way she could not explain. As the older girl watched, she knew a pang of envy.

Together the two brothers and two sisters went to the grand new Newtown Wesleyan Methodist Church. Mary had an impression that cousin William only went to be obliging; they had already had some vigorous discussions about Christianity. The church had only been opened a year and its high gothic facade soared above King Street. Mary followed her sister in through the arched cedar doors to stare in wonder at galleries overhead and the body of the building full of families in their rented family pews. The church at Cawdor paled to nothing beside the carved cedar panels, the sunshine streaming over the heads of the people through vast coloured leadlight windows. The preacher, Stephen Rabone, was lofty in the high pulpit. The congregation rustled to their feet to sing a hymn and Mary heard Lydia's treble and William's firm bass beside her. She felt a great happiness, and a certain fear. Surely this pleasure of worshipping in such a place – and being with these people – could not last. Today they would worship together, then later over Lydia's Sunday dinner they would laugh and talk, and she and William would probably have another friendly argument about the sermon. But soon she would have to go home again and William would go back to his goldmining at Hill End. When the people bowed in prayer, she brushed away a tear. 'Lord, what do you want for my life?' she prayed.

The canary-yellow horse tram stood waiting at Redfern railway terminus, a vehicle of fantasy to carry Mary away on a day of delight. Decorated with devices of lions and eagles in the brightest of paint, the brand-new tram with its cargo of dozens of holiday-makers ran down the hill along Pitt Street, past the shops and crowds and fine sandstone buildings of Sydney, all the way to the harbour and Circular Quay. The sun glinted from the waters of the harbour, bright, almost metallic. The four of them, Lydia and Richard, Mary and William hurried from the tram onto the Phoenix wharf.

'Let me pay, I'm almost a rich man!' William announced, and bought bottles of sarsparilla and gingerade from a vendor and their shilling ferry tickets with a flourish.

The paddlewheel steamer stood at the wharf with 'The Phantom' painted along its bow. Mary took William's hand as he helped her up the boarding plank. Somehow it didn't seem strange, even after the plank had been drawn up and the great paddlewheels had begun to churn their circles of spray across the harbour, to find her hand still firmly held in the curve of his arm. She was too aware of his presence beside her to look directly at him, but even as she looked away across the blue of the harbour to the dark greens of the headlands and coves, watching small craft and seagulls in flight, she knew with great intensity the touch of his work-roughened fingers on her hand, the pressure of his arm against her own. They stood at the ferry rail with the wind in their faces, laughing when the fine seaspray damped them, the men teasing the girls as the breeze tilted their wide skirts into an unseemly display of ankles. Never was weather balmier, never was conversation wittier, never was scenery more lovely. Mary breathed deeply of the smell of the sea, tasting the delicious flavour of the day. The paddlewheel steamer came at last to the far side of the harbour, to Manly in a sheltered cove. The four left the vessel to walk along a path scented with wildflowers which led them across a narrow neck of land to the open sea.

With Lydia's picnic basket and William's bottles of aerated waters, they sat on the sand in the sunshine, watching long lines of breakers rolling onto a glittering curve of golden beach. Mary had seen the harbour before, but never the wideness of the ocean. Even ants in the sandwiches and the sun reddening her nose did not spoil it. Resting against William's arm, she felt that she had never been happier in her whole life.

'It wouldn't be like this always, you know.'

It was dusk at last and the harbour was behind them. The horses of the horse tram laboured up the hill back to Redfern station. It had been raining and passing carriages sent up sprays of mud from the unpaved road to dirty the lions and eagles. Mary was beginning to feel chilled and pulled her mantle more tightly around her.

'It couldn't be like today,' William said again. He did not explain what could not match their golden day at Manly, but he began, awkwardly, to speak of the goldfields.

'Rough — a lot of things are rough there — on the goldfields, I mean. Good blokes, most of them, but a mixed lot — you can meet all the nations of the world in an afternoon. And not all the nations are friends, either — there are some bad troubles between the Celestials — the Chinese, that is — and the rest of the diggers at most places, and it has been very bad at Lambing Flat this year. But it's not only that. Some of the men are a wild lot; not all of them, but some have very coarse manners, not fit for decent company. Houses, too — very rough, not like Lydia's new house. Tents or bark huts put up overnight, or if you're lucky a wall to the waist of mud and straw with a canvas roof. My bed on the field is the ground, or a couple of poles with cowhide nailed between them. And food — we hardly ever see fresh vegetables or fruit. Not like you have at the farm; just mutton and damper — and pickles for a treat.'

He rushed on and, with a chill in her heart, Mary felt that he was busily piling up obstacles, one on top of the other, to block a path along which she had imagined she might one day walk.

'And there are not many ladies on the goldfields — well, not what I'd call ladies — and some of the miners' wives always look so tired all the time. People are sometimes falling down open mine shafts and breaking bones — it's quite dangerous — or getting very drunk, or brawling... What I'm trying to say is it's no place for a woman.'

Mary nodded silently, holding her face stiffly as disappointment swept over her. Today she had thought — even been nearly sure — that he liked her, too. She'd thought that one day he would ask her to marry him. Now she drew away from his side and stared blindly away at the city streets as they darkened. The gaslights of Redfern station were just ahead and, as soon as the horses stopped, she stepped out of the tram without waiting for his hand. They sat in silence in the train, with the noise of the engine filling their ears. She couldn't look at him.

Lydia and Richard were quick to walk on ahead to light the candles in the cottage. William caught Mary's arm as they reached the gate.

'Wait, cousin!'

At last she looked at him and saw deep love in his face.

'Mary, the goldfields are no place for a woman. I wouldn't take a bride to a place like Hill End. But if I leave goldmining and find a regular job here in Sydney, will you marry me?'

The bride took one last look in the mirror before she turned to take her father's arm. The face reflected seemed somehow unfamiliar, with the wreath of white flowers and veiling framing the silken sheen of her hair. 'Is that really me, plain Miss Mary Rootes of Marshdale Farm?' she wondered. 'I look nearly — nearly beautiful.'

'Are you ready?' Her father offered his arm and her mother dropped a sudden kiss on her cheek as she moved from the privacy and security of her little bedroom in Lydia's house, down the hall and to the door of the crowded parlour.

For a moment Mary hesitated in the doorway. The room was full of elbow-to-elbow Rootes and Playford relatives all decked out in their best. Then through the crowd she saw William, solid and sure, waiting for her, and in his eyes she saw welcome and love. Not daring to take her eyes from his, she walked across the room, released her father's arm and stood beside her bridegroom.

The minister, Stephen Rabone, stood before them. Mary knew that he was a very busy man, with responsibility for a large parish, chairmanship of the Sydney district of Wesleyan Methodism with its multitudes of committees and his continuing interest in the work of missions in the Pacific. Yet he had been kind to her, the girl from the country coming for her wedding, and had won her loyalty with the way he encouraged her for her four years of faithful collecting for the work of mission. Now Mr Rabone acknowledged her arrival with a smile and began the service, the solemn words a counterpoint to her thoughts.

'Dearly beloved, we are gathered together here in the sight of God and in the presence of this congregation, to join together this man and this woman in holy matrimony, which is an honourable estate. . .'

(In the sight of God. Mary had an intense feeling of God's presence, of her Father with them in the intimacy of the words of marriage, even more truly than the audience of relatives. She hoped William felt it too.)

'William Playford, wilt thou have this woman to thy wedded wife. . . Wilt thou love her, comfort her, honour and keep her, and forsaking all other keep thou only unto her, so long as you both shall live?'

('The goldfields are no place for a woman,' William had said. 'I reckon a man should only go mining if he is so rich he can afford it, or if he is so poor he has nothing to lose. I'm not gambling on losing you, my Mary. Work at the brickworks in Newtown will do me.')

'I will,' said William.

'Mary Rootes, wilt thou have this man to thy wedded husband . . . so long as you both shall live?'

('Oh, William! The awful news of Mr Burke and Mr Wills, lost in the middle of Australia on their expedition – dead. If you had gone with them, perhaps you'd be dead, too. I want to live with you for years and years, until we are both old.')

'I will,' said Mary.

They spoke their vows, echoing the words of Stephen Rabone, their hands clasped in promise.

'. . .to have and to hold from this day forward, for better for worse, for richer for poorer, in sickness and in health, to love and to cherish till death do us part, according to God's holy law. . .'

(Behind her stood her parents, James and Anna Rootes, with more than thirty years of marriage behind them; she had seen lived out in her own home a marriage that had faced the better and the worse, the richer years and the years of flood and drought, the sickness and the health. She knew it could be done, not lightly, not without pain, but it could be done.)

'. . .and thereto I give thee my troth.'

William took the ring and gently slid it onto her finger.

'With this ring, a token and pledge of the vow and covenant now made betwixt me and thee. . .'

(The ring gleamed, soft gold, gold wrested with the sweat of his brow from the mine at Hill End; the roughened hands that dug it and separated it from its earth now clasped her own.)

'. . .I thee wed.'

The service was over. Somewhere in the background, Mary was aware of loving laughter, with Mamma and Lydia and the girls starting to bring out the bridal feast. She stood in a little island of happiness with her husband, songs of thanks to God singing silently in her heart.

When at last the feasting was over, the bridal pair escaped from Lydia and Richard's house in a shower of rice and flower petals.

They walked along in silence, hand in hand. Behind them, Mamma Rootes was crying into the washing-up and Lydia was resting her tired legs, now heavy with pregnancy. On either side of the road the businesses of Newtown ran beside them: grocer and corn dealer, milliner and dressmaker, drayman, dairyman and druggist, coppersmith and carpenter, hotels and a ladies seminary. The towering chimneys and brick kilns of a number of brickworks thrust up into the sky, pointing them to their new home at St Peters, just down the road.

Mary clung to William's arm as they walked along a hilltop with the wind whipping her skirts. Spread widely below them was the place she must learn to call home, a panorama of Sydney. The brickworks were nearest, dominating the scene at the top of the hill with the rawness of a clay pit gouged out of the grass. A line of green marked the point to the east where sand dunes and mangroves made a horizon beyond which moved the Pacific Ocean. Dairy farms and market gardens, factories and shops, stands of bush timber and suburban webs, a glimpse of Botany Bay to the south with the gothic grandeur of new churches and a university to the north: this was to be her new home. There seemed little to build a bridge between this and the lush pastures, bush and river of Cobbitty.

'Let's go home and light a little fire in the grate,' she said urgently. 'I'm getting cold.' She pulled her mantle tight against the autumn winds.

Their cottage waited for them in May Street, St Peters, of good brick from the brickworks, square and neat with steps leading directly onto the street. There was a narrow front verandah with a central door and a window on either side. She thought of home, with the stringybark roof, and knew she should be very thankful indeed.

William unlocked the door and swung it open. She giggled and said, 'I'm too heavy, silly Will,' but he scooped her up, hoops and all.

'If I'm strong enough to carry a 150 pound bag of flour a mile, then surely I can carry my bride over the threshold of our home!'

Inside they held hands and explored the house, suddenly very shy of each other. It became important to look at all the work members of their family had done to prepare their cottage, to peep into bundles and baskets to discover Marshdale Farm eggs, pickled pork, yellow pats of butter from Mamma's churn, a fresh loaf. William set match to the fire laid in the grate and lit a lamp, while Mary untied her bonnet ribbons and hung her bonnet on a peg beside William's wideawake hat.

'There's another package here – shall we open it?'

She brought the square bundle to the fireside and they folded back the wrapping. A leather-covered Bible lay before them, a gift from her parents. Mary turned the pages slowly, enjoying the feel of fine paper and the texture of leather, recognising familiar passages as the pages turned.

'They hope we'll read it together,' she murmured. 'I hope so too.' She was learning that, though William was quite willing to attend church faithfully and was morally upright, he did not care so deeply about things of the spirit as she did. But he'd change, she felt sure.

William picked up the book and discovered the Family Register, blank pages at the beginning of the book.

'Look at this, a place to write our wedding day and all our family births and deaths. Good – I'll start with the first entry right now!'

He jumped up and fetched pen, ink and blotter and sat down again with a broad smile on his face. 'I think we'll fill this whole page with the names of our children,' he declared.

Mary blushed a fiery red and watched with hammering heart while he proudly wrote, as the first entry in the new Bible, 'William Playford and Mary Rootes, married at Shepherds Paddock, 2 May 1862.'

It was only the next morning when she woke beside her husband that she noticed one more package to be unwrapped. She gathered up the heavy bundle and scrambled back into William's arms to open it. Inside she found bulbs, daffodils, jonquils, freesias and a thick clump of violet plants, only slightly wilted and with the earth of home and Marshdale Farm still enfolding their roots. Mamma had tucked a little note among the leaves: 'Something to plant at your new home.'

A winter, spring and summer came to the little cottage in May Street, St Peters and the violets bore a few tentative flowers in their first year in a new garden. Mary struggled with a strange mixture of emotions. There was delight in her marriage mixed with homesickness for her parents and the farm. She was loving Lydia's company and the pleasures of being auntie to Lydia's baby, but she suffered the miseries of morning-sickness. And though William sat beside her in church every Sunday among the families who filled Newtown Methodist Church, she felt he was probably thinking about bricks during the sermon.

She was very proud of William and his enterprise. He and his brother Richard had gone into partnership in their own brickworks. During the winter and the spring she had often wrapped herself in her widest shawl and walked to the end of May Street where the towers of the brickworks chimneys of St Peters and Newtown punctuated the landscape with their exclamation marks. Filling the vista across the city stood the great caverns of brick kilns, their chimneys sometimes belching clouds of dark smoke into the air and sometimes seeming to ripple with waves of heat. At the foot of the hill lay a creek and in the distance the mangroves. At the claypit, men tore into the shale with picks and shovels, loading the clay and rocks onto carts. A horse walked in endless circles, harnessed to the pugmill which turned round and round crushing the clay. Wheels turned, machinery thudded, steam engines powered the work, piles of firewood and stacks of completed bricks waited to be put to their purpose.

Mary would search for William among the workmen. Sometimes he would be loading unfired bricks into the kilns, or supervising the pugmill. She would stand at a distance watching him fill the great curved doorway with loose bricks ready to be plastered over with damp clay to seal the kiln for firing. The young wife would watch shyly, proudly, secretly; watching the strength and purpose of him, the energy and confidence, his old hat daubed with dust and clay. He seemed at home when he was handling the earth, knowing and comfortable with rocks and clay, sand and minerals, gems and coal. Then he would turn and see her, and grin his special grin for her, returning in his eyes his love and pride in his tall young wife who now carried his child. They might exchange a few words and she would walk home, satisfied.

In the heat of summer, she watched Lydia and Richard and several hundred children and teachers set off in a convoy of wagons for the annual picnic of Newtown Sunday School.

'I wish I could come, too,' she whispered to Lydia, and Lydia looked shocked.

'In your delicate condition? It wouldn't be decent!'

'But you're going down to Phoenix Wharf and you'll have a lovely day with a ferry ride across Middle Harbour, and there'll be flags and a band, a sea breeze, and singing and games for the children . . .'

'My dear girl, you're a married lady now and you know perfectly well you can't go on picnics in your state. Just imagine it!'

So Mary stayed home that hot February day, restless with

pregnancy, discreetly away from the public eye. She wandered around the house, finding everything already clean and ordered as she liked it, then fingered through the baby clothes she had prepared. It was too hot to sew. Mary picked up her library book and then laid it down again. Usually she was happy to read something from the Sunday School collection of over a thousand books, but today it was too hot to read.

'Lydia's baby is lovely,' she thought. 'Mine will be beautiful, too, mine and William's.' Yet a prickle of fear stabbed her. Babies died, she knew. And women died in childbed. Mamma had promised to come to help her with the birthing, and she trusted Mamma, but she'd been hearing stories about other families. No woman could be sure of a live baby anyway, though in the country more babies seemed to survive and thrive than in town.

'I'm just a bit worried,' she said sternly to herself. 'And I don't feel very well – it's all those bad smells. . .' Here in the summer in town there was always the heavy aroma of cesspits and the droppings of a thousand horses, the smells of bad drains and rotting garbage, and it made her long for the simple earthiness of farm smells.

'You'll feel better when your mother comes,' William assured her as the days passed. 'She's a clever woman with babies. Maybe it's just that it's our first time.'

He often picked up the Bible, not to read it but to stare at the page of the Family Register. Mary knew that this was the place where he would record the birth of an heir.

In March 1863 Mary lay with her son in her arms while William wrote in his most careful penmanship the name of his first son, James Playford. She had lived, and the baby was alive, too, though not strong and Mamma looked anxious. Within the month William made another record on the family page. Their first child was dead. Mary lay prostrate on her bed, pleading with tears for God to help her in her pain. William's grief was coloured with deep anger.

'If God is a loving God, as you say,' he demanded, 'why couldn't he have saved our child? Our little boy didn't even begin to live – just long enough for us to love him. Religion may be all very well in its place, but what good is it now?'

It was not that William did not believe in God. Nor did he mind going through the Saturday night rituals of the hipbath, the washing of dusty hair and the polishing of Sunday shoes by the fire. He would dress in his decent suit, comb his whiskers, don his good round hat and sit beside her in church.

Yet Mary felt sadness that William did not disguise the fact that most of his churchgoing was because he wanted to please her. The Bible her parents had given them was read by her, and William had recorded the birth of Anna Mary, their second child, in it, but he rarely picked it up himself. However, he encouraged her to take an interest in the excellent school which was conducted through the week at the church, and to help with the new Juvenile Missionary Society. Mary still worked actively for missions in the Pacific, but she couldn't persuade him to come with her to hear the returned missionary John Watsford speak on Fiji, or the young Fijian convert with him. 'I'll stay home and mind the baby,' he said cheerfully.

Mary came home full of enthusiasm, describing the big Fijian man in modern suit and bare feet who spoke with such feeling of the changes that the gospel was bringing to his once violent country.

'He said he was sure we all had more gold at home to give to help our missionary work,' she said, 'and he'd be happy to wait while we went home and got it!'

William laughed. Somehow she didn't think that he would lightly give much of his own hard-earned gold to such a cause.

From time to time her parents would write a note, carried by a visitor, to let her know that they were praying for William. It caused pain to her parents, she knew, that more than one of their children and the spouses of their children were not yet convinced Christians. After the first flush of bridal hopefulness, Mary was learning that William was William, and she would be wise to love him as he was because he wasn't planning to change. He loved her dearly, he worked very hard to provide for her, but he had too many hard questions about the painful mysteries of life to be hypocritical about his religion.

When his father, old Henry Playford, died, they talked again as they mourned his passing. He had respected and loved his father, and the deaths of both his father and his son left him raw. Even baby Anna Mary was fragile and, as they talked, Mary knew that he was alert to the sound of her breathing.

'What do you have to hold on to, if you don't feel you can trust the Lord?' Mary asked. 'Your gold in the bank? That couldn't buy our baby's life. Or your brick business? That's good, but even a fine business has been known to fail. Are you holding on to me? I'm strong, but I'm not strong enough . . . I only know that if I can't

trust God I have nothing.'
And he held her tightly in his arms in silence.

A stranger came to Sydney in 1864, an American fresh from San Francisco. His name was William Taylor. He was called 'California Taylor' because he had gone as a missionary to the cosmopolitan mix of men on the goldfields of California in the first rush of 1849. When Mary first heard of the man, she discovered that he had come to Australia to try to raise funds through an extensive lecture tour to rebuild his chapel and hall which had been burned down. But it soon became clear that this was no common lecturer. This man captured the imagination with his lectures on the Holy Land and the ancient travels of Paul, and captured people's hearts with his preaching. The churches around Sydney, at York Street, Bourke Street, William Street, Redfern, Chippendale, Newtown and the rest, were already filled with many families living in the area, but when California Taylor preached and spoke, every seat was taken and people still kept crowding in.

The night William Playford finally decided to attend one of California Taylor's meetings, he did not walk up the road with Mary with very good grace. He had been hard at work all day, stoking the fires of the brick kiln, and it had been hard to scrub himself clean and set out for an evening meeting when he would have preferred to go to bed. But Mary had been persuasive and friends had assured him that the man was worth hearing. The big man with the waterfall of beard and the curious accent began to tell stories about the Californian goldfields, and Mary knew that William was listening.

'There were men there from every nation of the world, and every man was after gold.' The preacher looked around at the grandeur of Newtown church. 'There was nothing like this, no smart pulpit. I used to stand outside the saloons and start to sing, as loud as I could, and sometimes when she thought they'd knock me down, my wife would come and stand beside me and sing, too. We'd sing them right out of the saloons and then I'd call, "What's the news?" I'd call one by one on men of every nation: What's the news from Ireland? What's the news from Italy? What's the news from the West Indies? And then I loved to tell them that I had good news. I'd jump up on a whisky barrel and I'd tell them the best news of all, that Christ loved them enough to die in their place, to take the punishment they deserved.'

William was nodding in recognition. It was clear that he was seeing the scene outside the saloons, and the miners, and the man on the barrel yelling at the crowd.

'And now I want to say to you men and women tonight, what is the most important thing in the world to you? Is it gold? Is it money? Is it security and fame? Listen to these words from the Bible, from the third chapter of Proverbs: "Happy is the man that findeth wisdom, and the man that getteth understanding. For the merchandise of it is better than the merchandise of silver, and the gain thereof than fine gold."'

The powerful voice went on. He spoke of those who seek gold, perhaps even find gold, yet miss the greatest riches of wisdom and understanding; those who struggle to fight their way through their lives, grasping, coveting, striving to achieve, yet miss the ultimate satisfaction and peace of trusting the wisdom and understanding of God. 'To trust in the Lord with all your heart – it's better than gold. It's better than the biggest nugget you've ever dreamed of.'

When he had finished speaking, William Taylor announced the final hymn. 'After the others have gone, those who want to pray and put their lives right with God are invited to wait and then come to kneel at the communion rail for prayer.'

The hymn was sung and people began to gather their books and top hats from under the seats. William sat where he was. Mary sat beside him with the sleeping Anna Mary in her lap, all kinds of prayers tumbling through her mind. Others moved away and as the building became more quiet, William slowly stood and moved to kneel at the communion rail. California Taylor knelt beside him. Mary could not hear their words; what was said between William and God was his business and if he chose to talk about it later that would be a special gift. But she sat very still with the tears pouring down her face, thanking God that her beloved William had discovered the most precious thing in the world.

A special day that was to burn itself in Mary's mind was 24 May. Methodists remembered it as Wesley Day, the date when John Wesley had experienced the 'warming' of his heart. For colonial NSW it was a public holiday for the Queen's Birthday. But in 1865, 24 May was a day of special rejoicing at Ashfield.

It was a time of new church buildings, as large families built their homes a little further from the centre of the city of Sydney. Networks of new roads, schools and shops were spreading out with the people.

The Newtown Methodist circuit had for a long time had up to eleven congregations worshipping in the area. One of these was at Ashfield and now all the Methodists flocked to celebrate the opening of a handsome new church building there. As William and Mary Playford arrived from the afternoon train, they joined a crowd of six hundred spilling outside the building as they were too many to sit inside. California Taylor stood on a tabletop, ready to preach, and William whispered, 'At least he's not on a whisky barrel!'

It was so good to have William beside her. There was a holiday spirit in the air, a spirit of hope and enthusiasm as people saw yet another fine new building standing in a new suburb 'to the glory of God'. The sense of hope went deeper than new structures of Sydney sandstone and Newtown brick. In the past year or so, many people had been profoundly affected by the preaching of California Taylor and other local men of God – Rabone, Kelynack, Watsford and others – and there was a great sense of the power of God at work among them. For William it had meant a change from religious form to a faith which was becoming more and more part of his life.

In a tent in the paddock beside the church, Mary happily balanced little Anna Mary on her hip and a plate of food in her hand. These days she felt more at home in a crowd of Sydney church people and greeted friends during the meal. By the time the crowd, well-fed and quite ready to be encouraged to give liberally to the church building fund, had moved into the church for the evening meeting, the sound of exploding fireworks in the neighbourhood reminded them that it was the Queen's Birthday. Speakers spoke glowingly of the Queen and the British Empire. One speaker suggested that an American Indian had said that the reason why 'the sun never sets on the Queen's dominions' was because 'God almighty could not trust Englishmen in the dark!'

'I have noticed,' California Taylor said, after he had spoken of the need for all members to use their gifts in the life of the church, 'that here in Australia you ignore the women and the children. That's why you have been getting on so slowly with the conversion of the world. Women, as well as men, have been called to prophesy – remember St Peter quoted the prophet Joel, ''Your sons *and your daughters* shall prophesy''. That does not mean extraordinary foretelling of the future. It means strengthening believers and waking up those without faith. This is women's right! Let the men debate the points of order and be the preachers, but let the women take their right place, too.'

Mary felt William's arm pressing against her own. Very gently, he covered her hand with his own.

The next time fireworks lit the night sky for the Queen's Birthday Mary and William were in no mood for celebration. Little Anna, two years old and with the delicacy which had frightened Mary every time yet another wave of disease passed over their village, was dying. There had been other epidemics – dysentery, scarlet fever, measles, typhoid, dyphtheria – and other people's children had been taken. Now the mother crouched over the little bed, all her desperate efforts to help her child to breathe freely in vain, and watched her baby die. Her hands shook violently, but she took her scissors and snipped off a curl, to be wrapped and cherished and wept over.

The walk to Camperdown Cemetery was an agony. Mary walked with head bowed, the streets and paddocks around her seen through blurring tears and the thick mesh of her black veil. She walked among the other graves, so many little graves with their headstones wreathed with stone-carved flowers, or doves or angels, each telling of other women's children who had died after days or weeks or months. Sad and sentimental verses were engraved, almost a pleading for it to be true that the children were better dead, better to be safe in heaven, a cry for some comfort, some explanation. She clung to William as they stood under the cypress trees. The grave of her first child, infant James, was there too. Even the knowledge that her new baby, Legh Richmond Playford, was safely at home in his cradle in the care of a neighbour, or that she herself was young and healthy and sure to have many more children, was no comfort. All around was the dark theatre that surrounded death, the tasselled hearse drawn by horses under high black plumes, the processional of mourners, the black costumes of grief, the stage-set of graven tombstones and fenced garden beds tended for the dead. It was her little Anna who was at the centre of this bitter display. She stumbled away with the sound of the falling clods in her ears, wanting desperately for William to have enough faith for the two of them.

A well-meaning family friend wrote a long poem for them called 'Our Babes in Heaven' in memory of their babies. Its verses pictured the Playfords sitting at their cottage door in the cool of the evening, listening to the sound of the voices of other children. It spoke of the

'. . .two mounds in the quiet place

With summer blooms o'er them creeping
Where Anna with the sweet pale face
And her baby brother lie sleeping,'

of scalding tears and 'angels bright in heaven'. Mary sat stroking the single fair curl with the lugubrious poem before her, and felt anger that she should not be allowed to grieve without a sense that she should be glad to have her children in heaven.

A small lamp was lit in her darkness on an evening much later when William read to her of Jesus and the children. He read of little ones creeping shyly to the Lord, and Jesus lifting them in his arms to bless them. When at last Mary fell asleep, it was with a simple picture in her mind of the fair curls of Anna Mary and her little brother held in the security of Jesus' arms.

In time, when William Playford needed a symbol to mark his bricks with the Playford identity, he marked some with a small 'P' and his bricks with an imprint made from a mould of the baby fist of his surviving son.

There were times, through the next few years, when Mary envied her sister Lydia. Lydia had lost none of her children, even though both families faced the same dangers of disease and both young mothers travelled together through pregnancies, births and childhood ills. But those times of envy were not very often. Mostly Mary was content. William in his mid-thirties was full of energy and, though his hair was just beginning to thin a little, Mary thought he looked very handsome with his luxuriant full dark beard; he was adding some of the polish of a successful businessman to his skills as a fine artisan. They now had two children, Legh and Harry, each child well and lively, while Lydia and Richard had three. Back at Marshdale Farm, her parents were ageing, but James Rootes was still a vigorous farmer and her mother was always available to her children and grandchildren. The two youngest sisters had married and moved away, Louisa to Richard Todd and Elizabeth to one of the Fryer boys from Camden.

The year 1869 was a year of change. Since William had left goldmining eight years earlier, he had worked in partnership with his brother Richard, but now Richard decided he wanted to buy a dairy farm at Petersham, a little to the west. The decision was made in a friendly fashion, with William buying out the brickworks and the two familes each building a larger house as near neighbours in Windsor Road, Petersham, with plenty of open pasture land around them. They transferred to the Ashfield Methodist Church and William and Richard began teaching Sunday School there. Mary was a little sad to leave her own first cottage, her bridal home, but the new house was so close to Lydia's, and so fine, that she soon settled in. The new gardens were dug, and for perhaps the first time that patch of soil was planted with iris and freesias, violets and daffodils. Mary and William began to buy grander furniture, vast cedar pieces with a glass-fronted bookcase for Mary's books, brass fireirons and coal vase for the parlour, the luxury of gas lighting and a new mangle and box iron for the laundry. William bought Mary a new machine for sewing seams and, as modern dress demanded great armfuls of fabric to trail away in elaborate draperies and long trains, she was grateful. Everything was larger, more embellished, more modern, more colourful.

'Even I am much larger,' Mary laughed to Lydia one day when they were visiting together. 'I was never a dainty little thing like you, but look at me now!'

'Childbearing, my dear,' Lydia replied. 'You've had four children — what can you expect?'

'And eating. You know how much I love to cook. Oh, well, it's good that William likes a good armful.'

William himself had never been busier. In the evening, he would come home, clothing thick with dust and clay, smelling of the smoke of the fires of the brick kilns, and talk about his business. Sometimes Mary went to visit the works with the children and he showed them his new equipment, specially his new iron pugmill which broke down and mixed the clay before it was formed into bricks. 'This is the first one to be made locally here in NSW — I ordered it from the foundry to my own specifications and it's good,' he explained. Drayloads of Playford bricks left the yards, hauled away by draughthorses, to become part of the fabric of the growing cityscape.

'We're building Sydney! The orders are coming in all the time,' he said. There were a dozen brickworks in Newtown now, but Playfords were still doing well.

One evening William came home with a look of triumph on his face. Even before he took his bucket of hot water from the stove for his evening wash, the news came spilling out.

'A new order, probably the biggest we've ever had! You know how the NSW Royal Agricultural Society has had displays of livestock and farm produce out at Parramatta for years? And how this year they set up their tents and cattleyards close to the city at Prince Alfred Park?'

Mary knew well. She had taken the little boys, with Lydia and her children, to explore the ten hectares of paddocks with their wealth of animals and tents full of displays of fruit, wool and grains. Her main memory was of wading through mud after heavy rain.

'I'm getting a contract to provide bricks for a grand new exhibition building, to be built for next year, 1870, to commemorate the visit of Captain Cook one hundred years ago. They like their new site in the park, and they want NSW to host a great intercolonial exhibition here, just like the British and their famous Crystal Palace, or Paris in 1855. People from all our Australian colonies and around the world will be sending their best products here to Sydney and we'll be recognised by the world.'

He was still talking as she poured his hot water. 'So they don't want the world to come here and have to walk in mud and horse manure. They want a huge building with space for thousands, and comfort — and lots of Playford bricks. We'll be rich!'

Mary went to visit the works on the day that the first load of bricks for the exhibition building was opened. One of the great cavernous kilns was loaded and being brought slowly up to full heat, the curved fire holes along either wall a sequence of fiery eyes, blinking and blazing from behind their metal doors. Keeping the children well clear of the workmen and the kilns, she moved along the alley of machinery and storage sheds to the other kiln. The fires along those walls were blackened now, after being built up for seven days to bake the clay bricks within the heavy walls, then extinguished to let the kiln begin to cool over more days. William stood before the mouth of the kiln with some workmen, knocking out the last of the sealing wall which had enclosed the bricks. He turned and waved at them. The heat from the kiln was so intense that the children shrank back, even though they were not near. Strong waves of heat shimmered in the air above the kiln, making the chimneys seem to bend and waver and causing ripples of heat along the ground.

The children peered at the ordered stacks of bricks revealed in the cave of the kiln. Small Legh called in surprise, 'But Father, the bricks are black — and red! Are they the ones for the big building?'

'They just look black, son, because they are just starting to cool. The red ones are so hot they are like a brick-shaped fire. Don't worry, when they cool down properly we'll be able to lift them out and they'll look fine.' William turned to Mary and added, 'These are going to be beautiful bricks — so pale they'll be nearly white, something like the colour of your best shortbread. And strong! These bricks won't crumble or melt and should last for hundreds of years. And, though nobody will see it when they are part of the building, they have our special imprint.'

The day Mary swept through the doors of the new Exhibition Building decked in her own new finery, she found it hard to believe that bedded into the vast structure around her was the work of William's hands, his imagination, his dream, his sweat. The lines of the building were very modern, with rounded arches, curves and half-circles.

'From outside, the roof looks a bit like an enormous jam roll, cut in half lengthwise,' she murmured, and William gave her a silencing nudge.

Inside there seemed to be acres of space, elaborate exhibits displaying the finest agricultural products from around the world, and outside were avenues of tents, entertainers, livestock, machinery. On William's arm, Mary walked among the bounty of the world, resplendent in her own feathers and draperies, interested, intelligent, observant, yet all the time watching for the lines of bricks which were pale as shortbread biscuits. It seemed a good time to be bringing another child into the world.

William's bricks were very good, there was no doubt about it. When, a year later, someone suggested that he should enter some of his firebricks in another international exhibition, this time in England, it did not seem a foolish idea at all. There was such a feeling of confidence and pride in things Australian, such growth in Sydney as a city, such development in technology at all levels, that everyone felt that any man could achieve anything, that nothing was impossible. Cathedrals thrust ornamented steeples to heaven, shops stocked and sold more and more luxurious items, railway lines pushed further into the countryside, opening NSW to wider settlement with better transport for wool and wheat. Even the new Sydney Town Hall which was under construction was being designed with the aim of being vaster, more heavily embellished, more richly finished than the town hall in rival Melbourne.

Mary encouraged William to select and send samples of bricks to England. 'Your work is good. At least you should try it,' she said. The bricks went, entrusted to a steamship across the oceans.

A package arrived from England soon after their tenth wedding anniversary when Mary was expecting her sixth child. Their small boys watched the unwrapping with excitement and Mary had to hold the toddler Sarah safely away while William untied the string.

As the wrappings were laid open, Mary startled her little girl by abruptly putting her down and hugging her husband with a mix of tears and laughter.

'I *knew* that your bricks were very good!'

William Playford's firebricks had been awarded two medals, in competition with bricks of the world, and the medals lay there, glowing on their satin cushions, reassuring them that their world was very good.

*   *   *

It is spring in 1872, the same year that William Playford won his medals. The wattles are in bloom along the Mitta Mitta River and there is still snow on the mountains of the Victorian Alps. A husband and wife say goodnight to their hostess for the evening and set off through the moonlight for the rowing boat they have left moored on Snowy Creek. Their home is on the far bank. Richard Caldwell is a popular man in the area, a new selector of land, member of the Good Templars and the Independent Order of Rechabites in Beechworth. His friends call him 'good-hearted Dick' and he and his wife Mary are known as genial, generous and hospitable people. His wife is the oldest daughter of respected Albury residents, the Gregsons, from the border area between NSW and Victoria.

People in roadside cottages hear them pass, hear their laughter and fragments of happy conversation. Someone says later that they thought they heard them cooee for another canoe, but perhaps after all it might have been a scream . . .

Next day they find the capsized rowing boat and Mary Caldwell's body trapped in reeds. Good-natured Dick is not found till later, further downstream, drowned. The coroner finds an open verdict of 'found drowned'. People discuss the tragedy with shock and sorrow. Perhaps she lost her balance stepping into the little boat in the dark, and the weight of her heavy skirts dragged her down. Perhaps Dick jumped into the icy water to try to save her — who could know? They were both convinced teetotallers and everyone is sure they were sober at the time.

The saddest part, people say, is the seven orphaned children left behind. Their father's land selection had not yet been paid for, so there will be no money, and the youngest is only six months old.

8
Stone upon stone
1873-1888

'THEY ARE TALKING ABOUT selling Marshdale Farm!'

Mary Playford put the letter down on her lap and turned to her husband. She felt shocked. Her parents and family had been at the farm for more than twenty years and she had thought it would stay in the family.

'Your father is getting older — he's close to seventy — so the farm is probably getting too much for him.' William was philosophical. 'And your sisters are all married and moved, and Jabez and his tribe have moved west to West Wyalong. That only leaves brother James, and he already has his place on Razorback Mountain near Cawdor. So of course your parents will have to sell one day. Where will they live?'

Mary hesitated. Before she spoke, she folded the letter with the familiar handwriting of her father and put it in her pocket. Her father had hinted that things were more difficult than appeared on the surface. Something was going badly wrong in the family.

'Father says they will go to live with brother James. Mamma will help with the children . . .'

She said no more, but began to make her own plans to take the children, four of them now, to visit their grandparents at Marshdale Farm before the property passed from the family. Without intending it, she felt her mouth tightening into a stern line. Brother James, she feared, had been letting the family down. Admittedly, the past few years had been very hard for him. First there was the death of a little daughter, then poor Jane's difficulty delivering the twins, and the babies both dying within a month. Jane herself never really recovered and she died before the year was out, leaving James with four motherless children. Of course it had been hard, no-one denied it. But for James to behave as the hints suggested, and take to drink . . . !

In the privacy of her own parlour, with Lydia, the sisters discussed the problem of James. Each of their brothers and sisters had had their share of sorrow, ill health and business worry, but this was different. Poor Mamma . . . poor Father . . .

'Do you think any of our friends at church might hear about it? I do hope not. It would be very awkward for us all, specially as we are such strong members of the Ashfield Band of Hope, and William is superintendent of that big Sunday School.'

The Band of Hope was a society in their church which worked for a temperate community. Both sisters had recited verses on the dangers of alcohol, helped to teach children that drinking would lead to all sorts of evils, and been righteously stern about the way the Devil could use alcohol to tempt people from the straight path. Mary's standards of behaviour, for children and for adults, were always very high and she found it hard to tolerate the thought of her brother deliberately abusing his body. She had walked past hotels with her sons, and when one of the boys had asked curiously, 'Is that the place that makes people drunk?', she had answered in her most scornful and ringing tones, designed to be heard by loiterers on the footpath, 'Yes, it *is* my son!' It had been easy enough when the drinkers had been anonymous men on street corners, haggard and unshaved, or someone else's relative who had fallen from grace. But this was James, her brother and Lydia's.

The visit to Marshdale Farm was difficult. Her father was looking older, white hair fringing his bald scalp and thick white eyebrows forming verandahs over alert, intelligent eyes. James Rootes often had a hand cupped around an ear, straining to pick up conversations as deafness increased. Mamma was in a state of bother around the house, worrying about what things they should sell and what would come in useful at James' house at Razorback. She poured her love and care into the lives of James' sons and daughters, but young Augusta Jessie whispered, 'Auntie Mary, Grandma sometimes gets muddled these days.' Mary helped with the sorting and packing of the old home, and knew that the scattered family would never again come back to that spot for Christmas.

Other things had changed, too. Matavai was in the hands of strangers and Denbigh had passed to the Macintosh family after the death of Thomas Hassall. Her father still spoke with emotion of the six hundred and more people who had gathered in the churchyard of St Paul's Church, Cobbitty, to farewell this good man who had been so influential and so beloved in their district. Now James Rootes was a friend to the new young rector, Arthur Pain, and he and Jabez had worked on the committee of men who had arranged and paid for the new rectory for St Paul's. For Mary, with no links to the new regime, there was a strong sense of loss at the passing of the man who had baptised and instructed her. Even the Methodist community at Cawdor had changed. Familiar faces of her growing-up years had gone, marked now by gravestones in the quiet churchyard. The Methodist minister was a stranger to her, and to her sorrow there were very few girls in the congregation and no young men at all.

And there was James. When they met, there was an awkwardness, a constraint. He knew that she knew that he had been drinking heavily, that sometimes Pa had to go to bring him home and there were times when he had no control over himself. For much of her visit, he avoided her, disappearing immediately after meals to see to the work of his farm. Only once did he talk to her. She had gone to collect the washing from the clothesline near the woodheap and found James chopping firewood. They went on with their tasks in silence till James spoke. His axe kept up a rhythmic rise and fall as he said, 'You're right, of course. I've been drinking more than is good for me. But you don't have to put that look on your face. . .'

He turned his back on her, splitting each block of wood with an angry blow. 'You can't know what the pain's like. You've lost children – I know that – but I've lost my wife, too. After Jane died, I started to drink just a little because it didn't hurt as much when I'd had a few. Then I needed more, or the hurt came back too soon. And now I can't stop. Sometimes I hate to go home. . .'

He looked at her briefly and in his eyes she saw herself reflected; a dignified woman encased in outraged respectability, offended by her brother. She had been about to speak but stopped. Mary realised that she didn't know what to say.

The night before Mary left the farm to travel home with the children, she knelt to say her prayers. She had been finding it hard to pray. Her reaction to the change in her brother shocked and troubled her. As she tried to pray, she realised that her prayer was entangled in anger, resentment at the way James' behaviour might affect her own standing in the church. He was letting her down, shaming the family, embarrassing her at the Band of Hope.

'Lord, how *could* he?' she muttered. 'What is the matter with him?

What's he doing to his poor children? What about our parents?'

The strange thing was that the more she railed against her brother in her prayers, the more she felt that she was missing something important. She tried to be still. With her face pressed into the folds of Mamma's old patchwork quilt, she found a picture forming in her mind. She saw Christ with his arm around her brother's shoulder, protecting him. Protecting him? Shielding him from her hurt pride and wounded respectability which was set to attack him at his most vulnerable. In her mind she stared at James, a broken man finding a place of shelter from the critical eyes of the world. Mary tasted tears trickling saltily past her mouth, tears of repentance, tears of compassion.

At the railway station next day, waiting for the train to take her home to William, she embraced James.

'Dear brother, I love you very much,' she whispered. 'I hate what this has done to you – I hate the liquor trade – I'm furious at the harm I see done by it! But I love you. William and I will be praying for you.'

*   *   *

On a farm out of the town of Albury, set on the banks of the Murray River which divides New South Wales from Victoria, a letter has arrived. The farmer's wife has held it all day, waiting for her husband to come home and open it with her. Her house is silent. There is no-one to share her days while her husband is out in the paddocks; no child to cherish, no family members to call in to see her. Her brothers and their families are far away in the colony of South Australia and there has never been a child.

She tries to steady herself by picking up a garment from her mending basket to stitch a tough patch on her husband's working pants. Nothing can steady the agitation of her mind. The letter lies on the kitchen table, keeping its secret.

They first heard of the little boy some months ago. People spoke of the tragic drowning of the parents and of how first one then another of the orphaned children had been found homes. All except the baby. No-one seems to want the responsibility of a two-year-old, though they were happy to take the older children who perhaps could soon help in business or on farm. At first she did not want to mention the idea to her husband: to ask to take this strange little boy is almost like admitting defeat. Yet they have been married for five years and have had no child. As it happened, her husband did not laugh at the idea and they approached the grandfather who was caring for the children.

Now the reply has come. At last her husband comes to the house. Leaning over his shoulder, she reads.

'Albury, 10 October 1873. Dear Sir, I write to you respecting the little boy. I would have brought him out next Sunday, but find I cannot. If it is convenient for you, you might come for him during next week some time. And I am quite willing to sign him over to you entirely as I have done some of the others as I am quite satisfied he would have a good home. As regards the religion he may be brought up in, it matters not to me so long as it is a Protestant one. I shall be at home all next week and if you come in would be glad to see you. I am, Sir, Yours etc, John Gregson.'

*   *   *

Mary opened her eyes slowly. The room was very quiet except for the gentle snoring of Mamma, slumped in a rocking chair in the corner. The cradle stood beside her bed. The days away from home in the nearby cottage hospital were behind her, the pain and fear, the physical struggle for her body to part with the baby. It had seemed strange to be cared for by a stranger and, though the nurse Mrs Drake had been efficient, she had missed her mother's touch.

This time William had been firm with her. 'You must go to the hospital for this child. Your mother means well, but we both know that she is not as strong as she once was.' He did not say it, but she heard the unspoken words as well. Her mother was slowing down, not only in body, but sometimes in her mind, and the birth of their seventh child was too important to risk with her mother's occasional confusions. The period when her brother James had not been himself had taken its toll on Mamma. Mamma had cared for the children, cooked and washed for James and prayed for him with great intensity. Even now, when the bad times were a memory and James had begun a new and stable life with his marriage to a gentle widow and membership in the abstainers' society, the Order of Rechabites, Mamma was still always unsure and anxious.

She eased her body cautiously into a sitting position. A gauze cover lay over the cradle to protect it from flies and dust and she lifted it carefully. The softly crumpled newborn face was peaceful, eyes closed in sleep, fuzz of fine hair, minute fingers curled. The mother listened for the sound of infant breathing. There were so many things which could snatch away such a new child – the act of birth itself, croup, convulsions, or waves of measles and scarlet fever which had just swept through their district. She thought of her dead babies, the ones who had had no chance to grow up. What was the future for this little one?

Beyond the cradle was the rocking chair. Her mother, Anna Rootes, was asleep. Over the years she had lost her teeth and her mouth sagged in a hollow fashion within the network of wrinkles. William was right. Her mother's small frame was no longer the energetic and brisk figure she remembered, and sometimes the sure mind was becoming vague and forgetful. The hands lying slackly in her lap were becoming knotted, but Mary remembered the touch of her mother's hands over the years to caress or discipline, heal or hurry her children.

The cradle and the rocking chair, her mother and her daughter, linked with her with bonds she could not explain. As she looked at the two sleepers, Mary knew a great tenderness for these two, bone of her bone, flesh of her flesh, one nearing the end of a long and fruitful life and the other at the beginning. 'Thank you, Lord,' she prayed, 'thank you for all that Mamma has taught me of life and loving, of compassion and generosity. Thanks for her strength, her ability to survive. And please give your grace to this little girl. May she be yours.'

The baby stirred and cried and the grandmother's eyes opened. Soon the older woman was stooping over the cradle, murmuring soothing words, and lifting the baby into Mary's arms.

When she and William named their new daughter, they did not use one of the old family names. They called her Grace, 'the unmerited favour of God'.

It did not seem such a big thing at the time. William mentioned it casually one evening.

'I'm thinking I might sell the brickworks.'

He wandered around the room, aimlessly poking the fire with the ornamented fireirons, lifting and replacing china ornaments, inspecting rows of books in the cedar bookcase, but Mary could see that his mind was on other things.

'It's not that the brick business is not successful. It has been very good to us. But I've worked in that dust and smoke for eighteen years and I need a change. Before we were married and I had the responsibility of a family, I had a number of jobs, and travelled all round Victoria and New South Wales. No, I don't want to travel. But I plan to sell the brickworks and buy into a local hay and grain store.'

It did not seem a big thing. Neither of them saw a fine hairline crack appearing in the stone of their family foundation.

The year was 1879 and Mary spread her arms as widely as they would go around her younger children as they rocked and swayed towards a new experience. William sat opposite her in the steam tram, very upright and dignified with the first hints of grey in his beard and a high gloss on his silk top hat. There were six Playford children to be steered through the day. Since the birth of Grace four years earlier, two more entries had been made in the family page of the Bible, the birth and death of Thomas who had only lived for a few days and the birth of little Will, still a babe in arms.

Mary was privately relieved that Lydia had not come with them today; Lydia's approach to discipline was more relaxed than her own and a combination of the seven cousins, Lydia's latest baby and her own family would have been lively but exhausting.

As they chugged along on the way to the Botanic Gardens on the harbour, over their heads clouds of black smoke and cinders gushed and thundered. Passengers grumbled that this new-fangled steam tram was frightening the horses, and that the city was no place for engines.

'I liked the old horse tram better, with its lovely painted lions,' said Mary.

'Nonsense, my dear, this is just sentiment. This is the modern age – with steam power, and gas. Wait till you see the international exhibition at the Garden Palace.'

The tram turned the last corner and passengers spilled out, pouring down through the lush lawns and shrubbery of the Botanic Gardens towards the harbour. The new Garden Palace lay before them, vast, with acres of building to house the gathering of the world's technology and the genius of the modern age. Gleaming in the sun shone the great dome, clad in the latest curved galvanised corrugated iron. It was said, with considerable feeling by some, that the Garden Palace was far too large for its site, that it blocked out what should have been one of the best views of Sydney Harbour, had cost twice the original estimate, was a foolish indulgence, but this morning the crowds were prepared to forgive its shortcomings.

William was ecstatic. At every turn he discovered something else to show his sons, Legh, Harry and Robert. Art treasures and works of science from all over the world competed for attention. He hurried from the latest in equipment for fire engines to inventions for underwater diving or icemaking, from a passenger lift from America to telephones and sewing machines. It was the year of the first successful shipment of refrigerated beef from Australia to England, within months of the first telephone system in Sydney, and memories were still fresh of the gentleman who had startled a Government House garden party by falling out of the sky into a tree from a failed Montgolfier fire balloon. The papers reported that one Mr Edison was so convinced of the possibilities of electricity that he said he could light half of New York with it, though most sane men saw that vision as sheer fantasy – 'Nothing is going to supplant gas or steam,' they said.

Mary walked till her feet were blistering. In between the demands of the little ones, she gazed at ceramics from China, fine glass from Italy, pottery from Japan, paintings, carvings, statuary, brilliant fabric pieces. The artistic riches of the world were laid out for her. She found a seat under the dome and sat down, Sarah and Grace beside her and baby Will on her lap. A pool of colour flowed down from the sun, flooding through the immense stained glass eye at the heart of the dome. Around her, passing through the rainbows of light, moved the residents of Sydney, proud in silk top hats and resplendent in vibrant colours of silks and satins, hooped and looped, swathed and flounced, bustled and bowed. In January she would come back, she decided, and look again, and hear the presentation of Handel's *Messiah* and perhaps the big temperance concert being advertised for Anniversary Day, 26 January. Sydney in the summer of 1879-1880 felt to her like the centre of the world.

*   *   *

The year is 1879 and the mother spreads her arms around her two children as they rock and sway towards a new experience. Her husband is ahead of them driving the first loaded dray with his partner following behind with the second. The woman can barely see her husband's battered bush hat above the load which fills the dray. In her own hands are the reins of the spring cart, loaded with pots and pans and blankets and all the things they need along the road. The two children leaning against her are asleep. The boy is eight years old and she loves him as if he had always been hers. When he is older they will tell him, perhaps, of his other parents buried at Mitta Mitta and the brother and sisters who are scattered around Victoria. The little girl is four, the child she had never expected to bear, conceived the year after they had adopted their son.

Over their heads, the branches of the forest giants spread, eucalypts and grey box, wattle and Murray pine. The bush presses around the track, almost defying the wheels of carts and wagons to come any further into its depths. They have left the comparative security of the Hume Highway behind, the long road they have followed north from the Victorian border with its scattering of hamlets and the comfort of the sight of other travellers from time to time. They have camped night after night by the road, rolling in their blankets to sleep under the dray when it rained, cooking their damper in the hot ashes of their camp fire and boiling the billy for tea.

Sometimes the woman looks back over her shoulder as the bush closes around them. Somewhere far behind is the substantial town of Albury, and their farm at Bungowannah. Even further out of reach is 'Rosemary Lodge' at Mount Pleasant, the family home in Adelaide where life had been gracious and she and her husband were married so happily by her clergyman brother. Hidden among the boxes and barrels of their cargo are her books to feed her mind in the years ahead. She smiles wryly at the thought of her book on the art of conversation and debating with notes on good literature. Where might she ever practise those arts again? She has brought little mementoes of her past like the exquisitely stitched sampler from her girlhood in distant Yorkshire. Her husband has warned her that it will be months before he will bring the dray out the forty miles to the nearest stores in Wagga, so she has brought a bolt of turkey twill, with needles, thread and thimble and a pair of strong boots each.

The procession of the drays and cart moves slowly. Ahead of them move their stock, the cattle and horses, and they can't be hurried. Somewhere before them is their destination, a selection of land for each of the men in the Riverina, part of one of the great sheep stations, North Berry Jerry, which has recently been declared open for selection. For years there has only been one fence between the Murrumbidgee and the Lachlan rivers, dividing the land of North

Berry Jerry from that of Big Mimosa, many hundreds of acres of land. The Wiradjuri people whose land it has always been have worked as stockmen for the squatters, but their tribes have been free to travel across their land, to seek the secret water and follow the game. But now selectors and fences are coming and the face of the land is about to be changed. The man in the battered hat drives forward with confidence. His wife's brother has been in the district for a couple of years and has called them to join him. He sees a vision for a land rippling with grain. Though he is surrounded by bush and scrub which must be ripped out of the soil before he can plant his first wheat, and though he's been warned that there will be no natural creeks or water supplies on his selection, he is not daunted. With his cargo is the latest in farm equipment, including a stripper, and at least he'll be independent, not like the days back in England when he was unemployed for months because of strikes. He has said to his wife and children more than once, 'With land and some tools and plenty of hard work, nothing is impossible for a man to achieve.'

The boy is awake now and takes a turn with the reins. The woman walks for a while by the spring cart. The bush around is alive with wild life: in branches of yellow box there is a glimpse of ringtailed possum and glider while in the grass move kangaroos and bandicoots. She watches for snakes and sees a goanna rustle through fallen bark and climb a Murray pine tree, clinging halfway up the trunk and watching her. The woman is a little afraid of the bush. She can see no landmarks, and she imagines her children wandering lost in a featureless landscape. Yet there is beauty and song. Above the noise of cattle and sheep rises the symphony of a hundred birds, and with a whirr of wings a rainbow of colour spreads overhead, cockatoo and parakeet, galah and rosella. The lad in the spring cart laughs and points up at the painted sky. He at least seems unafraid as they move forward on their great adventure.

*   *   *

Mary stood at her kitchen table whisking egg whites. The fire in her kitchen range burned brightly, hot enough for her sponge cake, and her hand kept up its steady rhythm with the whisk. It was spring, the time when her peach trees blossomed, violets scented her parlour and Sydney Sunday schools celebrated their anniversaries in a fanfare of new clothes, music and tea meetings.

For twenty years now she and William had been part of the annual sequence of tea meetings, anniversary services, picnics, Sunday School meetings, both at Newtown and now at Ashfield Methodist churches. The years tended to flow into each other, each anniversary only distinguished as 'the year one of Lydia's girls first put her hair up', 'the year Harry sang a solo', 'the year Sarah wore cerise with a huge bustle bow', 'the year Will was a baby. . .'

Footsteps sounded on her path and Lydia appeared at the door, her new baby in her arms and nearly adult older daughters following with baskets of food.

'Is this for the tea meeting this evening? Let me beat the eggs for a while and you hold baby.'

'Don't worry, I'm nearly finished. What have you brought? My other cakes are ready.' Mary found herself hurrying on, chatting about food for the tea meeting, turning the conversation from babies. She didn't want Lydia to see that she had no wish to hold the new infant. The only baby she would have liked to hold was her own — but that was impossible. Only months ago her tenth child had died, little Arthur just two months old, the fourth of her children to live briefly and then be taken from her. It hurt too much just now to hold another woman's child.

'Tell me about your girls' new dresses for the anniversary,' she said, and listened with only part of her attention as Lydia began to list the details of ruffles and flouncing which their sewing woman had been creating. Mary dropped egg yolks into her satiny mixture, bright yellow suns against white which broke and swirled into a marbling of yellow veins till the white had turned to palest gold. She stared at the cake batter without thought as she folded in the flour, filtering out Lydia's talk of dressmaking and the latest wickednesses of her young sons.

Why, she asked herself silently, do Lydia's babies all live? Why have so many of mine died? Am I a worse mother than Lydia? Is God punishing me for something? Is he teaching me something that I'm too slow to learn? Were William and I wrong to marry each other, being second cousins, and have we passed on some family weakness to our children? It was not the first time she had asked the questions, and she knew it would not be the last.

There had been a time, once, when she had felt sure that she understood God's ways, when she expected that the good would be rewarded and the bad punished. But now, in her middle years, nothing was simple any more. Why had James lost wife and children and suffered such a time of grief and loss of self-respect? Why was her dear mother, a woman who had survived so much and had been so generous with her practical care and loving, now living more and more in a private world cut off from reality? Why was William, so hardworking and honest in his dealings, having such a struggle with his hay and grain enterprise, so much so that he spoke of soon having to give it up in failure? She didn't understand. In herself she was discovering a new humility, a growing sensitivity to the pain of others, a new reluctance to offer advice as quickly as she might once have done. As she slid her cake into the hot cave of her oven, Lydia's voice still in her ears, Mary knew only that she and her family were all woven into the same intricate, unfinished embroidery; they were all part of the loose threads, the mistakes, the parts which needed to be unpicked and stitched again, each colour and texture affecting the total design. She knew that she could not see the complete design and was almost afraid to think what it might be, but she felt that her only choice was to trust the Designer.

'The kettle's boiling. Let's have a cup of tea before we pack up all the food and go down to the church.' Mary set a steaming cup before her sister and added, 'And let me hold baby for you while you drink your tea. . .'

Later that afternoon, the two women loaded Mary's phaeton with their baskets of sandwiches, jam tarts, cakes and the sponge cake garnished with piled cream and jam from summer strawberries. Armloads of green branches and buckets of flowers to decorate the church hall were packed between small children in their best clothes. With Mary at the reins, they drove past Richard's dairy farm, the Chinese market gardens and fine houses set back in spacious grounds and gardens. The village of Ashfield was developing into a respectable middle-class suburb.

Bearing baskets, branches and the baby, Mary and Lydia entered the school room behind the church, plunging into the noise of many voices and the activity of many women preparing for a special occasion. There was a fire to be lit under the copper for hot water, trestle tables to be erected and laid with cloths, flowers and silver, flowers and greenery to be draped and swathed round every door and window, mottoes and scripture verses on banners to be hung from every picture hook. These women were their friends. These were the ones who had come to her when baby Arthur was so ill, had wept with her at his funeral, who had brought food during the time when she had not been well enough to cook for herself. Each household had known its own times of trouble and distress, and each woman knew that the other women of that church would be there to support and care when the hard times came. Though it was always the men who were the preachers, committee men and leaders, the women formed the larger group of people in church each Sunday, teaching Sunday School classes, working for the Band of Hope, meeting for prayer, creating music, raising church funds and providing a sense of celebration and community in their church through shared meals, banners and flowers.

When all was ready, the doors opened to dignified men in their high silk hats, troops of young people and children in their brightest finery, women urging their children to good manners. By some social magnetism, the men moved to one end of the hall and the women to the other. Later, filled with too much cake, children stood in self-conscious rows to sing or recite, men with or without humour made speeches, William Playford read his annual report as superintendent of the Sunday School and the minister George Woolnough prayed for them all. Mary looked around her, at her big boys growing towards manhood, the younger boys itching for mischief, her daughters in slightly wilted finery, William so dignified and highly respected, her wider family and friends. Despite the appearance of well-being among them all, she knew that most families had their problems. Even so, their commitment to each other as a Christian group meant that none of them would be without support.

Before they left the church that evening, Lydia hurried up to Mary with a shocked look on her face. 'Those naughty boys! My Jabez and Abijah Jesse and your Robert . . . That gentleman is so *angry* and I can't blame him. Whatever am I going to do with those boys?'

And Mary set off for home, a chastened Robert in tow, knowing that in future this year's anniversary would be identified as 'the year some boys filled a gentleman's silk top hat with jam tarts . . .'

*   *   *

The woman drags the heavy camp oven from the hot coals onto the hearth. When she lifts the lid, the pleasant fragrance of hot scones drifts up and her children come to beg one.

'These are for this afternoon, for the concert,' she says, then relents and gives each child a scone spread with dripping.

Inside the kitchen this morning there is a sense of excitement. Later in the day, Father will come in from ringbarking trees and grubbing them out of the ground. He will harness a horse in the spring cart and they will drive across country to the woolshed of a neighbouring settler. To go to a concert, no less! The woman sweeps the earth floor of her kitchen with new zeal and the children swoop in and out of the kitchen door, too full of anticipation to be calm. Usually the woman likes to stay within the walls of her kitchen. Her husband has built it for her — the kitchen building itself and the separate hut for sleeping, the round saplings cut from the bush and planted upright in the ground, the tree he felled to cut boards for the walls, roughly adzed into shape. There is still a faint scent of pine from the young timber. He has built the fireplace, a wonderful thing with a great block of stone for the hearth. The space within the fireplace walls is so wide that she cannot span it, even with arms at full stretch. He has nailed a mantleshelf over the hearth, where she keeps her clock and her mirror, the tea pot and the precious caddy of tea. He has carved pegs for hats and coats, fitted thin saplings together into shelves for her pots and pans and turned kerosene cases into cupboards. He has driven stumps into the earth floor and laid adzed timber boards over them for a strong table, beaten smooth the sharp edges of kerosene tins and twisted wire to form handles to provide her with water buckets. He has cleared the ground around the house into smooth earth so that snakes are less likely to come close.

Stripes of sunlight fall on her table, the light edging through the cracks between the timbers of her kitchen wall. Somehow she feels safer in her kitchen, more sure of herself. When she is baking scones, or simmering a kangaroo tail soup in the cooking pot hung from the hook over the fire, or stitching patches on her son's worn trousers, then she knows who she is. When she sits at her kitchen table and reads aloud from her Bible to her children, she is reassured that God knows her name, even if she is somewhere out in the bush. Sometimes when she prays, she thanks God that he knows where she is, because she herself isn't quite sure. Her man says it takes about seven hours in the spring cart, or three days with the horse and dray, to reach Wagga, the nearest town. He has gone for stores several times in the year they have lived at Berry Jerry, but she knows that if she were to set out through the bush without him, she'd be lost within the hour.

Today is going to be different. Today she will see her neighbours, her brothers John and Robert Swann and their wives, the Jennings, the others. They all live scattered across the district, but on a few occasions they have met in a woolshed for a church service. Here in the bush the labels of Church of England, Presbyterian, Methodist and Baptist don't matter any more. They all know that they need courage and faith in God, hope and strength of spirit to survive, and each family knows that they need each other. They know that the squatters are sure they'll all starve to death on their selections, that they'll never be able to sow enough wheat to pay their way, that they'll die of thirst for want of permanent water supplies or dams, that their livestock will be lost before they have time to build fences . . . they know they need God's help and they need each other.

The woman comes to her door and looks out. The timber seems to spread forever. After the hills and hollows of the country round Albury, with the mountains of the Victorian alps beyond, their new land seems quite flat. If she pictured the land as an ocean made solid, their Victorian home is among high seas and their new land lies in a very gentle swell. They have built their house on top of a rise which looks out across grasslands and scrub and with humour they call it 'The Hill'. Other settlers have told them that the Aboriginal people of the area, the Wiradjuri, gave the district the name Berry Jerry because it means 'box trees', and the country is heavily timbered with yellow box and grey box. One day, she dreams, she would love to grow flowers around the house, but not yet – there is no water for flowers and their first need is for a patch of cabbages or carrots, to see the greenery of a pumpkin vine or a hill of potatoes. In a natural depression in the earth, the land holds water. A group of Aboriginal people come to camp by the water as has been their custom, and watch warily as the selector digs a deeper hole in the hope of catching more precious water when the rain falls, water for people, cattle, sheep, horses, plants. In the distance she can see his figure stooping, while he hacks, drags and pulls fallen trees together to be burned. His strip of land to be ploughed will only be won at great cost – cost to the man in toil and pain, cost to the dark people who have always belonged to this land and cost to the native creatures whose habitat is being altered.

At last her man comes to the house. He washes the dirt of his work away in a shallow dish of water and they set off for the woolshed. Each family brings an item for the concert and food to be shared; one man has a fiddle, another a tin whistle, a woman sings a song learned as a girl in England or a poem memorised in a school far away in Melbourne or Adelaide. There is story-telling and jokes, ballads and bush verse.

'What do we need first?' they ask each other.

'First, a church building – a union church that we all can use.'

'Build it on my place! You're welcome to pull down some of my surplus timber,' says Jennings.

'Then a teacher. There are enough children between us to warrant them sending a teacher to us – we can use the church building for a school as well.'

A new community has begun.

*   *   *

I'm so tired.' Lydia leaned back in the big armchair in Mary's sitting room and sighed. A young baby whimpered fretfully against her shoulder.

'And me.' Mary's voice was flat. Her own new baby, Daisy, had coughed and wheezed all night and Mary saw the same signs of weakness which had taken her other children. 'I'm getting too old for new babies. Forty-four years old and eleven babies so far. Is the end in sight, do you think?'

Lydia shrugged. 'Who knows?'

The women talked quietly, offering home remedies to each other for infant ills, passing on the latest news of their children. 'His teacher says that my bad 'Bijah is all set to turn into a bushranger or a cattlerustler when he grows up – he wears me out, I know,' said Lydia. There is news, too, of their husbands, William and Richard. William had given up his hay and grain store and bought a dairy in Ashfield, but somehow it seemed that cows could not be counted on in the way one could be sure of bricks.

In the well-furnished and richly decorated room, all provided by the hard and successful work of her husband, it seemed to Mary that it was disloyal to mention, even to her sister, that she was worried about William and his more recent business ventures. Somehow things had not be working out as well as he had hoped. She knew that it was not for want of hard work, and William had great integrity in his business dealings, but even so she felt an unease. For so many years the society around them had been inventing superior technology, building grander buildings, growing wealthier, expanding horizons. Why should she be anxious?

Yet she remembered that it was only two years ago, 1882, the year baby Arthur died, that the vast fabulously rich Garden Palace had burned to the ground in a brief conflagration which swept away in hours the entire collection of art works, technology and irreplaceable records housed in it. If the Garden Palace could be reduced to ash and twisted metal after only three years, it was not unthinkable that William might have problems in his business ventures.

The team of four horses paced with dignity along the road to the cemetery. Mary had travelled this way so often and so painfully. Only months before she had supported a sobbing Lydia as she buried her baby Ira and now she followed the vehicle which carried her own little Daisy. Today the undertaker walked before his special hearse, reserved for members of Lodges and Friendly Societies with its plate glass sides and black hangings fringed with gold. It cost more, but it didn't relieve the grief of adding her baby to the children already lying in that plot. Rows of houses were now pressing around the cemetery. Terraces, narrow dwellings shoulder to shoulder on narrow streets, and the cypresses of the churchyard cast wider shadows than they had done in earlier years. The rows of tombstones marched closer and closer.

William held her arm to steady her as she walked across the grass. Behind her she could hear the steps of her big boys and the soft weeping of her girls, Sarah and Grace. She found that she had no public tears. As she walked away at last, she hoped it was not wicked to ask God not to let her bear any more children.

*　　　*　　　*

The open cart comes to a halt under the aromatic pines. The rich red of the earth has been folded back, waiting. The little group of settlers cluster close together. There is no need to stand so close — open space and pine forest reach out to the horizon — but there is a great need to be near each other.

There is no other grave here. Under the trees the grass is green from the autumn rains and the native bush is unbroken. In spring there will be wattle and wildflowers here. Across the paddock where a settler has ploughed enough land with his single-furrow plough to sow his first crop of wheat, the people can see their church. It is their first public building and was opened with due ceremony last year, 1883, by an Anglican bishop, no less. There has already been a wedding there in the scented newness of wide slabs of sawn pine overlapped and set upright in the ground.

It is very quiet and peaceful here. Well, maybe peaceful isn't the best word, thinks the woman who stands at the graveside with an arm around her son and daughter. Lonely, that's the word. The coffin is lowered into the grave by husband and brothers. Her sister-in-law, young Mrs Agnes Swann, leaves behind the new baby born days before her death. There is no doctor out here, no minister at the graveside. The prayers and words of farewell are spoken by friends and relatives, the handful of selectors who mourn her passing. They move away slowly, leaving the heaped red earth alone in the bush.

*   *   *

She wished very much that she did not have to do the task before her. 'You'll need to go to the school and tell them that we are moving,' William had said, so Mary Playford walked with little enthusiasm along The Boulevarde towards Petersham Superior School. On either side of The Boulevarde stood beautiful new homes, large two-storeyed places surrounded by broad verandahs and balconies, bulging with bay windows, frilled with iron lace. Set in suburban gardens, they were residences of men of large families and large resources.

At the end of the street stood the school, still new and handsome with pointed gothic windows, a tower and weathervane. Mary crossed the school grounds resolutely and stepped along the stone-flagged verandah. Through classroom windows she glimpsed rows of children bent over slates, little ones in tiered rows learning their early letters and older ones chanting their multiplication tables. It was a good school which made her task all the more sad. Her daughter was learning things which she had not been taught in her day. The newest subject was history, only introduced that year, but they were also reading from a series called *Australian Reading Books* and *The Geography of New South Wales*. When she was a girl, the teachers had not supposed things Australian were worthy of being taught.

She rapped on the door of the headmistress.

'Miss Collins, I'm really disappointed to have to do this. But Grace will be leaving the Petersham school. Sarah, of course, already has her 'Certificate of Being Sufficiently Educated', but Grace is only ten and I regret this for her sake.'

She hurried on. 'We are moving from Windsor Road, Petersham. My husband is going to manage a brickworks at Merrylands, right out of town, not far from Parramatta. We'll miss your excellent school.'

The headmistress handed her the papers of transfer and Mary walked away quickly. She didn't want the other woman to see her disappointment. William couldn't help it. It wasn't for want of hard work that the dairy had failed. It wouldn't be like owning his own brickworks, but at least the job as manager of the Merrylands brickworks would put him back with the work he knew best – clay, stone, kilns, bricks. The house at Petersham would be rented and they would have to start again in a new community.

*   *   *

The chill of winter lies over the land. In the warmth of the kitchen, the woman watches her bread rising slowly on the hearth and stirs the pot where a loin of kangaroo meat is simmering. Soon the children will come in from school. This morning they left early, big lad of fifteen and little sister of ten, each with a lunch and a bottle of water. She watched them disappear among the trees, swallowed in the winter fog, and hoped that they would not be too cold today.

At least, she thinks, they have a school to go to – she had feared that they might grow up ignorant and unlettered here at Berry Jerry. There is a young man teaching them now, Peter Tweedie, and he has been urging them to send their son away for higher education. 'He's a clever boy,' he keeps assuring them. 'That boy could do anything with a good education.' It's not possible, of course. His father needs him on the farm. He's been milking and doing boy's jobs for years and in season he works beside his father and their neighbours after school on the cycle of farm work. Nor is there money to send the boy away to school, and of course there could never be a question of him attending university. That is for the sons of rich men.

The mother remembers with appreciation their first teacher. Young Miss McGinty arrived unannounced, sent by the Department, and was forced to walk the twelve miles out to Berry Jerry from the new railway siding at Coolamon, their nearest village. The children had not forgotten Miss McGinty; it is not every young teacher who can claim that her police sergeant father was shot by the famous bushranger, Morgan.

There is the sound of voices and the children come in. The boy has brought another book home. He reads all kinds of books — fiction, travel, poetry, instruction manuals on practical skills — and Mr Tweedie keeps lending him more. Father arrives as early dusk falls. The district is becoming more civilised these days. As well as having a new railway line, a church and a schoolteacher, there is a tiny store and post office. Father brings in a letter and speaks privately about it to the mother.

'Must you tell him?' she whispers.

'I must.'

The meal is over. Mother and daughter have gone to bed. The boy sits on his stool in the cave-like haven of the great hearth. A pine log glows and splutters, dragged into the kitchen days ago by father and son. The slush lamp casts its small and odorous light, the meagre flames wavering over the tin of animal fat. The boy strains his eyes to read his book. The father stands before the fire, arms propped on the mantelpiece staring into the flames. In his mind he frames his sentence over and over again, but it is almost impossible to say it aloud.

At last he speaks. 'Son, I collected a letter today. From Victoria. It said your sister died a few weeks ago. Of consumption.'

'My sister?' The boy's face is confused, unbelieving. 'But — my sister just went to bed — we ate our tea together. . .'

'You have another family. Five sisters and a brother, all older than you. Your mother and I are not your real parents.'

The boy jumps to his feet, book spilling to the floor and face very white. The man tries to calm him, to tell the story properly, to reassure him. The boy is afraid, disorientated, suddenly disinherited.

The man puts an arm around him and leads him to the door. Outside it is very cold, dark and still. Somewhere in the dark is the new deeper waterhole and the horseyard. Beyond is the first paddock which the man cleared and ploughed. The boy watched him sowing the wheat by hand last autumn, each handful broadcast in wide even sweeps, left hand and right hand, while overhead hovered multicoloured squadrons of cockatoos and galahs, waiting to steal the grain before it could be harrowed into the ground. The paddock is patchily green now, the wheat which survived the cockatoos growing up to be trodden down by kangaroos. The darkness is lightened by the bonfires to the north, great heaps of ringbarked, dead and dried trees — pine, oak, belah, box and the fruit of months of backbreaking work to kill, clear, cut, grub out of the ground, drag into piles — and the perfumed fires will burn through the winter to expose more land to the plough.

The man hesitates, there in the darkness beside the boy. He knows that the boy will need time before he will be able to come to terms with the knowledge that he is adopted, the child of people he can never know. But he says, with all the sincerity and love he knows how: 'As far as I'm concerned, you're my son — my only son. And all this,' — he waves into the dark space towards unseen stock, horses, sown paddock, distant bonfires — 'all this is for you.'

*   *   *

When they first moved to Merrylands, Mary Playford was willing to go with William, but did not feel obliged to like it. She knew that she was going to miss being near Lydia and all her friends very much. William was excited about returning to the familiar scene of brick kilns and chimneys. 'I'm happy to manage another man's brickworks for a while, while I build up resources again for my own business,' he assured Mary. He liked the atmosphere of their new district with the enthusiasm and drive of many new industries just beginning. As well as the brickworks there were the varied sounds and smells and chimneystacks of Byrne's woollen mills, the tannery, the abattoir, kerosene works, the wool-wash. Land was being bought and sold and there was a great sense of confidence. The area, which was called Holroyd, had just become a municipality with its first council. 'There is a lot of energy here,' he said. 'It's good to be part of it.' (She wasn't surprised, in later months, to find him elected as an alderman on the new Holroyd council.)

Mary viewed their Merrylands environment with little favour at first. After the grandeur of the churches at Newtown and Ashfield, the small square church just across the railway line in William Street, Granville, with its small square porch and new school shed at the back seemed plain in the extreme. Some of her children had complained about moving away from their friends and it was odd sitting in church among strangers. Even so, despite herself, she found herself being welcomed by the people of the Granville Wesleyan Methodist church and began to build friendships with the families there — Milgates, McDowells, Fletchers, Coulsons, Woodwards and the rest. When William agreed to become a member of their church Trust and was asked to be Sunday School superintendent, she knew that he was prepared to belong. She discovered that their home at Merrylands reminded her of her girlhood in the country, with open paddocks and space for Harry's beloved horses.

Someone in the family thought of it first, perhaps James, or Anne. 'Fifty years! It is fifty years since Mamma and Pa left England and sailed for Australia. And 1887 is the Jubilee of Queen Victoria's reign, too. We should get together again . . .'

It was a long time since all the brothers and sisters had been together, and even then not everyone was able to travel to Razorback at the same time. Anne, James and Jabez had each lost their first spouse and remarried and each of the seven adult children of James and Anna Rootes had their own growing families. When Mary arrived with her family from Merrylands, Lydia from Petersham, Jabez from West Wyalong and the others from around New South Wales, the cottage overflowed.

'You'd never fit your family around the table now, Mamma,' Mary said. 'If we were all here, there would be over sixty grandchildren and great-grandchildren!' The old woman smiled vaguely and nodded, but Mary did not think she understood. For so many years, Anna Rootes had been the one who was there for others in their need, but now the busy hands were idle, and others cared for her.

'Queen Victoria came to the throne a week after we sailed,' old James Rootes reflected. 'We didn't even know it had happened till perhaps a year later.'

'I went to a big public meeting in the Exhibition Building a few weeks ago,' offered William. 'Thousands of us were there to listen to speeches about a plan to hold a great children's fete to teach Australian children to respect Queen and Empire. They'd had to call in police to break up earlier meetings because some people had nearly caused a riot — they said they didn't want *their* children taught to bow down to a monarchy on the far side of the world — they said Australia ought to be a democracy and free of Britain!'

'Not honour the Queen?' James Rootes cupped his hand round his better ear to be sure he heard correctly. 'But Britain is Home!'

'Never fear, we outvoted and outshouted those who spoke for independence from the Empire, and we all sang ''God save the Queen'' and ''Rule Britannia'' before we went home.'

James Rootes shook his head. Britain would always be Home, even though most of his eight children and all of his grandchildren had never seen its shores.

'Do you remember Sussex still?' the old man asked, and Anne replied, 'Yes! Snow on the roof, and bluebells in the woods in spring.'

'I just remember the *Augusta Jessie*, and the sailors. . . Pa, you should write down the story for us. We were too little to remember much, and you are the one who can tell the story of our fifty years in Australia.' James shouted his message into his father's ear and the older man nodded, the spark of new purpose in his eyes.

Family news flowed from one to another. Mary talked of their new home and William's new job, the church at Granville with its fine singing group, Sunday School and active Mutual Improvement Society with its lectures, debates and lantern slide shows as well as their family enthusiasm for choirs. She whispered to her sisters that she thought her oldest, Legh, was falling in love with Florrie Milgate. Harry had bought a new horse, Sarah was growing into such a sweet seventeen-year-old, Robert had started shaving, and Grace was beginning to learn the organ. They compared notes on their ministers. Young William McCallum was the man at Granville, and becoming a good friend to the Playfords.

Sepia photographs were passed from hand to hand, solemn family parties grouped around a seated father, arranged in obedience to a photographer crouched under a black cloth. Mary showed pictures of her children, Sarah looking grown up with her silky hair piled on top of her head and Grace with her childish short skirts and flowing hair sitting on a cardboard rock before a backdrop of painted Grecian columns. Old James Rootes sat among his family, gazing carefully at each picture. He left his place and returned with some photographs of his own and passed them to Mary.

'Your poor mother didn't enjoy having her likeness taken,' he said. 'The photographer told us we must not smile and we had to stay completely still till he gave the signal.'

Mary looked from the picture to the old woman sitting by her in the rocking chair. Mamma had sat for the picture in her best bonnet with the black lace veil, an enormous ribbon tied under her chin and her mantle with the fringes draped around her, but the fine clothes did not disguise her anxious concentration and her face was frozen forever in a look of deep gloom. Mary remembered a comment by a minister who had only known Mamma in her old age who had said, 'she often takes her burden to the Lord, but she doesn't always leave it there'.

'She looks so grim, poor darling! She doesn't always look like that.' Mary felt sad that the face which had been captured on cardboard was Mamma's worried face, not her face of welcome, or love, or kindness.

'She didn't want to come, you know,' the old man said, nodding towards his partner, the small woman who had shared his life for fifty-eight years. 'To Australia, I mean. She said she didn't even know where it was. . . But she did it. She wanted me to have a chance, and our children. I'm not sure if she still ever thinks of Northiam, and Sussex — I think so. In many ways it has been very hard for my Anna — she's a brave girl. . .'

Mary sat quietly beside him. His hearing was so poor that she hesitated to speak. There was an unexpected sound beside them. The old woman began to sing, her voice quavering yet strangely certain. It was a song she had often sung, one she called her favourite, a song drawn up from the depths of her memory and her person. The toothless old woman who often looked so severe was singing of joy. She sang, 'O happy day that fixed my choice on Thee my Saviour and my God. . . Happy day, happy day.'

Anna Rootes died in the spring of 1888 when her violets were in bloom. The country of her adoption had just celebrated one hundred years of white settlement with a whole week of festivities, a new Centennial Park, dinners, speechmaking and fireworks. Anna had lived in Australia for half that time.

All her family — her seven children and sixty-four grandchildren and great-grandchildren — flocked to Cawdor for her funeral. The Rev. J.F. Orr read the words of scripture with their promise of resurrection. The crowd stood quietly to say goodbye to the woman who had lived in the district for so long. The young ones only knew a frail old lady of eighty-four, growing increasingly vague, but the older ones thought of a friend, a helper, a mother. They sang together a hymn she had loved: 'On Christ, the solid Rock, I stand, all other ground is sinking sand.'

Stretching away around the little church and graveyard lay the rolling hills of the Cowpastures, green with new spring growth, almost as green as England. Her daughter Mary knew that one day she would return to this spot and plant violets there.

9
Cracks in the brickwork
1889-1896

LIKE THE PROUD FIGUREHEAD of an old sailing vessel, Mary Playford swept into the Granville Wesleyan Methodist Church with her husband and children in close formation behind her. Since the death of her mother, her own children had become even more precious to her and she was very aware that the days when they would all be together, crowded into the same pew in church, were numbered. Legh was already twenty-three and planning to marry Miss Florrie Milgate soon. Harry was very popular. Sometimes she worried that his love of beautiful horses might draw him into a pattern of drinks-with-the-boys after a day out together. He had assured her that he was never game even to go through the doors of the pub, just in case. Sarah sat beside her, wearing her prettiest bonnet and pretending that she was unaware that Louis McDowell was gazing at her from across the room. Sarah and Louis – yes, thought Mary, that would be quite suitable, if the young people cared for each other. Robert fidgeted just a little in the pew and elbowed little brother Will: at sixteen years of age a boy might head in any direction. Then there was Grace, just entering that mystical time of change when a little girl slowly becomes a woman.

The mother dragged her attention from her children onto the preacher for the day. On the previous Friday evening at the meeting of the Mutual Improvement Society, this visitor from England had seemed to explode into their presence. The Rev. James Scott was a gifted storyteller and, as he described his journey from England to Australia, they had laughed and cried, seeing every picture he painted in their minds. As he stood in the pulpit ready to speak about Christ, it was soon clear that this time his story-telling was not merely to entertain, but to open windows on matters of deep significance.

He told them the story of a young girl of twelve years old, the child of a man of importance. He drew a picture of a beloved daughter who became very ill, so ill that the mother sent the father to find Jesus the healer — 'Tell him she's dying! Beg him to hurry before it is too late.' But though the father ran desperately with his message, Jesus waited to help someone else on the road, and the news came that it was too late. The little girl had gone. The father was broken-hearted, but Jesus said to him, 'Don't be afraid. Only believe.' Jesus and the crushed father went to the house. It was hard for the parents to put aside what they could see with their own eyes, or to shut out the wailing of neighbours. Gently, Jesus drew three of his closest followers into the room with the father and mother and the dead girl, and shut the door. While the mother held her breath, he took the limp hand in his and said, 'Get up, my child!' And the young girl opened her eyes and saw Jesus. With the father and mother clinging to each other in amazement, the girl sat up, still holding tightly to Jesus' hand. She never took her eyes from him.

Mary heard the story, so often heard before, and found herself acutely aware of her own twelve-year-old daughter beside her, the child called Grace. She had prayed so often for all of her children, longing for each of them to know Jesus, and had given each of them a Bible of their own.

The preacher urged them not to be afraid but to believe in the power of Jesus in their own lives. 'If any of you wants to put your life in the hands of Jesus, to let him bring you to life, then come and join me after the service and we'll pray together,' he invited. A stream of about twenty young people went forward, many of them from William Playford's Sunday School, and Grace was among them. It seemed to the watching mother that the child was holding tightly to the hand of Jesus and seeing him face to face.

*　　　*　　　*

It is Saturday and the minister has arrived for the Sunday service to be conducted next day. He has ridden from Junee and is warm and thirsty. The farmer's wife offers tea, and they sit by the teapot till it is empty.

'Would you like to join our men and the others in the hunt this afternoon?' she offers. 'They usually enjoy it.'

With a fresh mount and bush clothes, the minister blends into the crowd that gathers. One of the farmers, John Swann, has initiated regular Saturday kangaroo hunts and the men and some young women of the community meet to ride together in an attempt to reduce the numbers of kangaroos on their land.

The farmer's wife does not ride with the others. She watches the noisy and cheerful crowd of neighbours go, kangaroo-dogs running ahead, horses set to leap fallen logs and crash through undergrowth after fleeing kangaroos. Her son is nearly a man now and he has become a skilful shot. He is tall and lean and has begun to cultivate a beard like his father's.

At dusk they return. She sees in the distance the last of the neighbours disappearing through the bush on their way home to their places scattered through the district. There are about thirty residences in the Berry Jerry area now, in 1890, and everyone knows that they depend for their survival, material and emotional, on their neighbours. Not everyone has the same background or values, but everyone knows that they need the others.

Father and son bring the minister back to the house.

'We did well today,' the boy is saying. 'There are kangaroos everywhere around these parts. It's not so much that they eat the crops, but they lie down on the young wheat and trample it – one morning early I counted over a hundred kangaroos leaving my father's wheat paddock.'

'The next thing is rabbits,' adds the father. 'When we came here there were no rabbits. Then a few years later a few turned up and we didn't take much notice. But now – we are getting rid of the 'roos and being overrun by rabbits!'

The family sit to the evening meal. They talk and laugh about the day's hunt. They tell the young minister about their local progress committee, the new Amalgamated Farmers Union having their first meeting in Wagga to talk about getting cooperative grain storage, the piece of equipment brother Robert Swann has invented which will speed the work of clearing virgin bush for the plough – 'He calls it the Forest Devil,' they explain – and the excellent stump-jump plough which will relieve the backbreaking work of digging out every dead tree stump, or burning it out, below the depth of the plough share. The farmer has recently dissolved his formal partnership with Mr Bryant, with whom he travelled from Victoria, and they talk about how Bryant has taken a dray, a plough and a winnowing machine with some stock as his share.

'Our boy here has one small piece of land already,' the father remarks. 'Not big enough for a decent place, but a start. I bought it for him from Mr Bryant. Now the lad is eighteen he's eligible to select a block for himself.'

The table is cleared and the woman and her daughter wash the dishes. A kerosene lamp is lit, a luxury in honour of the visitor. The men continue to talk and the minister talks to the boy about God. He already knows that the parents believe profoundly in the central place of God in their world; he has seen their family at prayer and heard them speak of their faith, but wonders how much the eighteen-year-old understands or cares about religion. They talk, the young man from a city theological school and the boy from the farm. The mother smiles to herself. It is clear that her son has a sharp mind and is asking many deep questions about faith. The boy is no fool. The visitor is offering to lend him books on theology and commentaries on scriptures if he is interested. Knowing her boy's love for books on any subject, the woman silently prays that his mind and heart will be opened to the discovery of a faith in God which belongs to him, and is not merely a mindless imitation of his parents.

*   *   *

William Playford was on the move again. Mary listened with some apprehension as she heard the first clues of his intentions. She had begun to feel happily at home at Merrylands and her children liked it, too.

'But we'll be going home again,' he reassured her. 'Back to Petersham. I thought you'd be pleased.'

She didn't know what it was that made her so anxious. William was talking so enthusiastically about his newest scheme. He planned to go into partnership with a friend in another hay and grain business. 'This time it's going to be a great success. My mate knows all about the business side of things and I'll work with the customers. We'll be back in the Ashfield area again and we'll see all our old friends.'

He talked on about the money they would borrow to establish themselves again, and his new friend's business skills, and Mary wondered why she had mixed feelings. Was it, she wondered, because he had already tried and failed once in the hay and grain area? Or that she wished that he would stay with one business instead of moving on? This would be the fifth change since he sold out his brickyard ten years earlier. Or did she have some unease about his new partner?

Whatever the reason, Mary began to consider the futures of her children with great care. Legh was easy – he was qualified in his trade as a plumber and he and Florrie were buying themselves a home in Ashfield. Harry and Robert were buying into a dairy in Ashfield, too, and setting up their own business. Sarah was engaged to be married to Louis McDowell and so her future was settled. But Grace?

'I think Grace should be trained in some work.'

'Grace? But why? Don't you expect your daughter to be at home and help you?' William was puzzled. Sons were the ones who must be found work and established in life, and daughters should marry.

'She's a clever little thing. I'd like to see her given a chance to study further. If we're going back to our old home, perhaps she could be trained as a pupil-teacher in her old school.'

Mary had been re-reading some notes on women and their work in an old edition of the *Weekly Advocate*, the Wesleyan Methodist newspaper. The article began by suggesting, tongue-in-cheek, that to the 'lords of creation', women were 'charming creatures, when they content themselves with nursing babies and making puddings; but oh beware, ye young men, of women who have opinions, and express them, who criticise your sermons and laugh at the oratorical flights of honourable MPs. Very inconvenient creatures, these petticoated quizzers. You never know when you have them... If you would have a peaceful hearth, take not to your bosom wives who read parliamentary debates, who advocate the cause of woman doctors, and lawyers and editors, and who do *not* believe that marriage is a girl's only salvation here below from the horrors of a loveless, objectless old age.' Mary, who was known in her household as one who did not hesitate to express her opinions, read with approval the article which went on to quote one Harriet Martineau's statement that 'whatever a woman proves herself *able to do*, society will be thankful to see her do,' but suggested that for many women it was still true that 'we do nothing thoroughly... there is the trail of the amateur in all we attempt.'

'William, listen to this article,' she insisted. 'It is saying that girls should be better prepared for life. What would Grace do if something happened to you? If you were ill?' She did not add the other possibility – What if your business failed? – but read aloud this extract: '"grim poverty stares the girl in the face. What can she do? Crochet an antimacassar? Make a wool mat? Play a bit? ... What a relief it would be for the breadwinner if his daughter were qualified to occupy some honourable position that would be at once both suitable and remunerative. Why should they wait until dire distress is upon them before they launch into a praiseworthy attempt at being women of purpose?'' Why, indeed? Let the child be equipped!'

So it was that before they left Merrylands, William Playford made application on behalf of his daughter Grace that her name be put down as a prospective pupil-teacher. She was still a child, with her long hair flowing down her back and still wearing the shorter skirts of the young, but by the time the family moved back to live in Petersham during the winter of 1889, she had been accepted to enter the apprenticeship scheme of pupil-teaching at some future date.

The letter of appointment arrived. Grace was to begin her new work in the Infants Department of the Superior Public School, Petersham. She was fourteen years old.

'Your hems will have to come down!' Mary said. With the help of her sewing woman and lengths of suitable serge fabric, she cut and stitched to make Grace her first skirts to sweep the ground like a woman's.

On her first morning, Mary helped her dress. The new long skirt looked very grown-up and she twirled around the room in delight. Her first attempt at putting up her hair was a failure.

'Mother, it won't stay up!' Grace wailed, as hairpins slithered out of place in the glossy pile of hair. The mother brushed and combed it, adding a dab of coconut oil for shine, then pulled the strands uncompromisingly back up, twisting the hair high and pinning it into place. When the girl was ready the mother looked at her carefully.

'It does make you look older. Behave like a lady, then!'

Young Will followed her down the street, giggling at the transformation of girl-sister into pupil-teacher. Mary watched them go, setting off along the familiar streets, then went back into her empty house, strangely alone.

Late that afternoon, they were home again. 'The children have to call me "Miss Playford"! And some of them keep forgetting because only yesterday at Sunday school they were calling me Grace. They think it's funny!' The young girl was excited and scared.

'All the morning and half of the afternoon I have to stay in a classroom with a senior teacher and help her with small groups of children, hearing them read, checking their arithmetic and things like that. Then after the children go home, the other pupil-teachers and I have our own lessons – things like French, and History, and Freehand Drawing. It scares me a bit, but I think it's going to be good. And my best friend Gertie Elliott has started there, too!'

*   *   *

For many months it has been very dry. Sudden twirls of red dust lift and scud past the house and the leaves of the peppertree hang limp and dust-laden. Only the cactus in the kerosene tins in the shade seems to have survived so far; the geraniums and ferns have withered for want of water. The crop is sparse and unpromising. The farmer mutters that he might as well cut it with the scythe, the way he harvested their first crops before they used their stripper, there is so little of it. Often in the evenings they hear thunder and see lightning flashes light up the far horizon, but it always means nothing.

The dam on the gentle slope below the house is almost dry. Week by week, the level of water has been receding, shrinking into a smaller and smaller muddy pool surrounded by a cracked crazy pavement of dried and drying mud. A few days ago, a party of Aborigines camped near the dam. Two of their men approached the farmer about the use of water.

'What did you tell them?' the farmer's wife asks anxiously.

'I had to let them drink, even if we're short. It was their waterhole before we turned it into a dam, and how could I send any man away thirsty?'

The Aborigines have moved on again, but yesterday Furner, a neighbour from a block to the west came to the house door, water tin in hand.

He apologised. 'I know you said it was all right for me to take water from your dam when I ran out. But I've just been down there and you're just about out, too. I'd better not take any more.'

The farmer is generous. 'I promised you could have water while we had some – go ahead, my friend.' The farmer's wife sees their neighbour disappear over the bank of the dam with his tin and then walk away with his precious freight. Her stomach feels as if it is tied in knots.

Now they sit around the table. The evening meal is over. The woman's mind is full of frightened questions. Will one of her brothers in the district still have water in his tank or his dam which he can share? Will they be able to buy water from a train freighting water across the drought-stricken countryside if they take the cart to the village of Coolamon? They knew when they came here that there was no river, no permanent creek, yet they had thought they would be safe with their tanks and their dam. She knows that without water she will not be able to cook, to water their young fruit trees, to wash. In the end they will have nothing to drink.

The man says, 'This afternoon I went down to the dam and drained off the last of the water into a water cask. All that's left is mud. It's very brown water, so you'll need to boil it.'

The woman is conscious of the gaze of her son and daughter. She asks the question they are all asking.

'And what will we do tomorrow?'

'I don't know.' There is a long silence. 'I don't know what we are going to do tomorrow, but I know what we are going to do tonight. We are going to pray, as we always have. Surely we can trust God.'

Heads are bowed. The man's voice cries in prayer to his Creator, to the one who controls the elements, to the one who cares for his little ones. He reads the words of Isaiah: 'Say to them that are of fearful heart, Be strong, fear not: behold your God will come. . . he will come and save you. Then the eyes of the blind will be opened, and the ears of the deaf shall be unstopped. Then shall the lame man leap as an hart, and the tongue of the dumb sing; for in the wilderness shall waters break out and streams in the desert. And the parched ground shall become a pool, and the thirsty land springs of water. . .'

The woman stands beside her son later, outside the back door, staring up into the clear night sky. Every star is sharply defined, the moon riding high and free of even a trace of cloud. They hear the distressed sounds of animals who have not had enough to drink.

'Father really believes that, doesn't he?' The boy's voice is puzzled, questioning. 'He really thinks that God will make it rain. Well, it doesn't look too much like rain tonight!'

They are woken in the night by a drumming on their roof. It is raining. The family stands in the pale wet light of early morning and sees water running down the bank into the dam, off the iron roof into their tank, filling buckets, dishes, horse trough. 'Thank God!' shouts the father into the downpour, and his family shake their heads in awe and thankfulness.

The ring of metal on metal sings from the new blacksmith's shop, still-green pine sapling poles surrounding the bricks of the forge. The farmer's son watches the blacksmith with admiration. He is a young man now, curious, capable and keen to learn new skills. This is a district where every man and woman must find a way to make and do the things they need — there can be no reliance on the tradesmanship of artisans in some distant town. At the least, people improvise, cobbling things together with wire to keep them working. At their best, they become gifted inventors, designing tools and equipment to meet the district needs. Uncle Robert Swann has built a stripper for his brother-in-law, the farmer, on a Ridley design, as well as his 'Forest Devil' for land-clearing, and neighbour Pratt is producing his own designs of plough, threshing machine and poison-cart against the rabbit plague. Now here is another uncle, Uncle Jim Swann, come to visit from South Australia, and he is an artist as a blacksmith.

The farmer's son leans on the bellows and pumps air into the heart of the bed of glowing coals, orange-red under the blackened surface. Uncle Jim pulls a metal rod from the forge, almost transparent red with heat, and pounds the softened metal with his great hammer, shaping it over the anvil, controlling it as he wishes before thrusting it suddenly into a water tub where it hisses and steams. He has been making farm tools, each a fine piece, and the young man watches, asks questions, tries his hand under the guidance of the master blacksmith.

'Well, that's enough for today, lad,' he says. The latest piece is hung from the rafters to cool. 'I'm off to the Farmers and Settlers' meeting with your dad.'

The two men ride off to the meeting, disappearing down the slope through the trees. They haven't far to go. A roadside hotel has recently been opened, providing accommodation and refreshment to travellers on their way from Coolamon to northern destinations, a stopping place for the Cobb and Co. coaches.

When the farmer returns for his meal, he is alone.

'Where's Jim?' The woman's voice is sharp, anxious.

'He shouldn't be too long. The publican McManus and the blacksmith Pratt were still having a great discussion about whether we can run a race meeting or a ploughing match in this district. Jim said he'd wait to find out if anything comes of it.'

'That's all very well, but I just wish he'd come home with you...'

Her voice trails away. Husband and wife understand each other.

Jim has not come to visit them for a simple holiday. He needs help, and the new Springwood Hotel is not likely to give it to him. His successful blacksmithing business in South Australia has been in serious trouble. Over the years, Jim has come to enjoy more and more the pleasures of taking his clients over to the pub for a few drinks and now customers are leaving him because he is less and less reliable. His sister had thought that it would help him to make a new start, far from the scene of his problems and away on a farm where he is not likely to be tempted to drink. He has come, full of good intentions, but the hotel has opened its doors almost over the fence from their property and he is still as friendly and convivial as ever.

He comes home at last, full of enthusiasm for the way the men have resolved their differences. There is to be a ploughing match, a great social occasion for the community, and everyone is invited to a public meeting to plan it. 'You should go on the committee,' he urges the farmer.

The ploughing match proves to be a great success. The farmer loans his paddock over the road from the Springwood Hotel and the land is alive with men and women from every direction. Tents spring up where church people sell cups of hot tea and sandwiches and the publican sells a stronger brew. Wagers are laid on who will plough the finest furrows, some with three-furrow ploughs and some with a single furrow. Horse teams are admired and women from isolated farms relish the chance of a good talk with friends. It is a great day. For the farmer's wife, the one disappointment is to see her brother spend most of his day around the publican's tent. It is not going to be as easy as she had hoped to help Jim break away from his dependence on alcohol. She has watched her son carefully through the day – he is a great admirer of Uncle Jim and she worries that perhaps he will want to join him in his drinking.

At their evening meal, Jim excuses himself. 'Not hungry,' he says. 'Think I'll go to bed.'

*   *   *

It's easy to be wise after the event, people said, but we should have seen it coming. If we'd had our wits about us, men admitted over a pint at the hotel on the corner or after morning service at their church, we'd have worked it out that the 'land banks', those new combinations of banking, land, building and finance, were just built on bits of paper with precious little behind them.

In the early days of the eighteen-nineties, Mary Playford watched William with growing concern. When they had celebrated the centennial of the colony, back in 1888, everything was looking so promising and everyone felt assured of a brilliant future for Australia. There was wealth on all sides, it seemed, and the separate colonies were seriously talking about Federation to build together a powerful country. Certainly there had been a terrible fire in the centre of Sydney, city health and hygiene was generally poor, the country was suffering droughts and strikes and wool and wheat prices were dropping, but surely those things couldn't cause William to look so troubled. At the end of his working day, William would sit silently at the table, his thoughts far away. If she dared to ask about his produce business, his replies were evasive with a touch of anger.

She sat up in bed waiting for him one night, her candle growing shorter as she waited. At last he came, his face drawn and shadowed as he wearily pulled on his nightshirt and sank onto the bed beside her. 'Whatever have you been doing?' she asked sharply. 'It's so *late*. You're always late these nights – working on sums or staring into space. What's happening?'

'There's no need for you to think about it, my dear. Just let me take care of things.' His head was buried in the pillow and the breadth of his back formed a shield against her questions. Husband and wife lay silent, sleepless, facing the named and the nameless.

Little by little, the truth began to come out. It was not only William Playford and his partner who were afraid. Across the wide spaces of New South Wales and Victoria, men had been playing games with land. Men borrowed to put deposits on new selections, land was surveyed, divided, subdivided, bought and sold. Agents took potential buyers out to see new subdivisions of land, plying them with champagne luncheons as they paid their deposits. Land values went up, land kept changing hands, men became millionaires through land – and it was all based on an insubstantial web of paper, promissory notes, options, overdrafts, a fragile fiction. The crash was inevitable. The whole financial edifice was not supported by solid foundations and, first with minor rumblings, then more violent shaking and disintegration, the economy of the country began to collapse around them. The first to go were some of the less viable land banks, as one by one they suspended payment. Nearly forty land banks had failed between 1891 and 1893. The savings of many working people vanished overnight, leaving families struggling without financial help.

'But William, we've not invested in land like that. Surely these problems with land won't affect your produce business. Will it?' Mary persisted with her questions. There seemed to be something about William's worries which was not clear.

'Not exactly. But my partner has been dabbling in land deals. And I think, though I'm not sure, that he has been using money from the business. If things don't improve, we'll be in serious trouble.'

The months went by. More and more families found their fortunes melting like dew in the sun, substantial landowners and businessmen in deep debt. People sold what they could sell, let their house servants go, stopped giving dinner parties for their friends and were too proud to admit that their children sometimes went to bed hungry in a house bare of most furniture. The impact of the failure of the land banks undermined confidence in the great banking companies and people began to panic about their money. There were terrifying days when hundreds of people crowded around the doors of respected banks like the Savings Bank of New South Wales, desperate to take their money away, then hesitatingly depositing it again. In April and May 1893, twelve banks with nearly a thousand branches across the country closed their doors. Some suspended payment for days, or weeks, then continued their work, grimly clinging to their vital role in society. Many banks failed, dragging their investors with them into financial disaster. It was a year of frightening unemployment, financial panic and gloom.

At breakfast one morning, the Playford family waited for Father to lead them in family prayers. Mary waited for William to move, grieving for him. He sat slumped among the teacups and toast crumbs of breakfast. At last he stood up heavily and brought the worn Bible back to the table.

'This is a hard day – a hard thing to say.' He paused, then went on, tearing the words out one by one. 'Our business – it's finished – near enough to bankrupt. My partner – well, he says it was all a mistake, not how he thought things would work out. He says he wasn't expecting his investments to be lost in the bank crash, that he thought he'd be able to pay the business back . . . Anyway, the thing's done and I'm finished financially. I must assign my estate and even if they sell everything we own it'll go nowhere near paying our debts. All those good men who trusted me, who loaned me money – I've failed them all!'

He opened the Bible and Mary wondered what despairing psalm or grim prophecy he had chosen to read. He had turned to the final words of the prophet Habakkuk, a book full of the agony of a prophet who sees his nation falling apart from inward rottenness and guilt, who looks for the final answer of almighty God. In a voice that trembled a little, William Playford began to read.

'Although the fig tree shall not blossom, neither shall fruit be in the vines; the labour of the olive shall fail and the fields shall yield no meat; the flock shall be cut off from the fold and there shall be no herd in the stalls, yet I will rejoice in the Lord, I will joy in the God of our salvation. The Lord God is my strength. . .'

The royal purple of jacarandas in bloom stood against the cobalt blue of the Sydney sky that November. Mary stood at the door watching her daughter coming up the path, her eighteen-year-old feet treading lightly over the carpet of fallen purple blossoms.

'And how are you now?' she asked.

'Better – but there is still tomorrow and the next day. Exams make me so nervous!'

Mother and daughter sat together and Mary heard the story of yet another day of teachers' examinations for Grace. For months the girl had been studying and now her skills in French and Domestic Economy, Art of Teaching and History, Geography, Blackboard Drawing and Vocal Music were being tested. She had nearly finished an apprenticeship of four years before she progressed to being an assistant teacher. The girl looked tired, with dark shadows under her eyes. Hours of close reading had already revealed that she needed to wear spectacles, and the round rims sat solemnly on the young face. Grace knew that she must be successful or she would be unemployed. With the economic depression affecting all parts of society, teachers were losing their jobs.

The girl pushed back wisps of soft hair escaping from their pins at the end of a tiring day. 'Oh, Mother, it isn't just the exams – I know I always get in a state over exams – but I can't help thinking about Father. What's he going to do? He's always been such an honest man, such a hard worker. Everyone has always trusted him in the church and in the community – and he hasn't done anything wrong! But he must feel so – so ashamed. . .'

Mary reached over to take her daughter's hand. 'Your father is very shaken. That's true. But he is holding onto God's promises.

He is sure that somehow, at some time, God is going to make good come out of this – we don't know how, but we believe it. Have you noticed how often pain and joy are linked in the Bible – like Father's reading from Habakkuk?'

Later she watched Grace carefully underline passages in the Bible she had given her long ago. Over the years, Grace had begun to write little annotations in the margin, dates of special sermons, underlinings, a sort of spiritual diary. Now she marked and dated this passage from Habakkuk, 'Although the fig tree shall not blossom . . . yet will I rejoice in the Lord,' and this one from the first letter of Peter, 'Do not be surprised at the fiery ordeal which comes upon you to prove you, as though something strange were happening to you. But rejoice. . .'

The sale was set for a date in March 1894. There was a bitter irony when they realised that those organising the sale had advertised it for William Playford's sixtieth birthday. For weeks before the sale, large posters were pasted up around the community advertising a major sale of Playford house, furniture, personal effects, buggy, horses.

Grace came into the house after school and looked as if she might burst into tears. 'Mother, it's so *horrible!* Those posters are all along the road up to Petersham School and I have to walk past them every day, shouting to the world that poor Father has lost everything. It hurts so much!'

Mary moved stonily through the days, sorting and packing, selecting those few things which they must keep for their survival. Over the years she had been able to buy many fine pieces of furniture, silver, china, linen, and now they must all go. She ran a regretful hand over her tall cedar bookcase with the glass front. At least the family would not be out on the street, she thought. Legh's home in Ashfield was open to them all, and Harry and Robert's dairying business would keep them. But she mourned for her William, whose confidence in himself was so fragile, and braced herself to support and comfort him through his deep valley of failure and discouragement.

On the day of the sale, the house was crowded with strangers, poking, peering at her things, despising treasures, arguing over the merits of her household furniture. She felt exposed, naked in spirit. As the auctioneer shouted his wares and his hammer beat out the death knell of her home as it had been, Mary clung to William's arm, supporting and being supported. When it was over and people departed with their booty, William walked away from the house with Mary on one arm and a red-eyed Grace on the other. He paused in the street and looked back.

'I'm sixty years old today – and I own nothing!'

*   *   *

The new house is beautiful. The farmer's wife has watched it grow over the months from a smooth patch of earth just outside her kitchen door to a fine large house with wide verandahs running all the way around it. The cypress pine was cut from their own pine forest, milled by the McRae neighbours, fitted together with skill and care so that walls, floors and ceilings are knitted together with tongue-and-groove and mortise-and-tenon joints. The house stands square on the shallow hilltop, a bedroom at each corner and large kitchen and living room in the centre, protected under a shining roof of bullnosed iron. Even the tops on the verandah posts have been beautifully curved by hand with the spokeshave and every room has its own fireplace.

The woman is proud of her home and her family. She has lived here at North Berry Jerry for nearly fifteen years now and five of her brothers and their families live in the same district. Her nieces and nephews are often in the house, visiting her son and daughter, as are many other neighbouring families. The orchard which her husband planted near the dam has developed from a cluster of bare twigs to a flourishing display of fruit trees. Her son has surrounded her vegetable patch with rabbit-proof wire fencing and built another rabbit-proof barrier around the edge of the house verandah, leaving just enough room for a narrow garden bed which in spring is sweet with the perfume of sweetpeas and stocks. She and her daughter have filled rows of cut-down kerosene tins with geraniums and cactus, ferns and lilies and they are banked along the verandah in the shade, giving a patch of gentle green against the reds and browns of the landscape. There is a new organ for their daughter and books and tools for their son.

Other men in the district with their large families sometimes worry about the future for their sons. How, they ask, can one selection, even with the maximum of 640 acres, provide a decent living for four or five sons one day? All they'll need will be a bad year, a drought, a plague of grasshoppers and the never-ending plagues of rabbits and they'll all be done for. But this woman is not so fearful.

They have only the one son, and have already added more land to their farm. He's sensible and he loves the land.

There is only one serious darkness over her world. Her brother who had come to live with them to recover from his alcoholism is worse. He thinks that her family is being unreasonable when they plead with him to stay at home and not spend so much time down the road at the Springwood Hotel. 'You're turning into a lot of sour-faced wowsers,' he says. 'Never willing to have a bit of fun with friends.' At weekends the bush hotel is crowded with workmen, clearing gangs, dam-sinking crews, teams of men putting fences across the countryside, shearers and harvest hands in their season. Jim loves to be with them, to take his turn shouting a round of drinks, and he's always among the last to leave. She supposes that he has a private supply tucked away somewhere on the farm. When he is well, he is teaching her son the art of welding and the two spend cheerful hours working together in the blacksmith's shop. When he is not well, he is very ill indeed, and sometimes she fears for his sanity. Her son is becoming more and more opposed to alcohol because of what he sees happening to his uncle.

*   *   *

Things could have been a great deal worse for them, Mary knew. Most of the children were employed, though the boys teased Grace that she only kept her teaching job because she was a girl and therefore very cheap. 'Of course the Education Department will keep girls like you,' they said, 'when it costs them only about two-thirds of the salary they'd have to pay a man.' Legh and Florrie had fitted them all in for the time being and Robert was buying a house as well. She had been very touched to find that her sons had worked together at the auction to buy back some of their more basic pieces of furniture and had also rescued her beloved bookcase. Sarah's Louis had his shop and, to Mary's delight, Sarah had presented her with her first two grandchildren, little Grace named for her aunt and baby Stanley.

Although William found it such a painful thing to see his business career end in such an anticlimax, he was not totally without work because his sons encouraged him to work with them on their dairy. 'Just because you're sixty, don't think you can retire just yet,' they commented, and were pleased to see how physically strong their father still was. He was by no means the only man among his group of friends who had suffered from the effects of the economic depression.

Though it was in some ways a sad and difficult time for the people of Sydney, there still remained a sense of confidence and a toughness, a resiliance. Men who had sold their fine horses rode bicycles with aplomb. Women simplified their elaborate dress, now that many were forced to do their own stitching, and assured each other that the plainer styles were so much nicer – 'all that dreadful birdsnest of wire and horsehair to hold up our trains – such a thoroughly uncomfortable thing to wear!' Women like Mary Playford worked to provide help for the destitute, serving hot meals in soup kitchens to the hungry, and joining philanthropic societies to try to alleviate the sufferings of the unemployed. People on the streets developed a kind of cheeky spirit, prepared to thumb their nose at hard times, to be larrikins, to do more than survive.

In the warm twilight of the evening of Christmas Day, Mary sat beside William for a presentation of scenes from the life of Christ thrown on a screen by the most modern triple lime-light machinery, and joined with congregation and choir in singing carols. In the crowd around her she could see members of her own family, nearly all adult now, friends of thirty years from Ashfield and other friends from the newer church nearby in The Boulevarde, Lewisham. The continued friendship of fellow-Christians was like soothing balm on wounded spirits and the energy and enthusiasm of the many groups in the church gave William some sense of purpose. Their minister J.E. Carruthers and his wife were there, both people who had become close friends. Watching Mr Carruthers moving among the people at the end of the evening, Mary wondered whether he would be chosen as the new President of the next Wesleyan Methodist Conference in a few months. In the previous Conference he had come close to being elected and she thought he would make a wise leader. 'Nearly a new year,' she thought to herself. 'Perhaps 1895 will be better for us all.'

The new year began with promise. To Mary's delight, their friend J.E. Carruthers was honoured by being elected President of Conference for the year. With a group of other senior ministers, Carruthers invited the Sydney Methodist young people to attend an evening meeting of Conference, drawing together hundreds of young people who belonged to the newly established societies of Christian Endeavour. Mary and William Playford took their places in the gallery of the great new Centenary Hall, York Street, Sydney to watch their Harry, Robert, Grace and young Will join the crowds of youth streaming into the body of the hall. Conference had always been the preserve of men, mostly older men, but the young now filled the hall, under great banners bearing scripture words, garlands of flowers draping pillars and gallery and the sound of organ and orchestra. In their suburban and country Christian Endeavour societies, the young people were learning to lead, to take initiative, to study and pray and speak publicly about their faith, and the leaders of the church wanted to encourage them. Mary looked in vain for Grace among the sea of people below her – every girl seemed to be wearing an identical stiff straw boater hat – but as the crowd exploded into song with 'All hail the power of Jesus' name!', the mother gave thanks in her heart that her daughter and sons were part of it all.

That winter, William and his brother Richard attended the meeting in the church on The Boulevarde when church leaders formally divided the heavily overpopulated Ashfield Methodist circuit, with its eleven congregations, into two parts. Their church at Lewisham with Mr Carruthers was to be part of the new circuit. William came home elated about the signs of growth in the churches but worried about his friend Mr Ritchie, the Sunday School superintendent.

'Ritchie looked quite ill tonight,' he told Mary. 'Something wrong with his throat, he said. He would have been better home in bed.'

'Mr Ritchie wasn't there in Sunday School today,' Grace said. 'He's never missed before. Is his health worse?'

William shook his head sadly. His family sat around him at the Sunday dinner table. 'Poor Ritchie. He's been troubled for a while with throat problems but now the doctors have told him that he has cancer.'

Mary put down her knife with a clatter. Mr Ritchie was their friend, their Christian brother. How could such a thing happen?

'But can't they *do* something? Some medicine? Some surgery?'

'They've suggested surgery, but Ritchie has declined it. He says he'd rather leave himself in the hands of God. I must admit I don't blame him – they want to remove some glands in the neck and cut out his tongue!'

There was a gasp around the table and William went on. 'Now the medical people have told him that he can only prepare for the end. If he won't let them operate, there is nothing they can do for him.'

'But we can't just give up, can we? We can surely pray,' Mary said with passion. 'Do we believe that God can answer prayers for healing or don't we?'

Among the people of the church came a growing sense that it was right to pray for the healing of Mr Ritchie. Some were confident that God would certainly heal, others not sure what to think, but very eager to ask for God's hand on the situation. William and Mary Playford went with Grace and some of their boys to the Lewisham church one evening. Mr Ritchie was there, looking very ill. Their minister J.E. Carruthers led them.

'Do you remember the story of Jesus' friend Lazarus and his grave illness? When Jesus heard that his friend was dying, he said, ''This sickness is not going to end in death. No, it is for God's glory, that the Son of God may be glorified by it.'' Does the illness of our dear friend Ritchie have the marks of something which can be to the glory of God?' Mr Carruthers asked.

There was a murmur of assent. Those with great faith and those with only a little agreed that they wanted to pray for the healing of their friend. Mary knelt through the service of prayer, asking God to heal their friend. Some placed their hands on his head or his shoulder as they prayed, others stayed in their places. The whole building was full of a strong sense of the presence of God's Spirit. Mary felt tears flowing as she pictured Jesus Christ standing there among them, his arm around Ritchie's stooped shoulders, a gentle hand touching the diseased throat, the very energy of the Son of God passing through his fingers in healing.

Weeks passed. On Sundays and through the week, Mary heard news of Mr Ritchie as she continued to pray for him, with her family and in her private prayers. The news was gradual; 'he has less pain', 'some of the swellings and lumps seem to be reducing', 'he feels well again'. Then one Sunday, Ritchie was back in Sunday school, leading the singing and speaking with his usual strong and confident voice. 'He's been back to the doctors and they are baffled,' Mrs Ritchie confided. 'They can't find any signs of the cancer! They don't understand it at all . . .'

Just before Christmas 1895, The Boulevarde Sunday School invited the parents of their pupils to a social evening. For Mary, there were two special moments; one was seeing their friend Mr Ritchie welcoming the guests and children and the other was a surprise. During the speechmaking, her daughter Grace was called to the front to be presented with a fine new study Bible. Mr Ritchie and others had signed it, and gave it as 'an expression of our personal regard and high esteem of her as a Christian worker'. Immediately after Christmas, the whole congregation gathered once again for a service of thanksgiving for the healing of Mr Ritchie. J.E. Carruthers led the people in their thanks to God, and assured them that he had written a letter describing the whole story to be published in the church paper *The Methodist*, so that the people might be encouraged by their President to remember that God heals.

At the New Year's Day camp meeting on the banks of Cooks River, Mary Playford talked with her friend Mrs Mary Carruthers. They and their families shared an interest in the many activities of the churches: Band of Hope, Christian Endeavour, Sunday School, Mutual Improvement Society, choirs, tea meetings and prayer meetings, and missionary meetings with missionaries Dr J.E. Moulton and Dr George Brown.

'I'll be sorry to miss the performance of Handel's *Messiah* in a few days in the Centenary Hall. I'm going for a holiday with friends for a few weeks,' Mary Carruthers explained. 'We all have a busy year ahead of us.'

'But that can't be true! I was only talking to her just before she went away for her holiday. . .' Mary was shocked, disbelieving.

'Mr Carruthers told me himself.' William did not want to believe it either. Their friend Mrs Carruthers, wife of their minister, had taken ill with acute pleurisy while away from home and after a short illness had died.

Mary and William Playford were among the many who crowded into the church on The Boulevarde for the memorial service; with many other church friends she was shocked and shaken. How could God, who had saved the life of their friend Mr Ritchie, take the life of her friend Mary Carruthers? Surely poor Mr Carruthers needed her? What about her teenage daughters and her young sons? The lighted gas lamps shone on the drapes of black and white over the pulpit railing and lit the wall hanging which read 'She being dead yet speaketh'. Behind the masses of blues and mauves of hydrangea and agapanthus sat the choir, with Harry among them, and her Grace was at the organ, playing for the soloist who sang 'I know that my Redeemer liveth'.

Mary sat there, confused and sad. How could anyone begin to understand God's ways? Why was Mr Ritchie healed and Mrs

Carruthers dead? Did it have anything to do with their worth as people, or their goodness as Christians? Did it have anything to do with praise or blame? Was it related to the strength of the prayers of God's people, or the degree of faith they had? Was there some almost magical formula they had missed? Or was it part of some great cosmic meaninglessness or some terrible inconsistency in the nature of God? She did not know the answers, but many suggested answers were surely not the way Jesus Christ spoke or acted towards people.

The Rev. George Lane stood to preach. As she listened, Mary realised that he was preaching from the same story which Mr Carruthers had shared with them as they prayed for Mr Ritchie. Then they had remembered that the illness and dying of Lazarus was 'for the glory of God'. Now she heard again the next part of the story; Martha, the sister of Lazarus, came to say to Jesus, 'You are too late – if you had come in time, he'd not be dead now. But even now, God will give you what you ask.' Jesus said to her, 'I am the resurrection and the life. He who believes in me will live, even though he dies; and whoever lives and believes in me will never die. Do you believe this?' And Martha, still weeping, still not understanding the answers to her questions, answered with the one thing she was sure about. 'Yes, Lord, I believe that you are the Christ, the Messiah, the Son of God . . .' The only certain thing in the place of grief and questions was the belief that Jesus Christ was there, with her and her family, right in the middle of the pain of dying, weeping with them, knowing that dying is a part of living, offering life beyond dying, offering himself.

The preacher repeated the phrase of Jesus, 'I am the resurrection and the life. . . Do you believe this?'

Mary the wife of William echoed the response of Martha the sister of Lazarus. She still did not understand the answers to most of her questions, but the nature of Jesus reassured her. 'Yes, Lord, I believe.'

The birthday cake with twenty-one candles stood in the middle of the table, each little flame flickering a soft light on the faces of the family as they sat around. Everyone was there, all home for Grace's coming-of-age. Mary embraced her daughter, such a dainty little person and with such a special gentle charm about her – we chose well when we named her 'Grace', Mary decided. The boys were teasing Grace, asking questions about the intentions of a young man who sometimes came to call – 'He's going away, anyway,' Grace returned, rather flushed, 'he's going to sea soon, and he probably only calls in on Sunday afternoons because he likes Mother's good cooking!'

Sarah's little ones climbed onto Grace's lap, little Grace and Stan puffing at the birthday candles and snuggling up to their aunt. They were all giggling together as Grace tickled them.

William said with regret, 'Grace, I once had this great plan to buy you a beautiful gold pocket watch on a gold chain for your birthday. But, since the sale, and with no business of my own . . .'

His voice trailed away and Mary sensed the pain he must feel, that he couldn't match the gifts he had made to his older children on their coming-of-age. She knew how much he loved his daughter. Grace recognised it too and, spilling the children unceremoniously into Sarah's lap, she jumped up and went to hug her father.

'Just all being here tonight – that's the most beautiful present! I don't need a gold watch, Father.'

William's disappointment was far deeper than being unable to buy a gold watch. There was a loss of self-respect, an aimlessness, a deep shame that there were still old debts which he had been unable to repay. Mary had tried to reassure him: 'Now that your business has been wound up, no-one has any legal claim on you – you've done all you can. You just have to believe that your creditors have just put it down to the hard times and have forgiven you.'

She could not know that William's discontent was only one of the tremors that would continue to shake their family structure and that Grace's birthday party was to be one of the last times they would all be together for a long time.

The changes, when they came, happened within about six months in 1897. Robert's wedding to Fanny Evans had been planned for a long time and Mary watched him set up his home with Fanny with considerable contentment. The whole family was excited when Robert was able to buy a whole houseful of beautiful cedar furniture for twenty-five pounds from a wealthy merchant whose home was breaking up. Harry and young Will worked with Robert at their Ashfield dairy, but Harry was seriously thinking about looking for a dairy farm somewhere on the north coast as Ashfield was becoming too crowded for cows.

Then William came to his wife one day with a letter.

'Do you remember, years ago, my old friends the Boxsells? James

Boxsell has bought land out of Cootamundra at a place called Cullinga. He's written to say that he's heard I'm not in business any more and wondered if I'd be interested in going to Cullinga. He reckons there's gold on his land . . . He says another bloke has been looking for gold on his place, but has given it away, leaving the beginnings of a mine. His son-in-law Jasper Ingold is offering to provide my tools if Boxsell gives me access to the land, and my keep.'

He hurried on, as if he were trying to convince her. 'The three of us, Boxsell, Ingold and me, would be partners in anything I found. Oh, and you'd stay in Sydney, of course, and keep house for the boys and Grace — it will be rough living at first, and I mightn't even find a grain of gold . . .'

Mary sat very still for a long time. For the first time in many months she saw the light of enthusiasm in his eyes, an excitement, hope. How could she say to him, 'You're a foolish old man, thinking of setting off as a gold digger again more than thirty-five years after the first time'? How could she complain, 'What about me, left behind — I'll miss you so much'? How could she demand to know why he thought he would find gold in a mine that another man had already abandoned?

He came to sit close by her, and took her hand. 'Do you remember, long ago, I used to say that there were only two conditions when a man should go goldmining? I reckoned he had to be either so rich he didn't care how much money he lost on the business — or have nothing to lose. Mary, I've already lost so much that was important to me — I've failed as a businessman, not once but several times, I've let down other men, I've lost my purpose for getting up in the morning. Please don't stop me in trying just once more . . .' So William left home, carrying a simple bundle of bedding and a frying pan, little more than he had taken when he left home as a seventeen-year-old so long ago to follow gold.

Only weeks later, Grace's official letter arrived. 'What if they've sacked me? I've been worrying about it for months,' Grace said as she fumbled to open the envelope. Other teachers had been losing their jobs because of financial limits on the Education Department. The letter was addressed to Miss Grace Playford and was dated 31 August 1897. The formal notice read, 'Appointment to Upper Yanco for purpose of acting as Teacher of Provisional School there.'

'But where on earth is Upper Yanco? I've never heard of it!'

It was not easy to discover. Not many of their Sydney friends could help. When at last Mary stood on Redfern station to see Grace off on the train, they knew that she was going to what must be a very small school — provisional schools always had less than twenty pupils — somewhere far to the west along the new stretch of railway line which ran to Narrandera, then south to a tiny settlement called Coonong on a sometime watercourse called Yanco Creek. Mary watched the train pull out. Grace looked so tiny and defenceless leaning from the window waving. The last carriage of the train rushed past her and the lines stretched away to the west, empty.

William had gone. The boys had married or were planning to marry soon. Young Will talked about wanting to join his father. Sarah was expecting another baby soon and couldn't travel from Wollongong. Her old father, James Rootes, was ninety-three and, though his mind was as clear as ever, they both knew that his earthly life must be close to the end. Now Grace was gone, and all she could do was to pray for her protection.

For the first time, Mary suddenly knew what her William must have felt when his working life was snatched from him. She turned quickly and hurried to catch the train back to her son's house in Ashfield. With Robert's new bride Fanny, she had even lost her job as the boys' housekeeper.

'Dear God, don't let me be useless!' she prayed as the train carried her back to her nearly empty nest.

Grace's story

10
A barren land
1897-1898

SITTING BOLT UPRIGHT, sailor hat severely level and handbag clutched in her lap, the girl in the train struggled to choke back a sob. For a flying moment, she saw the Petersham Public School standing solidly among its Moreton Bay figs and jacaranda trees, then it too was gone. The train steamed on into the glaring eye of the setting sun. Behind lay the measured streets of the city, a patchwork of terrace and cottage, boulevarde and back lane, sandstone and sea, spire of church and barrow of fruit vendor, tramways and trains, university and hospitals, choirs and crowds.

And ahead of her? Maybe the place mentioned in the letter was a myth. Maybe she would find herself somewhere out in the depths of the country, standing by a roadside, bag in hand, and very lost indeed.

Grace reached into her bag and pulled out the letter again. 'Upper Yanco', it said. 'Miss Grace Playford'. Dated 31 August 1897. It was such an insubstantial piece of paper to have the power to uproot her from everything she knew, from the security of home. Yet without it she would not be in a train heading south-west across New South Wales.

Through the window, the sky was streaked with pink and apricot, gilt-edged, and the rich farming country on the Nepean shadowed in purples and blue-grey. This was familiar country where she had often come to visit deaf old Grandfather Rootes, or Uncle James and Auntie Mary Anne on the farm at the foot of Razorback. But beyond it? The train would steam on through the night – and tomorrow, who knew?

Around her, fellow passengers read their papers and talked among themselves. Though Grace stared out into the darkening countryside, she saw the faces of her family; Mother trying to pass on some of her own strength of character to her daughter, Father already somewhere out near Cootamundra, her brothers and Sarah. She saw her mentor Miss Collins from Petersham school who had taught her everything she knew of teaching and had opened the door for her wider education. There was the face of her special friend Gertie and the other girls. Gertie had cried, written her poem of farewell and embroidered a bookmark with the word 'Mizpah', 'The Lord watch between me and thee while we are absent one from the other'. There was her friend the sailor, almost offended by her going: 'Men are meant to travel, but girls should stay home where you can find them!' and he gave her three glowing cat's eye stones from his travels with the plea that she not forget him. And there were all her friends in her church, so many close friends.

The faces in her mind had become so real that she almost missed a fellow-traveller's question.

'I beg your pardon?'

The woman, surrounded by baskets and bundles, leaned towards her.

'I just said, how far are you going, dearie?'

'To Upper Yanco — the station is called Coonong.'

'You've got family out there, I suppose, have you? Don't know the place myself.'

'No. . . No, I'm a teacher.'

'Oh.' The woman inspected her closely. Grace flushed as the woman observed her neat costume, the set of her straw hat and her diminutive size which left her feet swinging a little when she sat back into the deep railway seat.

'Don't look old enough to me,' the woman decided. 'Can't think what the Education Department can be about sending young girls. . . Well, dearie, I hope it will work out all right for you. But I wouldn't be in your boots, thank you!'

Grace looked away, her carefully-mustered confidence escaping, leaving her shaken, tears prickling. As soon as the other woman seemed to have lost interest in her, she dug into her bag in search of a handkerchief.

Her hand in the bag touched the reassuring hardness of leather. She pulled out the brown leather cover of the Bible Mother had given her for her eighth birthday. Grace held the book, feeling the texture of leather, the embossed design on the cover and the fine edges of the pages, some loosened a little after years of use. It didn't really matter that it was now too dark to read it. With the roar and rush of the steam-engine in her ears, she leaned back in her corner, closed her eyes and remembered family prayers that morning. Mother had read aloud the comforting words of the Traveller's Psalm, Psalm 121, and later Grace had taken her pen and neatly underlined some of the phrases in her Bible, writing the date in the margin.

Now the words were marching purposefully around in her brain, strengthening, reassuring. 'My help cometh from the Lord . . . He will not suffer thy foot to be moved: he that keepeth thee will not slumber. . . The Lord is thy keeper. . . The Lord shall preserve thy going out and thy coming in from this time forth, and even for ever more.'

The hours passed slowly. At times she slept curled awkwardly, her hat drooping over one ear till she relegated it to the top of her suitcase. At times she woke to find the train standing somewhere in the dark, waiting, while the anonymous heaps of humanity sharing her carriage breathed and sighed. Ill-lit railway platforms swam into the frame of her window, half-observed with sleepy eyes: Goulburn, Yass, Cootamundra. 'Somewhere out there, Father is sleeping in his tent,' she thought, and wondered if he felt as alone as she did.

She finally woke fully to the gentle light of dawn. She was in a foreign land. Slipping by were wide spaces, paddocks and scrub stretching away to the horizon. In the alchemy of the slow night, hills had smoothed to widely undulating plains, soil had changed colour to a rich brick-red, and grasslands were pale, bleached off-white by a dry winter. Twisted skeletons of dead trees stood in sown paddocks, the lines of young green wheat curving in apology around their roots, recognising the last defiance of what had once been forest and native bush, untouched for thousands of years. Little clusters of farm buildings stood at long intervals and, where early morning smoke rose from cottage chimneys, Grace tried to picture the invisible women lighting their fires for porridge and tea. 'How can they live out here?' she asked herself. 'Where are their neighbours?' Corrugated iron and round timbers, stone chimneys, simple verandahs for shade with a water tank at one side were now in spring softened by the pink fluff of a peach tree in blossom or the white of apple. She tried to imagine what it would be like to live in such a place, but could not. Yet as she saw the gold of daffodils in cottage gardens, and saw baby clothes pegged to dry, she knew that women were there.

There was a brief pause at Junee, where passengers surged into the high ceilinged dining room for a railway breakfast, then on again, steaming west, and Grace watched the country unfold. Tiny country stations tugged at the train, forcing it to pause by the simple squares of platform – Marrar, Coolamon, Ganmain, Grong Grong – before they were shaken off as the train thundered on. At the greater dignity of Narrandera station, she changed trains for the southern line, a new stretch of railway which went part way to the Victorian border.

A fatherly conductor leaned from the door of the new train. 'Yes, this's the right train for Upper Yanco, miss. Get off at Coonong – it's only a couple of stations. There's not much out there, mind you, just mile after square mile of the big sheep holdings of Sir Samuel McCaughey.'

The last hours of the journey dragged more and more slowly. 'Only a couple of stations' the man had said, but this was not Sydney with stations almost in sight of each other. The country was flatter now and, as they travelled south-west, the sight of cottage or farm-shed became more and more rare. Wide expanses of tough tufty grass spread away, almost like dried-over swamps, and trees became rare.

As she felt the train losing speed, Grace suddenly became aware that the train had become a refuge for her. Perhaps if she were to stay on it long enough it would turn round and take her home again.

'Coonong,' called the conductor and the train shuddered to a halt. With a jump and a fluttering of skirts she landed on the patch of platform, dragging her bags after her. A youth with a flag waved the train off, and her refuge whistled unfeelingly and left her there.

The youth with the flag eyed Grace curiously. Solitary girls with suitcases did not jump off the train at Coonong every day. She stood as tall as she was able within the barricade of luggage and said, 'Could you please direct me to the public school?'

'The school?' He looked puzzled. 'But there's nobody at the school, miss. The teacher left, so the kids haven't bothered with it for a few weeks. Don't blame them, I say.'

She looked around anxiously. She was standing on a platform of railway sleepers with not even a small goods shed to grace it and beyond was a small cluster of buildings edging a wide dirt road.

'Well, could you please tell me where the teacher used to board – the one that was here before?'

'Board? At the hotel, of course. There's nowhere else. Are you looking for a place, miss? I'd try the pub – over on the other side of the road there. They'll look after you.'

Grace gathered her things and set off. The building he had indicated was nothing like any hotel she had seen before. Hotels she knew were solid brick and stone standing grandly on street corners. Her feet began to drag as she came nearer to the small, single-storey edifice of corrugated iron and split timber which appeared to be deserted. Never had she been through the doors of a hotel of any description. She had been brought up by Mother, Father and the Band of Hope, all vigorously against alcohol in all its forms and had been raised on the moving story of Uncle James and his delivery from alcoholism. Mother would be shocked.

Disconsolately, Grace approached the hotel doors. Up and down the dusty street she could see no other way. Band of Hope or not, at least the hotel had a notice reading 'Accommodation'. Taking a deep breath, she plunged through the door.

The plate in front of her was full, the greasy mutton stew defying her. She poked gingerly with her fork, nudging bones and gristle, thick layers of fat clinging to tough strands of mutton. The gravy was greyish and glistening with oil: the other guests were soaking it up on the thick slices of bread and eating with enthusiasm. Even the potatoes had been boiled to death, she thought, collapsing into sodden heaps. A glimpse of the hotel kitchen, the nature of the meal before her and the heavy and unfamiliar aroma of alcohol had all combined to kill her appetite. She struggled to reduce the quantity on her plate, even a little.

There was little conversation among the diners. As well as the man and wife who ran the hotel, there sat at table a silent traveller from a stock and station firm, the youth from the railway station and a bullock driver on his way through to Jerilderie. The owner's wife attempted to talk to Grace in a friendly fashion.

'It's a bit quiet here, through the week,' the woman commented. 'But on Saturday night things will liven up a lot. The shearers, you know. There's a lot of men out on Coonong station for the shearing at the moment, and by Saturday they'll all be ready to knock down their cheque in the bar. Good bunch of blokes, too, usually. A bit rough-and-ready, but they're all right. A lot of them come up from the mountains of the Monaro in spring for the shearing. Great horsemen.'

She inspected the table then shrieked towards the kitchen. 'Girl, get in here and take the plates! You had enough dinner, miss?'

'Yes, thank you,' said Grace faintly, watching with relief as her half-full plate was borne away. Probably the hotel dogs would enjoy it.

'Don't worry if things are a bit quiet, miss,' the woman went on. 'Just you wait till Saturday night!'

Thin slivers of sunlight lay in patterns across the school blackboard, adding texture to the rows of pothooks carefully chalked as examples for the little ones to copy. The little schoolroom was built of horizontal boards of adzed timber, roughbacks, allowing sunshine, wind and dust to filter through the cracks. Apart from the whisper of children breathing heavily over their spelling test and the scrape of slate pencil on slate, the room was very quiet as Grace read out the next word to be copied.

For the first few days, Grace had found it very strange to be the only teacher, and in such a tiny school. There were only about twelve children, the families of station hands and fettlers, and she had discovered that she could pace across the schoolroom in four steps and from the blackboard at the front to the fireplace at the back in twelve. There was very little in the way of school supplies; only chalk, slates and slate pencils, a few scratchy nibbed pens and exercise books and a set of school readers, but no maps, pictures, charts or library books.

Through the two small windows, the plains spread away in the distance. She could see the railway line shining, snaking its long path across the country, waiting for the trains which passed twice a day. Down the road further was the scattered village, iron roofs and walls blazing in the sun. (The school at Petersham had been near the railway line, too, and looked down the the the affluence of The Boulevarde. . .)

The last word of the spelling test was spoken, the last squeak of slate pencil was silenced. The teacher moved quickly among the children, correcting work.

'Well done, children! Clean your slates, and as soon as you are ready, I'm going to teach you a song.'

'Just wait till Saturday,' the woman at the hotel had said.

On Saturday morning, Grace woke to the sound of the other girl in the room splashing her face and hands at the washstand. The hotel keeper had suggested she share a room with a girl from a local family who worked at the hotel.

'It'll be busy today, I bet,' the girl said, talking through the folds of towel. 'The missus likes to have everything nice on Saturdays and anyway, what with expecting the shearers to come over here later on, she'll be wanting me to help with a lot of extra cooking. Though, if you ask me, the blokes are more interested in what they are going to drink than what they are eating...'

The girl disappeared briefly into a flurry of skirts and emerged to hook herself into her tight-fitting bodice. A rapid pass of the comb, a twist of long hair into a topknot, arms thrust through the straps of a vast working apron and she was off.

Grace sat up in bed. The whole weekend stretched blankly before her. At home it would have been different. Mother would have a list of Saturday tasks: baking, cleaning, silverpolishing, weeding, shopping. Then she would have her Sunday School lesson to prepare, and hymns to rehearse on the church organ, friends calling in, final choir practice, maybe a concert or church social to attend. And Sunday was always the best day of all; quietness and music, freedom from work and the discipline of the special day, time for reading and pleasure of teaching, being together with friends at church and meals, time for worship and hearing messages from God through the preaching of men she respected, being alone and at peace.

But here? Here she wasn't free to wander into the kitchen and announce, 'I think I'll make apple pie.' The woman in the kitchen would probably take offence if she offered to clean the hotel silver — 'though it could do with a good shine,' she thought privately. There was a sitting room for guests, but it was generally a haunt of the male guests and she didn't feel at home there. Tomorrow there would be no chance to go to church — 'Oh no, dearie, not every Sunday! A minister turns up here about once a quarter, I think it is...' and Grace had been given a clear impression that the kindly hotel keeper's wife did not feel herself cheated if the minister came but rarely.

She climbed out of bed. There was no point in staying in there, she thought: it wasn't even very comfortable. Dressed and washed, she left the hotel and set off for the little school. Around the school the plains spread away, flat and featureless to the horizon, and she felt as if she were almost invisible in that wide space. In the silence and privacy she re-read notes and letters from her mother and friends and let tears of homesickness flow. She pulled out a private exercise book which she had headed 'Gleanings' and had already begun to use to copy poems, scripture verses and cuttings which appealed to her from the church newspapers. Several friends had sent her on her way with poems, sad verses about parting, and leaving one's mother, and homesickness, and the stresses of finding God's way for the future. She copied them neatly into her book, pausing from time to time to wipe damp spectacles.

The sun was already on its downward path when she returned to the hotel. She had left her school blackboard carefully filled with school exercises for Monday's lessons, and had spent a soothing afternoon copying a large map of Australia onto a section of the board, with each major city marked. People said that within a few years there would probably be a federation of Australian states and, as she ruled up the colonial boundaries, she wondered whether it would be so. It had been peaceful in the silence of the school, but as she returned she found strange horses tethered to the hitching posts of the verandah and a few wagons stood free of horses beside the road.

As she slipped through the entry door, loud male laughter burst from the bar and she hurried down the hall to her room. Smells of cooking beef and boiling cabbage drifted in; the food seemed to be of unrelentingly poor quality and cooked with the least attention to hygiene or nutrition.

'I think I'll ask for some boiled eggs with bread and butter for my tea,' she decided. 'At least nothing nasty can have happened to the eggs if they are still in their shells! Yesterday's beef was as tough as old boots, and about as tasty.'

When the dinner bell rang, Grace walked reluctantly to the dining room. Though she kept her eyes down, focusing on the stained table cloth and the unappealing plates of food being placed before the diners, from the edges of her vision she saw the men in the bar. Without looking directly, she knew that they were leaning on the bar counter, drinks in hand, and were watching the scene in the dining room through the connecting door. Her friend the maid appeared, bringing her boiled eggs, and there was a burst of comment.

'What do you reckon, lads? A bit of all right, eh?'

'I like the big girl in the apron — she looks good for some fun.'

'Nah. The little one. Hey, turn round and let's see you, love!'

'Ooh, too much of a lady, eh? Too good and lah-de-dah to say good day to us blokes! Come on, love, give us a smile.'

'Leave her alone, fellers. That's what the city does to you. Maybe she can't stand the smell of sheep on you, Charlie.'

Grace choked on her eggs, red to the ears with confusion and humiliation. She had no idea how to respond, no experience to suggest a path somewhere between discourtesy and wantonness. Most of the men and youths of her world lived in the secure and familiar framework of home, school and church. Men outside the framework had always ignored her. Back in Sydney, people were free to choose whether or not they wanted to be part of hotel society, but here there was no choice. She tore her eyes away from the wreckage of eggshells on her plate to seek a clue from her hostess.

The older woman was unperturbed. She went on pouring black tea floating with tea leaves and tossed her head cheerfully towards the men in the bar. 'Don't let them worry you, Miss Playford. They mean well, I'm sure.' She leaned across the table and added in a hoarse whisper, 'Those fellows, shearers and that, they don't see too many single girls. . .'

Someone in the bar started to sing, and voices joined in with a song of the bush. Grace swallowed the last of her tea and fled from the table, running from the shouts of farewell – or was it invitation? – which clutched after her as she hurried into the dark hall. She fumbled for matches and lit her lamp from the hallstand, her hand trembling as she carried it to her room and thankfully pulled the door shut behind her.

It was a long evening. She sat at the little table with its cheap lace cover, a book open in front of her, but the words marched stolidly past her eyes without penetrating her mind. A rising tide of sound washed through the walls, with waves of song, then laughter. The aroma of alcohol seeped under her door and seemed to fill her room. She had always been brought up to be offended by alcohol and the invading smell of it assaulted her senses. There was no escape from it, nowhere to run.

There was a thump on her door. She stared at the twisting doorknob, immobilised by fear.

'Come on, miss! For goodness sake unlock it and let me in.' It was the voice of the other girl.

'Sorry – just a moment. . .'

She fumbled with the door and the girl came in, dragging off her soiled kitchen apron and kicking off her boots. Before the door was shut behind her, men's shouted phrases as pungent as the smell of their liquor floated down the hall towards them. Grace banged the door abruptly and sat down, twisting her long plait restlessly. She could still feel eyes staring at her, even though it was in her imagination. The eyes followed her on the breath of alcohol, on the sound of drunken voices. They heard a thump, a crash, the tinkle of broken glass: 'Somebody's chucked a bottle through a window again,' said the other girl philosophically. 'Tomorrow the boss will probably have to nail up the busted furniture. By Sunday morning it won't just be the chairs without a leg to stand on!'

At some point in the night, the sound of laughter turned to anger. Brief brawls spent themselves somewhere outside in the dark, behind the tankstand. Then the girls heard a voice shouting, 'Where did those two girls go? Somebody go and find the girls. Tell them to come and join the party. . .'

'No thank *you!*' said Sadie briskly. Before Grace realised what was happening, she was on her feet and dragging a chest of drawers across the floor. 'Come on, Miss Playford, give us a hand!' Between them they heaved the weighty chest in front of the door, barricading themselves in.

'Stupid shearers!' Her tones were scathing. 'In the morning they'll be sorry for themselves, and all apologies. Don't worry, miss. The bar closes at eleven o'clock and then the boss will send them on their way. They won't bother us now.'

The lamp was out, but Grace sat up in bed by the light of a candle, book open in her lap and, surprisingly, a pen in her hand. The other girl rolled over and peered curiously from under her blanket.

'What're you doing, miss?'

'Just underlining some Bible words I want to remember. I'll blow out the candle in a moment.'

She underscored the words thickly. It wasn't possible to make her usual fine, straight line, but she was sure God wouldn't mind. The words were from Psalms 4 and 5. 'Lead me, O Lord, in thy righteousness because of mine enemies. . .' and she added a line under the marginal note which described 'mine enemies' as 'those which observe me'. Another thick line marked the words, 'I will both lay me down in peace and sleep; for thou, Lord, only makest me dwell in safety.'

In the margin she wrote 'Coonong, 4/9/97' and then blew out the candle.

*　　*　　*

This is the day of the district ploughing match. From all over the area, families have come for the day of carnival, a high day of the year.

A young man grips the reins in strong hands. The team of Clydesdales pulling his plough is experienced and obedient; they have been with him round many paddocks and he trusts them to know their work. The horses move steadily across the ground, the steel of the coulter slicing into the soil before the plough foot, red-brown earth turning away from the mouldboard, leaving behind them a trail of furrows, even and very straight. He watches the line of furrows, guiding his horses up to the fence, sharp turn back, return along the first lines, his hand ready on the governor lever to adjust the width of the furrows if they threaten to be crooked.

Today there is no time to let his mind wander to the question of his own selection. His father has been urging him to start work on his own land. 'You'll be wanting to marry one day, son, and you'll need a place of your own,' Father said. But today is not the day to think about selection, or marriage. Today there is the roar of voices behind him urging him on.

'Keep it going there, I'm wagering my new bowler hat on you!' yells a friend.

As he turns again, he sees again the line of tents set up for afternoon tea under the trees, the side shows, the crowds of neighbours in their spring clothes, fine riding horses, girls poised sidesaddle, empty sulkies waiting with down-tilted shafts to take home the families. There is no time to look; he doesn't want his mate to lose his hat because he took his mind off the job. Further across the paddock other men are ploughing, and soon judges will walk across the uneven ground to inspect the work, looking for the best mark-out, those first critical straight lines between the marker pegs, the neatest crown on the ridged furrows, the neatest finish with the most workmanlike completed section.

His section is complete. His father congratulates him on a job well done, and his mates take him off for a drink.

'No use taking this bloke to the publican's tent,' they tease. 'Let him have his cup of tea!' They know that his close friend and uncle has recently had to be taken away to a hospital for the mentally deranged as a result of years of drinking, and they wouldn't be so tactless as to force their mate to drink.

The President of the ploughing match announces the next competition. They have already had the horse-jumping, the harness-racing and most of the ploughing events. 'There is a prize for the largest family and now — look smart, men — three young ladies are the judges in the "Best Looking Competitor Competition". Are you ready, men?'

His mates jostle each other, tugging hats over eyes, straightening ties. They have all come to the ploughing match dressed in their best suits and hats. Chests thrust out, swaggering gait, the young men parade themselves jauntily before the giggling girls who are advancing through the crowd carrying the blue prize ribbon. The young ploughman shrinks in embarrassment. A covey of his girl cousins and his sister surround him, certain that he is the finest young man present. The three pretty judges descend on a handsome young giant from another part of the district, drape the ribbon round his neck and present him with victory kisses. The ploughman turns away in great relief. It is not that he objects to girls, not at all. But he feels shy and awkward with girls beyond his own family.

'You might not be the best looking lad,' his father says, 'but you've just won four pounds and two pigs for the three-furrow plough section!'

*   *   *

Grace spent her twenty-second birthday at Coonong.

It was the first time she had been separated from her parents and family at the time of a birthday, and the day seemed very strange indeed. That morning at the school she had very nearly said to the children, 'Today is my birthday', but it had seemed too silly and she had stopped herself.

After the children had gone home from school that afternoon, Grace stayed on in the quietness of the schoolroom, writing another sentimental poem to add to 'Gleanings'. It suited her mood. She lay the pen back in its groove and leaned her chin on her hands. There was a smudge of chalk dust on her cheek and her hair was beginning to escape from its hairpins, but she didn't care. She was remembering that last year the whole family was there for her birthday. Now she was alone.

It was getting late when Grace finally locked the door of the school, planted her hat squarely on her head and set off for the hotel. There seemed no point in hurrying. No-one would be waiting there for her with birthday hugs and a cake ready as a celebration. Though things had been quieter since the shearers left, every weekend was still a wilderness. The hotel food still verged on the poisonous, and she was very sick of boiled eggs.

A flock of newly-shorn sheep, pathetic and unprotected without their fleece, ran beside her along the fence. The ancient words of the shepherd Psalmist came into her mind: 'The Lord is my shepherd, I shall not want. He maketh me to lie down in green pastures... He leadeth me in the paths of righteousness for his name's sake. Yea, though I walk through the valley of the shadow of death, I will fear no evil, for thou art with me... Surely goodness and mercy shall follow me all the days of my life; and I will dwell in the house of the Lord forever.'

She walked on, comforted. As she walked through the door of the hotel, the voice of the host called her from the bar. 'Some letters for you in the dining room.' Snatching the precious bundle up, Grace hurried into her room to read them. Then it was that she read her mother's letter, and saw a picture in her mind of a mother hen, feathers fluffed up hugely, rushing to the defence of her chick.

Mother wrote, 'When I learned from your letters that the Department had sent a girl to a place where there was no proper arrangements for board, I decided that it was not acceptable at all. So I went in to the Education Department and demanded to see someone in charge of appointments. You should be having a transfer to another school any time now...'

Grace almost shouted with a laugh of relief. Dear Mother! So it was that Grace Playford received a transfer to another country school, boarding with the family of a German bullock driver, and a year later she found herself in still another part of the Riverina. This time she was to board with the family of a settler near the little bush school at Gwynne, a few miles out of Old Junee.

*   *   *

The axe handle is smooth and a little greasy with sweat. He grips it firmly and attacks yet another tree, sending chips flying as he circles it, hacking a deep ring around its bark. The tree stands tall above him, curves of gum leaves shuddering with every blow. Today the tree breathes fragrant life, but as the circling wound is axed, its dying begins.

The young man works on. Somewhere behind him is a fence separating this stretch of thick scrub from the ploughed and sown acres of The Hill. On The Hill the wheat is ripening, but here on his new selection there is nothing but scrub, native bush that has been there always. Once, this land belonged to the Aborigines, and for many years it had been part of a vast cattle and later a sheep station where stock roamed across the wide plains without the barrier of a fence. Over the past few years, the Aborigines have rarely been seen. Now it is his, these acres of pine and grey box, eucalypt and wattle, thistles and nettles, paddy melon and tiny grass flowers. He leans on his axe and tilts back his wide hat, thoughtfully scratching the back of his head.

'What sort of a fool am I?' he says aloud. There is no-one to answer. His dog pricks up his ears but makes no remark.

'Just look around you, dog. What do I think I'm doing? Father's worked nearly twenty years on The Hill but he's had the Swann uncles to help, and me, and now it's looking a good place. But it is still hard. If the cockatoos don't eat the seed, the kangaroos will knock down the grown wheat; what the rabbits leave, the grasshoppers will finish off; if a drought doesn't get you, a bushfire will.'

He spits on his roughened hands and picks up the axe again. Around him the section of ringbarked trees is expanding. Further back, a small stand of dead trees wait, skeletal, dessicated, waiting for the man to pull them down with chains and horses and pile them into monster bonfires. The forest surrounds him, defying his efforts as long as it can. But the bearded young man with the axe sees open acres, golden in the sun with ripened wheat, dotted with sheep, bush alternating with fallow paddocks. He sees an orchard and vines. He sees a house.

The axe rings, biting wood, and the work goes on.

*   *   *

At last it was Friday afternoon again. The sun had been burning down on the corrugated iron school roof all day and the children were drowsy and lethargic. It was too hot for playing many of the usual Friday afternoon games, so Grace took them out under the shade of the peppercorn tree and read them a story until it was time for them to go home.

Around the little school the paddocks of Gwynne were spread. Harvest had begun, and in the distance she could see the movement of horses across a crop as one of the local farmers guided the harvester through his wheat. The little school stood alone among the paddocks, there being no village store, railway line or church at Gwynne.

'Miss Playford, how many weeks now to our Christmas concert?'

'Only one week left now. Do you know your poem properly yet? Next week we must practise all our songs and poems, and the tableau, and pin up all your best work – because your parents will all be coming to see you. It's going to be a beautiful concert – just wait and see!'

She smiled at the children around her. She was growing very fond of them. School was, for many of them, the one window open to them on the rest of the world. These farmers' children would have no other opportunity to learn to read, write a good hand, build skills in arithmetic, learn songs and poetry, discover the wonder of maps and books. There was pride in their careful pages of fine handwriting, in books ornamented with illustrations copied from the drawings their teacher had drawn on the blackboard, in detailed maps studded with names of places they perhaps would never see. She stood up under the peppertree and closed the book she had been reading to the children.

'Everybody stand, please.' There was a shuffle as children stood, brushed off grass seeds and came to attention. 'Good afternoon, boys and girls.'

'Good afternoon, Miss Playford.'

Children scattered, gathering school bags, retrieving boots discarded on the verandah. Some began a long walk home, while others mounted two and three together on the family pony. Grace set off for the Butler home where she boarded, riding neatly sidesaddle on a fine horse name Jack that Harry had chosen for her.

She was in no hurry to get back to the house. The farmer and his family were very kind and friendly, but Grace cherished a little time by herself. In a strange way, she found herself in this setting almost never alone and yet always alone. All day long she was with others; the child who shared her room, the farmer's family, the children at school. Some of the farmer's children were her pupils, so they were together at breakfast, together over their school dictation, together at the end of the day. Even on Sundays, when she liked to ride the eight miles down to the crossroads at Old Junee where a tiny church stood, her pupils would say cheerfully, 'Hello, Miss Playford.'

Never alone, and yet always alone. In the family home, she was a welcome guest, but not truly a member of the family. At school, she was 'the teacher', the only one, the one who must always stand apart from the pupils. In the community, she was the odd one out – 'that girl from the city' – with the implication that she would be incompetent and ignorant of the realities of country life. In the church, she was the sole single person in a congregation of families. Riding along the shaded side of the road, she leaned forward to stroke the neck of her horse. 'Only a few weeks, Jack,' she murmured, 'then I'm going home for Christmas!'

The two girls lifted the hems of their skirts just enough to clear the gutter and stepped out across George Street in brilliant sunshine. It was Christmas week 1898 and Sydney was vibrant with colour and crowds. Passing horses pulling cabs and coaches seemed to have an extra lift in their step, and cable trams lumbered cheerfully along city streets, gathering and scattering passengers in rainbows of summer dress. Sober-suited gentlemen with bowler hats marched briskly into banks and business offices, while mothers with families of holiday children moved in droves through the streets and arcades, overburdened with parcels. Somewhere at the end of George Street lay the harbour, glittering blue and gold, and on all sides were the treasure troves of tall buildings, arcades, market barrows and tiny shops tempting with their wares.

In front of Grace and Gertie as they crossed the road loomed the Town Hall, splendid with its ornate stone carvings and clock tower looking down on the summer multitudes at its feet. The new Queen Victoria Markets stood astride an entire city block, copper dome gleaming, statuary and stained glass expressing the ebullience of the age. The girls stared with open mouths.

'What are the shops like in Gwynne? Like this?' Gertie was teasing. She had spent the past two years teaching in small country communities, and was as enthralled as Grace by her return to the city.

'You know perfectly well there aren't any shops in Gwynne. Let's go in and look!'

The girls walked through the wide entrance and gazed around them. Before them stretched a vista of wide colonnaded space, parquetry pavement and spiralling staircases, and curving balconies high overhead. The sun streamed through the rich colours of leadlighting in the windows and skylights, rows of elegant gaslights were suspended and opulent carvings and stonemasonry embellished the grand interior.

'After Coonong and Gwynne, this belongs to another world. What a pity we're not extremely rich!'

They plunged into the melee of shoppers, two young schoolteachers from the country returning to their native place. After their time away in remote settlements, everything looked grander and more exuberant than it had ever done.

'Where is the rusty corrugated iron?' Gertie giggled. 'I can't see any mud bricks, or adzed timber with bits of bark still on. Come on, Grace!'

Among the people they went, moving happily between stalls heaped with summer grapes and glistening cherries, peaches and apricots, plums, pomegranates and pale green figs. Buckets of fresh flowers scented the air, pinks and purple-blues of hydrangea, bells of fuschia, daisies, and pink-tipped Christmas bush. The girls stooped over cages of puppies, poodles, cockatoos and paraqueets.

'I don't need to buy birds!' Grace turned away. 'Out at Gwynne the parrots and galahs fly in their hundreds. The farmers would think I was quite mad if I went back there with a parrot in a cage!'

They pored over the stalls of brightly coloured fabrics, fingering silk scarves and coveting lace-fronted blouses and feathered hats. They hunted through arcades and searched in bookshops and music stores.

'Just think — if we really were rich,' Gertie confided. 'Imagine what we'd be able to buy for our families!'

'Well, I don't think that's likely on teachers' salaries. And since Father lost his money and had to sell up, money has been very tight in our family. Poor old Father, still digging away on his abandoned goldmine. I do wish he'd come home to Sydney and stop hoping to find a fortune.'

As they walked through the streets of the city, rubbing shoulders with elegant ladies, sailors off island vessels, street vendors of boiled peas or gaudily dressed larrikins, the girls talked of their schools. The little bush schools seemed remote and of the stuff of fantasy as they passed down canyons of city thoroughfares. They talked of isolated buildings, the strain of teaching twenty or thirty children at five and six class levels all at once, the poverty of schoolbooks and equipment, of loneliness and homesickness.

'How long do you think we'll have to teach in very small schools?' Gertie wondered. 'Sometimes I miss home so much...'

Grace grasped her friend's hand tightly for a moment.

'Oh, so do I!'

The telegram arrived just days before Christmas. When Mary

Playford opened the door to a telegraph boy with a bicycle, she was afraid at first, but the telegram read, 'Home for Christmas arriving Christmas Eve', signed 'Playford'. The older woman returned to the kitchen, aromatic with Christmas baking, and said, 'At last he must be giving up. He had such high hopes of that mine, too.'

'Are you sure that he isn't just coming back to Sydney for Christmas?' Grace suggested. The lid was off the jar of spicy fruit mince, wafting fragrance into the kitchen as she spooned the dark mixture into delicate cups of pale raw pastry.

'No, I think not. In his last letter he sounded really discouraged. Another disappointment. . .' Her voice trailed away.

Mother and daughter worked on in silence, cutting pastry lids and crimping the fluted edges of the mince pies before they were slid into the oven. Another piece of wood was added to the glow in the firebox of the stove. Rows of pale buttery shortbread lay cooling and the mother covered any signs of emotion under the steady clatter of the whisk, beating eggs for another cake. It was hard to talk about Father. He had always worked so hard at all his enterprises, had always been such an honest man, had always made such fine plans. Yet he had suffered so many disappointments in business. It didn't seem fair. Grace had never heard her mother utter a word of criticism of Father, yet it must have often been difficult for her, too, when new projects had not lived up to expectations, when the family had moved house so often, when Mother had had to relinquish treasured objects from her home. Even now, Mother was living in someone else's home, sharing a house with Robert and his Fanny and their children. The kitchen in which they were working was not really Mother's kitchen; it was Fanny's.

'Well,' said the mother at length, 'I must say that I'll be very glad to have Father home again. And our young Will, too. I've been missing you all while you've all been off in the country.'

William Playford and young Will appeared as expected on Christmas Eve, travel-worn and grimy.

'Mother, sit down. We have some news.'

Grace watched her Father's face for a clue, but the only hint was the dancing of Will's eyes.

'Family, we must all praise God. Will and I have struck gold!'

11
The colour of gold
1898-1899

'BUT WE ALL THOUGHT. . .'

'Gold!'

The family was awe-struck. Mary Playford was overcome: she had never put much faith in the idea of finding gold at Cullinga. Grace flung her arms around Will in delight. Not only was the whole family home for Christmas, with Sarah's family and all, but now gold!

'Tell us – what happened? We thought you were ready to give up.'

'We always thought that there ought to be gold in that area,' Father said. 'There was so much about the rocks and soil of that place that reminded us all of Ballarat, and my friends Ingold and Boxsell had found traces of gold at different times. But never enough to be really sure.'

For two years father and son had worked. In the darkness under the surface they had burrowed along a tunnel, sturdy father hacking into the rockface with his pick while son dragged loads of rock and soil up and out into daylight. They had worked long hours, growing pale from lack of sunshine, the earth staining their skin with its chocolate tones. Muscles ached from long hours of stooping in shallow tunnels, ears became attuned to listening for the whispering of timber props which would give warning if the tunnel became unsafe. In the dark, each man saw the roughness of the rock face in the wavering light of the lamp on his hat, and watched the looming shadows of himself and his partner cast up around the roof of the shaft. They watched eagerly for a line of gold-bearing quartz running along the shaft wall, like a yellow-cream filling in a vast cake of rock, smooth and a little lumpy against the rougher texture of other stone, yet it eluded them. For month after month they had

211

swung their picks, gouging their way along, toiling without success in the claustrophobic gloom.

'In the end,' the older man explained, 'I said to young Will here, ''Son, if we haven't done any good by Christmas, I think we should give it away. Two years is enough. You'd do better finding a job somewhere, or getting an apprenticeship. And I'll just have to accept that the goldmine idea has been a failure.'''

Christmas was approaching. Several promising leads had petered out and the pair grew more and more dejected. In the paddocks above them, Boxsell was harvesting, and Ingold in the town of Cootamundra was working at his business. They had each supported the search with confidence, but even they were beginning to think that perhaps they had been badly mistaken.

Father and son paused to rest one day. Out on the surface was the fruit of their labours, heaps of crushed rock, a grey slag heap, a dam of water for washing — and scarcely a hint of gold. William Playford squatted silently, his head resting against his pick handle. He felt old and tired, aching in every joint. He pictured himself going home to Mary and admitting that another business venture had not worked out as he'd hoped. 'Failed — again,' he thought.

Will leaned against the wall of the shaft, idly scratching patterns in the clay surface with the point of his pick.

'Father — why don't we strike out through this wall behind us, instead of going straight ahead?'

'Lad, that makes no sense. You know it doesn't. That wall is pure clay — gold doesn't lie in clay like that.'

'But Father, what if beyond it. . .?'

There was silence. The older man said, 'Let's pray about it.'

They bowed their heads. William had prayed about everything that had ever affected him: his family, his work, his future. He had never seen prayer as a magical formula which produced instant prosperity, but as deeply personal conversation with his heavenly Father through every phase of his life.

'Lord,' he prayed. 'We don't know what to do next. Perhaps we should leave goldmining and try some other kind of work. We don't know. Please Lord, can you give us a sign? Can you show us whether you want us to stay here, please? We really want to do the thing that will please you.'

He paused, searching his own conscience. Then he added, 'Lord, it isn't that I want to be a rich man. That's the truth. But I would so much like to be able to repay those men who lost money when my business failed. Please, dear Lord, guide us now.'

Together they said, 'Amen.'

'Right, son, let's put our backs into it.' And William raised his pick and struck deeply into the clay wall. Together they swung, alternating the rise and fall of pick, dragging earth aside. Shadows swooped and quivered round them as they drove into yielding clay. Then a pick head shuddered to a stop. It had struck rock. Behind the veneer of clay they found solid rock, layers of rock spread one over the other through thousands of years. Flowing through the layers was marbled the creamy yellow of gold-bearing quartz. Staring at the vein of rock, the two men recognised the signs of the presence of gold. Overwhelmed, they attacked the rockface with new energy, tearing chunks away to be carried to the surface for crushing and washing. The gold was there, they knew it! Beads of sweat rolled down William's head as he strained over his work, salty sweat running into his eyes and mingling with the tears that threatened him.

The story was told on Christmas Eve. The rush of questions was answered. The gold was there, a seam of gold running strongly. Already they had taken a payable quantity to the bank, though only Boxsell and Ingold knew yet what was going on. After Christmas they would return to the diggings, and who knew what fortune might be waiting for them under Boxsell's lucerne paddock?

When the mine was formally registered, William Playford called it 'Christmas Gift'.

Grace and Gertie stopped at an open-air coffee stall in the city, tempted by the aroma and the wisps of smoke rising from the chimney above the bed of charcoal. All through the school holidays they had done things together; shopped for school things, sung with the church choir, been part of the great crowds singing gloriously in the flowery pillared splendour of the Centenary Hall at the annual Wesleyan conference. Gertie shyly showed Grace her newest poems and they talked about the questions they each had about their futures. They had been buying serviceable fabric to stitch into dresses for school, neither very confident that they'd be able to produce the beautifully tailored garments of women's magazines.

'When we marry very rich men, we'll pay a dressmaker. . .' On the occasions when they said, 'When we marry. . .', it was always said flippantly, with a laugh. Neither girl saw marriage as something which might really happen in the near future. Grace's sailor was a dear friend, but she didn't take him very seriously.

'When we were at the Centenary Hall, with all the crowds and that wonderful preaching,' Grace said, 'I felt that I could be strong enough to do anything at all that God called me to. Maybe he wants me to be a missionary – they need single women, and teachers can be useful. Mother has always passed on her interest in missionary work. Or maybe I could be a deaconess. It's when I'm by myself at Gwynne that I wonder whether God is calling me to anything at all...'

'You'd be an excellent deaconess!' Gertie enthused.

'It would be nice to know for sure what God had in mind for us, wouldn't it?'

Near the end of the school holidays, Grace went with her mother to visit the gold mine at Cullinga. They travelled by train to Cootamundra then on through pleasant rolling hills to the mine. The men proudly showed Grace and her mother the mine shaft, the towering crusher, the grey slag heaps and their tents. Father had begun to build a solid house among the trees, and already some other men had come to work with him.

'Come and look at something,' Will said, beckoning Grace out into the warm evening.

Moonlight lit the paddocks, silvering the gum branches over their heads. The looming shadows of the crusher crisscrossed against the high-starred sky and moonlight reflected a gleam from the surface of the dam. Grace followed Will down the slope from the house to a corrugated iron outhouse where tools were kept. He pushed open a door and drew her inside. The little hurricane lantern shed its small circle of light over picks and shovels, buckets, mysterious metallic shapes. Will quietly bent over a kerosene tin bucket of cold grey ashes. His hand stirred the ash, sifting the floating substance, seeking something beneath the surface.

'In there.' His voice was barely audible. 'Ready for tomorrow.'

Before the ash settled again, she saw the fibres of a sugarbag, brown and hairy, submerged under the floating greyness. Will dusted the ash back across the surface, turned to the door and led her back through the stillness of the summer evening to the house.

Later, sitting with Father and Mother around the table, the Bible still lying open from their family prayers, the hidden sugarbag was mentioned.

'Will showed you where we've put it, did he?' Father said and then shrugged. 'I don't really think anyone will come to steal it.

Most people don't think we are doing much good with the mine, so they don't expect there is anything here to steal. But you never know.'

'Is there much gold there?' Grace found it hard to believe that here in this quiet country place there could be anything like a fortune in gold.

Will's grin was very broad. 'There's enough. Since Christmas, the rock we've been crushing has been producing very nicely. Tomorrow Father will know what his gold dust is worth.'

In the morning, Grace watched her mother hoist herself up into the sulky beside Father. She wore her neatest dark dress and her dignified matron's bonnet. Mother had never been a small woman, and now her solid bulk in its yards of heavy fabric spread formidably across the sulky seat. Father sat beside her, grey beard neat and big hat hiding the shine of his bald head. They looked a picture of respectability, an aging couple off to town to do their shopping, or perhaps to attend a prayer meeting.

'Are you ready, Father?'

William nodded. His tall son disappeared into a toolshed and returned, dusting ashes off a sugarbag. Will lifted the bag, Mother raised her feet from the sulky floor for a moment and the sugarbag disappeared under the heavy folds of skirt which enveloped not only her politely hidden feet but also the bag on the floor.

'Are you quite sure you don't want to take the gun, Father?'

'We don't need a gun. If God has given us this Christmas gift, I don't think he'll let any highway robbers hold us up on the road to Cootamundra. And anyway, what robber would be brave enough to find our sugarbag today?'

Grace and Will watched the sulky roll off through the trees on the solitary ride to town. Mother had been laughing, but as they set off she wiped the smile from her broad features and replaced it with a look of steel, her indomitable spirit ready to face anyone foolhardy enough to threaten her.

When the sulky returned that night, and William and Mary Playford told of their day in town and the visit to the bank, their children learned that gold dust to the value of one thousand five hundred pounds had been carried to town that morning in a sugarbag.

Riding to school at Gwynne at the beginning of the school term, Grace felt that both the thrill of the gold find and the excitement of her holiday in Sydney had evaporated very suddenly indeed. The nearest thing to gold was the spread of pale, glittering stubble paddocks and the only colour was an arc of pink and grey galahs. Only yesterday she had been with her own family, and excited about the possibilities of the goldmine, Harry's wedding and Sarah's new baby. Now the world around seemed empty and she rode on alone.

In her mind's eye she saw herself and Gertie happily shopping in the vast expanses of David Jones and Anthony Hordern's spreading floor space, tempted by objects for sale. Yet now, gazing across open country, the world of the huge emporium vanished. Only the new books and pictures in her bag across the saddle convinced her that such a world still existed.

She tried to sing as she rode along, but the songs that came to her lips were songs sung at the Centenary Hall, her solitary voice small in the limitless spaciousness of the sky and the wide paddocks. The deep resonance of hundreds of young voices in the Hall was only a memory, only some of the words remaining: 'He will keep us, he will guide us. . . And if our ways be far asunder, Still doth our Lord watch between'.

When she opened the school door, the small room was sun-warmed and stuffy, the scents of last term's chalk and homemade ink still on the enclosed air. Long narrow desks stood in their rows, scarred with the use of years, inkwells unnaturally clean and innocent of ink. She walked slowly in, feeling the silence already peopled with the children soon to come: lanky youths longing to be free of schooling and out with father on the farm, big girls nearly ready to be women, naughty children who would send her home exhausted at the end of the day, delightful children whose minds were opening up to discover everything she could bring them. Today there would be one or two new tiny ones, clinging to big brothers or sisters as they entered into the strange unknown of school. She drew a deep breath and put her bag on the teacher's desk. A parcel of things had come from the Department and she opened it. There were new slates and a whole box of new white chalk, long unbroken sticks of it. As she drew out a fresh piece of chalk and laid it on the ledge of the blackboard easel, she found herself smiling. Lonely or not, still a 'visitor' from the city or not, she suddenly knew that she loved to teach.

When the first of the children came clattering into the schoolyard, they found their young teacher standing in the sunlit classroom at the blackboard, preparing their first work for the term in her smooth handwriting.

'Hullo, Miss Playford!'

'Come in! Come and tell me about your holidays till the rest of the children get here.'

*   *   *

Furrows roll back from the cutting edges of the plough, running straight and true across the paddock. The horses know what they are doing and the man behind the plough works with only part of his mind on the work.

To be asked to preach at services! Him, a farmer's son with only lessons in the bush school to count as his education. He thinks of some of the preachers who come to lead services in the Berry Jerry Union Church on Jennings' property; men of education, clergy of the Anglican, Methodist and Presbyterian churches. Yet other country men have taken responsibility for local services, and with so many country congregations scattered so very widely, and so few clergy, isolated groups of Christians need their help.

Yes, he agrees with the need for lay preachers and he greatly loves the times of worship with his neighbours. But – to be asked to be a preacher himself! He speaks to the horses as they reach the corner and swing back for another march along the paddock, then lets his thoughts return to Mr Pennington's request.

'We certainly need more men in the pulpits,' the minister had said. 'And you are a great reader and a thinking man. Most importantly, I know that you really love the Lord, and that always makes up for any inadequacies you may feel about preaching. People won't mind if you can't give them the original Greek of the New Testament reading, but they will expect to hear God's Word from soneone who believes that God is still speaking to us now.'

'Well, *that* is true enough. But...'

He is not quite able to say to Mr Pennington, 'The thought of standing there in the pulpit, with people waiting to hear God's word, and only me to offer it, frightens me! What if I fail them?'

He stares down the paddock between the heads of the horses, but he is not seeing the red ridges of his father's land, or the scrub beyond with its tangle of partly cleared land which will one day be his own farm. He is praying for strength, but feeling weakness. In his room at home is the slip of paper neatly ruled up for the next three months with the Methodist preaching plan. As well as the name of the Rev. H. Pennington and the names of the other lay preachers, at the bottom of the list under the label 'Helper' is his own name. Three times he must travel to other country places and lead the people in worship.

As the young man with the long brown beard follows his team through the cooling afternoon of early autumn, he is both scared and excited. Perhaps God is opening some new doors for him.

*   *   *

As she slid down from her sidesaddle that Sunday afternoon, Grace saw an unfamiliar pony tied to the church fence. The little weatherboard church stood on the corner where it had been a focal point for the community for twenty years, since the days when the Lord and Storey and Robertson families had helped to build a place of worship. Grace tied Jack under a tree and walked to join the people who were gathering outside. Women smiled and greeted her, folding back the dark gossamer veils which had protected them from dust as they drove to church. Families from the farms for many miles around were beginning to move in through the tiny front porch. Men were nodding to their neighbours and looking forward to a good yarn after church. Young people were happy to be with friends and sweethearts and small children were filing into their family pews prepared to sit through church for the fun of playing with their friends afterwards. Over the months, Grace had met them all and been welcomed. They were all friends and, in some cases, relations, and there was a sense of family and belonging between them. There was no sign of a stranger.

Edging into a pew, Grace knew that once again she was the only 'outsider' among them. As she closed her eyes for prayer, feeling the congregation around her, she could almost imagine herself back in the dark timber of the pews at The Boulevarde, or the stained glass of Ashfield, or even, but with more difficulty, the soaring space of Centenary Hall in York Street.

'Lord, I know you are here with us. You know how much I miss being in church with my friends in Sydney,' she prayed. A thought struck her, and she suddenly felt contrite. 'Lord, could it be that I've loved to go to church because of my friends? And not from a pure wish to worship you? Forgive me! Help me to want to be here just because you are here. Please show me what you want me to learn today...'

Slowly her eyes opened. The floor beneath her feet was still the scrubbed bare boards of pine, and the pews were simple. A woman sat at the small organ, playing quiet music while they waited for the preacher to enter. Grace felt a sense of peace, of waiting.

Footsteps sounded at the open door behind them and a stranger strode the short distance up the aisle into the pulpit.

'Let us pray,' he said in a deep voice. Grace bowed her head again and joined in the prayer of invocation. It was only after the prayer was over and they had stood for the first hymn that she looked at the preacher.

The first thing that she noticed were his hands. They were the hands of a working man, large and strong and scarred with nameless marks of whatever his work might be. The hands held the hymnbook firmly, even tightly, and she noticed then that his eyes were fixed unswervingly on the pages of the book, as if, as if. . .

'That poor man is nervous!' The thought sprang into her mind clearly. Perhaps he was not used to preaching. Perhaps he was one of the settlers from the backblocks somewhere, or a small store owner in the growing township of Junee Junction, or perhaps a workman from the railway. Perhaps books and preaching were something far outside his normal world, and the minister had been forced to ask for his help because of all the preaching places in the wide district. Poor chap, she thought. How awful to have to stand up before strangers and speak publicly like that.

The hymn ended and the service moved on to the reading of scriptures and more prayers. The man with the long brown beard dragged his eyes from his notes and his books to look directly at the congregation for the sermon. As he began to speak, Grace heard a slight quiver in his voice, but it soon strengthened till he was speaking with more confidence. The young teacher felt a certain sympathy; she pictured him at home somewhere, perhaps in a bark hut or a rough place of wattle and daub, sitting in the lamplight laboriously writing out his sermon notes while his wife hushed the little ones so that he would not be disturbed. The words he was saying were thoughtful and he was obviously very sincere in his faith.

'Quite a good sermon really,' thought Grace, just a touch patronisingly; she was more used to hearing the fluent messages of the presidents of Conference, other senior ministers or prominent laymen.

The final hymn was sung and the people moved out to enjoy the pleasure of being together. Introductions were made as people shook hands at the door with the preacher.

'Miss Playford, this is Mr Jim Higman from North Berry Jerry, west from here. Miss Playford is the teacher at Gwynne.'

'How do you do?' A large rough hand enveloped her small one briefly and she moved outside to speak to the friendly women of Old Junee.

Riding home later that afternoon, Grace decided that after all God had not shown her anything new for her life. She felt a little disappointed.

It was Thursday, mail day and, as she passed the kerosene tin mailbox on the top of the gatepost, Grace pulled out the mail from under a rock. Three times a week she looked there hopefully on her way home from school, and today she found several things for herself. As she rode to the house she skimmed the pile – something from Mother, a church magazine, a letter from one of the girls she had taught in Sunday School – and a letter with a foreign stamp.

'Mail for you, Mrs Butler.'

'Any for you, Miss Playford? Oh, you've got yours. Do you want a cup of tea with me in the kitchen while you read them, dear? The kettle's just on the boil.'

'A cup of tea would be lovely, thank you.' She hesitated, then said, 'I'll just take off my hat and wash my hands first.'

Grace opened the door into the small bedroom she shared with a little daughter of the family. It was not often that she had complete privacy. The letters she slipped into the pocket of her big protective apron before she rejoined Mrs Butler at the kitchen table. 'I'll read them later,' she thought.

Grace was aware of the letters as she sat there. The kitchen was pleasantly warm and smelled of fresh ironing, stove blacking and scones. Her landlady was looking rather tired; with a large family and a boarder, she worked very long hours every day. As she put down her cup, Mrs Butler said, 'Well, I'd better go down and help the boys with the milking. Come on, little one, you can help me feed the chickens.' Watching her go, Grace realised how demanding was the life of a farmer's wife.

Grace walked away from the buildings, past the chicken run and the pigsty, past the house paddock and the stables. When she was hidden on the far side of a clump of wattles, she found a fallen tree to sit on and pulled the letters from her pocket. The foreign stamp she left to one side and began with the others.

Mother's letter was exciting. 'Father and Will have been doing very well indeed. You'd never guess how much they took in to Cootamundra last month — nine thousand pounds! More miners are coming to work at the mine and it is turning into quite a little village. You would hardly recognise it since Christmas. They have a little store and a post office already and, now he's finished our house, Father is building a small school house and the Department will send a teacher next year. Some people say that Cullinga could prove to be another Mount Morgan, a really big goldfield. It is quite astonishing. . .'

It was only putting off the last letter, she knew, but she slipped the cover from the little Methodist paper with 'Glad Tidings' across the top. She turned the pages, pretending to read, and paused at a poem entitled 'The Missionary Call' by the famous missionary Hudson Taylor. His words, she saw, were some of the questions that had been tugging at the edges of her mind for a long time.

Why live I here? The vows of God are on me,
And I may not stop to play with shadows
Or pluck earthly flowers till my work have done
And rendered up account.
And I will go! I may no longer doubt
To give up friends and idle hopes
And every tie that binds my heart
To thee my country.

With slow fingers she folded the magazine and picked up the last letter. Grace was angry with herself when she found her heart bumping.

'He's only a friend. It isn't important,' she muttered fiercely to herself. It was only Mother who used to sometimes call him 'Grace's young man' in tones that hinted at family expectations. Will and Harry called him 'Grace's sailor' and teased her. It was months since she had seen him, or even had a letter, and when he wrote it was always with a careless lightheartedness that promised nothing. It disturbed her to find herself disturbed. He was just an old friend.

She slit the letter open. He wrote from a distant port in Asia, unimaginable to a schoolteacher sitting on a hollow log in the middle of New South Wales. He wrote of funny events, of life on board ship, of bartering with Orientals for exotic curios — 'I'll bring you something from here when I come back to Sydney.' There seemed no point of contact; he had no understanding, and perhaps little interest, in her life in the country. What had been a happy friendship seemed a very slight thing now. 'I should be in Sydney at the end of the year when you'll be on holidays. Perhaps we can have dinner together?'

Thrusting the letters back into her pocket, Grace stood and walked restlessly round the dead tree. Her feet kicked up fallen twigs and twists of bark. Grass seeds caught in the folds of her skirt as she paced and she pulled them out without thinking. The letters had thrown many questions into sharp relief. What did God plan for her life? Was she to be a schoolteacher, travelling from one little country community to another all her life, growing into a brisk little spinster, always slightly outside the community where she taught? Would Father become a wealthy man, against all expectation, and might she return to Sydney to live in luxury in a lovely new house without having to earn her own living at all? Should she take seriously the challenge which kept coming to her in a number of forms to offer her teaching skills and her life in missionary service in some far-off place? And what about 'Grace's sailor'?

As she walked back towards the crowded loneliness of the farmhouse, she prayed a silent prayer. 'Lord, please show me the way you want me to go!'

The knock on the school door startled her. Once she and the children were safely inside with a fire burning to warm the cold winter morning, the door was closed and no-one expected parent or neighbour to intrude. The children looked up, surprised, as their teacher went to open the door. A tall man stood on the step, wide hat in hand, and at first she didn't recognise him.

'Miss Playford, good morning. We met at Old Junee last month at church. Jim Higman. Would you mind if I had a drink of water from your school tank, please?'

Now she knew who it was: the tall, bearded lay preacher.

'Of course, that's all right – there's a mug on the tank stand.'

He backed away down the steps and moved towards the tank. 'Thanks very much. I'm just on my way home after preaching at Junee Junction last night. Just a bit thirsty – thank you . . .' He seemed polite but a little confused. She stood at the door for a moment watching as he filled the tin mug and drank, gave a little wave, mounted his pony and rode off.

With a puzzled look on her face she shut the door behind him and went back to the intricacies of third class subtraction sums. That was odd, she thought. Most men carry a waterbag, and almost no-one ever calls at this school. A child struggling with the Fourth Reader soon commanded her full attention and she forgot the incident.

On a winter evening, Grace sat toasting her toes at the fire of new friends the Penningtons, the Methodist minister and his wife at Junee Junction. Lamplight and firelight glowed and flickered and she nestled into the cushioned chair, relaxing in the comfort of the good company and mutual understanding. The talk had ranged through books and poetry, favourite music, gardens and theology. The young teacher and the young couple had discovered many shared interests and common friendships from their backgrounds in Sydney and Grace loved to accept their invitations for weekend visits. The conversation turned to the difficulties of finding enough lay preachers for the six preaching places in the circuit which spread to Coolamon in the west, all many miles from each other.

Henry Pennington stirred the fire with the long fireirons and remarked, 'I think Jim Higman is going to be a help. He takes preaching very seriously and his Christian faith is very real to him. I've loaned him some of my theology books and last time I saw him he told me that he was ordering a new Bible commentary for himself.'

Mrs Pennington added, 'Such a nice young man, too. A bit solemn sometimes, but he has some unexpected flashes of dry humour. They say that he is a very hard worker. A very eligible chap for some girl, I expect.'

Grace leaned back in the cushions and said nothing. She had almost said, 'But I thought he was a married man . . . !' She felt her face flushing red. More than once now he had preached at Old Junee and she had supposed that his intent gaze had been equally distributed among all the worshippers. She had ignored his visit to Gwynne school. Even when Mrs Storey, whose house was just over the road from Old Junee church, had invited the preacher and the teacher both home for a cup of tea after church, and the lay preacher had sat quietly watching her, she had paid no attention. The awful thought struck her that perhaps she was to be troubled by the completely unwanted attentions of a single man from the bush. 'I have enough questions to answer about my future without that!' she thought.

For her birthday, Gertie sent her a birthday book to record the birthdays of friends and family. Gertie had ornamented the flyleaf with her name in elegant script, decorated with scrolls and flowers. 'I think I'll use it to write down something good about each day to cheer myself up,' Grace decided. There had been times over recent months when she had been feeling very low and discouraged. Too often she found herself suffering from bad headaches at school, from the stress of work and from recurring neuralgia.

The countryside around was in the grip of drought after several very dry years and sometimes she felt that the parched paddocks and dying stock was a picture of the dryness she often felt in her spirit. In her Bible she underlined a verse in Psalm 63: 'O God, thou art my God, early will I seek thee: my soul thirsteth for thee. . . in a dry and thirsty land where no water is. . .'

The birthday book was renamed the 'Book of Blessings' and day by day she noted one small thing. Sometimes it was Mother's letter, or a visit from one of the women from the church, or 'freedom from headache' or even 'Jack' − simple things. It was in the Book of Blessings that she noted in October, 'Visit to Berry Jerry'. When she spent another happy weekend with them in Junee, Penningtons had said, 'Why don't you come with us on Wednesday when we go out to Berry Jerry for a church meeting? We could pick you up straight after school, stay overnight with one of the Berry Jerry families then get you back in time for school on Thursday morning. You'd enjoy it − and we'd love your company!'

It was only after she had agreed to go that they added, 'We'll be staying with the Higman family.'

Sitting in the high buggy with Henry Pennington and his wife, riding through the blue and gold of a spring afternoon, Grace travelled with slightly mixed feelings. Even though Mr and Mrs Pennington had assured her that Mr and Mrs Richard Higman were fine people, and had a daughter her own age, she felt a little awkward about meeting their son again.

'I'm probably making the whole thing up,' she said firmly to herself. 'I'll just enjoy a good outing.'

The buggy spun down hills and pulled slowly up rises to offer successive vistas of a back road and country she had not seen before. The soil was deep rust-red, richly coloured and very unlike the paler earth of Sydney. Belts of native timber, grey-olive and olive-green, were lightened by an occasional late flowering wattle and fences edged struggling crops of wheat and oats. The sky hung widely blue and cloudless and the fragrance of spring floated around them. As they travelled west, the country flattened into gentler undulations and when they reached a farm gate at the foot of a slight rise, it seemed appropriate for the gate to bear the notice 'The Hill'.

On top of the rise, standing a little above the surrounding countryside, stood a solid house sheltering under encircling verandahs. Grace sat stiffly in the buggy as they drove up, a little apprehensive. The front door opened and a girl hurried out, followed by an older woman. A retinue of dogs dashed up and barked around the buggy wheels, but there was no sign of any young man.

'Welcome! It's lovely to see you – come in!' The women drew them warmly into the home.

'Mrs Higman, I'd like to introduce Miss Grace Playford who has come out with us for the meeting,' said Mr Pennington. 'Grace, this is Miss Evelyn Higman.'

'Come and take off your hat and coat in my room,' said Evelyn, and Grace followed her around the wide verandah lined with ferns and cactus. Along the verandah edge, poppies and sweetpeas sheltered within a high fence of wire netting from wandering sheep, cows and rabbits. Evelyn's room was dainty and feminine, bright with modern wallpaper, ornaments and plants. Grace unpinned her hat in front of the mirror over the carved mantelpiece and in its reflection saw Evelyn watching her. She had an uneasy feeling that she was being assessed.

Laying the hat on the bed, Grace tidied her hair at the mirror, trying to discipline the tiny curls that always wanted to escape into a greater softness than she allowed herself. Out of the corner of her eye she was watching the other girl in the mirror. The two faces were oddly alike. The features were different and Evelyn was taller and darker than Grace, but the two girls were very close in age, both girls having smooth brown hair piled in high topknots, each with a high lace collar on her spring dress, each wearing round spectacles on her nose.

'We could be sisters!' thought Grace, startled.

The other face in the mirror suddenly smiled and said, 'Come and look around the place before it's dark. We'll be having tea early, as soon as the men come in.'

In the dusk, the girls walked around the house. From the vantage point of the rise where the house stood, the country lay in the last glow of the setting sun. The last of the spring blossom coloured the trees in the orchard and the girl talked enthusiastically about the fruit trees and vines her father and brother had planted and how hard it was to keep them alive through the drought. They strolled past granite boulders to the fence around the house dam, a burnished sheet of water reflecting the sunset sky shrinking within its banks until the rain would come at last. Evelyn pointed out the rows of spring vegetables in the house garden, all safely enclosed inside rabbitproof fencing. As they walked around, Grace caught herself watching for another figure among the farm buildings, and thought she saw men bringing in horses beyond the trees.

'Are you interested in things like the cowbails or the blacksmith's shop?' Evelyn asked.

'Not really! My father and brothers have had a dairy farm over a number of years, but I'm not really so keen about cows or metalwork myself. But tell me – how long has your family been out here? I somehow wasn't expecting. . .' She didn't explain what she had been expecting; it would have been ill-mannered to say to this self-possessed and gracious young woman that she had expected to find a bush family in a rough hut, scratching a living as settlers, not a fine new timber house pleasantly furnished.

'Oh, we've been here just twenty years now. I was only little when we left Albury and can't remember much. But Jim was eight, and he says he'll never forget the long journey sitting up on the back of the wagon among the furniture and chicken coops! Some of our uncles came here before us. It was all virgin bush, too; terribly hard work. I can just remember the tent, at first, and then our first kitchen. That's still used of course.'

As they walked back to the house, Evelyn added, 'Jim is beginning all over again, on his own selection, just like Father did. He wants to do it, but it is going to be years before it is anything like The Hill.'

Inside the living room the atmosphere was comfortable and warm, the table laid ready for the evening meal. A fire burned in the grate and the lamps were being lit. The scent of stocks and sweetpeas mingled with woodsmoke and the rich aroma of baking meat from the kitchen. Tantalising on their bookshelves waited rows of books – classics, poetry, theology and farmers' manuals. A well-thumbed Bible lay apart, bookmarks dangling, just as a Bible might be found in the Playford household. An organ stood open with familiar music propped on the music stand.

'Who is the organist in the family?' Grace asked.

'Mostly me. But Jim can play a bit. We both learned when we were young.'

There was a tread of men's footsteps along the verandah and an interval while they went to wash and prepare for their meal. Grace had begun to relax and feel at home with Evelyn and was listening with interest to the conversation of the older woman and the Penningtons. She found herself strongly reminded of her own home, also a house where the minister was a natural and frequent visitor, and felt The Hill was a little like an oasis for her in a desert land. 'I wish they didn't have a son – it would be much nicer that way,' she thought privately.

Two tall and bearded men entered, father and son. The younger man smiled widely at her but had little to say. After everyone was seated and a blessing had been said, Grace addressed herself to her dinner, conscious as she ate of a man's eyes watching her. As the table conversation flowed around her, she found herself continuing to revise her original estimate of what life would be like for a settler living out as far as Berry Jerry, miles from the railway and hundreds of miles from Sydney.

'. . . Mother will stay in Melbourne later in the year when I take Evelyn with me to visit our relatives in England. Jim will have to stay on the farm, of course. . .'

'. . . our brother John Swann's prizes for his best bushel of white wheat at Wagga and Sydney and now a huge cup from the Chicago Exhibition for his wheat. . .'

'. . . in touch with the scientist Mr Farrer who is experimenting with drought-resistant seed – we are offering to try out some of his new wheat varieties for him. . .'

Listening, she realised that it was a much wider world than she had imagined. Even so, she hoped very much that she was mistaken about Jim. He seemed a good enough young man, but she certainly did not want him interested in her.

Next morning, riding back to Gwynne, Grace sat silently beside Mrs Pennington. Her companions chatted amiably to each other, reviewing the business of the meeting on the previous evening, the good attendance of local people of Berry Jerry, the kindness and friendship of Richard and Caroline Higman. Grace said nothing. Last night had been a mixture of real pleasure, with the homelike atmosphere and the gentleness of Mrs Higman and Evelyn, and the uneasiness as she had tried to avoid the gaze of Jim. She had been forced to admit that she had gone to their home with a false and preconceived idea of what she would find. She had been wrong. But even so, she didn't want to follow any further the path which was being hinted at by the tall young man. He had helped her up into the buggie that morning, had said, 'I hope you'll visit us again one day,' and had offered her the loan of books of poetry she had admired. As the buggy had run down the slope from The Hill, he had stood watching till they were out of sight.

Thoughts of young men, be they sailors or settlers, left her completely during the weeks of October as soon as she received notice that Mr Lawford, the School Inspector from Wagga, was coming to inspect her and the school at Gwynne on 24 October 1899. Her horse stood patiently waiting till late every afternoon after school while she worked to prepare everything as well as she could. The school rolls and records were checked, maps drawn, children's books marked, ranks of spelling and multiplication tables displayed across the blackboard in her most careful writing. Desks were scrubbed and flannel penwipers washed and replaced around the china inkwells. The children chanted over and over their patriotic poems of Queen and country, and sang their little songs until Grace felt that the tunes were burned forever into her brain.

On the morning of the great man's coming, Grace and the children were scrubbed and polished to a high sheen. Even the boys had been persuaded to wear the boots which they preferred to discard, and some of the girls had honoured the occasion by torturing their hair into fat curls like very long sausages, with curling rags. Grace looked at the twenty-six children with pride. She had done the best she could.

They heard the hooves of the Inspector's horse well before he pulled into the schoolyard, and when he came to the school door they were all sitting up in their desks in frozen innocence. As Grace invited him inside, every child jumped to attention ready to chorus 'Good Morning, Mr Lawford'. The gentleman seemed to fill the whole schoolroom with his presence, and see every page, hear every hesitant reader, staring stonily while she taught and drew and sang. Then, after the children had gone home in the afternoon, she faced her own examination. When at last the Inspector drove away, Grace was exhausted and certain she had failed.

A few days later a large official brown envelope waited in the kerosene tin under the stone. She tore it open and found a document headed 'Certificate of Classification'. Quickly Grace read the words under her own name.

'Grace Playford had passed an examination in the subjects hereunder, and has been placed in Class 111, Section A, subject to the Inspector's reports upon her schoolwork being of a favourable character.'

Tucked in the envelope waited another paper, Mr Lawford's report of satisfactory work at Gwynne. She rode up to the house singing.

The year, and the nineteenth century, began to move quickly towards an end. A letter came from a distant sailor announcing that he had enlisted to go to the Boer War and was sailing soon; and from Sarah and her children, promising picnics and happy reunions. Father drove all the way from Cootamundra to Gwynne to collect her for a happy weekend with her parents and Will. And at school the big children studied for their final examinations.

Father was making plans like a boy with a secret, excited, revealing fragments of his idea. 'Before the end of the century. . .' he began. 'We'll all be in Sydney before Christmas and that's when I'll do it. The Christmas Gift has been a gift indeed!'

The last traces of jacaranda purple-blue lay on Sydney footpaths under the greening trees when the Playford family arrived in Sydney. Grace was absorbed into the warmth of family life, with Legh and Florrie, Robert and Fanny, Harry and his bride Minnie, Sarah with Louis and four little ones visiting from Wollongong, and Will full of enthusiasm for all that was happening. Her parents looked vigorous and cheerful, her father's financial worries behind him. Father returned from the tailor with a fine new suit, and Mother spent hours at the dressmaker's, being fitted for new clothes.

'I don't need many new things for Cullinga,' she explained to her daughters, almost in apology. 'But Father wants me to have something good for his special party.' She turned slowly in the new dress, displaying the sleeves edged with braid, elaborate buttons and scalloped edging on the bodice, generous volume of gathers encasing her ample person.

'You look very dignified, Mother,' they encouraged. 'Father will be proud of you.'

The horse cabs stopped outside the Loong Shan Tea House in King Street, Sydney, and the Playford family alighted. Sons and daughters with their families gathered on the footpath, all in their best clothes and waiting to be ushered in by their parents. Grace knew very well that this was no small thing for her father. She had never forgotten the despair on his face that day years ago when he had watched people come to buy his furniture and almost everything he owned at the sale. She had said then, 'Father, this sale will raise some money to pay back your creditors *something*, and you can't do more than that. You are only one of hundreds of men in the same trouble – try not to be too discouraged.' But his face had been bleak, uncomforted, and she knew that the thought of men who had lost money because of his business failure continued to haunt him. It made no difference to explain yet again that legally he owed no man. He didn't forget, and had even kept detailed records of everything he had once owed.

William Playford stood at the door of the restaurant, erect and dignified. The earth-stained miner from Cullinga had become a prosperous Sydney citizen. He had chosen carefully, and the special banquet tonight was at one of the most sophisticated restaurants in Sydney, one of several owned by the well-known society gentleman, Chinese merchant Quong Tart.

'Are we all ready? Then let's go in.'

The family moved in under carved and ornamented wooden panels, Chinese characters embellished with carved flowers and gold painted peacocks. Grace stared around her at the unfamiliar elegance. Overhead soared the balconies of two upper floors, with stairs leading up to private rooms for chess and writing, and the ladies' reading and retiring rooms for country ladies. They followed a uniformed waiter across the floor of the main dining hall, threading their way past ferneries and grottos, playing fountains and pools of goldfish to the tables prepared with a banquet. Grace caught Sarah's eye and almost giggled. The luxury and sophistication was so unlike the normal simplicity of home.

William Playford drew the attendant to one side and Grace heard him murmur, 'Have you followed my instructions?'

'Certainly, sir, just as you asked. Everything, including. . .' and he bent his head to speak inaudibly into William's ear.

William looked across the tables. There were fine damask cloths with elaborately folded linen napkins, silver epergne heaped with the bloom of peach and grapes, tall candles lit and delicate porcelain vivid with hand-painted parrots, butterflies and flowers. He nodded in satisfaction.

Other guests began to arrive. As the beautifully dressed people made their way through the ferns and fountains, waiters ushered them to their places at the tables. Grace recognised some but not all of them. They appeared to be people who had been linked with her father through business connections at the time of his financial failure. She took her place near her sister and waited.

The hum of conversation was silenced as her father stood to speak.

'Before we ask a blessing on our meal and the staff brings in the first course, there is something I want to say.' He paused, looking around at the faces of men and women who had been hurt by his business failure, people he had always felt he had cheated. 'Nearly six years ago you lost money because of me. I regretted that bitterly, but there was nothing I could do. Since then I've been through some deep waters – no business, no funds, no job. I tried goldmining and for two years that was useless. But now God has blessed me. It wasn't something that I deserved, but that is the graciousness of God who gives good gifts whether we deserve them or not. The Lord led us to gold. Now I'm able to do what I've wanted to do for six years, to pay you back everything I owed.'

With the flourish of a conjurer performing magic, William Playford commanded, 'Please, look under your plate before the waiters pour the soup!'

As each guest lifted the plate of fragile Chinese porcelain, each one discovered an envelope with their name. In each was the sum of money William Playford had once owed, with interest. He cut across the sudden response of astonished voices and a smattering of applause, his strong voice tinged with emotion.

'Let's sing the doxology for our table grace!'

As Grace stood with the others, the voices joined in the words of praise: 'Praise God from whom all blessings flow, Praise him, all creatures here below. . .' and she found her eyes were full of tears.

12
A land chosen
1900-1905

THE FAMILY STANDS ON THE railway platform, surrounded by
luggage. Caroline Higman is still trying to explain household details
– her last minute anxieties – to her son.

'I'll manage, Mother, don't worry about me,' Jim assures her. 'You
go and have a good holiday. If I can't stand my own cooking, I've
plenty of cousins to rescue me!'

The train is coming and there is a flurry of hugs and handshakes.
Then at last they are all on board, Mother off to Melbourne for
several months and Father and Evelyn on their way to join their ship
to travel to England. Evelyn waves goodbye with delight, Mother
is weeping a little and Father is still giving instructions about the
farm as the whistle blows.

The last thing Jim hears as the train pulls out is Father shouting,
'Don't forget to grease the buggy, son!'

At last they are gone. Jim drives home to the empty house at The
Hill. All around him the paddocks are green with grass growing
high and thick, weeds growing into monsters of their kind, young
crops looking better than they've done for years. At last the rain
has come; good rain at the right time, coming with a new year and
a new century, a fresh beginning. Jim wishes he had the funds to
buy more sheep – last year with the long drought they were
worthless and now, with plenty of feed, the price has soared.
Thinking about farm decisions to be made, he knows that he's going
to enjoy being 'boss cockie' for some months. Then there is his own
new place as well.

The weeks pass. It is winter, 1900, and Jim is building a house
for himself on his own selection. The building of the chimney was
his first attempt at stonemasonry and bricklaying and he is pleased

with it. For the walls he has dug narrow trenches and rammed upright pine poles into them, edge to edge. The house is to be wattle and daub. He works to combine earth with water from the dam; a stiff red-brown mixture of mud clay which he spreads thickly over the posts, covering, filling, smoothing till he has solid walls.

Jim rubs mud from his hands and stands back to admire his work. Sooner or later one of his mates is going to turn up to look at how he's going. He imagines the raised eyebrows: 'What do you want with all those rooms? A single bloke like you!'

He works on, working long hours to get the iron on the roof. After four years of drought, they've been getting good rains but, unprotected, rain will soften his new walls back into mud. It is going to be a good house, with wide verandahs, standing in its cleared space enclosed by rabbitproof wire to give a little safety for vines and vegetables from the rabbit plague which is continuing to drive farmers to despair. He dreams of fruit trees, grape vines, shade trees.

Back at the empty house at The Hill that evening, Jim reads his newspaper and finishes a letter to his natural brother Will Caldwell who is in America with an invention he has made. The newspaper has items on the Australian soldiers fighting in the Boer War in South Africa, on the Boxer rebellion in China and the excitement over the forthcoming first federal parliament of Australian states. Jim has just received a formal invitation to go to Melbourne as a representative of his district to see the Duke of York open parliament. It sounds interesting, but he considers all the work on the farm and thinks that perhaps he'll be too busy.

He is still thinking of his new house as he writes to his brother. He has been daydreaming as he worked, dreaming of a small and dainty girl, a young schoolteacher with a special quality to her. Jim knows that his girl cousins have often said, 'When you marry, Jim, you must choose a good country girl — you'll need someone strong who knows about cows and poultry to help with your new selection.' He doesn't find himself caring overmuch whether the young schoolteacher is good at milking cows.

Jim writes, 'I am building myself a house of wattle and daub about ten chains behind the old hut. Married, did you say? No. Not yet. People think that I am going to be, so they say. I wish I thought so. I'm willing enough.'

*   *   *

The notice of transfer came to Grace early in 1901. She was to move to the country town of Young. It was a time of changes for her and her family. Only Legh remained in Sydney now, with Harry and Robert leaving wives and babies in Sydney while they went off on a journey of exploration on the north coast of New South Wales to buy a dairy farm – the one in Ashfield was being overtaken by city growth. Sarah was with Louis and the four children on the south coast, Will was away studying at the Ballarat School of Mining in Victoria and her parents were at the mine at Cullinga. Dear old grandfather Rootes was gone, of course – he'd died in 1898, a very old man. Even the Penningtons were moving from Junee to another district, and Grace's ties with Gwynne were happy, but never meant to be permanent.

On her last Sunday at the little church at Old Junee, the district people wished her well. They had been good friends. The Butler children hovered around, sad that their friend Miss Playford was leaving. Behind the people she saw another face, a sometime visitor to Old Junee, the face of the young man who seemed to be attacked by thirst whenever he was passing the school tank at Gwynne on his way home from weekend preaching. As other families began to move away, Jim Higman followed her to her horse.

'Do you mind if I ride back with you as far as Butlers?'

She flushed. His presence embarrassed her and she was sure that every departing family was watching, digging each other in the ribs and chuckling. It was impossible, she knew, but she felt that all the neighbours knew that once he had asked her, awkwardly and without success, to marry him.

'I suppose. . . are you sure it's not out of your way?'

'I'd be riding that way, anyway,' he said.

She mounted, spread her skirts across the side-saddle and nudged Jack with her heel. Jim followed. They rode in silence much of the time. He told her his family news, how his father and Evelyn were home from their visit to relatives in Plymouth in England, how his mother hadn't been well, and how one of his natural Caldwell sisters had come to work for a Swann uncle and had married a cousin.

'I was asked to go to Sydney in February,' he said shyly, 'by our church. They asked me to represent Junee circuit at the Wesleyan Methodist Conference.'

Grace looked at him with new respect. She had been to enough of the public meetings of the annual conference to know that it was no light thing to be chosen as a delegate. The men who represented their circuits met with the key church leaders of New South Wales and carried the heavy responsibility of decision-making for the whole church. She watched him from the corner of her eye as they rode side by side. It was not lack of respect which made her shy of him, she decided: their minister admired him, his district selected him for important church work, his community had put forward his name for an invitation to the opening of federal parliament, he was always full of enthusiasm and ideas for developing his land and his district, he was clearly intelligent and well-read. But that didn't mean she felt close to him, or that she was obliged to wish their slight friendship would grow stronger.

'Tell me about Conference!' Conference was a good general topic of conversation and might keep him off anything personal till they reached Butler's gate. 'When I lived in Sydney, I used to love to go to the public meetings – the singing and the preaching and the whole atmosphere was marvellous. I miss that in the country.'

'It was the last of the Wesleyan Methodist conferences – you know all about the plans for union, don't you?'

'Of course.' For years she had heard her minister the Rev. Carruthers and the Rev. Rutledge and others talking often about the long-drawn-out efforts to bring together the fragments of what had begun as the Methodist Church which grew out of the ministry of John Wesley. The New South Wales Wesleyan Conference of 1900 had finally decided to move to organic union – most other states had already decided to do so.

'In a way, it was sad,' Jim said. 'Older men were sad to see the "Wesleyan" name go, and found it hard to think that things will be different from now on. But there was a lot of excitement and hope that this union will be to the glory of God. Some churches have been experiencing revival recently and now are eager to share with others the new things that God is doing. Straight after the meetings that I was at, they were having a united conference in Sydney to make plans to formalise the union.'

He laughed. 'At the end of the last Wesleyan Conference, they lined us all up on the steps outside the Centenary Hall for a photo. I was only one of the lads, so I was up the back, with all the greybeards and church fathers at the front. I'm not used to that sort of thing!'

They rode on and he asked her about Young and her plans. Grace sensed that now was the moment when he was going to want to say more personal things, and she had a sudden urge to escape. Answering briefly about her time of departure, she said suddenly

'Let's have a race!' and urged Jack forward, leaving Jim and his pony behind in their dust.

It wasn't fair, of course. Jack was so much faster and Grace was so much lighter. Jim's pony was not nearly the quality of Harry's Jack and when Grace pulled up at the Butler's gate, Jim was well behind. He came up laughing, but Grace was quickly repentant when she saw the hurt look in his eyes. She knew that she was glad to be moving to Young because, among other things, she was relieved that she would no longer need to respond to Jim Higman, one way or the other.

'May I write to you?' He looked anxious. She hesitated. She had thought this would be a tidy end to his interest in her.

'Oh. Well, if you really want to write, I suppose so. But,' and she added a hasty caution, scared that he might think she was even a little eager, 'please don't write more than once a month. At the most, that is. And please don't think I mean to be rude, but I'd rather not promise to answer if you write.'

Grace felt confused, hot with embarrassment and awkwardness. Why couldn't the man see that she didn't want him to follow her with his letters?

The young farmer nodded and raised his hat to her.

'Goodbye, Miss Playford.'

She saw his backward glance, but could not read his mind. She had no way of knowing that, as he rode home, Jim Higman was thinking, 'Grace Playford is the one woman I've ever met who I want to marry. It probably isn't possible – she doesn't seem to think much of me – but I'm not going to give up till there is no hope left, even if it takes years.'

Grace had to admit that Jim Higman was doing just as she had asked. Only one letter a month appeared on the hall table at the home of the Starr family where she was boarding. But, as she picked up the latest thick envelope with her other mail, she thought, 'If these letters get any longer, he'll have to post them as a parcel!'

She carried her mail to her room, calling out as she went to the Starr girls that she would come out soon to join them for tennis. As she pulled off her hat, she glanced quickly at her other mail – Mother's regular letter and one from Harry. It was a long time since she had heard from her sailor friend. Last Christmas he had given her a vase as a gift with part of the Kipling poem, 'The Absentminded Beggar', printed on it – satirical verses about men leaving to fight in the Boer War who were remarkably 'absentminded' about the girls and wives they left behind them. She had taken the oblique message to heart and dismissed him from her mind.

Outside the bedroom window, she could see the other girls running around the family tennis court at speeds that she suspected her mother would find quite unladylike. Grace left her letters until later and went out to play with them.

Young, she found, was very different from Gwynne. In Young the school was a large, handsome brick structure with many classrooms and a tall square tower over the imposing front entrance. For several years she had taught alone, responsible for both tiny children and adolescents. In Young she was only one of a full staff under a headmaster. At Gwynne she had valued the Sunday services at Old Junee, but in Young they also had a lively Christian Endeavour Society, a Sunday School where she could teach, an organ she was invited to play, concerts and friends who prayed together regularly. The town of Young was prosperous, having grown out of a gold rush when it was known as Lambing Flat and now the streets were lined with columned courthouse and town hall, banks and offices, shops and churches. The railway linked the town with Sydney and the rest of New South Wales and the town was very proud of being the first community in New South Wales to have electricity lighting both private homes and streets, even before Sydney suburbs. One other thing about Young which Grace liked was that it was not so very far from Cootamundra and the mine at Cullinga.

It was much later before Grace was free to go back to read her mail. The letter from Harry was important in that it described the plans he and Robert had made for their future. They were home from their trip north, having covered hundreds of miles by horse and sulky. They had travelled far up the north coast searching for farms, even past Ballina, and had finally rented a good dairy farm at Springvale on the Richmond River near Lismore. Harry and Minnie with Robert and Fanny and the children would soon be on their way to settle there. Harry wrote vividly of the hazards of the month on the road — rough camps, a lame pony, poor roads, homesickness, but his main complaint was about flies, mosquitoes and fleas. One camp, he wrote, was 'a regular mosquito den. We pitched our tent and the Black Varmints pitched into us and we were battling the whole night!' Grace knew she was going to miss her brothers when they moved so far away; she loved them very much.

The letter from Jim Higman ran for page after page. She had tried to be discreet, only sending an occasional letter, and other months substituting a copy of a church paper or a postcard, but still the letters came. He shared his world and his mind, sending news of the district. He and his father were experimenting with the use of superphosphate, though their neighbours assured them it would be useless. It was another dry year, but Mr Farrer's experimental wheat, 'Federation', seemed to be going well, despite the dry. He wrote of books he was reading, quoting British and Australian poets who appealed, and his latest thoughts about God as he prepared to preach.

She pushed the letter back into the envelope while she stared blankly out of the window. He was making no demands, but they both remembered very vividly the day at Gwynne when he had asked her to marry him. She cringed to think of it – her embarrassment and awkwardness, the shock making her less gentle than she might have been, both of them stumbling in their words, she confused and agitated in her refusal, he distressed and miserable. He had pleaded, 'Can I still be your friend? It would help if I knew that you still thought of me as a friend.' 'We can be friends,' she'd said, but there was no promise of more. Then a few months before, he had appeared, unannounced, in Young for the weekend, coming to call on her formally. 'I just wanted you to know that I haven't changed my mind. If ever you feel that God wants me to be part of your future, then remember that I've loved you since the first day I saw you, sitting there in the little church at Old Junee. I always pray for you . . .'

Little by little, Jim Higman was invading her mind, building a friendship by slow and careful degrees, and she didn't know what to do about it.

Another year had passed when Grace sat with her red leather writing case open and began to write yet another letter. Her face felt stiff with dried-up tears. On the table beside her was a letter to Harry and a letter to the Education Department, both letters to redirect her life. With a sigh, she began a last letter to Jim Higman.

'I thought I should let you know,' she wrote, 'that I'm leaving Young very soon. So perhaps you will want to abandon our correspondence as I'll be so far away. I'm very sad to write that my dear brother Harry's wife Minnie has just died, leaving a two-year-old and a new baby. I've just written my resignation as a teacher and have written to tell Harry that I'm coming to Springvale to help him with the little girls and keep house for him. Thank you for your friendship. Goodbye.'

She blotted the letter and folded it carefully. Nothing was happening as she had imagined. She felt that God was asking her to go to Harry and that this was his place for her. Dreams about being a missionary or a deaconess had only been dreams, but this task was clear and real. Poor Harry — he and Minnie had only had three years together. Harry had always been the popular one, the one who could make other people laugh, but now he was alone and sad.

As she wrote the Berry Jerry address on the envelope, she was surprised to discover in herself a profound and unexpected sense of loss.

The little girls, Maude and Minnie, were delightful and demanding, as all tiny children can be. Harry was working very long hours on the dairy farm, up well before daylight and falling into bed wearily at night. The hard physical work seemed to help him live with his grief. Grace settled into the busy life at Springvale with the work of the home and children and often spent time with Robert's wife Fanny with her babies at the neighbouring cottage on the farm. Her own work was tiring and there was little to make the household work lighter.

Letters still came every month from Jim. Her brothers teased her. 'Grace, you mustn't encourage this poor bloke. Here's this country hayseed from the backblocks, not a wealthy squatter but a poor selector, hacking away at a living in the bush. You're a city girl, so this chap's not the right man for you! And the papers say that out that way they've had two of the driest years ever, and the selections are just turning into dust and rabbits, with this year's harvest a dead loss. Don't you think about it, Grace!'

'You haven't even met him.' She surprised herself to hear the tone of defiance in her voice, to realise that she was springing to Jim's defence. 'He may not be rich, but he and his father experimented with superphosphate last season and they are among the only farmers in their district to harvest a crop at all this year. And he's *not* a hayseed, he's an intelligent, good man.'

She turned her back on them, busy with saucepans on the stove, and missed the grin her brothers exchanged.

'And anyway,' she said, swinging around abruptly, 'who's a city girl now? Look at this farm, miles from anywhere — it looks like the bush to me!'

The months passed quietly. The little girls were growing, Harry was becoming more settled and the dairy was more established. The area around the Richmond River was very beautiful, hilly, well-watered, lush with subtropical timbers and bush. In her mind, Grace saw two contrasting landscapes, the multiplied greens and blues of the Richmond River and the browns, ochre, pale straw with a little olive-green of Berry Jerry. One seemed always moist, fresh, rainbowed waterfalls and flowing water courses. The other was remembered as dry, dusty, with spirals of red dust spinning across bare earth. And yet a half-remembered face of a bearded man kept on returning to her mind, a man whose friendship was growing more and more important to her.

Even when Jim's letters said nothing directly of his love, he sometimes copied out a poem for her, and often the theme was love. When the little girls and Harry had fallen asleep at night, Grace sat quietly to copy the poems, and others of her own choosing, into her 'Gleanings' exercise book. Turning the pages, she realised how often her choices of verses spoke of love or of questions about an unknown future. There was 'To love one maiden only, cleave to her, and worship her by years of noble deeds until he win her', and words of Shelley, Longfellow and lesser versemakers. Revealingly, she realised, she had copied the words of Elizabeth Barrett Browning:

> Methinks we do as fretful children do
> Leaning their faces on the window pane
> To sigh the glass dim with their own breath's stain,
> And shut the sky and landscape from their view.

She buried her face in her hands, pouring out her sense of unease and questioning in a painful prayer to God.

Sarah, Grace's older sister, died suddenly in 1903 just after giving birth to her fifth child. The baby Sadie survived. Four of Sarah's children – Grace, Stan, Alice and the new baby – were taken to live with their grandparents, William and Mary Playford, at Cullinga, and the other little girl Mary went to their father's sister, to be cared for till they would all be old enough to live again with their father.

After Sarah's funeral, Grace sat with her gathered family, feeling the pain. Harry's children and Sarah's children had lost their mothers and Grace felt a great swell of love for the little ones. Legh and Florrie were childless but loved the nieces and nephews, and Robert and Fanny had three little boys. Her father was not looking well, and her mother whispered to her that he was having to give up much of the heavy work at the mine, though he was still the mine manager with responsibility for the workmen. He was nearly seventy years old and the work was getting beyond him. Her brother Will had a girlfriend in Cootamundra now, and he had returned from his studies to take over the mine work from his father. Even though she was in the heart of her family, Grace had a sense of loneliness. There was no shortage of nieces and nephews for her to love and care for, and yet she longed for her own partner, her own home, her own children. The love which she had once rejected in haste had reached out to her over years of faithful, gentle, persistent letter-writing; the man she had once rejected had only been her imagined caricature of a selector in the bush, not the real Jim. The quality of the real man was now drawing a response. After the funeral gathering had parted, Grace underlined these words in her Bible: 'He setteth the solitary in families.'

Back in Springvale, struggling once again with primitive kitchen conditions and still shaken by the loss of Sarah and the thought of how little time her brother and sister had known for their marriages, Grace decided to send a little gift to Jim Higman instead of her usual brief postcard. With care she chose a small book, finely bound, and spent much time thinking about an inscription on the flyleaf. In the end, her inscription was restrained in the extreme. She wrote, 'J.R.C. Higman, from G.P. Easter Greetings 1904.'

When Jim unwrapped his parcel, he was close to tears with joy. The simple inscription was not a disappointment. The book was by Henry Drummond, 'The Greatest Thing in the World' and, as he read, he saw that it was a beautiful essay on what true love is.

It was very strange indeed being together again. Grace sat nervously in the sulky with little Minnie wriggling on her lap and Maude bouncing up and down on the seat between them, chattering without pause. The presence of the children was both a help and a hindrance; the little ones saved the need for conversation and formed a simple link, yet the little girls imposed their own restrictions on the adults. 'Take a picnic to the falls on Cooper's Creek,' Harry had urged, and now they were on their way.

With her arms full of small Minnie, Grace found herself too shy to turn and look squarely at the man beside her. She looked at his hands; large hands, strong hands scarred with hard work, determined hands holding the reins as they drove along the bush track to the river.

He had written asking if he could visit and, though her brothers and Fanny had raised their eyebrows and given each other significant looks behind her back, she had invited him to come. When he had first arrived, both she and Jim had been painfully shy. If it hadn't been for Harry's easy manner, welcoming and friendly, perhaps Jim would have turned round and caught the boat again! She herself had been barely able to hold out her hand to shake his and, all the way back to Springvale, each of them had been acutely aware of the physical presence of the other, so different from the distance and control of letter-writing.

Now Jim had been at Springvale for a week and the first awkwardness was wearing off, though Grace still felt scared of what was happening to her feelings. It was two years since they had seen each other, and the changes which had happened in her own heart and mind were mysteries which she was afraid to explore. All she was sure of was that if Jim Higman were to walk out of her life now, if she were never to receive another letter sharing his wide-ranging mind and deep spirituality, the hurt and loss would be extreme.

Jim pulled up the pony near the creek and lifted the children to the ground. He reached up and took Grace's hand in his own as she stepped down onto the grass. His fingers felt warm and rough and she clung to him for a few seconds. The picnic basket over Jim's arm and Grace holding the hands of the little girls, they walked together along the path by the creek. The water flowed past, washing over smooth stones, rippling like caramel silk. Along the water's edge, the green lace of ferns and bracken rested the eye and the little girls laughed at bright butterflies floating and bush flowers hidden among leaves.

'How far would you like to walk?' Jim asked.

'If we go a little further we'll come to the waterfall – Minyon Falls. It's pretty there.'

They spread a rug on the grass near the foot of the falls. Far over their heads a creek poured over a clifftop, spilling bright water in diamond-studded spray over the edge and far down into the river below. The sun struck through the sheer spray, painting a rainbow against the white. They ate their picnic lunch to the music of rushing water, leaning against cushions of bracken, fanned by fronds of maidenhair fern. The chatter of the little girls subsided at last and Minnie fell asleep with her head on Grace's lap while Maude lay on the grass absorbed in watching ants carry away the last crumbs of the picnic. At last the man and the woman were able to look at each other, face to face, and to see the love that was there.

The children broke in, at last, tired and irritable, complaining of a mosquito bite, hot and thirsty, wanting to go home to Daddy. Grace and Jim packed up the picnic things and folded the rug in a daze. They walked silently back to the sulky, following the little girls who skipped down the path ahead, and Grace discovered the comfort and security of being tucked under the arm of the tall man beside her. There was no need for more words just now. The words had been spoken, the pledge given. As she leaned against Jim's arm, feeling his warmth, Grace had a strong sense of the rightness of what was happening, the assurance that even if they had to wait some time for the next step, this was God's plan for them both. She had a frond of maidenhair fern tucked in the basket – 'I'll press that in my Bible, just as a memento!' she thought to herself.

Harry came in from the dairy that evening to find his sister in the kitchen with Jim's arm around her.

'Harry, we have something important to tell you,' Grace said. 'I've already said to Jim that I won't leave you to manage the girls alone till they are older, but Jim and I are engaged to be married.'

They had thought, Grace and Jim, that perhaps they would have to wait a long time till Harry's little girls were old enough for him to manage alone. However, Harry announced that he had met a woman whom he planned to marry very soon and so Grace did not need to feel bound to care for his children.

'We're really happy for you, Grace,' Harry said. 'I used to think that you'd be mad to marry some cockie farmer from that new land out there – everyone says it is pretty hard. But now I've met Jim, I like him. A bit solemn sometimes, but he came up here to Springvale on serious business. And if you're happy, we'll all support you.'

The two little girls clung to Grace for their goodbyes. Their young auntie had mothered them for nearly two years and they loved her. Robert's family had become very close to her as well and in many ways she was sad to leave the beautiful green land on the Richmond River. She travelled the long train journey from the far north coast of New South Wales to Cootamundra in the central west, joining her parents at the mine village at Cullinga. Again she was enveloped in family love, with her parents delighted to have her with them again for a time and Sarah's children thrilled to have their favourite Auntie Grace to themselves. 'Auntie Grace is better than Christmas!' said one of the nieces, as they looked forward to the games and songs, picnics and small adventures which Auntie Grace always seemed able to produce for their happiness.

Jim invited her to visit his home and family. Staying at The Hill, walking with Jim through the orchard, admiring their wheat crop and their flock of sheep, Grace confessed to Jim how very surprised she had been when she first visited The Hill.

'I thought I was going to find bark huts or corrugated iron houses with one room, and people who had never read a book in their lives! I thought it must be awful to have to live here always — and I know I didn't want to have much to do with you. You made me nervous.' Grace reached out to him and took his hand. The more time she spent with Jim, the more she was thankful to God for bringing them together. 'Now I'm finding that I love your family. Evelyn is becoming a special friend and is going to be my bridesmaid with my niece, Sarah's Grace, and your parents are so lovely to me. And do you know, I'm learning that this country around here is really very beautiful with its own special colouring.'

He took her to see the house he had built, the mud walls fresh with whitewash, the wide fireplace in the front room. They walked through the house hand in hand, shy of each other, dreaming their private dreams for the future.

'I've put one more poem in my book of "Gleanings",' she said. 'It's called "Together" and one little bit says: "We can toil on and hope and sing together, Because you love me dear, and I love you . . . Thou art God's richest blessing to me . . ."' and Jim held her close, still finding it hard to believe that at last his love was being returned in full measure.

She sat late one afternoon in her room at The Hill brushing her long hair. The uneven sound of Jim's mother's footsteps came along the verandah and the older woman tapped on the door.

'Come in!'

They sat side by side on the bed together. Caroline Higman was looking very frail; she had had a stroke some months earlier and since then her movements had been limited and her speech difficult. She sat wordlessly beside Grace smiling at her, touching gently the soft fluffy brown hair which fell around the young woman's shoulders, looking at the fine features, looking deeper into the spirit of this girl her son had chosen as his bride. Grace felt that the older woman was studying her, testing her.

At last Caroline Higman leaned forward and kissed her, patting her hand with her one good hand. As she carefully levered herself onto her feet and moved from the room, Grace heard Jim's voice. He had been waiting for her on the verandah.

'You like Grace, don't you, Mother?'

With an effort, Caroline Higman spoke firmly. 'I *love* Grace.'

In the months while Grace was preparing for her marriage, many things changed in the family. Caroline Higman died in July 1904. She had been ill for a long time. She was buried at the Berry Jerry Cemetery, one of only a handful of graves, and the people of the district flocked to the funeral. Neighbours and friends honoured her as a mother-figure to many over her twenty-five years in the district. Grace was sad she had not lived long enough to see her son married.

That year William Playford and his partners decided to sell out their shares in the goldmine. 'I'm too old for it — let young Will be the manager, but let some other man have the responsibility of owning it,' he said. 'There's more gold there, I'm sure, but let someone else have the worry of it.' Playford, Boxsell and Ingold sold the Christmas Gift Mine for 900 pounds, but by this time they had all made a considerable amount of money from the mine. William had not been as well as he used to be, and Mary worried about the heart pains he often suffered.

William chose not to sell all of his gold, but used some to be fashioned into things of beauty for his family. To Grace he gave the gold for her wedding ring and a beautiful pocket watch on a long chain made from Cullinga gold, the watch he had once hoped to give her for her coming-of-age. To his wife Mary he gave several brooches of gold. 'This one is special,' he said, when she opened the jewel box on the newest gift. A small twisted nugget, glowing as it had when first gouged from the rock by William long before, was set on two smooth gold bars with an engraved inscription. 'Do you remember, at Lydia's wedding, when I showed you this nugget? The inscription on this is where and when I found the nugget and the gold for the bars — and it's also a record of the years I've loved you!' On the bars bearing the nugget were the words 'Hill End 1860, Cullinga 1904'.

It was also in 1904 that Harry had another heartbreak. The lady he had hoped to marry died in an epidemic only months before their wedding. Before Grace had time to feel that she should cancel her wedding and go back to help Harry, Robert wrote to her. 'Fanny and I want to care for Harry and the little girls. You know what a wonderful mother Fanny is. We are all giving up this place here on the Richmond and moving further down the coast. We are buying a dairy farm at Nana Glen on the Orara River, inland from Coffs Harbour, and we're going to build a big house where we can all live together.'

For Grace and Jim, their wedding was planned for February 1905, after harvest. It was to take place at the little schoolroom William Playford had built for the children of the mining village and the Cootamundra minister, William McCallum, who had been the Playford's minister many years earlier in Granville, was to conduct the service.

January 1905 was bad bushfire weather. Day after day, fierce temperatures burned down on the countryside, drying grass and stubble to crisp tinder, ready for the torch. Hot winds gusted across the paddocks and when afternoon thunderstorms crackled and flashed, lightning strikes lit the match that set fires ablaze. From the house at Cullinga, Grace watched distant grey-black clouds of smoke on the horizon. It was too hot to sew, too oppressive to plan, too awesome to rest. News travelled through of great fires sweeping round Young and Gundagai, Wagga, Temora and Junee, and Grace feared that they would come nearer to Cootamundra and Berry Jerry. She pictured Jim's farm, his wheat harvest still to be carted to the railway, the house he had built for them – and was afraid.

It was almost as if their growing love for each other was something which might be thwarted, that circumstances were trying to conspire against their marriage. As she wrote out orders to Sydney bakeries for a wedding cake and special festive cakes, she prayed for protection. As she threaded finest baby ribbon through the edges of the deep lace fichu on her wedding gown, she prayed for Jim. Even her wedding gown was linked with him and his world: it was of palest cream in a very light, fine wool fabric and in the lace over the bodice she could see delicate ears of wheat in the design. It was a long way from the heat and dust of Jim harvesting, or the earthiness of Jim hunched over a sheep with his blades deep in the fleece, but somehow it made him feel closer. Her parents watched her anxiety, and day by day the family sat around the meal table, William and Mary Playford, Grace, Will and four young McDowell grandchildren, and William prayed for them all.

The bride paused for a moment in the doorway of her parents' house. The bridal veil fell before her face, transparent and delicate, shielding her in a thin cocoon of orange blossom and bridal flowers, lace and silk ribbons from the rest of the world. Through the veil she could see the village of Cullinga, dominated by the tower of the battery crusher and mounds of earth and rock, corrugated iron humpies, earth-floored huts of pitsawn timber or mud walls, the little post office and the store. Miners' children waited, fresh from washing their faces at tin dishes set on boards outside their huts, eager to see their first wedding. Across the grass stood the school hall where the children had lessons through the week and her mother taught Sunday School at the weekends. She and her mother had searched for flowers to decorate the hall, but the hot summer had shrivelled the last of them. Now the hall waited for the bride in the fragrance of gum branches, young leaves bronze-tipped and fresh green. Father had erected a large marquee for the wedding breakfast and she knew that all the special things ordered from Sydney and the home-baked foods were ready for guests.

Behind her, Evelyn Higman and thirteen-year-old Grace McDowell gathered up the back of her veil, held their own posies and followed her down the steps in their bridesmaid finery. Grace stepped carefully across the grass. Beyond the little community lay rolling hills, paddocks, mossy rocks, the shadows of sheep against dry grass. Far beyond that, miles distant, was Jim's farm, a world she barely knew, a community where she was unknown, far away from her own family. As she walked, her heart pounded so hard that it seemed that her bridesmaids would hear it. She knew she was afraid.

The door of the hall stood open, waiting for her. Children crowded on either side, open-mouthed. From the brightness of outdoors it was hard to see inside, but from the interior shadows Grace could see heads turned, smiling. Her hands were trembling. One of them slid up to the high lace collar of her gown and she touched the gold brooch she had pinned there. Her fingers felt the smoothness of the gold bar, the feel of filigree edging, the slight indentations where three tiny jewels were studded. She touched the catch which held closed the secret lid, and was satisfied. Ahead, standing among the showering cascades of gum leaves, stood Jim. This was the man she loved. This was the man who had given her the brooch with the secret lid; if she were to open it now she knew she would find his private message, 'I love thee', engraved inside. This was Jim who had waited for her faithfully for nearly seven years. This was her dearest friend who had said, 'Grace, I love you from the top of your head to the soles of your feet!'

With a deep sense of thankfulness and peace, Grace moved forward to stand beside Jim and echoed the words 'for better for worse, for richer for poorer, in sickness and in health, to love and to cherish till death do us part. . .'

Their honeymoon was in Sydney. After the first week or so of privacy and intimacy, Grace and Jim joined the crowds of Methodists streaming up York Street and between the pillars guarding the doors into the Centenary Church. Holding Jim's arm, Grace saw one after the other of her old friends coming to her with welcoming smiles as she proudly introduced the man beside her: 'This is my husband.'

For the new bride, the meetings of the New South Wales Methodist Jubilee Conference, meeting to celebrate fifty years of Methodism in Australia independent of British Methodism, brought together most elements of her life. It was as if a slice of the concentric rings of the tree of her life and growth had been exposed so that every year, every growth point was visible at once. On the official platform was Mr Carruthers, greeting her as a daughter. Among the lay people were those who had taught her in Sunday School, shared with her in church activities and been on committees of Christian Endeavour with her. There were ministers from Sydney whose preaching had influenced her over the years. Henry Pennington was there, one of the few who knew both herself and Jim – 'Surely I've had a little part in bringing you two together!' he said – and William McCallum who had so recently joined them in marriage in the little bush schoolroom. Her past and her future were clearly part of the one design.

Jim had come to Conference as an official delegate, representing Junee circuit, and for both of them it was a joy to sit together in the public meetings, the great missionary rally and the crowded meeting for youth. They knelt together at the Conference communion service and listened to the 'Conversation on the Work of God' when for three hours men took turns to share what God had been teaching them, spontaneous song breaking out among them and never a 'point of order' to be heard.

The days of honeymoon and holiday passed quickly. On some days, Jim was occupied with the weighty business of debate and decision-making in the Conference and on those days she joined her mother who had come to Sydney to help prepare for Will's wedding the same month. On one day all the ministers and laymen at the Conference were sent to the Crown Studios to have their photographs taken for the souvenir Jubilee Book, and Grace and Jim took their bridal garments into the studio for a wedding portrait. With the photographer giving instructions, Jim sat stiffly in a studio chair with Grace standing solemnly beside him, her small figure almost obscured by the floral bouquet the photographer had handed her, feeling very odd in her wedding dress after several happy weeks as a wife.

The music of 'Oh, for a thousand tongues to sing my great Redeemer's praise!' welled up around her. The richness of thousands of voices multiplied, resonant; a high-flying balloon of sound, lifted on the peal of organ, coloured by the orchestra, decorated by the treble descant and anchored by the men's deep tones, floating above the fluted pillars and flowered balconies of Sydney Town Hall. The hall was full for the Jubilee demonstration, with guests from other churches, a great choir and singing which brought tears to the eyes.

Grace couldn't sing. She mouthed the words, but her throat was full of tears and no sound came. From her place in the gallery, she gazed across the kaleidoscope of faces and feathered hats. Below among the Conference delegates, she could see Jim's dark hair and the heads of many of the men and women. Looking at each face, she knew how much she loved these people. Her eyes devoured the scene, storing it for the future; the scripture banners, the soaring organ pipes, the garlands of flowers, the people – the people. . .

Her chin had begun to tremble uncontrollably and she bit hard into her lip. When the people bowed for prayer, she took advantage of the privacy to mop her eyes, blow her nose and wipe her spectacles. She knew that Jim was down there, but she knew that she was saying goodbye to something which had been important to her, and the words repeated themselves in her mind, 'Never again – never again.' Soon Conference would be over, then there would be Will's wedding to his lovely lady from Cootamundra at Ashfield, and then she and Jim would leave Sydney for Coolamon.

Grace and Jim sat in the railway carriage with their luggage. The lights of Sydney glittered past as the train pulled away from the rail terminus at Redfern, jewels of house lights and street lights scattered against the dark geometry of triangles, circles and rectangles of suburbs, terraces, pubs, shops.

Jim stretched his long legs and watched the city flowing away behind them.

'It's good to be going home!'

Grace snuggled against his shoulder and smiled at him. 'It's good to be going with you,' she said.

But later, when the train ran on through dark countryside and Jim had fallen asleep in his corner, silent tears ran down her face, soaking into her high collar. One day, perhaps, she too would call it 'home'. But not yet. Tonight she was beginning a journey into exile.

13
Spring growth
1905-1914

THE GOLD FOB WATCH lay in the little pocket on her belt, suspended on its long gold chain, and she willed herself not to look at it yet. Already that afternoon she had pulled it out several times, snapped open the ornamented lid where her father had had her initials engraved, and looked at the time. The hands seemed to crawl with infinite slowness onto the next numeral on the watch face and the afternoon dragged on.

Once more she walked through the house. Everything was ready for Jim's evening meal, covered with a gauze throwover to keep off the flies. Her mornings were always busy; cooking Jim's hot midday dinner, washing, cleaning, butter making, baking. The house was immaculate, every drawer neat, everything dusted and swept. She had written letters daily, but she'd have to wait till Jim had time to drive to the Berry Jerry Post Office before she'd know if there were more letters to answer. She had milked the cow, separated the milk, fed the fowls, worked in the garden — and waited for Jim. This afternoon she had read, embroidered, thought, prayed, and always in a deep silence. Sometimes she talked to herself or talked to the cat, just for company.

Perhaps if she were to go back out into the garden and dig another flowerbed, the time would pass and the sun would start to go down and Jim would come home. She walked outside, past the strong timber and earth walls Jim had whitewashed, along the verandah, past the young peach and almond trees Jim had planted. All around the house ran a strong fence of rabbitproof wire, bedded deep under the earth and forming a rabbit-free haven for her garden and Jim's new grapevines. Somewhere, across the farm beyond the trees, Jim was sowing his wheat on the land he had wrested from the bush and he wouldn't be back till it was nearly dark.

On the hill in the distance she could see Evelyn's house, but she couldn't set out to visit Evelyn again so soon – she felt as if she was always going over to Evelyn's, or hoping Evelyn or Richard Higman would come to visit her. Miles away stood the little timber church at Berry Jerry. Every Sunday afternoon she loved to drive with Jim to the church, to worship with her new neighbours, but in between Sundays everyone was too far away and too busy to come calling on a lonely new bride. To the north of Jim's farm there were no neighbours at all, just the spread of Mimosa Station running for hundreds of acres.

'It's not that I don't love Jim,' she said aloud. The cat rubbed against her skirt and looked up at the sound of her voice. 'I *love* being Jim's wife. The better I get to know him the better I like him! But he's out all day long, and I can hardly run along beside the team. And with only two of us to look after, I seem to finish my own work too soon.'

Grace picked up the spade and began to dig over a new bed Jim had begun. Some young vegetables were already planted and there would not be much more time for growing, Jim said, before the winter frosts. She missed having children around. Ever since she was a fourteen-year-old, she had been in the classroom with lessons to prepare, her own studies for examinations, daily work with children in class and out. Even when she was with Harry at Springvale she had the daily care of two little ones, and recently at Cullinga there were Sarah's four. She had always been busy with church meetings. Now there was nothing. Everything was new and different now; a new family in Evelyn and Father Higman, new neighbours, a new house, a new relationship with a husband, a new church community and a new daily work. She was shocked at herself to think that perhaps she did not find the care of her husband quite enough to fill her days.

'It's the quietness – nobody to talk to, no children to cuddle through the day, just waiting all day for Jim to come home,' she said to the cat, who yawned widely and just stared at her.

She put away the spade and went to the front room. Her fine organ stood proudly there, and her music. For years she had thought about God's guidance for her life, trying to follow step by step where he wanted her to be. She believed that God had brought her and Jim together. Now, though she found it puzzling to have no way to reach out to others, no extra tasks and few relationships, she supposed that God knew better than she did what his plan was for her and Jim.

Grace opened a hymn book and began to play and sing, songs of hope and trust, and when Jim came up to the house as the sun was setting, he came in to the sound of singing.

One Saturday at the end of April, she and Jim drove to Junee in the sulky. Jim was to preach in Junee on Sunday morning and Old Junee on Sunday afternoon, and Grace looked forward to seeing old friends in Junee and hearing Jim preach again.

They were nearly at Junee when it happened. Perhaps it was the unfamiliar ring of metal under its hooves, or the dazzle of the sun off the railway lines, or perhaps the horse caught its shoe against a railway sleeper. Everything happened so quickly that they could never be sure what caused the horse to shy. All Grace knew was that at one moment she and Jim were happily talking and riding up over the railway line and the next the horse was rearing, forelegs flailing.

She screamed. The animal was fighting away from Jim's control, hooves smashing down, first splintering one shaft then the other. She saw in one long second the horse towering over them, the sulky tipping, the weight of the rear hooves crashing onto the front of the sulky, then she was thrown violently onto the ground.

Jim held her closely, terrified that something dreadful had happened to his beloved. She leaned on him, clinging, letting herself sob in the safety of his arms. The horse was tied to a fence, panting, while they comforted each other.

'My dearest, are you hurt? If anything has happened to you . . .'

Carefully she checked the damage. She felt bruised and shaken, bleeding where arms and shoulders had struck the ground, but nothing seemed to be broken. Jim was distressed but unhurt, appalled at what might have been.

In the end, after the mended sulky had carried them home behind a chastened horse, her bruises had faded and the broken skin had healed, the accident opened new doors for her. An account of it was written in the new local paper, *The Coolamon Echo* and, for weeks after, little messages of sympathy and kind gifts of food came from neighbours she had barely met, sent through the post office.

When, on a beautiful autumn day in May, the farmers and their families from the surrounding district gathered for the annual Empire Day picnic at the Berry Jerry cricket ground, the accident gave the farmers and their wives something to talk about with Jim Higman's bride. They had all known Jim Higman for years: the Stinsons, the Jennings, the Swanns and Pearces, Manglesdorfs, Bryants, Furners, Mark Lyndon and the rest. But Jim's new wife was a city girl, a schoolteacher, a stranger, and the women were a little shy of her. Now they came to her in friendship, asking about the accident, concerned for her well-being, offering homecures for abrasions and good advice about horses.

Sitting with the women under the pine trees in the sun, Grace felt welcomed and comfortable. Jim had introduced her proudly to neighbours she hadn't met before, and Evelyn Higman sat with her. Together they joined the others for tennis and cheered the winners of the children's foot races. When the children of the communities of Berry Jerry, Rannock and Winchendon Vale competed in sack, egg-and-spoon and potato races, she helped Evelyn hold the finishing tape. She had been hesitant about putting her own cakes and sandwiches on the loaded picnic tables, feeling that she was still an inexperienced cook, but women encouraged her and one even asked for a recipe.

As the families crowded around the tables of picnic food, Grace felt a strong sense of community solidarity among them, even though as a whole group they only met three or four times a year — at the Anniversary Day sports carnival in January, the Empire Day picnic in May and the ploughing match in August. She could see that the scattered households had a tradition of mutual support, in their work and in their family lives, and it was not hard to imagine herself being gradually absorbed into the network, too.

The men grouped at one end of the table, talking about their land. The autumn rains had been excellent and they sounded happy about prospects for their newly-sown crops. Farm dams were full and the country looked green and beautiful. Even so, they complained of the never-ending rabbit scourge, and spoke of the offer by the Pasture Protection Board of a bonus on the scalps of rabbits, dingoes, hares and crows. They muttered about the problems of grasshoppers — 'Are we supposed to build grasshopper-proof fences thirty feet high?' — and the price of wheat. Another hazard of farming which also concerned them was the existence of 'rings' which trapped men into a credit system from which it was hard to escape, and which dominated the price of cereals.

At the end of the day, as families prepared to drive home to their farms, women said to Grace, 'It's been lovely to meet you, dear.

It does you good to have a talk, doesn't it? Did you know they are thinking of putting a telephone from Coolamon to Springwood Hotel near your place, and from Springwood to Berry Jerry Post Office? Then it won't be so hard to send messages between us.'

By the time the rural communities gathered again in Coolamon for the ploughing match in August, Grace knew that she would have a child in the new year. In the peace of her home, she and Evelyn had begun cutting out and stitching baby clothes, with Evelyn almost as excited as she and Jim about the news. Tiny garments, soft and delicate with exquisite stitchery, were made as the two young women talked together. Evelyn loved her brother very dearly. 'It really upsets me,' she explained to Grace, 'when someone talks about Jim's "people" and they don't mean us, they mean the Caldwells. He's my brother, part of my family all my life, and your baby is very important to me.' Grace had written to her parents and her brothers' families with the news, and was happily looking forward to a visit from Sarah's Grace, who was coming to be a companion for some weeks.

On the day of the ploughing carnival, amid the excitement of ploughing and riding competitions, the talk of the people was about the new land ballot. Hundreds of acres of Mimosa Station due north of Jim's land at Rannock were being thrown open for selection, and applications were being invited.

'How much chance do you think you'll have, Jim?' men asked. 'We've put our names in, too, but they say that they give you a numbered marble in a barrel, and it all depends on which marbles are pulled out!'

'I'm keen to add to my land,' Jim said, 'though I don't know how I'll go in the ballot.' And Grace knew that he was dreaming privately of his unborn child – a son, perhaps.

The results of the ballot were published in October 1905. None of the local men had won land, to Jim's disappointment. Two hundred and sixty-one people had put their names in the barrel and only ten marbles were drawn. Nearly all the new people were to come from Victoria. Grace saw the news in the paper and read the unknown names; Grinter, English, Allen, Moncrieff and others.

'These people will be living nearer than most of our Berry Jerry friends,' she said to Jim with pleasure, 'and they'll be even newer than me!'

Grace opened her eyes slowly. Over her head the canopy of white cottonlace bed curtains hung, cheerful with bobbled fringe, and the enclosing folds of the mosquito net. It was still very early, but the morning cry of the rooster had begun and soon she would hear the cow. Jim lay beside her, just beginning to stir, and his beard tickled her cheek. She moved cautiously, shifting the weight of her unborn baby. It was going to be another clear, hot day, good for harvest.

It was very strange to think that this was Christmas morning. Today was the first Christmas she had woken to find her husband beside her. The house was very still. On other Christmases, growing up with her family or coming home on holidays, this morning had always been full of voices and laughter and children. There had been a special church service on Christmas morning with all her friends, and favourite music for the season, and a crowded table for dinner with everyone talking at once, and giving and receiving little gifts. Today her own family was scattered widely, there were no children in their home and there would be no Christmas service at Berry Jerry because the minister had come to them last Sunday. Jim was in the middle of harvest and had hinted that he'd probably do a few hours with the team this morning before they went to The Hill to share Christmas dinner with her father and Evelyn.

Jim had just finished building her a fine separate kitchen of weatherboard lined with hessian. She had helped him with the hessian, holding the long strips of fabric against the ceiling on the broom. Yet even with her much-improved cooking facilities, her contribution to Christmas dinner had not been quite as happy in preparation as she remembered on other Christmases. Then Mother had been in charge, with her array of recipe books and fine skills in cookery, producing delectable festive foods with the ease of long experience. Her own first effort at a Christmas pudding didn't seem quite right: she burned the shortbread and then there was the Christmas bird. Somehow she had expected Jim to catch and kill the fowl for Christmas dinner as her father always did, but he'd expected *her* to do it as his mother had always done. Grace had been horrified – 'But Jim, I'd have enough trouble even catching one, and then I'd *hate* to kill the poor thing!' – and Jim had looked perplexed. What sort of farmer's wife was this who couldn't kill a hen for dinner? The bird was now safely cooked and under the wire meat cover, the least-burned of the shortbread were in a cake tin, and she hoped Evelyn wouldn't realise how harrowing her preparations had been.

She lay quietly, watching the square of blue sky through the window and holding the swell of her body between gentle hands. Her baby was kicking, pressing against her hand, alive. For weeks now she had been thinking about Mary, the mother of Jesus, another young mother waiting for the birth of her first child. For the first time she had known a little of what that long-ago girl must have felt; the excitement, the tenderness of spirit, the sense of looking inwardly toward the promise of a new life. She knew the bodily changes of pregnancy, the tiredness, the weight, the aching back, and thought of Mary riding toward Bethlehem, clinging in exhaustion to the donkey. Mary had ridden away from her parents' home to a strange place where she would bear her child among strangers; at least, thought Grace, there is no question of me having my baby out in the barn, and the cottage hospital in Coolamon will look after me well. Evelyn will be near and, of course, Jim. Yet there was a great sense of awe at the very thought of the mystery of childbirth, and a certain fear.

Suddenly she was no longer troubled about burned shortbread and the loss of the familiar from her celebration of Christmas Day. The child who had been born was the one born for all times and places, city or bush, with a family or alone, coming into the life of humanity to rescue his people. The child would not care who had, in the end, killed the Christmas hen.

She circled Jim in her arms and kissed the tip of his nose. 'Happy Christmas, my darling!'

The telegram lay yellow and threatening on her kitchen table, brought across from the little post office at the Springwood Hotel. Her father, William Playford, was dead. Grace sat, shaken, at the kitchen table till Jim came home. Her mind churned with thoughts; of her father and how terribly she was going to miss him, her mother now alone in the house at Cullinga mine, the new baby due to be born this week or next. She had known he was not well, seventy-one years old with a weak heart, retired at last after so many years of hard physical work, but even so she had not been ready to lose him.

'Of course, with the baby due, you certainly can't travel all the way to Cullinga, my dear.' Jim was concerned for her. 'But I'll go, for the funeral. I'll take you up to stay with Evelyn and leave as soon as I can.'

'Jim, I don't know what Mother will do now. Without Father, I don't think she'll be happy staying at the mine. She hasn't a house in Sydney any more. If Sarah were living she might have gone to Sarah – Robert and Harry's house is so full already – there's Will and Martha, or Auntie Lydia and Uncle Richard but...'

'Would you like to invite her to come to us?'

'Will you ask her, please? And I'll send a letter with you.'

As Grace packed her bags ready to go to Evelyn and then on to the cottage hospital for the baby, she could not know that almost never again would she be quite alone in her home.

Everything changed in so short a time, it seemed. Her father died in March 1906 and within twelve days baby Caroline Gertrude was born. Jim returned from the funeral with the news that her mother would be very glad to accept their invitation, and would drive herself across from Cullinga in a few weeks. Mary Playford arrived at Rannock alone, very weary but undefeated. She had driven her four-wheeled phaeton with its little canopy across some eighty miles of dusty roads from Cullinga east of Cootamundra to Rannock north of Coolamon. On the way she had spent a night at the big stone Bethungra Hotel. Her larger furniture had been committed to the railway for transport. The old Bible in which William had recorded their family history and the vast new leather-covered family Bible with metal clasps, her glass dome full of stuffed birds and the jewellery William had given her were carefully packed around her in the phaeton. Near her feet she had carried a package of Cullinga soil with cuttings of her favourite plants, bulbs and a clump of violets.

When she stepped down from her vehicle, solemn in widow's black from her bonnet to her boots, Grace hurried out to greet her with a great thankfulness. Her mother was so strong and determined, grieving for the loss of her life partner, yet willing to come to help her daughter. At sixty-five she was vigorous and capable and Grace knew that she and her mother would be able to lean on each other.

The two women held each other closely with tears in their eyes, each thinking of William Playford whose grave was in Cootamundra. Later, Mary Playford would talk about his last few days, when he knew he was dying, and they had talked quietly of their confidence that his death was not the end of life. She would tell Grace of the two hymns which her father said were singing in his mind, 'O God the spring of all my joys' and 'My God, I am thine', and Grace would gently play them on the organ, the two of them weeping a little. She would tell how the Rev. William McCallum at the memorial service had spoken of their family life which he had known over twenty years. 'He said that our home was just like the family in that poem by Robert Burns, "The Cottar's Saturday Night", with the love between family members, and parents leading in prayer and good counsel,' she said.

For now, Grace clung to her mother and drew her into the house. 'Come in, Mother, I'm so glad you're here. Come and see your newest granddaughter — she's so lovely.'

'I'll just put these violets on the verandah out of the sun — I've brought a little bit of our old home with me. There. Now, where is baby Caroline?'

A new baby in one room, her mother in another and then Grace and Jim were asked to provide board for the teacher at the new little school at Rannock. With ten new families just arrived to take up their selections on what used to be Big Mimosa, and the prospect of another ballot and more land opened up next year, the community had built a little school a mile or so north of Higman's property. It was five years since Grace had been a teacher herself, but she greatly enjoyed the interest of a close link with the new school and the young man who came to teach there. Meal time conversations expanded her world. Jim talked with enthusiasm of farming, theology, the latest in inventions for agriculture and schemes for the community good through Farmers and Settlers. Her mother talked of her lifelong interest in her church, literature, goldmining and of news of missionary work in the Pacific. The teacher entertained them with school stories and engaged in heated discussions about education.

The new families were arriving. Men were working on fencing, clearing land, building their own pisé or wattle and daub cottages, the women anxious and a little afraid, looking back wistfully to their old homes on established farms in Victoria and wondering whether it was such a good thing for their men to have won this raw and uncleared block, so far from anything they knew. Jim's farm by comparison was so much more advanced, and The Hill had the benefit of nearly thirty years of hard labour. New men sometimes didn't know that the rabbits could clean out their whole crop if they hadn't put in rabbitproof fencing, or hadn't learned the benefits of the stumpjump plough over their root-ridden land.

'I'd like to visit some of these women,' Grace said to Jim. 'I think I understand what it must be like for them, coming here new, and they don't know anybody yet.' So sometimes with her mother holding the baby, Grace set out to call on women, many similar in age to herself, offering friendship, inviting them to come to see her if ever their husband was passing that way.

Before many months had passed, Grace knew that she was to have another child. Mary Playford announced that, as she had inherited a large amount after her husband's death, she would like to pay for a separate room to be linked to Grace and Jim's home by a breeze-way. A fine large weatherboard room was built and furnished with Mary Playford's large cedar furniture, her heavy bookcase and chest of drawers, her glass dome of birds, lace curtains and ornaments. Some of Sarah's children came to stay for some months and, with the teacher, the house was full. Evelyn discovered in Mary Playford a new friend, a woman of wisdom and commonsense whose thoughts Evelyn began to value.

The new pattern for Grace's life was being set. The last verse she added to her collection of poems was called 'Christmas Child'. It spoke of a new mother's relationship with her baby:

I hid her safe within my heart,
My heart, I said, is all for you,
But lo, she left the door ajar
And all the world came flocking through.

Grace paced quietly to and fro across the kitchen, her new baby supported against her shoulder. Baby Mary had been born prematurely and her first months of life had been very difficult. Several times Grace had been afraid that she would lose this little one altogether. Her mother had been a great strength, suggesting practical things for the baby's diet, arranging for goats to join the other farmyard animals to provide their milk for baby, and carefully browning flour in the oven to make a paste to feed the tiny child. When Grace was busy with the baby, the grandmother took little Caroline on her own wide lap and cuddled her, sang her songs and held her hand for staggering infant walks in the garden. There were times when the young mother came late to the kitchen to prepare a meal, tired and anxious after spending hours with a fretful and fragile infant, to find the grandmother had already finished most of her work for her – 'Mother, however would I manage if you were not here?' – and the older woman only smiled, thankful that she still had a significant place and a purpose.

When at last the day's work was over, Grace sat down wearily at the kitchen table with Jim. Jim sat opposite her, papers, pen and ink spread around him.

'What are you working on? Will you be long?'

'Not long. A couple of things. Read this for me – it's a letter to the Coolamon paper about the local option vote soon about whether public houses and liquor licenses should be continued as they are or be reduced. You know how I feel about the whole question! Ever since poor Uncle Jim died in that asylum, and other friends of mine have ruined themselves and their families, I can only see the evils of the trade.'

She picked up the carefully written letter, an impassioned statement about the effect of the liquor trade on the homes of New South Wales. Her Jim didn't mince his words.

'And this other thing is the report for the annual meeting of our North Berry Jerry and Rannock Progress Association. It's a great report, too! It wasn't till I started writing it down that I realised how much we've done this year. There are twenty-four members, including some of the latest group of new settlers who've come during 1907 – Furnells, Downies, Holdens. The telephone link and post office at Springwood Hotel has been set up. Then there's the new road we've cleared, trustees for the new Rannock cemetery, a local polling booth for the elections, the ground marked out and surveyed for the Rannock recreation reserve, and a decent fence for the school, as well as arranging for the survey and auction of more blocks on the Rannock village reserve. With all the new familes and the hope of still more land opened for selection, Rannock could turn into quite a good little town, with shops and offices, like Coolamon.'

His enthusiasm bubbled up and, even through her tiredness, Grace caught something of the vision he was seeing. He loved this area so much, and saw such limitless possibilities for it. At the moment around the Rannock village reserve, all that could be seen was bush and gently undulating paddocks with the spring growth of young wheat, a tiny school house inside its fence and the beginnings of two small weatherboard churches under construction, one Roman Catholic and the other a combination of Methodist, Presbyterian, Anglican and Baptist, set suitably away from each other on invisible streets in the imagined town.

'And what about the railway idea!' he went on. 'Just think if they follow up the idea of the Coolamon Progress Association to put a line through running north from Coolamon, right through Rannock up to join the Temora-Barellan line. A railway station in Rannock! We could send our chaff to Sydney – we could even make dairying pay. This is going to be one of the best districts in the state! We meet tomorrow night in the meeting room at Springwood Hotel, and some men plan to nominate me again for secretary-treasurer.'

Grace stood up and picked up the lamp. 'Put it away tonight. You're not going out surveying sites for railway stations before morning. Come to bed.'

The new church at Rannock was opened on a hot day in February 1908. Nearby the Catholic church was also nearly completed for the growing population of Catholic families. The larger group of Protestants were the Methodists, and they had had a lot to do with the new building, but the people as they gathered were neighbours and fellow-Christians first, and denominations second, and they all planned to worship together. For many of them, they thought of it as the 'Union Church'. Earlier the previous year they had read with interest the news of 'the proposed basis of union between the Methodist, Congregational and Presbyterian churches . . . the qualification for membership in the proposed united church is defined simply as the confession of faith in Jesus Christ as Lord, such faith being evidenced by obedience to him.'

Grace and Jim joined the crowd who gathered outside the new building that Sunday afternoon. Buggies and sulkies were lined up under trees and horses tethered to the new fence. With their little ones, the families filed in, nearly all young couples making a new start on new land. They passed through the tiny front porch to sit in their rows, staring up at the varnished pine ceiling and the organ where Evelyn Higman sat. Berry Jerry friends, visiting for the church opening, smiled across at Grace. Her two babies had both been baptised among them at Berry Jerry and, though the new church was so close to her home, she would miss seeing them regularly.

After the service, the people spilled outside and gathered in the shade of the tent set up for lunch. Grace and her mother helped to lay out the cups and saucers, pour strong tea from the big teapot and hand out food to the guests. Little ones ran around underfoot, women talked about their families and the men talked about the weather — 'It's pretty good having a fine day for the opening, but we could do with an inch of rain . . .'

Twirls of red dust spiralled across the ground and women fanned themselves, conversations rising and falling in the heat of the afternoon. Soon it would be time to gather their things and their children and go home to their selections, back to the quietness and loneliness till next Sunday. But now they had a school and a church of their own, and their own busy progress association. Their community was taking on a defined shape and a focus.

Evelyn sat on the edge of the verandah with her lap full of fresh peas to shell and Grace watched her quick fingers among the pea pods. The little girls Carrie and Mary sat beside her, swinging their fat legs and opening mouths for peas like baby birds waiting to be fed. The rocking chair squeaked a little as Mary Playford rocked to and fro with Grace's third daughter Constance on her lap, while Grace cuddled the newest baby, her first son Legh. Beyond the verandah, the grapevines draped along their trellises were sending out bright young growth, tightly curled leaves unfolding, and peach, plum and almond trees tossed blossomed branches at the sky. The song of ewes and lambs calling to each other could be heard from the paddock beyond the stable and across the yard hens shepherded running fluffs of chickens past the woodheap. Mary Playford's violets were in bloom, and her daffodils and crocus.

'Do you know,' Evelyn said with her back turned to them, 'that I'm beginning to dislike spring?'

Her dark head was bent so low over the little girls that Grace almost missed her next words.

'Everything is new and young — lots of baby creatures, blossom, even little things like spring vegetables growing after the frosts. And here am I, thirty-six years old, single and likely to remain so for the rest of my life. . . I'm glad to keep house for Father, but I can't help envying you your husband and babies, Grace!'

'But Evelyn, of course you . . .' Grace faltered to a stop. She had been going to say, 'Of course you'll marry!' Now she thought better of it. There had been a time when Evelyn had thought she would marry, but then there had been sadness and pain, and she had come to tell her sorrows to Mary Playford. That time was in the past and Grace realised that it was not easy to imagine who her friend might find as a congenial husband among the men of the district.

'Just tell me *who*, in these parts, I could marry!' Evelyn demanded, reading her thoughts. 'All the new settlers are married men, and the boys of the old families are too young by far, or too wild, or Catholic, or just not the kind of person I could ever be happy with. And I can't imagine me finding a man to love and share my life with among the travelling gangs of shearers, or dam sinkers, or timberfellers, or one of Father's workmen. Can you?'

Grace tried to think of something comforting to say. She knew that Evelyn's need was deeper than a wish for romance. Her friend was always busy with house, church and community, but the day must one day come when her father would no longer be there. What would she do then? Hire men to run the farm? Sell and live alone in town? For a single woman without a profession now in 1911, life could be difficult and limited and Evelyn had always lived in the security of the family farm at The Hill. She knew how much Evelyn loved Jim's children and how happily she helped to care for them. It was also true that Evelyn was Jim's sister and, like him, had very high standards in what she meant by 'love'. Only recently Jim had preached in the Rannock church and among other things had referred to books of light fiction – 'Such books are often called "Love Stories", yet there is scarcely an ounce of real love to a hundredweight of such books. The essence and proof of real love is self-sacrifice, yet how many of these imaginary lovers deny themselves at all for the sake of the one they are supposed to love?' – and Grace knew that Evelyn desired for her own marriage something that she saw modelled in her brother.

With her own baby on her hip, Grace stooped to kiss her sister-in-law. 'I don't know, dear. Perhaps God has someone planned for you – perhaps you haven't met him yet.'

Richard Higman always hired workmen to work with him on The Hill now that Jim had his own property. Sometimes young migrants came for a few years, to learn the skills of farming so that they could attempt it independently. There were workmen's huts at The Hill, but the men needed to be fed and some workmen always went to Grace's house for their meals.

It was at her table, among her children and with the other workmen who sat waiting for their dinners, with Jim at the head of the table, that Grace first met the Welshman. The other workmen were teasing him. 'This bloke's a real foreigner – listen to him talk – him and his brother talk to each other in some weird lingo. Can't make out a word of it!'

The stranger spoke, his words musical and accented with the sounds of Wales, even as he spoke English. 'My brother and I have just migrated. My name is Will Thomas and we've come to learn about farming in Australia. Yes, Welsh is my first language and hard it is to understand Australians!'

When the other men had finished their meal, Grace talked for a little while with Will Thomas. Her first impression was of a man who was a gentleman in workman's boots, courteous, well-spoken. He seemed very homesick for Wales. She learned that he was a Christian, eager to find out where he could attend worship and delighted to know that the community had recently begun a Christian Endeavour group. Many workmen did not want to be bothered with church and were much happier down at the Springwood Hotel.

The Welshman became a friend as for two years he sat at the Higman table. After meals he sometimes stayed to talk politics, theology or world news with Jim. He played with the children, Carrie, Mary, Connie and Legh. On Sundays he was always with them in church, his fine singing voice lifting the singing of the congregation, and a welcome friend at the tea meetings, helping the men put up the tent beside the church. When the neighbours gathered with the new young minister, Winsleigh Murray, for their Christian Endeavour metings, Will Thomas took his turn in leadership with the others. He asked the group for permission to pray in Welsh — 'It is the language of my heart and that is how I need to talk with God' — and the farmers and their wives bowed their heads and listened with their spirits to the voice of their new friend praying in the language of his far distant home.

There had perhaps been some clues earlier, Grace realised, yet it wasn't till the day of the first Coolamon Agricultural Show on the new showground that she realised something was happening to Evelyn. It was late August 1912 and Grace travelled in to Coolamon with Jim and the children, her mother driving her own vehicle with visiting McDowell nieces on board. The Coolamon Show had only recently grown out of the traditional ploughing carnival and the developing district and town was delighted with its new facilities, cattle yards, sheep sheds and industrial hall as well as the established racetrack. As they drove into the showground, the area was full of vehicles with even a few motor cars. Special trains from

Wagga and Narrandera had brought many extra guests and there was a high sense of holiday among the people.

Jim disappeared to see whether the fine fleece he had entered had won a ribbon in the competition. Grace and her mother walked among friends through the industrial hall, admiring the jams and pickles, needlework and knitting, cut flowers and prize vegetables, cakes and preserved fruit. She had not entered anything this year, because her newest baby, Richard, was only a month old, but her mother marched around inspecting all the homecrafts with a judicious eye and announcing in an undertone whether or not she agreed with the judgment of the judges. To their delight they noticed that Evelyn Higman had won prize ribbons for crochet edging lace and for a plate of scones.

It was when they began to tire that the McDowell girls took the bigger children away to look at the baby animals and to watch the competitions on the racetrack. Grace McDowell was nineteen years old now, and a dear friend and helper to her aunt.

'Let's go to the Presbyterian tea tent for a cup of tea,' Grace suggested.

Under the shade of the tea tent, they found long trestle tables set up and women busily pouring cups of tea and serving cream cakes to their customers. At one end of the table they saw Evelyn. She did not notice them come in because she was watching Will Thomas walking towards her with two cups of tea and a plate of cakes. It was only after their tea was finished and Evelyn was walking away that she noticed her friends. She walked to their place at the table, flushed and embarrassed. Will Thomas was behind her.

'Good morning, ladies!' he said. 'I just wanted to buy Miss Higman some morning tea to congratulate her for her success in the display of work. Goodbye, Miss Higman,' and he tipped his hat to the ladies and was gone.

Inevitably, the discussion later came round to Will. 'It's impossible, of course.' Evelyn's voice was determined.

'Why?'

'I'm too old to think of marrying now. Older than Will, too. And maybe people would misunderstand and think I was snatching at straws, marrying one of my father's workmen.'

'But what is the truth?' Grace persisted. 'Do you love Will?'

'Of course I do! Don't you like him? You know him well, seeing he's been in your home every day since he came here.'

'Will is a lovely man and being a workman has nothing to do with his character. He came here to learn how to be a farmer and there's nothing to be ashamed of in that. With both of you in your mid-thirties, a few years either way seems to me to make no difference. Does he love you, do you think?'

The answer was whispered. 'Yes.'

That was the year when the Rannock community added two tennis courts to their village, and a little shop, though the dreamed-of streets of houses had not eventuated. Jim was not well again that winter, as he had not been well for several winters, suffering severely from chest problems turning to pleurisy or pneumonia and, though Grace worried about him, he insisted on driving around the countryside with parties of men, inspecting possible sites for a railway line. He had not given up hope for it, but no further action had been taken by anyone in authority.

It was the same year that the village of Coolamon was proclaimed an urban area. Once bullock teams with wool bales, teams of Clydesdales pulling freight of bagged wheat or flocks of sheep, had toiled through mud or dust along a track to Coolamon railway station. On either side of that wide roadway, houses, shops, banks and hotels had sprung up. Now the community was to become a town and a proud town council demanded asphalted footpaths outside their shops, thousands of pounds worth of roadmaking plant, council chambers and the beginnings of a park along the middle of the wide thoroughfare.

For the farmers of the district it was a good year, too. Jim was among the men who carted wheat and truckloads of hay and chaff to the Coolamon railway, bringing a record delivery in both bagged wheat and chaff. He came home excited by the news of the fine harvests and delivery of wheat – 'Up to 1908, we'd never ever been up to 100,000 bags for the year, and this year, only four years later, we have topped 230,000 bags. Things are just going to get better and better!'

For a birthday, there was always cake for tea. Though she kept meals plain and nourishing most of the time, Grace always liked to make a special occasion of birthdays, making a festive treat out of whatever she had in the house. Today was Carrie's seventh birthday and Grace wound the handle of the telephone Jim had set up to link his home with The Hill.

'Evelyn, can you come for tea? Bring Father over, too – we're having Carrie's birthday tea.'

The table was set with the best china with a little posy of flowers and the birthday cake as the centrepiece. Grandfather Higman and Evelyn walked across from their home on the hill and the children ran to greet them, pulling them happily into the house. Richard Higman went to congratulate Jim on being given life membership in the local Farmers and Settlers association. Grandmother Playford sat in her chair and on her lap was baby Richie who tried to tug at the starched perfection of her crisp white cap with its tiny black ribbon bows. Grace McDowell had brushed the hair of the three little girls till it fell in long glossy waves down their backs, and tied coloured ribbons on top. The new table which seated twelve filled quickly with her extended family and the workmen. Her little house was becoming more and more crowded as her family and responsibilities grew.

As they ate, Grace poured tea and watched the faces of her family. Evelyn talked to Carrie and the other little girls, but she rarely looked to the far end of the table where the men sat. Yet Will Thomas was there, and she was sure that he was watching her.

When it was time for the birthday cake, Carrie ran from one to the other around the table and was given a birthday kiss and a hug from each of the family, with the men looking on a little wistfully, perhaps remembering distant families. They sang 'Happy Birthday' with enthusiasm, the little girl's face bright with excitement and pleasure, and then they cut the cake and Carrie passed a slice to each of the guests at the table. She had already received her birthday gift, a book. There were never dolls or toys for birthdays. What did the children need with dolls when there was always the newest baby to play with, and baby animals on the farm? Grace's children had a lovely life with picnics in the bush, old farm equipment to climb over, cubbie houses under the peppertree made of dead sticks to mark out the rooms, mud pies on fragments of china, imaginary schools and imaginary church services with a pretend organ made of twigs. Grandfather took them riding round the farm in front of him on his horse and Grandmother taught the girls to knit and sew. She told them stories of their family; stories of their great-grandma losing her bonnet overboard on the way out to Australia, and helping convicts, and stories of her own girlhood, reciting long poems to them. In the hot weather, Grandmother sometimes scrubbed the verandah then tossed the water over the boards, letting the children roll in the damp coolness. There were always friendly adults to talk to, and she herself taught them childhood games and read them stories, snuggled around her in evening lamplight. Grace looked around at her household with great contentment. It was hard to even remember that she had once felt lonely here.

The meal was over and the cousins took the babies off to bed. The workmen left, all except Will Thomas. Evelyn left the table and walked to stand beside Will.

'Jim, Grace, Mrs Playford, we have some news. Will has asked me to marry him. And I've said yes.'

The winter of 1913 was a time of very mixed blessings. For the farmers it was a very bad winter with the rains failing. For Jim it was a time of winter illness, as he had known for a number of previous winters. For Evelyn and Will it was the happy winter of their wedding.

Evelyn was very shy about her engagement, and Mary Playford had to take her to task for hiding her ring under gloves when she went to church for the first time. 'My dear, don't hide it! Everyone thinks a lot of Will, and they've loved you for years, so be proud that you are going to be Will's wife. All the neighbours will be happy for you both.'

The wedding was very quiet and private in the best room at The Hill. Evelyn stood beside Will, bridal in rich satin and heavy lace, as Winsleigh Murray read the wedding service. Grace McDowell and little Carrie and Mary stood with them as bridesmaid and flower girls. Grace sat with the family and chosen guests and thanked God for Evelyn's happiness.

As Mary Playford had predicted, the rest of the Rannock community was very happy for the newlyweds and crowded the Rannock church to wish them well. Friends sang solos and recited poetry, produced large quantities of refreshments and presented the bridal pair with a handsome silver tea and coffee service on a silver tray.

Yet that same winter was a very hard one for the farmers. Waterless crops struggled, thin and patchy. Jim was worried about his crop — 'We'll be doing well if we harvest half as much as last year,' he muttered.

Grace was worried about her husband. This year, his chest problems were more severe than they had ever been. Through the months of frosts and fog, with the house never warm enough to ease him, he had been ill and the town doctor, Dr Buchanan, sent him to hospital in Wagga, suffering from pneumonia.

She sat by his bed, listening with disbelief to the doctor.

'Your husband is not at all well, Mrs Higman. He needs surgery, and he'll be in hospital here for some weeks.'

She held Jim's hand tightly and listened to his laboured breathing. It was hard to believe that there had been a time when she had not known this man, or a time when knowing him she had not recognised him for the man he was, and had not loved him. Now their lives were totally intertwined, their care for each other mutual, each needing the other to make the other whole. He needed her to help him anchor his dreams to reality, to laugh when he was too solemn, to be the go-between and interpreter of children to father, to share in bringing love and open-hearted hospitality into his home. She needed his strength, his wisdom, his confidence and visions for the future, his enthusiasm for so many projects that lifted her mind beyond the immediate cares of the family. Each needed the prayers and depth of spirituality of the other, lifting up, enriching.

'Jim, my love, don't leave me,' her mind said. 'Lord protect him – help the surgeons – please heal him. . .'

As she sat waiting for news on the day of Jim's operation, Grace was conscious of physical pain in her own body, but she thrust the thought away. Their minister had come to pray with them at the hospital before Jim was taken away for surgery, and she almost mentioned to him that she was not feeling well, but somehow it didn't seem suitable to share with a young man and she said nothing. She knew that she was expecting her sixth child early in November and told herself that it was just that she was tired and worried about Jim. Yet the pain was like nothing she had known in previous pregnancies and she knew that this too was making her afraid.

The dry winter turned into a spring with little rain. The days were clear and very bright, but wheat and gardens suffered. Jim came home from hospital, thinner but glad to be safely home again. Harvest was going to be very disappointing, he knew. Dust storms were very bad that year, whipping up soil which lay dust-dry and unprotected since the forests and virgin bush had been stripped away. Dust lay over everything, coating butter in its dish, bread almost as she sliced it, filtering over brush and comb on the dressing table and reddening the washing on the line.

Grace found herself working more and more slowly, wanting to fight the dust which intruded into her home but without energy.

At last she admitted to herself and to Jim that something must be wrong. Last year, when little Richie was born, he had been born safely in her own home, but Jim was not accepting that this time.

'Wagga Hospital is the best for miles. We'll go there in plenty of time and have the best care for you. Anything that needs to be done, so long as you are safe.'

Even though it was a bad year and both he and Grace were not well, Jim's vision and optimism asserted itself. He began doodling designs on the back of the brownpaper wrapper off the newspaper and announced, 'We'll build a bigger house! When I built this house I was a single man with hopes, and just look at us now. . .' It was true. It had become difficult to fit in parents, grandmother, five children with a baby due soon and often nieces and nephews or other guests visiting. 'And the doctor said I should have a bedroom facing east for winter sun, for my health's sake.'

His pencil sketched in his ideas: more bedrooms, an enormous kitchen as the heart of the house, a long narrow pantry on the coolest corner, breakfast room and formal dining room, a private room for Grandmother, fireplaces in every room, a study for himself. 'We'll build on the other side of the farm, closer to the school and church so the children can walk there easily.'

Jim took Grace's hand. 'My dear, this house will be all for you.'

The journey to Wagga before her baby was born was an agony. Jim tried to drive carefully, but there was nothing he could do to relieve her pain. This was not the pain of labour but something else, something more sinister. After the child was born, the doctor had examined her again. It did not come as a surprise when he came to her with grave face to give her the news.

'Your little boy is well, Mrs Higman, a fine healthy baby. But I'm very sorry to tell you that you have cancer and should come back to hospital in about six weeks for a mastectomy.'

Little William was born in November 1913 and Christmas dinner a few weeks later was a subdued affair. Jim looked haggard as he carved the festive turkey, and Mary Playford seemed to have aged and shrunken almost overnight. The older McDowell girls had taken charge of the new baby and the other children, and Grace was thankful for their kind and sensible help.

On New Year's Eve, Grace had her bags packed for hospital. The doctor had been able to promise her nothing. He was a young man, newly qualified, and he said, to encourage her, 'I have the advantage of knowing the latest methods in this kind of surgery so we'll hope for the best.' Winsleigh Murray had spent time with them that day and his gentle spirit and prayers had been a comfort to her.

Now she couldn't sleep. Jim lay beside her, exhausted, snoring a little and she didn't want to wake him. In her own room her mother was sleeping, and she thought of her mother, now seventy-three and no longer as strong as she had been. Grace stepped outside onto the verandah. The moon was bright over her garden, her fruit trees heavy with peaches and plums, the scent of honeysuckle, banksia roses, rosemary and lavender on the air. Close around her mother's room clustered the greenery of flag lilies and violets, nerines and lilac, helping to make a lovely home on what had been bare earth. Silvered by the moon lay the paddocks, white gold stubble after harvest, Jim's beloved land.

Grace tiptoed from room to room. Sarah's children, the McDowells, were there, young Stan come to work on the farm, Sadie to attend school and the big girls to help her. One by one, she walked to the bedsides of her sleeping children. Each one was infinitely precious to her. There was Carrie, her firstborn, so clever and sensible, already 'big sister' to the little ones. Mary slept soundly, long dark hair across the pillow, the dear child who had had such a struggle to survive her early life and was such a solemn little thing. Connie was the fair one, and pretty: the mother remembered how hard it had been giving birth to this child, and how often the child was not well. Then Legh, bright and lively, already showing a strong personality, needing a mother's guidance and control. Richie lay asleep, dark curls tousled, the child who was little more than a baby himself: the poor little lad seemed of all of them the most insecure and distressed when she had to be away from him or was too sick to cuddle him. And the new baby, little Willie, only six weeks old. The big girls had done all his mothering so far, yet he was her child, and she longed to see this beautiful little boy develop and grow. At each bed she knelt and laid a gentle hand on her children. She prayed for them, one by one.

'Lord, you know best,' she prayed. 'I trust you with my life. But Lord, I ask you to spare my life till my little ones are older. They need me so much . . .'

When the travelling photographer came to their home some months later, Grace greeted him with an enthusiasm which surprised even herself. She was alive even though diminished in body and in strength, Jim was alive and well, their children were beautiful, and here was a rare chance to record their family. She sent one of the big girls to find Jim and bring him home, while she gathered the children, insisted on well-scrubbed hands and faces, and dressed the three girls in the beautiful dresses they had worn for their Auntie Evelyn's wedding. When Jim arrived, he was grumpy about having to change into his Sunday suit in the middle of a working day, but Grace was persistent, brushing the three girls' long wavy hair and parting it neatly in the middle and straightening the collars of the three little boys.

She and Jim sat surrounded by their children outside Mary Playford's room while the photographer did mystical things under his black cloth. Her mother watched, smiling, and later submitted to having a photograph taken of herself in her big chair under the peppertree, newest baby in her lap.

When, some time later, the photograph arrived, large and impressive with seven of them staring solemnly at the camera and only Legh with a happy grin on his face, Grace gazed at it for a long time. She was glad to have it. Life could change so suddenly and without warning. The doctor had been pleased with the results of her surgery, but who knew whether the disease might still be waiting for her? Her mother wasn't as well as she once was, and Jim worked so hard and was straining his own health sometimes, she felt. Even her home was going to change soon; the walls of the new house were rising on the far side of the farm, ochre cement blocks a paler shade of the land with which they were blended. Jim had already built his new barn and stable with the beginnings of an orchard planted near the house.

In the newspaper office of the town of Coolamon, the editor selected material for the next edition of the *Coolamon Farmers Review*. Earlier in the year his pages had been enlivened by stories of the sometimes violent confrontations between local farmers and men working on chaffcutting machines. At one point Coolamon chaff had been declared 'black' by the unionists, and in a year of drought there was a lot of anger in the community. Then people had turned their attention to the coming elections.

He had earlier decided that news of a distant assassination and the declaration of war by Austria on Serbia would not be of local interest. Now he set the type for his editorial, choosing the smallest typeface to describe the alarming mobilisation of troops in Europe, expressing anxiety over the momentous events abroad which he said must seriously affect Australia and great surprise that despite this 'the public mind continues to possess itself in considerable tranquillity. . .'

The editor sighed and went on to set, in bold type, the new syllabus for the Coolamon Mutual Improvement Society, the Church of England Grand Dance in Bradshaw's barn and 'The event of 1914: the opening of Tara Hall, ball and supper.'

14
Drought
1914-1917

THE WIDE GATE SWUNG BACK into position and Grace fastened it behind the loaded buggy. Jim was waiting, and there was no time for being sentimental. As she climbed back into the buggy with the little boys and an assortment of bags and bundles, she looked back. The house under the peppertree stood empty.

Mary Playford had gone on ahead, the phaeton carrying her freight of potted geraniums, stuffed birds in their glass dome, nerines, violets and cuttings of banksia rose and lilac. Mother was already planning a garden to surround the new house, 'Caldwell'. The visiting nieces and her daughters had walked across the farm, wheeling the baby and herding the pets.

Behind her, there was nothing left to do. Another family – the sharefarmer Charlie Pearce and his wife – would move in and life would go on there. Yet the empty house held a large part of herself; her bridal time, the babies, guests, many memories. Now it was disappearing behind them, obscured by their dust.

Jim did not look back. Jim, the eternal optimist, looked ahead to his new home with all its comforts and, though dust rose in the wind from his meagre wheat crop, he was confident that God would provide. Things were going to go well now, he was sure.

It was Tuesday, 4 August 1914.

The next day, after a busy morning moving furniture under his wife's supervision, Jim set off to attend an election meeting in Coolamon. Election talk was running strongly among the people of the district and the respective merits of Mr Joseph Cook, the Prime Minister, and the Right Honourable Andrew Fisher, Leader of the Federal Opposition, were regularly discussed in saleyards and churchyards. The Leader of the Opposition was to come to Coolamon that afternoon to address a public meeting in support of the candidature of Mr Chanter, the local member.

Young Stan McDowell, who had put the horse into the sulky for his uncle, came back into the house to go on moving more furniture with his sisters. 'Uncle goes to a lot of meetings, doesn't he, Auntie Grace?' the boy commented, as he manoeuvred one end of a vast timber dining table through the door into the breakfast room.

'Oh, he's always been interested in public life,' she said. 'He enjoys committees, I think. But this time he is just going because he is very interested in the federal elections — he hasn't any responsibility this time. This meeting won't be so very important, I don't expect. . .'

The Oddfellows Hall in town was moderately well filled that afternoon, the small town basking in the importance of having a former Prime Minister and Leader of the Opposition dignifying the proceedings. The local man standing for parliament was on his feet, presenting his electoral speech, pleased to have Andrew Fisher on the platform beside him.

A latecomer entered the hall. Instead of slipping into a back seat, he hurried forward to the platform, and the audience recognised him as the telegraph messenger from the post office. A slightly disapproving murmur began to buzz, and Mr Chanter hesitated momentarily, but after the telegram was handed to Mr Andrew Fisher, the messenger withdrew and the meeting went on.

After a formal welcome and an exchange of politenesses, Andrew Fisher unfolded the paper in his hand. 'I have just received an urgent telegram from Prime Minister Cook. It reads, ''England declared war on Germany midnight last night''.'

There was a strange silence, broken by a little uncertain applause and an enthusiastic person shouting, 'Hear, hear!'

Mr Fisher spoke carefully. This was clearly something which had exercised his mind for some time and the implications for Australia were plain to him. 'I am not one to say, ''Hear, hear'' to war,' he said, 'but what I do say is, now that we know that war is really on, and that we are responsible for our share in the protection of the empire, it is the duty of Australia to stand by the mother country. Yes,' he went on, his voice rising with emotion and passion for what he believed, 'we must stand by mother England to the last man and the last shilling!'

Wild applause broke out, the men of the district seeing themselves as true patriots, the healthy young adult son faithfully defending his motherland, the place so many families referred to as Home even though their fathers had never seen its shores.

When the meeting concluded, Jim Higman saw the reporter from the *Coolamon Farmers Review* hurrying up the street to telegraph the scoop of his lifetime to the Sydney papers, and the phrase 'to the last man and the last shilling' was on its way to becoming a part of the national consciousness. Jim untied the horse and soberly headed for home to tell his family that Australia was at war.

'Are we expecting visitors?' Stan called.

'Mr Andrew Downie asked if he could call in this evening.'

'It's more than Mr Downie. Look!'

The children crowded to the front door with their cousins to see the astonishing sight of one sulky after another, lanterns swinging and crowded with families, pulling up by the grand new front door with its coloured fan light.

'It's a housewarming! May we come in?'

The door was flung wide and friends came crowding down the hall and over the highly polished new lino into the warmth of the bright kitchen. A fire blazed on the whitewashed breakfast room hearth and soon Stan was set to lighting a fire in the best room. Guests explored the house, guided by Jim, Grace or the children and assured them that it was beautiful. 'We're very happy for you,' they said.

Most of the friends were people who were part of the Christian Endeavour group, settlers' families whose lives were bound up with their own. They made themselves at home now, found places to sit in the dining room and announced that several friends had come prepared to recite verses or sing solos. The kitchen table was covered with delicious cakes brought specially for supper and Evelyn Thomas helped Grace set out her wedding cups and saucers and every other cup and saucer she could find.

Grace looked around her new room filled with light and laughter, the organ open ready for the music, the fire crackling in the grate. Apart from her mother in her rocking chair in deep conversation with the new minister, Walter Theobald, there was Jim's energetic old father Richard Higman, Evelyn and Will, Jim and her girls and three boys, her nieces and nephew, and over thirty cherished neighbours and friends. Some of the men were talking about the elections in a few weeks and some about the distant war in Europe — 'A chap was in Coolamon during the week buying horses for the expeditionary force, some of the local boys are quite excited about joining up – they'd better hurry, it will probably be all over long before troops from Australia can be trained and travel to the other side of the world!' – but most seemed more interested in the coming Coolamon Show.

Andrew Downie spoke on behalf of the visitors. 'We have come to express our best wishes to you both. We are delighted to see you move into such a handsome building. All of us are here because we value very much the kindness you both have shown to each of our families during your time in our district. We all hope you'll both long be spared to enjoy your home and a happy and prosperous future!'

The two women walked slowly around the verandahs at The Hill. Evelyn carried a kerosene tin bucket of water and a dipper, pouring a ration of precious water on each of her potted plants. Grace watched her carefully, seeing the deliberation with which she moved, slow with the weight of the child soon to be born. 'Only six weeks till baby is due,' Grace observed, watching water drops slide from the leaves of a geranium. 'How are you feeling?'

'How am I feeling? A strange mixture. It's so wonderful to look forward to being a mother, after all these years, and I'm so very, very happy with my Will. This child will be such a gift to us both. But . . . here I am having my first baby when I'm nearly forty! Some people probably think it's odd, and not very safe – Dr Buchanan has warned me that it may be very difficult.'

They moved to water the plants on the corner, where the country spread below them pale with drought, and the roof of Caldwell lay somewhere to the north beyond a smudge of trees. 'I'm having a baby too.'

Evelyn's hand stopped, frozen in midair with the dipper poised over a fern. She stared at her sister-in-law. There was a long silence. 'Are you sure?'

'I'm sure. The baby is due in February.'

Evelyn lowered the bucket and dipper to the floor and put her arms around Grace. 'God be with you, dear sister,' she whispered.

'And with you, my dear.'

Jim was planting out young trees when Stan first talked to him about enlisting. The boy swung his spade with the energy of a healthy eighteen-year-old, turning the rich soil and digging a hole deep enough for the tree roots. The uncle lifted in a small tree and was firming the earth around it when the faraway war in Europe took root on his own land.

'I'm going in to Coolamon to enlist with some of the other boys, Uncle,' the young man said. 'We've been talking about it and we're all really keen to go. It'll be a great chance to do something for the mother country – and for Australia. I reckon I should be accepted, don't you think? They are looking for men aged eighteen to thirty-five who are really fit, and I'm nineteen in a few days and strong as an ox!'

He talked on, about what the other boys had said, and when they might leave for training camp. His enthusiasm bubbled up and he pictured uniform and heroic deeds and patriotic fervour. Jim began digging another hole, his mind on reports which were appearing in the local paper of massing armies and nations in conflict.

Stan McDowell was not the only boy enlisting in those months of spring in 1914. Young shearers left the shearing sheds of the district as soon as the shearing was over, farmers' sons made arrangements to return from army camp for harvest, youths disappeared from behind the counters of Coolamon stores and banks. Their sharefarmer Charlie Pearce came into Caldwell one day with the news that two of his brothers were off to enlist. Boys departed for training camps and returned on leave in later months, estranged by uniform, puzzling with new knowledge of weaponry and the mysteries of the discipline of army life. Older men looked back fifteen years to the excitement of farewelling a group of Coolamon boys off to the Boer War with the Bushmen Contingent. Only the strongest and fittest were chosen, only young men who were perfect. Rejected men returned angry and disappointed from their medical tests, bitter at being cheated of being part of the great adventure.

Stan was among the chosen ones, and set off with others to training camp at Liverpool near Sydney. Grace stood on the railway platform watching the train steam away, waving still, though she could no longer see the boy. 'Whatever would poor Sarah say, if she could see her little boy going off to be a soldier?' she murmured.

'Don't take it too much to heart, my dear,' Jim said. 'He is unlikely to be any nearer to real war than the training camp. The fighting in Europe is sure to be over by Christmas.'

Evelyn's baby was a daughter. Dr Buchanan had been right and it had not been easy for her, but now she and Will had a beautiful dark-haired tiny girl whom they called Jean. The baby was born in the spring, that same spring which saw some boys of the district exchange the tools of the land for the tools of war. For the first time, The Hill was home for a baby, and Will and Evelyn delighted in the presence of their child.

The intertwining threads of the embroidery of their lives showed light and dark, dramatic and sombre. Joy in Evelyn's baby wove through continuing anxiety over Grace's seventh pregnancy. Delightful district picnics and church concert preparations shone in contrast to the enervating drought which dragged on through summer. The laughter of children chasing the pet lamb past the house lightened the effect of letters from army camp of a boy being turned into a soldier.

Christmas 1914 came. Caldwell hosted its first Christmas, with Will and Evelyn happily bringing the baby and Grandfather over to Caldwell for Christmas dinner with the Higmans, Grandma Playford and the cousins. Yet the war was not over as people had so confidently predicted. The King of England called the British Empire to prayer on New Years Day 1915, asking his people around the world to pray for a speedy end to the war in Europe. But the end was not in sight, and Australian troops were sailing, setting off amid jubilation and city processions, splendid in their ranks, frightening in their innocence, sailing for Egypt, the Middle East, France.

Boys from district and church came to say goodbye. Boys came specially to seek out Grace Higman; her home had been open to young workmen, single men who had cherished the chance of a family meal and friendly conversation after days of solitary work on farms. They had been at her table, drunk tea in her kitchen while she heard their worries, sung hymns around her organ on Sunday evenings. One boy came with rooted cuttings of rosebushes for her new garden.

'They are the tiny pink roses, Mrs Higman – the ones they call Cecil Brunner. Maybe they'll help you think of me sometimes.'

'They'll be beautiful, thank you, Walter,' she said. 'I'll plant them just outside the room where we always eat. I won't forget to pray for you.'

Stan came home for his last leave before sailing. The meeting hall at the back of the Springwood Hotel was used again and again for farewell meetings when boys in uniform were honoured by their community and proud families smiled and clapped as their sons were presented with a wristlet watch. Admiring girls recited patriotic verses and soloists sang of king and country. Vainglorious lads suggested the fierce things they planned to do to the faceless enemy. Flags were flown and draped in country halls and churches, schools and civic buildings. The whole Higman family attended the farewell for Stan and his friends, the children bursting with pride that their cousin was resplendent in polished army boots and the honour of khaki.

A few days before he left, Grace was working at her stove when she heard his footsteps. The fragrance of blossom reached her before she saw him. When she turned to the doorway, she saw Sarah's son, strong and tanned, and in his face she caught glimpses of her sister's face. In his hands he carried a branch of cedar in bloom, and the perfume was heady, filling the kitchen.

'Look, Auntie Grace, isn't it beautiful? I've just been visiting some neighbours to say goodbye and I found this in flower. I thought you'd like a bit.'

He stood there talking happily, his face framed by fragrant needles and flowers of the cedar branch. He was talking now of when he would be 'over there' with the troops, and would remember home. It seemed that he saw his future in heroic terms, but to the woman war was war – separation, loss, pain, relinquishment. If Sarah could see her son now, she thought.

She took the flowering cedar branch. 'Thank you, Stan, it's very beautiful,' she said, but her eyes were on the youth rather than on the blossom.

Stan McDowell was to be among the men in the earliest troopships to sail for the far side of the globe where war was raging. He was to sail with the 13th Battalion under Colonel Monash, leaving from Broadmeadows camp in Victoria. After the public farewells, his adopted family with his own sisters were there to say goodbye.

Jim said, 'Don't forget the things that have been important to you here, son. You've learned a lot in the two years here, not just about farming either. You have learned a lot about the Lord, too. Hold on to him, son. He will be there with you, always.'

The boy went to his old grandmother and his aunt. The old woman held his hands and looked into his face with the loving severity which spoke of high expectations and strong faith. The boy knew that she demanded the best he could give and he would not willingly fail her.

Grace held him with the love of the mother he had lost and said,

'I'll be praying for you every day, Stan. Most of the time I won't know where you are, but our loving Father will always know.'

The boys were leaving and even the weather seemed to grieve for them. The people waited for rain but no rain came. The growing season of 1914 had begun with such promise of fine crops across Australia that wheat stocks had been heavily sold overseas, leaving stocks depleted to be replenished with the harvest of 1914-15. As that harvest approached, the farmers of the Riverina knew it was going to be a very bad year after all, with some farms barely harvesting enough grain for seed. Then, before Christmas, a freak hailstorm thrashed a destructive swathe two miles wide, curving across the countryside, leaving damaged town buildings and a trail of hail-struck crops, broken and spoiled. The dryness of the country extending for many miles further west, bereft of original timber and ground cover, left thick, soft layers of dust to shift endlessly across the land, eddying in spirals across paddocks and drifting to coat vegetation. In December, a severe black dust storm had passed over the country and ever since every wind, small or great, had created its own private storm of dust. On one very hot dry Sunday, ministers of several churches had set off to travel to country churches to lead worship, but each one had been caught in dust storms and had crept home reddened with dust and frustrated by the blinding element floating through the air.

Grace was nearing the time for the birth of her own child, and the heat and dryness were exhausting. After days of extreme heat, her father-in-law came to visit her, anxious to see that she was well. The three little boys played outside the kitchen door in the shade of the back verandah and Grace sat inside with the company of the cherished old ones, Jim's father and her mother. She felt safe and very loved with them; for her and Jim their parents were the stable centre of their world. The two old people were growing more frail, Richard Higman thin and fine-boned, Mary Playford softly bulky, bright eyes observant. Neither was in full health because of heart problems. She watched them now as they sat quietly drinking cool homemade fruit cordial, her mother gently fanning herself, though the fan seemed little help in the intensity of that hot afternoon.

'It's so *hot*,' Grace said. There seemed no escape from it. The three little boys on the back verandah had become irritable and quarrelsome. A strong fiery wind had blown up and the verandah was no longer a pleasant place.

Grace eased herself slowly from her chair, awkward with the weight of late pregnancy, and shook free her long skirts which clung damply. She walked to the door to look at the boys and to check the thermometer on the wall. Even in the shade it read 108 degrees Fahrenheit.

She sighed. 'When is it going to ease?'

A child tugged at her skirt and pointed away to the western horizon.

'Mother, look, look at the big dust coming!'

She turned to look. Across the distant fringe of timber to the west boiled a dust storm, the father of all dust storms. Its clouds seethed up and up, higher than any bushfire, huge with darkness.

The old man said, 'I must go! Evelyn is home alone with the baby.'

She heard the sound of the horse's hooves as it was urged down the road and moments later, the schoolgirls arrived home from school. 'We ran all the way and we're boiling!' they panted.

'Boys, come inside. Richie, bring Mother a nice picture book and I'll read to you in a minute.'

She moved as quickly as she could around the house, doing her best to seal out dust by laying mats or bags against outer doors. The nieces ran from room to room ahead of her, anticipating her requests. Jim, she knew, was somewhere on the far side of the farm and would find shelter where he could.

'Auntie, come and look now. It is a real black dust storm.' Grace McDowell stood at a window beckoning her aunt. A strong wind was blowing, tossing the newly-planted young saplings about and gusting across the fragile new garden around the house. The great cloud loomed up out of the west, bringing dust from Narrandera or Hay nearer and nearer, towering up, ominous, threatening, and they watched it come. The base of the cloud was inky with blackness, its waves rising up through amber and merging into red, rolling terrifyingly on towards them, riding through the heated atmosphere on a tidal wave of burning wind, to descend on their home, engulfing them. Inside the house of solid blocks they were protected, but as the pall of dust fell over them, stifling and awesome, Grace felt her heart thumping. Outside the window the world was totally, fearfully dark, with not even the nearest garden bed visible through the blackness.

For the woman watching, this was not a simple dust storm. She had seen many dust storms, large and small. This one, early in 1915, seemed to give form to fears which had no names yet, and she had a sense of darkness descending on her home.

Abruptly she turned from the window. On the big table glowed a lamp, its tongue of light shining through the tall glass of the chimney, illuminating the faces of the children who watched her anxiously.

'Let's say a prayer first and then have a story,' she said, gathering wriggling small Willie onto her lap and drawing the other little boys in beside her on the settee. Her girls had dropped sunhats and were dragging off hot school boots, sitting on the cool lino. She looked across the lampshine to the nieces, including them as close friends in her gaze, and her mother too, sitting nearby so calmly, her mending lying still in her lap.

'Thank you, dear Jesus,' she prayed, 'for being here with us now. It is very dark and dusty outside, but you are here, too, in the dark. We are glad about that.'

Grace's seventh child was born in the new house with the help of a midwife relative. She had been reluctant to go to Coolamon and somehow the solid walls and roof punctuated with chimneys had already become a symbol of security. Already after only six months, a young grapevine was planted by a back verandah post and banksia roses battled against dry weather with the rest of the newly-planted garden. For Jim, the act of building a fine strong house in the face of a very bad year and the prospect of a failed harvest was a practical demonstration of his care for his wife. It felt like home already.

After the baby was born, Grace lay exhausted in her room. The midwife and the nieces, her mother and Jim had all come to care for her, quietly moving in and out of the room, staying to attend to tasks or pausing to stand silently by her bed. Through the haze of weariness, she was specially aware of her husband; he was nearby, his large hand enclosing her own, long brown beard framing a smile of intense love.

'Is baby well?' she whispered.

'Our new daughter is perfect. Sleep now – the girls are looking after her.'

'The other children?'

'Evelyn has them all at The Hill – they'll come to see you tomorrow.'

She lay still, thinking. So yet again she had crossed the threshold of childbirth. Once more she had a live baby and she herself, though utterly drained, had lived through it. 'Jim, please say a prayer of thanks,' she murmured, her voice coming faintly from a face almost as pale as the pillow on which it lay.

Jim clasped her hand gently in both of his and in his deep, measured voice he began to pray; a thanksgiving for his beloved wife restored to him, for the great goodness of God to their family, for the new baby Muriel Grace. Before the prayer had come to an end, the mother was asleep.

In the months that followed, though her baby was well and she herself gradually regained her strength, Grace found herself seeing an approaching storm cloud on her private horizon. At first it was still in the distance, but its dark threat was there. Week by week, their local paper carried increasing material in the column headed War News, with details cabled from Europe of battles in France, of Australian soldiers in camp in Egypt. Coolamon women established a branch of the Red Cross and their sewing circles sewed for parcels of 'comforts' for the soldiers. Schoolchildren learned patriotic songs and farming communities began patriotic funds. Jim Higman joined neighbours in planning a patriotic sports day for Rannock for Empire Day. The weather continued to be very grim with no rain right through April, the very time when farmers needed rain for crop sowing. Dust storms slowed trains, carried good topsoil for many miles, then dropped it on clothes lines full of clean washing, and eroded the land. People started to suggest that perhaps this year, what with the war and another terrible season, they should abandon the annual Coolamon Show, but others felt that they were not in such straits as to warrant that.

Grace knew that Stan had landed in Egypt and was somewhere along the Canal. As she had promised, she prayed for him and the other young men she knew every day. She knew that her mother also prayed for Stan, and had discovered the old lady sitting by the beds of her grandchildren as they knelt to say their evening prayers and commanding firmly: 'And now pray, "God bless and protect cousin Stan and the other boys, and bring them safe home."'

She had been praying for protection for the young man from disease, from accident, from evil influences, for comfort if he were homesick. It seemed unthinkable to her that Sarah's boy could be faced with real battles, real bullets, but her prayers included even the unthinkable.

Then on 29 April 1915, the new Prime Minister Andrew Fisher announced to Australia that the nation's young men were at war. The news was garbled and people seemed unsure of what had happened for some days; people spoke of the Dardanelles and no-one seemed quite sure where it was or why it could be important. It wasn't till more than a week later that the first newspaper reports began to appear and the word 'Gallipoli' first began to brand itself on the consciousness of the nation. Jim studied his atlas and discovered a narrow neck of land north of the lands of the Bible, a site where the battles of ancient civilisations had been waged. Turkish troops in their thousands were entrenched there and Australian, New Zealand and British troops were landing with the aim of forcing the Turks back and making a way through to the Dardanelles, a narrow strait – part Europe, part Asia – which would give access to Russia and open the way for allied shipping.

It wasn't till much later that the full force of what had happened began to be known, as letters started to filter through and newspapers published the earliest eyewitness accounts. By then, Grace knew that Stan had been there, in the heart of the horror, there among the soldiers desperately running up the beach towards the cliff face under a rain of bullets and shells there on 26 April, the second day of the landing at Gallipoli.

Later, when she read the descriptions of the battle which was to go on painfully, fruitlessly, cruelly month after month, she could scarcely read for trembling and the pounding of her heart. Stan was still there; still alive when last she heard, but who could know? In the local paper a letter from a young Coolamon Private was published. Grace knew the boy and tried to imagine him – and Stan, and the others – in the scene he described. He wrote of being among hundreds of troops being taken as close to that rocky Gallipoli shore as the troopships could go, moving closer to the shore in boatloads, then jumping into the water in full kit and wading towards the shore in neck-high water. Around him men were falling, weeping, cursing, drowning and the hail of machine-gun fire sprayed over them from the looming cliffs above. Boats sank. Men screamed with mortal wounds before they had even reached the shore. He had run up the beach to shelter among a few rocks and watched his major shot down before he had reached safety. He wrote of the urgent digging of trenches, of forcing their way forward and being forced back, of slaughtering and seeing the slaughter of his friends, of the hideous task with the bayonet, of fearful, ever-present death, of himself crawling wounded for three miles from the front line back towards medical help, under fire all the way. The letter ended: 'Talk about hell! That was it, all right. It is to be hoped that the people in

Australia will never know what war is. When a soldier feels it most is when a mate is killed at his side.'

Grace read the paper and dropped it on the table. She found it hard to look at her family, her own little sons cheerfully playing before a warm winter fire, as she hurried from the room, tears spilling down her cheeks. In her own room she fell on her knees by the bed to pray and grieve for Sarah's son and the sons of her friends who were living and dying in a stony hell.

A cold wind was blowing and the sky was heaped with massed grey featherbeds of cloud, dark and promising, when the Higman family drove away from the house on Empire Day, 24 May 1915. The buggie was crowded to capacity, with children perched on bags of chaff for sale and everyone clutching trays and tins of food. Grandma was in her phaeton with her own cargo of children and foodstuffs.

As they drove along the road and through a thick pine forest surrounding the Rannock Recreation Reserve, other buggies and sulkies approached with loads of other Rannock farming families and visitors from neighbouring rural areas – Methul, Trickett, North Berry Jerry and Winchendon Vale. Farmers watched the leaden sky and compared notes on the rain which had fallen on their properties over the past few weeks, breaking at last the long weary drought. Women greeted each other as they unpacked boxes of crockery and set out quantities of food. Children from each of the tiny rural schools eyed each other suspiciously at first, but soon began to revel in the rare chance to play with a larger group of boys and girls.

'Time for the races!' called some of the men, and scattered children rushed back to watch and take part. First the schoolboys raced across the new grass towards the tape, then the girls, in a great flapping of skirts, and the men set off at a brisk pace in the gents walking competition. No less than thirty-six starters jostled at the start of the mystery race and one lone competitor wobbled his way with infinite slowness to be the only one to complete the course in the slow bike race. Grace laughed and consoled as one after the other of her children lost their hardboiled eggs, toppling from the spoons held in clenched teeth in the egg-and-spoon race. She held the smallest ones firmly in check while riders put their horses through the walk, trot and gallop and tilted at the ring. After the prizes were presented, everyone sat down to the vast luncheon waiting for them. A small fire burned nearby and several kerosene tins of water were hung from green forked sticks to boil for tea. Now and then the sun broke through the clouds and shone briefly on the people, sitting in the scented pine forest under their bower of gum branches, sipping their hot tea and choosing another cake from the rich array before them. Laughter and conversation mingled with the sound of the cool wind in the trees and distant birdsong. The homelike sound of washing up, plates rattling through the tin dish of the hot suds and being stacked by cheerful women flourishing teatowels, was interleaved with the loud joking of men and sometimes the fretful cry of a tired child.

The peace was sliced through by the speechmaking. With all the children sitting quietly with the adults, and Jim Higman presiding, the Church of England vicar, the Methodist minister and the town doctor made speeches. Grace sat in silence, listening. The men spoke about Empire and history, about past glories in other parts of the world and about the present conflict. With every other adult present, she was picturing the lists of Killed in Action which were beginning to be published and thinking of the boys who were at that very moment locked in mortal combat with the foe. 'Empire' had ceased to be a noble word speaking of the parts of the school map of the world coloured in red. Empire was no longer a pretty tableau of young students dressed as India or Africa, parading before parents. Empire was responsibility, interdependence, commitment to a cause far beyond Australia. Empire was Sarah's son leaving the place where he had played cricket with friends to be with others on a barren cliff, waiting to kill or be killed.

The town doctor was speaking. 'Australia's heritage is greater than all the gold and all the grain and the leagues of pastureland from the furthest west or east. Our chief pride now lies in the doings of our Australian soldiers at the Dardanelles. . . Children, never let your flag go down as long as honour can uphold it. Be true to yourselves, your country and your king!'

Grace watched the faces of her children as they listened to the speeches. The Church of England vicar and the Methodist minister spoke, each referring to the deeds of the boys away in the army and using words like 'sacrifice' and 'men who are willing to be heroes'. The children listened with open mouths, picturing who knew what of noble youths with rifles held high. The parents listened with heads bowed. The full force of what was going on at Gallipoli was still unknown, beyond the beginnings of news coming through. But each adult saw a son, a nephew, a neighbour's boy, a farmhand of long association who was now in grave danger or who would soon enlist and be plunged into the agony of war.

Despite several years of disastrous drought which had ruined crops and left many of them with very little in the way of cash, they had come prepared to be generous for the patriotic fund, and Jim announced the auction. A fine home-cured ham, bags of chaff and bags of grain, poultry and bouquets of flowers prepared by one of the girls were brought forward.

The auctioneer called, 'And what am I bid for this fine bag of chaff? Good Rannock chaff, too, none of this crook imported stuff they have been bringing in since our bad time last year.'

Men outbid each other, buying and reselling the same bag several times over, each time tossing the money into the hat. A knife, fork and spoon in a case was put up by the auctioneer: 'What am I bid?'

'Two bob!'

'Sold!'

'Hang on, I'll buy it off you for another two bob.'

'Hey, I'll give you another couple of bob — pass it over.'

The small set of cutlery changed hands nine times, with rising excitement and laughter. Each item became an object of theatre, turned into a priceless and coveted thing just for the moment. Children chuckled and jumped around as they watched their fathers tossing coins into the hat, multiplying the patriotic fund.

Later, when they were driving home again under skies which were still dark but had held their rain till everyone was safe home, Grace cuddled her baby in her lap and supported sleepy little boys. The bigger girls were walking home to leave room in the back of the buggie for the pair of turkeys and the pair of black Orpington pullets which were all making offended noises at their imprisonment. One of the bouquets of flowers shifted around on the floor among the empty cake tins, and Jim's bags of chaff were coming home again, having been 'bought' back.

The bearded man by her side was looking a little sheepish.

'Do you think I was a bit reckless with my buying, my dear?'

'Well, you did seem to have your hand in your pocket for almost everything that was offered.'

He said nothing for a while. At the gate he waited while little Legh scrambled down to open it wide. Driving up to the house he muttered, 'When a man hears what is going on with our boys over at Gallipoli, he feels he has to do *something*!'

On a fine autumn day in 1916, Richard Higman asked Evelyn to help him by leading the horse while he directed the garden plough through the orchard. He was cheerful and seemed very well, though he mentioned a twinge of indigestion. When they had finished, Evelyn went back into the house while her father went to let the horse go in the horse yard. That was where Will Thomas found him when he brought the working horses in at midday.

Will rang Higmans and Jim hurried straight to The Hill with Grace. The doctor and the constable were called, but everyone knew that at last Richard Higman's heart had failed and he was gone.

The funeral was held on Sunday afternoon. The older grandchildren were brought solemnly into the front bedroom of The Hill and led by Auntie Evelyn's hand past the open coffin where their grandfather lay. They didn't want to look. The Methodist minister, Walter Theobald, conducted a service in the home and then the procession began, winding through quiet country back roads to the Berry Jerry Cemetery. Looking back down the road, Grace saw a long line of vehicles following: buggies, sulkies and the occasional motor car – people said later that the procession was over a mile long. Richard had been a pioneer. He had come nearly forty years earlier, one of the first in the district, an initiator, an inventor, a hard worker.

They stood around the open grave with the sun shining through the kurrajong and cypress pines and illuminating wide paddocks spreading away into the distance. The great crowd stood silent, remembering the man they had respected. The only sound was a gentle wind in the trees and the voice of the minister reading the words of hope for a resurrection and the promise of life.

'Those who knew Mr Richard Higman intimately,' he said, 'wondered at his depth of vision, of interests and of sympathies; but above all these things, the light of his Christian character shone undimmed.'

Grace stood beside Jim, her hand on his arm. His grief was mingled with pride that his father was being honoured. There was a sense of completion about Richard Higman's death, a good man full of years who had achieved much in his life and had the dignity of a solemn funeral surrounded by friends. As the clods of red earth fell on his coffin, she turned away, blinded by tears for so many young boys, far away in Europe, whose lives were being cut off daily and had no chance to live to see their grandchildren, or even children. For them there was no funeral with plumed horses pulling a hearse through quiet paddocks. For them no weeping wife at the graveside, no children, no neighbours, no flowers. For them only mass graves, lost graves, or no grave but the mud of Flanders or the harsh stone of Gallipoli. Local boys were dying, and Stan was still there.

The knowledge came to her slowly and fearfully that her husband might feel called to enlist. Earlier in the year people had said of the war in France, 'It will surely be all over by the end of the summer in Europe', but the year of 1916 dragged on and even in the wheat belt of NSW, far from the scene of battle, it was becoming clear that the struggle must go on and on. They had had news of Stan. He had survived Gallipoli, though many of his closest friends had lost their lives. He wrote of a mine exploding in his trench, killing men beside him, but his letters were guarded and they guessed, from talking to men who had returned, that there was much he was not saying. He wrote of 'being privileged to be among the last to leave' on 20 December 1915, when a masterly evacuation had been engineered by their officers so that 90,000 troops were safely withdrawn from those barren shores in such secrecy that the Turkish army did not realise till too late that they had gone. People had difficulty in explaining how they saw the months of carnage at Gallipoli: it looked remarkably like a defeat for the Australians, yet they were turning it into the stuff of legend in their pride in their young men.

Stan had travelled by sea to France and wrote glowingly of beautiful countryside, spring flowers, green fields. He had sent postcards to his young cousins and Richie treasured one with a smiling and cherubic little figure in Australian uniform wrapped in a flag. But that was before he had gone to Flanders and they had begun to hear dreadful stories of battles being fought in the mud of the Somme.

The local paper began to publish regular lists of men who had enlisted – and lists of those killed and wounded in action. Men of eligible age found themselves under pressure when recruiting officers visited the town, and at every public meeting, speeches were made on the theme of the need for more recruits. Along with the vicar and the doctor and the Presbyterian and Methodist ministers, Jim Higman was often among those urging young men to respond to the needs of their country.

Posters were pasted up around town urging men to enlist: *Come*

Over to Help Our Boys. The town was divided on the question of conscription: Catholics and Labor voters tended to be against it while Protestants and many people on the land were in favour. Jim was of the opinion that all Australians should be obliged to take some formal part in the war effort, though not necessarily at The Front, and was disappointed when the referendum in late 1916 narrowly went against conscription.

One man after another was farewelled in the hall behind the Springwood Hotel or in one of the churches. Groups of friends were seen regularly at the little railway station, saying goodbye to men leaving for embarkation.

'How can I keep on talking about the need for more enlistments when I'm not willing to volunteer myself?' Jim asked. 'If I'm all words and no action, no-one can possibly take me seriously.'

'But Jim . . . surely they wouldn't pass you! After all your chest troubles, and your operation – and at your age! You're forty-four!'

It seemed a ridiculous idea, simply an offer to state a principle. He went to town to volunteer, but came home slightly disappointed. 'The doctor says he can't pass me for the medical,' he said. 'He says I'd be much more usefully employed if I made up my mind to stay home and accept nomination for Shire Council.'

'Yet another committee,' Grace murmured with a wry smile. Jim's list of committees, both community and church, went on and on.

But that was before the later months of the year brought increasingly serious news of endless battles being waged in France and army recruitment officers becoming more and more willing to turn a blind eye to deficiencies in volunteers.

One morning in the early days of the harvest of late 1916, Grace was pouring tea for the family and for Jim's workmen who were breakfasting with them. A young Irishman who was with them for harvest, Paddy McKenna, took his tea politely then turned to his boss.

'When harvest is over I'll be enlisting,' he said. 'It's a funny thing – us Irish Catholics haven't much time for the idea of going to the help of "mother England". Old mother England isn't too sweet a name in Ireland. But I keep thinking about my mates, the boys from around here, dying in that hell in Europe and the Middle East. I'm not going for the Empire: I'm going for my mates. After harvest I'll be off, boss.'

Across the clear skies of summer, Grace felt clouds building up, waiting to darken her world.

'But Jim, you *can't* go!'

Her words were not plaintive but fierce, the kind of ferocity that cloaks fear. They lay in the heavy darkness of a hot summer night, the sky beyond the open window spreading without limit into the unknown. In the paddocks the harvest was almost over. She looked at the faint outline of his profile against the pillow, lying there staring at the ceiling.

'I have to try again to enlist – there is nothing else for it.'

'But the farm!'

'Charlie Pearce is a good man. He can manage the place for you instead of just being a sharefarmer. And he's already been knocked back for the army.'

'But what about all the other things, family things, that I couldn't ask Charlie Pearce to help me with?'

'We'll contact Harry. He said he'd be willing to come to Caldwell to help you, if I was accepted for war service. And of course you have Evelyn and Will – and your mother.'

They lay in silence, the quietness shouting with unspoken questions. Both of them knew, with agony, that the war was not going well. From the safety and peace of the farm, they heard the cries of the nations at war. Telegrams arrived for neighbours to say that a son was dead or missing. Names of distant rivers and districts of France and Flanders were household words – the Somme, Ypres, Fromelles, Pozieres. Every letter which arrived from Stan – or from any other lad at the front – was cherished as a sacred object; you never knew which letter might be his last. Women knitted battalions of socks, armies of woollen scarves, the knitting wool rubbing unpleasantly in hot sticky hands as they knitted through the heat of summer for their boys wading through the icy mud of European winter.

At social events, a bitterness was building up between young men who had been abroad and returned, often damaged in mind or body, and the men who had chosen not to volunteer. Simple friendships and courtships were being rippled by the undercurrents of antagonism between the young men of the district. Local brides stood at the altar, clutching bouquets of blossoms and the arm of their khaki uniformed groom, knowing that they had a week, maybe only days, to cherish their beloved and then he would be gone, perhaps for years, perhaps forever. Longtime friends and neighbours found themselves divided on questions of conscription, and on prohibition of alcohol sales at particular times and places, as well as the ever-present conflicts of politics. People lived daily with a sense of unease, of impending doom that was always just beyond the edge of the corner of one's eye, waiting. Recruiting officers kept coming to town, appealing again and again for more men to enlist. On every public occasion the Church of England vicar, the Presbyterian and Methodist ministers, Dr Buchanan and the local member for parliament were on the platform speaking in favour of recruitment.

Only days before, Jim had gone to yet another recruiting rally where the cry for more men had been more desperate than ever. Grace had read the report in the *Coolamon Farmer's Review*, where the local member had said, and been reported in bold capitals as saying: 'Do not *hesitate* – the time is now -*your help is urgently required!*'

Earlier in the evening, she had seen Jim lay down the latest edition of the church newspaper the *Methodist* and walk away, absorbed in some private thought. Grace had walked to the outspread pages and looked. There, under large headlines reading, 'Recruiting. Appeal to Australian Manhood. Appeal from Heads of Churches in Australia' was a long letter signed by the Anglican Archbishop of Australia, the Presbyterian Moderator-General, the Chairman of the Congregational Union and their own Rev. Dr George Brown, President-General of the Methodist Conference.

Grace stood before the wide pages, reading the appeal of the clerics: 'We appeal to all citizens for a yet fuller response to the call of duty and patriotism. We believe the hour is critical . . . During the progress of the war, we understand better than we did that we are fighting for our hearths and homes, the honour of our women, the lives of our children and the future of our race. Our men have gone forth in their thousands to defend these, and many have died for them . . . The power of the enemy is not yet broken . . . many of us fail to realise how evenly the issue still lies in the balance.'

She had turned the page quickly to obliterate the terrible demand, but only found instead more news of the war, memorial notices of beautiful, gifted, treasured young men killed in action, letters from army chaplains. There was no escape.

Now she turned in the darkness to cling to her husband. 'Jim, you surely can't enlist. What of the children . . . and me? Surely they couldn't pass you with your bad chest. And what about your nomination for Shire Council? Your name is already on the ballot papers!'

'If they accept me, I'll write to the paper and tell everyone to give my votes to one of the other candidates.'

His voice cracked unnaturally for a moment as he held her tightly. 'My dearest, I cannot bear to stand even once more on a platform to ask other men, other people's sons, to go to war if I'm not willing to go myself. I must go to Cootamundra to the regional enlistment officers – I *must* volunteer again.'

She knew then that there was no turning back. For a time she lay in his arms but at last, when she knew that he was asleep, she rolled over so that he would not be disturbed by the hot painful tears which were soaking her pillow. Before she slept, she found herself praying a confused prayer asking God to make sure her husband's health was not perfect.

'The doctor passed me.'

The man standing in the doorway was clad in khaki. The woman with a baby in her arms and little ones around her feet closed her eyes. She didn't want to face what she saw. When she looked again, she saw that his face reflected relief – and pride. And she knew that, whether or not he had expected to be passed as fit by the army doctors, it meant a great deal to him to wear the dignity of uniform. He was a man whose actions had always supported his words and now his words would have much more credibility.

'They are very keen for recruits at the drill hall in Cootamundra,' he said. 'The officers were most courteous and they told me that any reasonably ablebodied man of military age would be almost sure to pass.'

'Military age!' she accused. 'What does that mean? They used to say that thirty-six was too old – and you'll be forty-five in two weeks!'

'They say Germany is having "slave raids" and forcing every man from seventeen to sixty into the field. We have to make a supreme effort too. They'll find me something useful to do.'

'And what about your bad chest? Is that miraculously healed?'

'The doctor who looked at me said that it was "just a slight defect, almost nothing at all" and he passed me. Though,' Jim admitted reluctantly, 'I had the feeling that he didn't really want to do it. He almost apologised to me.'

Grace turned away to do something meaningless with the saucepans on the stove. She wanted to hide from Jim and the little ones the twisting of her mouth, the burning of her eyes, the feeling of being barely in control.

At last she spoke, in a very small voice. 'You are a very stubborn man, Jim Higman. And a brave one. When you have made up your mind about something...'

The man in khaki moved to stand beside her and she fled to the safety of his arms, her face pressed against the military buttons and pockets of a new uniform, leaning against the comfort of his height and strength.

'I have six weeks to put my affairs in order and then I have to be in camp at Liverpool in Sydney for military training. I'm in the 12th Light Horse. Our Paddy McKenna will be coming with me. Then I'll come home for leave before I am sent – wherever I am sent.'

He held her tightly for a moment. 'Grace, you do understand, don't you, that I have to go because I love you, and the children, and our home so much?'

Much later that night, Jim sat down to write a letter to the editor. Among other things he wrote: 'The further I go the more certain I am *that every man is wanted*. Every indication shows that the war, though very likely not ended, will be won or lost during this year... We can only win one way – everyone do something towards that end. Liberty, justice and our beloved Australia are in extreme jeopardy. No matter how important our work may seem to us, weighed in the scales with these things it is nothing...'

Jim proceeded to organise his affairs. He said, confidently, 'You'll have Will and Evelyn nearby while I'm away. Charlie Pearce will be able to look after the farm – no need for you to worry about it. And Harry will be arriving any day.' It sounded reasonable enough. He spent time discussing the farm with Charlie, and family affairs with Evelyn and Will Thomas. Piece by piece, he was releasing the things in his life which were important to him; handing over his preaching appointments, taking his name from the nominees for Shire Council, finding someone else for his Sunday School class, resigning as secretary of the local Farmers and Settlers.

Grace watched the process with a feeling of anxiety which rarely left her. The year 1917 stretched away ahead; most of the time she was thankful that she didn't know what it held. Her Bible became more and more a place of safety. The pages almost fell open of their own accord at words which she had read and re-read, words of comfort and hope.

She went to visit Evelyn, knowing that Evelyn loved her brother

Jim with great loyalty and pride, and would understand something of what she was feeling. Evelyn was expecting her second child very soon. At The Hill she found Evelyn lying on her bed, looking very pale.

'You don't look at all well – are you in pain?'

'I don't know what is wrong, but I feel dreadful. Maybe it is the heat – or the baby due so soon. Forty-one is not the easiest age to have babies. Maybe it is just that I can't bear the thought of Jim going away to war. Grace, what is happening to our world?'

Grace shook her head wordlessly, not trusting herself to speak, and the two friends sat quietly, looking through the open door across the shaded verandah out across the spreading patchwork of paddocks, palest tones of cream and stone against brick red earth. The sun shone across their world, yet the eyes of their hearts saw clouds.

Evelyn Thomas went to Coolamon for the birth of her baby, and she and her gentle Will were delighted with their new daughter. Little Jean was lifted up in her father's arms to see the new baby. But Evelyn was ill. It was not just the exhaustion of giving birth to a child, but something else. She went to stay with a cousin in Coolamon and the doctor came regularly. He called in the doctor from the next town for another opinion and both spoke of an operation when she was well enough. Grace and Jim visited, and they prayed together, placing each other into the loving hands of God.

On Monday afternoon, with the new baby ten days old, the Higman schoolchildren came running into the house after school, very offended by something that had happened on the way home from school. They had gone with other children to the post office, and the other children had been told some news. 'But they said they wouldn't tell *us*,' Carrie complained. 'It's not fair – why should we be the only ones not to hear the news?'

Their mother was sitting very still, with a strange look on her face and traces of tears around her eyes. 'The people at the post office thought I should tell you the news myself,' Mother said. 'Your Auntie Evelyn died today. The funeral will be at the Berry Jerry Cemetery tomorrow.'

Looking back on the time later, she was to recall the next months as a sequence of formal ceremonies, each tense with pain and emotion, and the indecency of a plague of mice playing out a cruel farce in the background.

The procession of sulkies and cars gathered from the surrounding farms and township for Evelyn's funeral which drove through the first rain which had fallen for months. The community was stunned by this unexpected loss. Evelyn had lived at The Hill since she was a tiny child, long before many of the neighbours had come to settle in the district, and people knew her as a real friend. They remembered her as a maker of music on the organ and as a very active and respected member of her church. Grace stood in the rain at the graveside, grieving for the loss of her sister and friend, and listening to Walter Theobald read the funeral service.

After the funeral, she and Jim sat with Will, who slumped exhaustedly in his chair, his head in his hands.

'What about the children, Will?' Grace asked gently.

'I don't know. . . I can manage little Jean, I know what to do for a little girl, but a new baby. . .'

'Would you like me to take the baby, Will? I'll look after her for you until she is old enough for you to manage yourself.'

Will nodded dumbly. Perhaps he remembered that she already had the care of seven children, or perhaps he didn't, but he knew his child would be safe with Grace.

After Jim had left for the army training camp at Liverpool near Sydney, Harry Playford arrived from his dairy farm at Nana Glen on the north coast, and Grace was thankful to have him. Harry had always been her close friend, and old Mary Playford was overjoyed to have two of her children with her. Harry brought his horses and his younger daughter Minnie, who was a 'big girl' in her late teens to her admiring younger cousins. Harry said, 'I know practically nothing about wheat and sheep, you know. Horses and cows, specially horses, now that's different! But I'll do my best for you while Jim's away. Robert can manage the dairy at home.'

The tiny new baby came home to Caldwell and the cousins loved her. The baby things which Evelyn had so carefully prepared for her child were arranged in little Muriel Grace's room, next to Grace's own room, and Grace took up again the familiar role of mothering a newborn. It seemed very strange to attend to a restless little one in the middle of the night and to return to her bed to find it empty of her husband. The people in her world were unexpectedly altered – Harry instead of Jim and young Minnie instead of Evelyn.

The young minister came again to Caldwell for the baptism of the baby. Will Thomas, looking desperately forlorn and lost, stood beside Grace in the dining room. His little Jean clung to his legs, not willing to let go of her father and very distressed that her mother had not come back. The other children were there; Carrie, Mary and Connie subdued and wide-eyed at the service being led in their own house instead of the church, and the three little boys, Legh, Richie and Willie, trying hard to be good. Grandmother Mary Playford cuddled little Muriel Grace on her lap and watched with deep sorrow the grief of her family.

Mr Theobald took the infant from Will's arms and began the words of the baptismal service. They all knew that Will would have found it too cruel to have stood in the Rannock Church for the baptism of his child without his beloved Evelyn at his side, and the privacy of Caldwell provided a haven.

'Name this child,' he said carefully, knowing what the answer would be.

'Evelyn Mary.'

'Evelyn Mary Thomas, I baptise you in the name of the Father, and the Son, and the Holy Spirit . . .' and with the mark of the cross still wet on her little forehead, the child was laid in the arms of Grace Higman.

Letters began to arrive from Jim. Grace remembered the days when Jim Higman's early letters had been received with faint embarrassment and awkwardness, when she didn't really know him. It was very different now: they were from the man she loved, who had shared her life for twelve years. He wrote to the children, sometimes speaking more directly and personally to them on paper than he seemed able to do when he was sitting with them at table. He drew word pictures of the camp — line after line of tents in ranks across open paddocks, the mess hall, the Methodist Soldiers Institute where he often retreated to write letters and read and the big hall where the men were entertained with concerts and films. He didn't often go to the big hall. He described standing outside the door on a cold evening looking into the misty atmosphere inside with almost every man smoking, and decided to forgo the concert for the sake of his chest. Jim had never lived away from his home district apart from occasional holidays and church meetings and, like many others, he was homesick.

With her husband away, Grace had to face the problems of the mouse plague alone. Right across the district, thousands and thousands of mice were running, destroying, multiplying, crawling through haystacks, chewing through wheatbags, nibbling sleeping pigs, stealing the grain from the chickens. They were everywhere on the farms and in the houses. Householders devised all kinds of systems to try to keep the vermin from foodstuffs and out of houses. People tried poison and they tried drowning. They laid traps and sank kerosene tins of water into the ground with the surface of the water sprinkled with chaff to trap the mice. Thousands of mice were dying, but still they came. Grace found mice running in the house, mice in the children's rooms, gnawing at clothing, alarming her mother by running across her bed.

The smell of mice, alive and dead, was everywhere. It was nasty enough around their own home and even more sickening when she had to visit the town. The schoolchildren made a game of snatching the long dark mouse tails dangling through the cracks in an outside shed and dragging the mice through to their deaths. Grace found herself furiously angry with the mice. They had invaded her home in a way which appalled her, assaulting her haven, infesting her place of safety. All the anger which had been hidden in the face of bereavement and loss was channelled toward the invading mice. When she found that mice had chewed baby Evie's dummy and even run into the baby's basket, she shut herself in her room for a little while to control her angry tears.

The week of the farewells was a strange one. Jim came home on his final leave in April without his full beard, but wearing a lordly moustache.

'He looks just like Lord Kitchener in that uniform!' people said.

Jim was home, yet he was not home. Instead of his usual dusty working clothes or his best suit and hat, he wore khaki. He went around Caldwell with Harry and Charlie Pearce, but he would not be there for all the sowing, or for the harvest. He was shocked at the substantial damage by the mice, but he would not be there to see the problem solved. He seemed to be studying his beloved land, not as a farmer analysing his property, but as a traveller who is looking his last on home.

On Sunday evening, Jim lit a fire in the hearth in the dining room. The lamps were lit and the fire leaped in the grate, reflecting light from the brass fireirons and filling the room with the fragrance of woodsmoke. On the dining table were set out the cups and saucers of the best china with the blue rims and flowers, and the special glasses kept by the children for Sundays, with Sunday cakes waiting under a gauzy cover. All the family was there; old Grandmother

Playford in her rocking chair, Will staring sadly into the flames with little Jean on his knee and the baby in her basket. The seven Higman children were there, sitting on fireside mat and hassock, waiting for Mother to read the next chapter of their Sunday book. The mother sat at the centre of the group with little Gracie on her lap and a book open in her hands.

'Last Sunday we left our story at an exciting place,' she said. 'Let's see what happens in tonight's chapter.'

As she read, she was conscious of Jim sitting opposite her, watching her. The scene was just the normal one. The family was gathered at the end of Sunday at peace. It was a time to read aloud and sing and pray, a time to look your best and use your nicest things and eat the tastiest foods. Jim's eyes were moving from one family member to the next. At last his eyes stayed on his wife. She looked up from the page and met his gaze. Her voice faltered. Her mind had left the story she was reading aloud and had leapt forward to the unimaginable future. 'When will we all be here together again?' she thought. '*Will* we all be together again?'

After the children were all in bed, husband and wife sat by the fire together, staring into the bed of coals which glowed and sparkled. Jim slipped his hand in his pocket and drew out a tiny box. 'I've been thinking. I don't want to go unless you have my ring on your finger. After the other ring was lost in the garden, we said we wouldn't worry about it, but now. . . Anyway, I've brought you a ring.'

Very gently he slid the ring onto Grace's finger. 'I still love you from the top of your head to the soles of your feet,' he said. 'And I mean what I said with the first ring — I promise to be faithfully yours, for better, for worse, for richer, for poorer, in sickness and in health, to love and to cherish. . . till death us do part. . .'

That week she sat through three formal farewells to her husband. In some ways it was incongruous, but it was typical of Jim's attitude to life that one farewell was held in the Masonic Hall in Coolamon, where the Loyal Orange Lodge hosted a fine farewell for their member whose Protestantism was militant in its singlemindedness. Yet a few nights later he happily shared the platform at a Rannock community farewell with his good friend Trooper Paddy McKenna who was also in the 44th Infantry and was a staunch Catholic. Jim did his best to avoid confusing strong opinions with personal relationships. Paddy's own family were far away in County Derry, and the young workman gave Carrie a green silk handkerchief inscribed 'Greetings from Ireland' – 'I don't want you all to forget me,' he said.

The third of the farewells was held in Rannock Methodist Church. Grace sat through a succession of eulogies from neighbours and friends. She was very proud of Jim, but as the evening progressed and she sat through soloists and rounds of social games after the speeches, she was aware of two dark threads through the evening. Not everyone present agreed that Jim Higman was doing the right thing, leaving his family. Hints of strong criticism had filtered back to her, and she knew that, as with so many other controversial questions, her Jim had taken a stand which would not necessarily be popular. The other dark thread was the sense that she was hearing not so much a farewell as a funeral. 'They don't think he's going to come back!' she thought.

Her husband stood to speak in response to the speechmaking. He said, 'When this war began and they first called for men, I was sure it didn't mean me. I thought it was just for the young fellows to go. But the more I have read letters written from the trenches and followed the war news, the more I have weighed it all up and come to the conclusion that the call to serve comes to me and every man. I haven't come to this lightly. I know what it means. There is a picture of my dear wife and seven children printed indelibly on my mind, and that picture will go with me wherever I go, strengthening me to fight for the liberty of our country and our families.'

That year was a very wet one, with one grey miserable day following another. The overcast weather with mud underfoot and dark clouds overhead blended in with her mood. Jim had gone. She and the children had stood bleakly on the windy railway platform with the stench of mice reeking from the nearby wheat stacks in the railway yards, and watched him go. Driving home again in the sulky with the children huddling for shelter under umbrellas, she knew that for her, war would not mean heroic feats in a far country: it would mean being responsible to drive the horse and sulky for fourteen miles through rain, disciplining naughty little boys without the strength of Father to give weight to Mother's word, an empty bed, the chair at the head of the table always vacant, making decisions which she had always left to him. She set her mouth firmly. 'If I must, I'll do it,' she thought, 'but dear God, help me!'

In the winter, she travelled to Sydney to spend a week with him before he sailed. Other wives were there, waiting in accommodation near the camp where they could spend what little time they could with their men. She was not the only woman with a large family, she found. While the troops of 1914 and 1915 had been young and very fit and single, the troops of 1917 were men of more mature years, men with family responsibilities and often not as healthy as the recruiting officers imagined. These men were men with no illusions about empire and glory. They had not been forced to enlist by conscription, but by a sense of duty, or revenge. They, and their wives, knew that many of them would not come home to their children.

She met and heard about the men who would be Jim's companions. There was his officer Lieutenant Stewart Menzies, a young grazier who had already served with the 6th Light Horse, and many men from country districts who were experienced horsemen and skilled with their rifles; farmers, labourers, drovers, blacksmiths, a 'bushman' and the odd bank clerk. Paddy McKenna was there, greeting her with as much delight as if she were his own mother and asking for news of the children. The lines which had once been drawn between Jim and Paddy as boss and farmhand were already fading rapidly and they were fellow-soldiers, mates. 'Carrie treasures your Irish hankie, Paddy,' Grace told him.

The two of them talked as often as they were able, with long periods of silence when few subjects seemed worthy of filling those last hours together. Together they sat with the Bible open before them, clinging to the promises of God. Grace turned to one of her favourites, the 'traveller's Psalm', Psalm 121, which she had underlined in the years long ago. Jim read it aloud, his voice slow and careful, taking each phrase with its weight of meaning and holding it before them.

'My help cometh from the Lord . . . The Lord is thy keeper; the Lord is thy shade upon thy right hand. The Lord shall preserve thee from all evil . . .'

Grace took up the words of the last verse, holding tightly to her husband's hand as she read. 'The Lord shall preserve thy going out and thy coming in from this time forth and even for evermore.'

Grace was at the wharf when the *Port Lincoln* sailed. Beside her were other women, each one staring up to the line of figures on the deck, looking for that one man — a husband, a son, a brother, a beloved friend — from whose arms she had so recently been torn.

Paddy had said, 'I'm just as pleased not to have a girlfriend just now — it would be so rotten to say goodbye to her!' Grace stared up, searching for Jim. In their uniforms they all seemed to look alike, and all of them were waving to someone in the crowd. As the troopship began to move ponderously away from the wharf, she saw him. The ship moved slowly on, and Jim became a distant speck, then no longer visible, becoming one with the mass of troops in the 12th Light Horse. And Grace, too, was lost to him, engulfed by a wave of women weeping, their crumpled faces set to watch the *Port Lincoln* till it vanished round a point in the harbour and then they turned away, bereft, to struggle back to their lives alone.

She stared blindly across the water, the words in her mind pleading: 'The Lord shall preserve thy going out and thy coming in . . .'

15
Storm-clouds
1917-1918

THE WINTER OF 1917 was long and bleak; days draped in the pall of fog, nights of rain and wind beating on the house and rattling at the windows in the dark. Damp washing steamed before the kitchen stove. It hung on the wooden clothes horse and over the backs of chairs, the multitude of garments and babies' nappies discouraging in its volume and wetness while the sun refused to shine. There was little time for Grace to sit and be miserable, because the demands of the family were always there. There were always men to feed, Harry and the workmen, and her mother was becoming more and more frail. The active old woman who had supervised the planting of many of the garden beds which surrounded the house and had marched around, tomahawk in hand, staking up her chrysanthemums, seemed now content to walk with shuffling feet from her bedroom to sit by the fire, sometimes turning drying socks and underwear toward the heat and sometimes just sitting. The long winter rains turned the roads into quagmires so that few people willingly travelled to visit others and, as most farms still had no telephone link, there was little contact with friends. Will Thomas had hired a housekeeper to help look after little Jean and care for the house, but Grace missed her regular phone conversations with Evelyn. Even Walter Theobald and his wife made no visits to Caldwell for some time as the young minister had been ill for weeks during winter. Grace sometimes wondered whether he was supporting her in her struggle with Jim's absence, or she supporting him in the bitter task of being a wise pastor during the grim years of war.

Spring came with watery sunshine and then sparkling days with a hint of warmth in the wind. Clumps of violets showed purple against their green leaves, the violets which had come from house to house, and Grace took the little ones out with her to sniff the new warmth of the air and the perfume of the violets. Daffodils burst up from the soil, with scented jonquils and freesias. Banksia roses along the verandah posts showed bronze and glossy new leaves and the rose bush which the young soldier had given her was bursting with tiny pink buds. Along the back verandah, softening the workmanlike area of milk separator and meat safe, Jim's grapevine had sent up new and lively branches, the new leaves curled tightly into a myriad of knots waiting to be untied. The children ran in from school with tiny posies of buttercups – burnished gold, sunshine trapped in petals.

'Mother, do you like butter?' they called, dragging her to sit on the kitchen chair. Mary held the single buttercup under Grace's chin and the three giggled and looked to see whether a yellow glow would be reflected on their mother's skin.

'Mother likes butter! Willie, come; do you like butter. . .?'

With the spring came the magpies nesting and protecting their young with great ferocity, swooping on any children who approached their trees. Trixie the mare had a foal, and the little creature wobbled around the horse paddock on spindly legs. Children feeding the fowls scattered seed among hens and tiny chickens. The fruit trees Jim had planted in the new orchard broke into blossom – peach, plum, apple, pear – and beyond the nearby bush the paddocks of oats and wheat spread vividly green. Wattles washed gold through the greens of the bush paddock, and Grace took the children out for little Saturday picnics, carrying sandwiches and cake away from the house to walk among the Murray pines, the yellow box and the grey box, picking tiny wildflowers studded yellow and blue, purple and white. The yellow daisies with black hearts spread themselves joyfully through the young grass, and Grace was among them in the sunshine with baby Evie on her lap, little Gracie toddling around among the flowers and Legh, Richie and Willie poking sticks down rabbit holes. With the daisies, Grace and the older girls threaded garlands and crowns, and they processed home through the trees with crowns proudly on their heads and chains of daisies wreathing their necks. The boys teetered along the top of a fallen tree, clinging to its upturned roots and shouting, 'I'm the king of the castle!'

And Jim was not with them. Shearers had been hired for the few sheep, but Jim was not there to shear and supervise. The crops were doing well, but Jim couldn't see them. The mice plague had ended as suddenly as it had begun, with the mice dying of a mysterious disease which carried them off in their thousands, but Jim was not there to organise the disposal of the noisome bodies. The children demanded every moment of her attention and discipline, but Jim was not there to carry part of the load.

Nor was Stan around, or the other young men. Stan had written from France when he could, and they had heard the dread names of the places where he had been fighting and where several times he had been wounded: the Somme, Bullecourt, Passchendaele. He wrote excitedly of being promoted to Captain, and being presented with the Military Cross for bravery at Bullecourt, the Cross being pinned to his uniform on Anzac Day 1917 *by the king*! But Stan was still in France, and the newspapers carried weekly news of continuing battles and lists of the dead and wounded.

It was in spring, too, that Grace went to visit the sharefarmer's wife at the old house where she had lived as a bride. She drove across the farm joylessly, despite the beauty of green spreading around her. What could she say to Mrs Pearce, Jim's kinswoman? Charlie had just heard that one of his brothers had been killed in action on the other side of the world. She found Mrs Pearce at the copper, poking down her dresses into boiling black dye, ready for the months of mourning for their loss.

The two friends sat at the kitchen table later, having a quiet cup of tea together. 'We've been praying for him, and the other boys, all the time,' the woman said, her voice breaking. 'And we can't even go to his funeral.'

Through that spring two threads wove, two colours, two tunes, two tastes – the light and the dark, the gay and the mournful, the sweet and the bitter. On two Sundays in October, the two strands tangled themselves together at the Rannock Methodist Church with the Sunday School anniversary and the unveiling of the honour roll.

For weeks before the anniversary, Grace drove the horse and sulky up to the church each week and the children from the Sunday School ran across from the nearby school in their lunch hour. Grace enjoyed teaching the children the new songs. These days, among the little girls with hair sternly plaited and starched white pinafores protecting their dark school dresses and young boys nudging each other in the church pews, some of her own children sat.

On the day of the anniversary, the church was full of flowers. The sun was shining and every family for miles around was there for the children. Every child was dressed in their best, some in new spring clothes and everyone scrubbed and starched and polished to a high sheen. All the little girls had their hair flowing out in all its glory, rippling waves from yesterday's plaits or cascades of fat ringlets painfully achieved with tight, curling rags. The Sunday School teachers had made wreaths of fresh spring blossoms for the little girls and, as the children were marched into the church, the girls came innocent and beautiful with flower-wreathed hair and the boys came proudly, or bashfully, glowing with hair oil and soap, a flower buttonhole in their jackets.

Sitting at the church organ, Grace could see the faces of her neighbours as they watched their children. As the children sang and spoke, presenting their little dialogues and stories from the Bible, speaking of things like love and joy and peace, she saw that some parents could scarcely look at the children. They were too beautiful, too young, too vulnerable, too unaware of the wounds that the world might deal them.

A week later, Grace was invited to come forward during the church service. A flag was draped over the new oak honour roll which hung on the church wall. Carefully she lifted the flag away and heard the shuffle of feet behind her as the congregation rose to sing the National Anthem. The board read: 'To commemorate the brethren who served in the great war, 1914-. . . .' and then the names. Stan's name was at the head of the list, and the lad who had given her the rose bush. Two of the Swann boys' names were there and the men of other families sitting in the church. And Jim's name – J.R.C. Higman, there in gold letters with the others. Another honour roll was being unveiled that day in Coolamon which included the brothers of Charlie Pearce, one marked with a small gold star: 'Killed in Action'. There were no gold stars on the Rannock board. Not yet.

The congregation began to sing very softly as Grace returned to her seat.

> 'I fear no foe with Thee at hand to bless,
> Ills have no weight and tears no bitterness. . .'

She looked up at the honour roll, glossy with new varnish. What other names would need to be added to that list before the war was over? And how long would they wait before they knew what year the war would end? How long, O Lord? The people sang on.

'. . .Where is Death's sting? Where, grave, thy victory?
I triumph still if thou abide with me.'

It was in the spring, too, that Will Thomas came to talk to her.
'Grace, I'm not well. I don't know what the trouble is, but I'm
suffering a lot of pain in my hip. I thought perhaps I had cracked
it against something, or it was rubbing on the metal plough seat,
but I've been to Dr Buchanan and he says I should watch to make
sure it doesn't get worse. I don't think he is sure what the trouble
is. Still, it is probably nothing.'

The shadow of war fell even more deeply over the district as the
year ended. Through September, October and November the
cruellest battles raged and the names of Ypres and Passchendaele
cut deep into the hearts of families. A gold star had been added to
the Rannock Honour Roll for young Walter Allen, and Charlie
Pearce's feet moved even more sadly around the farm with the news
that his second brother was dead too. Walter Theobald said to Grace,
'I'm afraid to go visiting families unannounced these days – they
see my buggy coming and they think I'm coming to tell them
someone has died at the war. And it has often been the truth. . .'

On mail days, Jim's letters were gathered and treasured, but each
letter emphasised their separation. In the paddocks the harvest was
being gathered by Charlie and Harry and the workmen, but Jim
was writing of the Sinai Peninsula, Cairo and lonely patrols across
sandy desert. After sailing from Sydney on the *Port Lincoln* he had
spent further time at the army camp at Seymour in Victoria before
sailing from Melbourne in early September on board the *Kyarra*
for Egypt and the Middle East with the 19th Reinforcements.

Postcards began to appear in the roadside mailbox with exotic
pictures of pyramids, the street scenes in Cairo, palm trees and
camels. Grace and the children pored over the letters and cards.
Although their father had often appeared to be aloof and above the
earthy activities of the children around his table, the father who
was far away became a man whose family was more to him than
ever. Children who had wondered whether Father even noticed that
it was their birthday found birthday postcards in the mailbox. Their
father's notes were charming, speaking to them of the things they
knew: to five-year-old Richie about the tame magpie which had been
visiting the house, to four-year-old Willie about the vegetable garden
and how he was helping his mother to water the tomatoes,
encouraging Carrie for the way she had acted responsibly in taking

an important package for many miles on horseback. To the children
he said nothing of the war.

Grace carried Jim's letters in her apron pocket, even when she
knew every word, then collected them in her drawer. Each letter
was very personal, reassuring her of his love for her. This was
something she had never doubted; Jim was a man who gave his
word and kept it faithfully. Yet he was so far away.

Christmas 1917 came to Rannock, but it was a subdued Christmas.
Father was away, Will Thomas was ill and in mourning, the Pearces
didn't feel like celebrating. Grace tried to make Christmas Day
special for the children, but though the coming of Christ was more
needed than ever, it was hard for her to conjure up the lighthearted
magic of other years. The editor of the Coolamon paper gave words
to the feeling of many when he wrote: 'We cannot say "Merry
Christmas" to our readers, and the gloom which is war's despicable
shadow falls over the whole world . . . We cannot ignore the needs
of weeping ones nor can we feel in our own heart the joyous thrill
of Christmas in other days.'

'What do you think Father is having for Christmas dinner?' asked
the big girls. 'Would they have something nice? What about
Christmas pudding with money in it?'

'I've no idea,' Grace said.

Old Grandma Playford smiled at the children over her spoonful
of rich fruity pudding. 'When your father comes home, you must
ask him what he had — if it was nice he'll remember.'

*   *   *

The man with the packhorses knows about drought. He has lived
with thirst. Bare earth and dessicated vegetation has always been
part of the known world, since childhood when the dam dried up.
But not this. Not shifting desert sands, not men fighting each other
for the water in desert wells and cisterns, not seeing men killed
around you by shellfire while watering the horses. He knows all
about not wasting a drop of water, making a cupful enough for a
good wash, but here in the desert the officers plan 'ablutions days'
when camels are used to draw water from wells and pour it into
tarpaulins sunk in sand for queues of men. The lack of water in
the desert means that troops going to battle ride to meet the enemy,
then give their mounts to the horseholders to take back to the wells

— the men will fight dismounted till their horses return the next day.

Jim jolts along the rough tracks through the desert behind his team. The draughthorses are unwilling and he is cajoling them with voice and forcing them with whip to drag the laden wagon with its load of ammunition toward the front line. In the distance, beyond the harsh hills, the flash of shell and stutter of machine-gun fire reaches him and he goes forward with the grit of sand in his eyes and fear in his mind. It seems a long time since they were in the Arab town where he bought oranges and sent postcards to the children. He pictures the children — his children, not the ragged children of the villages — and his wife. Yet he dare not think of them. If he thinks of them now, he won't be game to go on. Since he arrived in the desert, the 12th Light Horse has been part of the fighting at the Battle of Beersheba on 31 October and other more scattered engagements, always under threat, always on patrol, always alert to the danger from aircraft. In his first month, of just over five hundred men, over fifty have been killed or wounded and nearly thirty evacuated sick. He and Paddy talk together about home when they can — 'It doesn't feel much like Christmas coming up, does it, mate!'

On Christmas Day 1917, the rain pours down, cold and dismal, soaking away into the sand. It is winter in the desert. The soldier in the chilly isolation of the listening post strains to hear sound other than the patter of rain, distant movement other than the flowing of water. He has been waiting, alert, silent, for hours. On Christmas Eve the news came through the officers that the Turkish army intends to attack their line any time in the next two days — 'They think that, being Christmas, we'll take our minds off the job — and Christmas means nothing to most of them, anyway. Sorry, men, but Christmas is off for us this year. Every man at full alert, all listening posts manned, patrols as usual.'

Jim shivers in the dark. Back in his tent is the parcel which arrived from home, gifts from those who love him. They have never seemed further away.

*   *   *

'I don't like to have to ask you to do this, Grace, but could you please take Jean for a while — maybe a few weeks? Dr Buchanan says I must go to Sydney to see other doctors and perhaps have an operation.'

Will Thomas looked gaunt and pale, troubled by the pain which had become part of his days. The family sat at the table eating their Sunday meal, but Will was barely eating. Will had come on Sundays with Jean for months now, and Grace had watched him slowly growing thinner.

'Of course I'll look after Jean for you, Will,' she said. 'The three little girls will be happy together. Just bring her over with her things when you are ready.'

Her mother's chair at the table was empty.

'I don't think I feel quite up to going to church this afternoon,' the old lady had said. 'If you'll excuse me, I think I'll stay in bed today. And no, I don't feel like anything to eat, thank you.'

Grace took her a cup of tea and sat by her bed for a while. Mary Playford seemed very peaceful and content, but very tired.

'Don't worry about me, my dear,' she had said. 'At least whoever is preaching this afternoon won't need to worry about this old woman with such high expectations. Next week, perhaps, I'll be back in my pew ready to correct any signs of weak doctrine.'

Grace held the soft and wrinkled hand in her own for a while, drawing strength from the wisdom and resiliance of her mother, a woman who had survived so many things and become such a powerful personality. Her mother had always been there: strong, forthright, just. A world where her mother was not present was unimaginable.

Sitting with the fragile old hand cradled in her own, Grace suddenly chuckled. 'Do you remember, Mother, some of the times you have taken advantage of your years to be quite wickedly direct with preachers who have not met your standards? I can think of a few times!'

'We should never let our men get away with rubbish, should we?' Mary Playford was unrepentant. 'They just need a few lay people who are not afraid to give them a little straight advice. Do you remember me telling you about the visiting preacher I had occasion to admonish once? I'd been hearing very upsetting stories about his character before I heard him preach. Then I heard him in the pulpit and his sermon was good. But I told him, I said, "That was a good message, young man, but I prefer to eat my dinner off a clean plate!" One of your brothers was with me, and I think I embarrassed him...'

Grace was still laughing as she went back to the children, but she knew, as she had on many previous occasions, that her sharp-witted and perfectionist mother was providing her with vital emotional strength.

One day a large parcel arrived, borne carefully to the door by the mailman. When they had finally freed it from its packing, they found the speech which had been made to Jim at the church farewell now glorified in an Illuminated Address, surrounded by a vast carved and ornamented timber frame. A portrait of Jim in Light Horse uniform was encircled with a laurel wreath, a Jim in riding breeches and high polished boots. Delicately painted Australian wildflowers and three patriotic flags filled a corner, with his initials elaborately designed and interwoven, the whole a marvel of embellishment.

'They really do respect my Jim,' she thought. 'But fine words, even framed and decorated with flags and flowers is not the same as having my husband here beside me, sharing my life.' She peered closely at the photograph, arranging her round spectacles on her nose. Yes, it was Jim there, under the military peaked cap. But had her real husband become a carved figurehead, a still photograph to hang over the dining room mantelpiece, companion to postcards of pyramids and Port Said?

'I can't remember his voice!' she thought. 'He has gone.'

The darkness began to thicken over Caldwell in early 1918. A private, invisible burden pressed down more and more on Grace. Will's illness was only one part of the gloom. Will had come home from Sydney after surgery, assured by the surgeons that all would be well.

'It was cancer, Grace,' he told her. 'But they say they have taken it all.'

Less than two weeks after he came home, Will was attacked by terrible pain and needed to be taken back to the doctor. After a return visit to Sydney, he came back to Coolamon to be cared for at Nurse King's cottage hospital.

Grace drove his two little girls in to Coolamon to visit, anxious little Jean only two-and-a-half years old, and Evie having just had her first birthday. The little girls crawled around on Grace's lap, awed by the sight of the pale man against the pillow. Jean knew her Daddy, but Evie wasn't sure of him.

'Grace, they've told me now that it is hopeless. It is just a matter of time.' The soft Welsh voice was blurred as he spoke, trying to control himself for fear of frightening his children. 'I'm not afraid for myself,' he said. 'I don't like the idea of dying – and I can't talk about the pain – but I trust God to keep his promises and I'll be safe with him. I'll be with my Evelyn again. But Grace, I keep thinking about my little girls!'

He watched the children who were now sitting on the floor beside the bed tasting some of the grapes a friend had brought. It was as if he were trying to picture those childish faces as mature girls, or as women, trying to see his daughters as they would mature and develop.

'Grace, would you consider taking my girls into your home as your children, bringing them up with their cousins? If you were willing, I could die knowing that they would have a beautiful home life.'

There was a catch in her voice as Grace answered, 'You know I will! Evie has been with me all her life already, and I love your Jean as my daughter, too. Don't be afraid for them.'

'But Grace, I'm very worried about the financial side of things. With the farm and everything it is going to be very complicated and I don't want you to have to look after all the legal side of things as well as caring for my children. So I have asked two of my friends from the district to be my executors. . .'

Grace nodded silently. It was only later, as she drove home in the dusk with the little girls drowsing on the seat beside her, that she allowed herself to think about the implication of what Will had said. If Will had made arrangements for other men to take care of his children's estate and finances, it meant that he did not expect Jim to come home from the war.

One day, Carrie was knitting a scarf for Father. The child sat in the kitchen, head bent over her work, slowly forming her stitches. The wool was a colourless khaki, part of the Rannock school effort for the Red Cross and, though Carrie was concentrating on every movement, the shape widened and narrowed mysteriously as it grew longer. 'When you post the scarf to Father, will you tell about Sunday – and Holy Communion?' Carrie asked.

The mother watched her oldest child with tenderness. She was growing taller and more mature and it would not be long before she would leave childhood behind and blossom into adolescence. On the previous Sunday Carrie had, for the first time, responded to the invitation for 'all those who love the Lord' to stay with the grown-ups and receive Holy Communion. Grace knew that it meant a lot to the twelve-year-old girl.

'I'll tell him, dear. You miss Father a lot, don't you?'

The twelve-year-old's face was wistful. 'I wish he wasn't so far away.'

There had always been a special bond of understanding between father and oldest child. Would Jim be there to see his Caroline grow to womanhood, Grace wondered painfully. And the other children, each one a unique personality, what of them without their father? There was careful Mary, who struggled with school work, and clever Connie who was often ill, Legh who was growing into a determined character and needed guidance, Dick with his sensitivity and anxieties, Willie lovable and naughty, Gracie with her need to love and be loved. Then there were Evelyn and Will's girls – Jean suffering from a sad insecurity and baby Evie who didn't know what she was losing. They needed Father – Father to be there, Father to lead the family in daily prayers, Father to teach the children by example and word, Father to see the school prize, the pet lamb, the new tooth. How could she be mother and father, too, to these young ones, she wondered.

She watched the khaki scarf, with its dropped stitches and wavering outlines. It is as if I'm trying to knit this family together with only one hand to manage both knitting needles, she thought – it is not possible to avoid some dropped stitches and lumps in the family fabric.

In the autumn of 1918, Grace watched her world disintegrating. One by one, each foundation stone of her world seemed to crumble, making her world tilt and wobble treacherously.

Old Mary Playford was ill. She no longer sat cheerfully in the kitchen, but stayed in her bed. The old energy was gone. She spoke of indigestion, but the doctor had said that her heart was weakening as well as other ailments. Grace watched her mother quietly fading and wondered how she could go on without the strength and faithful prayers of her mother to support her.

Family members who had not seen the old lady for years came to visit, her brother James with his Mary Ann and her sister Lydia with Richard. Grace listened to their stories of growing up on the farm and memories of their parents – 'Do you remember Lydia and Richard at that picnic?. . . And your William with his gold nuggets?. . . I can just remember the "Augusta Jesse" – that's eighty years ago!' Her children gathered to spend time with their mother. There was a dignity and sense of completeness about it, but Grace could not deny the knowledge that her time with her rocklike mother was running out.

And Will was very ill. Grace visited each week, but he had already said goodbye to his little girls.

Jim's birthday card for Connie arrived late in May. He had written it in February from Cairo, where he was having seven days leave from the army camp at Belah. The troops were having three months rest and training during the winter, after forcing the Turks into a partial retreat just after Christmas. Each letter that came from Jim was such a thin thread to connect them, so fragile. He wrote of strange sights and friendships with soldiers she would never know, of working on salvaging operations collecting engineering material and ammunition left by the enemy in the Gaza area, of regimental sports and boxing competitions, gas drill, the inspection by the Duke of Connaught. Sometimes he hinted at his own deep loneliness, and his sorrow at seeing the standards of home disintegrating. 'We expect to return to the front – somewhere in Palestine – marching off from here about 1 April. April Fool's Day...'

Each week the local newspaper brought news of the war in Europe. The War News column wrote of the Great Offensive, with decimated armies locked in a death grip across the fields of France. In many of the descriptions of battles, won and lost, the news was noncommittal and a reader would find it hard to know whether the real news was good or bad. Stan McDowell was somewhere there, somewhere in the death-filled trenches. Grace prayed for him, but sometimes felt that she was beating the air: Would God protect one solitary boy, just because she loved him, while he was permitting the world to have its own way and choose its own path to self-destruction? Walter Theobald called to see his old friend Mrs Mary Playford one afternoon that autumn and, after he had been with the old lady for a happy time of conversation and prayer together, he talked with Grace.

'Our five years in this circuit are up soon, and we've just had word that we are to move on to Junee,' he said.

'Oh dear! Oh. I suppose I knew that it must be soon, but somehow, with the war and everything, I'd forgotten... We are going to miss you and your wife so much – you feel like our brother and sister.'

They sat in silence together, remembering family times, church services, parties, enthusiastic Christian Endeavour meetings, debates, recruitment rallies, community picnics, family funerals and baptisms.

'Let's pray together before I go,' he said. Grace bowed her head and listened as her friend spoke to their heavenly Father on behalf of her whole family, but the tears squeezed from under closed eyelids as she prayed. Yet another human support was being taken from her.

Even the small country town nearby was not stable. The next time she went to see Will Thomas in Coolamon, she drove the horse and sulky over the rise which led down into the town and was shocked by what she saw. Along one side of the wide main street lay smouldering ruins. Smoke rose up into the autumn air from blackened timbers and the skeletons of a line of shops lay twisted and exposed, heaps of rubble still glowing red where once had been the bakery, saddlery, general stores with their wide assortment of goods, the photographic studio, the refreshment rooms, the agents' office. Even the Oddfellows Hall was gone. People were standing around talking about it, trying to discover how the disaster had begun, who was insured, whether anyone was injured. There was confusion and shock. As Grace drove on to the small cottage hospital, she looked back over her shoulder at the ruins of almost a third of the little town's business properties. Even the small township was not immune to change and loss.

Will Thomas died, as Grace had known he must. The funeral was on Anzac Day, 25 April 1918, and Grace stood yet again in the quietness of the Berry Jerry cemetery. This time Jim was not here to help her. Who knew whereabouts in Palestine Jim was? It was little more than a year since they had laid Evelyn in the grassy plot not far from her parents, and now the earth was thrown back beside her headstone to receive her husband.

Walter Theobald had been Will's good friend and, though all his things were packed to leave Coolamon, he came with the new minister to conduct Will's funeral. As he farewelled his friend, he seemed to Grace to be saying goodbye to a whole community with whom he had been sharing the griefs of war. After the funeral, when at last the house was quiet again, Grace sat with her mother talking.

'You are going to have your hands full, Grace.' The old woman watched her daughter lovingly, observing the dark circles under the eyes, the tired lines forming on her face. 'I wish I were feeling stronger and then I could help you a lot more. Perhaps next week. . .'

'The big girls do a lot, Mother, and Minnie is a great help. The McDowell girls are planning to come to visit soon, and they'll help, too – don't worry about it.'

'At least I could supervise their shoe-cleaning and their silver-polishing. Naughty rascals, they try to get away with shiny boot toes and scuffed heels – they know that I expect a job to be done properly! You just send them in to me, dear.'

Grace looked at the tired old face under the snowy cap with its tiny black bows. Even now, her mother demanded excellence and rightness and, if at all possible, perfection. The younger woman reached out a hand and gently patted the hand of her mother. 'I do love you,' she whispered.

Five days after Will's funeral, Grace went to take her mother a breakfast tray and found that she had gone. The heavy old body lay still in the bed, but Mary Playford was no longer there. Grace stumbled from the room, calling for Harry, calling for help. It was more than she could bear.

People were very kind, coming to the house, bringing food, taking all the children home with them for a few days, and Harry took charge of all the arrangements for her. Grace struggled through the day, writing a bald little letter to Jim. It seemed a futile exercise – he would not read it till long after Mary Playford had been lain to rest in the new Rannock cemetery, and Grace wanted him with her now more than ever before. Jim was not with her – and she had lost Evelyn, Will, her familiar minister and now her mother.

The people of the district travelled with the bereaved family from the Rannock church out to the Rannock cemetery. In a patch of natural bush, a slice of the original growth left by those who had cleared the land, a handful of graves were laid in a clearing. Over the heads of the mourners swayed perfumed pines, one dusted with fine yellow flowers, and gum trees, with spiky dried grasses rustling around their feet. The sun shone peacefully, warmly, but Grace felt a bitter chill. In the middle of a crowd of close friends she felt very much alone.

In the evening when the children and Harry were in bed, Grace sat by the fire and tried to pray. Her Bible was open on her lap. Her mind told her where to look for comforting words, soft words of joy, but her fingers turned the pages to find the words which echoed her grief. Through the pages there were many who cried out in agony, struggling for meaning in the middle of pain, shouting at God, demanding to be heard, but feeling separated from him. Men and women through the ages had cried, why? Why can't things stay stable and safe? Why do good people die from terrible diseases? Why do men make war against each other, one young man ordered to destroy another young man for national pride's sake?

She found the cries of the Psalmist saying, 'Have mercy upon me, O Lord, for I am weak, O Lord heal me. . . O Lord, how long? I am weary with my groaning, all the night make I my bed to swim; I water my couch with my tears. My eye is consumed because of grief. . .' She turned to the outpourings of the bereaved Job and those who tried, clumsily, to comfort him, and found his questions and his struggles to understand very like her own. The words and questions of Jeremiah echoed her own, as he agonised over a whole society which turned its back on God, and grieved for the people he loved who were destroying themselves. The painful poetry of Lamentations spoke of tears and despair, hard questions and feelings of separation: 'Thou hast wrapped thyself with a cloud so that no prayer can pass through. . .' Again she turned to a Psalm, looking for something to strengthen her, but found 'My tears have been my food day and night, while men say to me continually, "Where is your God?". . . my soul is cast down within me. . . all thy waves and thy billows have gone over me. . . I say to God, my rock, "Why hast thou forgotten me?"'

She sat rigidly, holding the book in still fingers. Her brain knew that the Psalm ended with the words 'Why are you cast down, O my soul, and why are you disquieted within me? Hope in God; for I shall again praise him, my help and my God.' Her mind knew that the words of hope were there, but her spirit was not ready to hear them. Grace closed the book and put it back on the bookshelf. She lit the candle to carry to bed and turned out the larger lamp.

As she walked along the dark hall to the emptiness of her own room, the little candle flame was the only light. It wavered and bent and, as she opened her own bedroom door, a sudden draught caught it and blew it out. Complete darkness had finally descended on her.

16
Blackened land
1918

CONFLICT AND A BITTER UNEASE marked that winter of 1918. The war news continued to be grim, with the lists lengthening of those killed or wounded. Politicians tried to convince Australians that the war was being won, but men and women receiving letters from the trenches were not easily convinced. The community tried to go on with their normal lives, but nothing could be normal any more. Coolamon Primary School presented an elaborate pageant for Empire Day, with the children dressed as the nations of Europe, but to some who watched, it was a mockery of the very real conflicts being waged between political forces. Local groups held fancy-dress balls in someone's barn to raise funds for the Red Cross Comforts Fund, but under the draping greenery and among dancers bedecked in outfits labelled 'Peace' or 'Lily of the Valley', there were strong undercurrents of feeling towards men who had never worn uniform, or anger that any man should be forced to go to war. Girls without partners had their own private cause for bitterness. The community was again at each other's throats on the question of Prohibition; people held public meetings to speak in favour of having their Coolamon Show without the usual well-patronised liquor tent because so many of the officials would need to be women this year, but others wrote furious letters to the local paper listing the many horrid attributes of such 'wowsers'.

Then there were the memorial services in every church in the district. The churches were draped in black, flags hanging overhead, women in black garments and men with black on sleeve and hatband. The church organists played the 'Dead March' from *Saul*, the sombre tones blending with the dark drapery and the deep communal grief for young men lost. The Methodists remembered their former minister, Winsleigh Murray, who died in battle in France. The story came back how he had fallen in battle, but waved the stretcher-bearers past him to help a wounded mate. He had been wounded again and before he could be rescued the German troops had recaptured the area and he was lost.

The black drapery was hung around the Rannock church yet again for a memorial service for Will Thomas. Grace helped prepare the building, and added purple drapes and masses of white flowers. The new minister spoke on Christ's words from Revelation 1: 'Fear not, for I am the first and the last. I am he that liveth and was dead, and behold, I am alive for evermore, and hold the keys of Death and Hades.'

'We don't understand why good, loved, young people die. Death sometimes seems to be lawless, out of control,' he said. 'Christ suffered death, too, but we believe he is alive, and the keys of death are safe in his pierced hands.'

Grace sat with her family around her, the bigger girls helping to care for the younger children. Today they were all trying to be very good. There had been a recent Sunday when she had stood up part way through church, taken one of the big girls firmly by the hand, marched her outside, smacked her briskly and marched her back to her seat. The children now watched their mother with a healthy respect.

After speaking of Will Thomas, the preacher went on to mention the charitable work of Christian people who provided care for the orphaned. 'These institutions do a fine work,' he said, 'but it is a great source of pleasure to know that these little children,' and he smiled at Jean and Evie, 'are not left to the care of an orphanage, but are in the keeping of one who will be in all ways everything that a mother could be.'

The woman in the pew drew a deep breath. It was such a daunting responsibility. Nine children, the oldest only twelve. What if she were ill again? What if she were permanently alone?

*   *   *

A tall man sits erect on the wagon, reins held in his strong hands and his eyes on the mules labouring through the heavy sand in front of him. The 12th Light Horse are on their way, the Belah camp near the Mediterranean now far behind. Men and animals are glowing with health after the months of training. The camp rhythm of drill, church parades, football matches, band practice and regular training have stopped, and the adventures of men on leave in Cairo have become the stuff of bawdy tale-telling.

Day after day they have moved north, hearing the first note of reveille before dawn, watering the horses, breaking camp, moving on from the barren dryness of the land of the Sinai desert and the open sand-dunes of Beersheba to the orange groves and villages of Palestine. Nearly five hundred men and twenty-five officers ride on, a long procession of men on horseback, with the limbers and wagons driving slowly with loads of machine-guns, equipment, stores, tents, water. Heavily loaded packhorses trudge along, with the mules and the donkeys. Each day the regiment stops at an oasis or a village, always searching for wells of precious water.

The older man with the heavy features drives on through the rising dust, watching the road, but always aware that he is driving through Palestine, the Holy Land. The column moves on, passing parties of Bedouins, men and women in flowing Eastern robes, camels and laden donkeys, Jewish children, Arab children. An officer calls back along the line, 'See that city? Jerusalem!' and they ride on by, staring across to the ancient walls, each man occupied with his own thoughts. Jerusalem had fallen to the British shortly before Christmas. They ride beyond Jerusalem, coming to the edge of a plateau and pause, looking down into the depths of a barren valley spreading widely far below sea level. A narrow strip of road clings to the edge of a cliff face, winding its way gingerly down past twisted chunks of rock, down to the distant oasis green of a town away on the valley floor almost obscured by dust.

'That's Jericho down there,' someone says. 'And that river is the Jordan, and the Dead Sea is that water to the south of it. That's where we're going — down past Jericho and beyond the Jordan. Somewhere on the other side of that river there's a strategic railway line and that's where the Turkish army is waiting for us. . .'

Jim looks back over his shoulder once again at the trees and groves of Palestine, then urges his team on, down the steep and treacherous road built so long ago by the Romans, past the rocks striking fire from the sun, remembering that once his Lord had told of another traveller who had gone down that road from Jerusalem to Jericho and had been rescued by an enemy.

*   *   *

Grace woke with a start and sat rigidly up in bed. She was shivering. The house seemed quiet enough. Even little Jean was asleep now. With shaking hand, she felt in the dark for the matchbox and the candlestick and lit the candle, the gentle flame lighting her safe corner of the bedroom with its shiny brass bedknobs and white net bedcurtains with their cheerful white bobbles. As she wrapped a warm gown around her, she caught sight of her own shadowy reflection in the dressing-table mirror, long hair loose, anxious face looking odd without her spectacles. With candle flaring, she walked from room to room, but every child was safe and sleeping peacefully. Even Harry was snoring gently in his room. Within the walls of Caldwell everything seemed to be well.

Even so, the woman with the candle felt a powerful sense of urgency. She went back to her room and closed the door again. Dragging a blanket around her shoulders, she dropped into her rocking chair and sat staring blindly into the moving shadows of her room.

'Dear God, what is it?' she cried in the silence. 'Is it Jim? Is it Stan? Are they in danger? Are they dead too? Oh my Lord, save them! You are there – you are beside them – you can save them – please build a wall of protection around them!'

She did not need to turn to her Bible for promises of hope – the words were printed on her mind. Phrases from the Psalm she loved, Psalm 121, wove across her thoughts – 'My help cometh from the Lord . . . he that keepeth thee will not slumber . . . the Lord is thy keeper. . . the Lord shall preserve thee from all evil; he shall preserve thy soul . . .'

The candle burned lower and lower and still she sat, fiercely battling against the powers of darkness which threatened to overwhelm her, the evil powers of this world set to destroy and poison, to bereave and defeat. Before the candle guttered out, she had fallen into exhausted sleep, still not knowing how her prayers would be answered, but clinging desperately to the Father she trusted.

As she slept, far away on the other side of the globe, Captain Stan McDowell sat disconsolately looking at his leg.

'You've done your leg in, sir,' the orderly said. 'That will probably score you a good six months' leave back home if you're lucky – you'll be on crutches for a bit.'

Stan almost laughed. He'd survived Gallipoli, he'd lived through

Bullecourt and Passchendaele and now he was to be invalided home for an unheroic accident playing football!

*   *   *

Worse than the heat, worse than the sandflies and the mosquitoes, even worse than the sight of distant rifles edging over the protecting rock, is the thirst. A man's water-bottle is his cherished possession and troops are prepared to fight for access to wells and springs to water their horses. In this deep crack in the earth's crust, the yellow rocks almost seem to writhe in the heat, a haze shimmering across a stony wilderness. No trees offer shade and little vegetation appears to soften the harshness of the landscape.

It is early May, and Jim's regiment has been on the east of the Jordan, struggling forward and edging back across the waste of barren hillsides, steep and rocky cliffs rising above the plain, the sound of artillery echoing across the valley. The enemy is there, visible in great numbers on the hills, and a fringe of rifles and bayonets moves raggedly among the rocks. Troops work to put up defences of barbed wire and to dig trenches, but barbed wire is no defence against shell and shot and men are falling, wounded. The horses are frightened and Jim fights to control the animals pulling his wagon. A water cart has driven up from the river with its freight of precious water, but shells explode on the cart and, when the air has cleared, the men see the water gushing out onto the ground. Ahead of him, Jim sees the horses pulling a limber rear up into the air in terror, smashing the poles and bolting away, with the limber overturned. Men on horseback come back clinging to their horses, bleeding from their wounds, and others struggle back on foot, leaving their dead horses behind them.

Fear is always there, and thirst. Men barely have enough water to wet their own lips and there is no water nearer than the Jordan river, four miles away, for the thirsty horses, mules and donkeys. The atmosphere is veiled in red dust that dries throats, fills noses — not the dust of the Riverina, but the dust of Palestine, dust of ancient battles, dust of long-gone armies. An officer orders Jim, among others, to take half the horses of the regiment back to the river to be watered, one man to four horses, riding and stumbling with two hundred horses and thirty mules across the stones back over the four miles to water. Horses with noses thankfully dipped into the Jordan's waters have been without water for fifty-six hours;

the other half of the animals must wait till tomorrow to drink.

Men are alerted to stand at arms at 3.30 in the morning, waiting in the dark for the firing to begin. Orders come to withdraw and the regiment begins the slow movement back, back down the precipitous terrain under machine-gun and artillery fire, trudging through the whole day and part of the next night and crossing the bridge over the Jordan at midnight, straggling back at last to their bivouac near Jericho some hours later. Exhausted men sleep, thankful to be among those who return unscathed.

*   *   *

The winter months of June, July and August bit bleakly into the family at Caldwell. The autumn rains had not fallen and the crop had to be sown dry, with winter bringing cold but little rain. Bitter frosts stung the land, spreading a cloth of sharp whiteness over the dry grass and the struggling crops.

Grace hurried out of the house carrying the clothes basket full of wet washing, a warm scarf wrapped around her head and an old coat donned against the cold, but her fingers were clumsy with numbness as she pegged out the children's clothes and wrestled with heavy wet sheets. Minnie ran out to help, and aunt and niece worked quickly, with their breath clouding into the cold air. Patterns of frost lay on the ground, pools of frost lying in the shade of the peppertree, in the shade of the wood heap, echoing the southern shadow of the house, chimneys and all, where the sun had not touched. Near the verandah, a crust of ice sealed the dogs' water tins and, in the vegetable garden, the last remnants of summer's vegetables were blackened leaves.

'Auntie Grace, do you think it would be cold where Uncle Jim is?'

'No, dear, I believe it is summer there. He doesn't say much about the weather. Uncle mostly seems to write about all the special places in the Holy Land he's had a chance to see – he's already seen a number of places mentioned in the Bible. It must be wonderful to be able to walk in so many places where Jesus walked. Uncle always takes such an interest in everything, too.'

She gathered up the last of the socks, pegged them firmly, then hoisted the clothes line high above the dirt on the forked clothes prop. A wintry sun shone down, with a feeble promise of dry clothes later in the day. Grace stooped to gather an armload of frosted wood from the woodheap to carry in for the fire. As she lifted the wood in chilblained fingers, she felt loaded down with self-pity. Most of the children were miserable with bad colds or other childhood ills, but Dr Buchanan had been away in Sydney for three months now, a very sick man. She missed her mother terribly, and Will and Evelyn. The war news was frightening, with talk of a Great Offensive in Europe. Her dear friends the Pearces were feeling the loss of Charlie's brothers, and she found it hard to comfort them. Even the new minister no longer came to see her — the poor man had been ill almost the whole time he had been in Coolamon and would probably have to resign. There was little hope for a good 1918 harvest. She herself hadn't been well, and somewhere deep in her mind lurked the fear that the cancer was waiting to attack her now at her most vulnerable. She needed Jim! And where was Jim? Somewhere where it was warm, exploring sacred sites when he was on leave, enjoying himself in the Holy Land!

*   *   *

June, July and August, the months of a northern summer, spread their heat over the valley of the Jordan, baking the land and the foreign regiment in its depths. People say that no white troops can survive a summer in the valley, but the 12th Light Horse stubbornly stay on, watching the strategic length of railway line, patrolling, worrying the enemy, taking their turn to relieve other regiments in the front line. Food is scarce and, without the usual variety of a canteen, the water is always short. Men complain of sandflies and mosquitoes — the latter not simply an irritation, but carriers of malarial fever. Diet and hygiene are a problem in the conditions and more men are battling with illness than with war wounds. Over their camp site near Jericho, and wherever the lines of horsemen move across the plain, great palls of dust rise, cloud-high, choking, obscuring. Hot winds swirl the dust, fine as powder, burning eyes.

Enemy planes fly overhead and drop their bombs. Horses trample each other in fear and men shout or throw themselves to the ground, waiting for death to strike them. Sometimes the planes leave destruction behind them and sometimes men and horses get up, dust themselves off and go on. The horses and men are daily growing thinner.

When at last the regiment is ordered to leave the Jordan Valley and move back up to the gentler heights near Jerusalem, back to the softness of orange groves and vineyards, date palms and olives, their officer pencils in his official war diary: 'The transport when leaving the Jordan Valley was in a frightful condition owing to the very hot weather and the state of the roads... The period spent in the valley was a most trying one...'

Jim is among the last to leave, driving his straining team up the treacherous mountain track. In his pocket is a handful of stones, picked up in the valley where Christ faced forty days of fasting and confronted Satan himself in his hours of temptation. Jim will not forget the wilderness. As the team presses up the road, always staying close to the cliff face and away from the crumbling road edge dropping steeply below, he remembers that other traveller on this road. Long ago, Christ, too, had left Jericho behind, the rich city of palms where he had healed the blind and encouraged a repentant Zaccheus down out of a tree and, walking up this same steep road, had said to his friends, 'Behold, we are going up to Jerusalem; and the Son of Man will be delivered to the chief priests and scribes, and they will condemn him to death, and deliver him to the Gentiles to be mocked and scourged and crucified, and he will be raised on the third day.'

*   *   *

On a grey foggy day, the mailman's buggy brought their twelve loaves of bread, the papers, a postcard from Jim and a letter from Stan.

'Minnie, listen! Stan's on his way home! His knee is "out" and he has been ruled unfit for combat. He'll be home in July... Praise God!'

The postcard was written to young Richie from Ismailia on the Suez Canal. Jim had written, 'Father does not forget his boys and hopes they are doing all they can to help Mother while Father is away. Pray God that the war may soon be over so that Father may return to his boys and girls and Mother. Make up your mind to grow up a good man, son. With love from Father.'

The hall behind the Springwood Hotel was crowded on the night of Stan McDowell's welcome home. In the wide dark around the little hotel and its hall, paddocks lay bleakly, crops blown flat by cold hard winds. The night was bitterly cold and sleety rain slashed around faces as guests climbed out of buggies and hurried inside. Grace struggled down out of the sulky, juggling children, food and an umbrella and, stepping around icy puddles, followed the swinging lantern into the light of the room. Stan limped in out of the rain, leaning on his grandmother's hawthorn stick and followed by small cousins.

'Good on you, Stan,' men called, and came to shake his hand and slap him on the back. 'Good to see you, mate.'

Women crowded around to give him welcome, with their daughters hesitating behind. Families greeted him in quiet voices, remembering their dead, and others asked for news of sons and brothers.

'Come and get some decent Aussie tucker, son,' they said, piling his plate with homegrown lamb and beef, home-preserved vegetables, buttery cakes, fruit tarts oozing sweetness under their blanket of thick cream. Grace watched his face carefully. It was an older and harder face than that of the lad who had left home in the spring of 1914. Now in the winter of 1918 he wore the face of a man who had suffered, a man who had seen things which perhaps he would never be able to share, a man who had lost one close friend after another as the carnage of war had swept across Europe. Shyly, back at Caldwell, he had shown her and the children his Military Cross, the fine silver cross hanging from its purple and white striped ribbon. But he didn't want to talk about the thing that had happened which had earned him the Cross. Even now, watching him chat cheerfully to old friends, Grace sensed that it was hard to bridge the gulf between the farmers of Rannock and the bloodstained fields of Gallipoli and Flanders.

After the toasts to 'The Boys at the Front' and some solos, neighbours made welcoming speeches and Stan stood to speak. He spoke of Gallipoli with its cruel losses and the evacuation. He talked about their first sight of France in the spring, after the horrors of Gallipoli, which was 'like a vision of Paradise'. Stan mentioned the woollen socks which had arrived through the War Chest – 'the mud would have beaten us more than the guns if it hadn't been for getting dry socks!' – and women who had knitted endless balls of khaki wool beamed at him.

He stood looking around the room at the faces of his friends. Everyone was aware of the boys who were gone – the Pearce brothers, the Swann lads, young Walter Allen, the Kellys, Paddy McKenna. The girls he had known were still there, older and more mature, but many of the boys were missing.

'One last thing I want to say,' he said, looking at his Auntie Grace sitting among the children. 'I can say that I am still a Christian.' People looked up, slightly surprised. This was a community welcome, not a church meeting. 'Yes, through everything that I have seen and experienced that is something I am sure about. I can testify that there is no temptation in a soldier's life that Jesus Christ cannot help him withstand and overcome.'

He sat down. Grace stared down at her hands, tears brimming. She had prayed for that. She had prayed that he would be protected, protected from violence and protected in the face of all the other kinds of destruction which could bring him down. The crowd had sung the National Anthem and pushed back the tables to make room for games for the children and young people. In the space in the middle of the noise, Grace sat quietly. God had answered her prayers for Stan. Would his answer be 'yes' to her prayers for Jim?

The dinner box bumped gently on the floor of the sulky as Grace drove across the farm with the meals for the shearers. A strong aroma of wattle drifted through the air. She had spent the morning cooking a hot dinner for the hungry men, but it still seemed very strange, even after such a long time, to have the shearers around without Jim coming home in the evening smelling strongly of sheep.

With spring and shearing came school holidays and a house full of children. A few young nieces rode with her in the sulky. During the morning, she and Minnie had tried to keep all the children occupied with household tasks or happy with their dolls while they worked, but there were nine children of her own and three small nieces under twelve: children wanting a cuddle, grubby ones needing to be washed, aggressive ones, tearful ones, enthusiastic ones wanting to have mother's help in some ambitious project. The demands were endless: 'Mother! please come and help us with our game. . . Mother, don't let him . . . Mother, can I . . . Auntie Grace, look what I've done. . .' All morning there had been the pressure of having the food ready on time for the men and she felt very tired.

Driving through the farm, listening with a fraction of her mind to the chatter of the little girls with her, she thought of the most recent letters from Jim. Jim had been for some time working at Moascar on the Suez, but was rejoining his regiment late in September. Many of the men had been ill and had been hospitalised with malaria, dysentery and cholera, but though he and Paddy were very thin, they were both thankful that they had kept out of hospital. As always he wrote with enthusiasm of the things he was seeing: the wonders of the pyramids, the wilderness through which the Children of Israel had wandered for forty long years. With a new friend, an Armenian Christian pastor in Jerusalem, he had visited sacred places around that ancient city. He wrote of how 'we stood under the olive trees in the Garden of Gethsemane on the Mount of Olives. . .' But behind the words describing exotic sights, Grace saw a homesick man, longing for his family and his native place. There were hints, too, that something serious was being planned by the generals, something in Palestine and Syria to match the Big Offensive in Europe, something which would perhaps reveal whether the armies of Germany and Turkey, or the armies of the allies, would finally be victorious. The thought of what such battles could mean twisted still tighter that knot of anxiety which had become an almost permanent part of her.

Beside her, the little girls jiggled and bounced on their seat. They chattered happily, laughing at the rabbits which dashed across their path, pointing to a big goanna watching them pass from his spot halfway up a gum tree. They loved to go to the shearing sheds, to hear the noise of the penned sheep, to watch the flash of the blades through thick wool and the dramatic flight of the severed fleece flung out across the woolclassing table. Grace became conscious of the gaze of a small niece beside her.

'Auntie? Auntie, you have such pretty red cheeks today!'

'Have I, dear?' She tried to smile cheerfully at the child, but the fiery band which was tightening around her head made smiling hard. 'Perhaps it's because I have a little headache today.'

*   *   *

The man behind the wagon sways with weariness. Ahead of him the columns of mounted men wind along the northern road stirring the dust. Under the reins, the skeletons of his animals show painfully through their hide, beasts exhausted and underfed after their months in the valley of the Jordan. They have been moving up through Palestine for ten days, ten days of constant marching, brief pauses for rest, then on again. Jim is tense, tired, aware of the effect that dysentery has been having on him, but determined to keep going as long as he can. Paddy has been a good mate, and the two friends have tried to help each other in their illness. Beside the road he watches the vista of rural Palestine: the vineyards and date palms, the olive groves and fig trees, the small villages, the laden donkeys, the children calling for money.

The enemy is there, waiting. They meet, confront, attack each other, take prisoners. The enemy is retreating. Only days ago they met face to face at the railway station of Semarkh, fighting man to man till the station was theirs, and a loaded train, and prisoners. They have camped by the Sea of Galilee, Jim standing in awe on the pebbly water's edge watching the sun rise across the waters where Jesus once walked. Again they have crossed the Jordan to the eastern bank, not this time across a solid bridge, but crossing a hastily built bridgehead. The men are faced with the almost impossible task of forcing horses in poor condition up the steep and rugged banks of the gorge in front of them. Jim tries not to think of the fear of that ride, the rocks towering above, the scrambling, sliding feet of horses, the uncertainty of whether Turkish machine-guns are waiting above them.

Above his head the roar of aircraft makes his animals shy in terror. Two German planes are following the columns of troops. He feels the whine and thud of bombs falling among them, explosions of flame and sand. A stuttering of machine-gun fire from the planes sends the columns into disarray. Jim fights to keep his team on the road. A British plane appears to do battle and sends an enemy plunging to earth, trailing smoke and flame. Jim is almost ill with fear and horror. 'What am I doing here? I should be home, shearing. . .' A young soldier rides by, sobbing, others pass with faces of stone, hard, grim. Horses have fallen by the road, not struck by bullets, but dying of exhaustion and weakness. Men ill with fever and dysentery cling to horses, longing to reach the bivouac where they can report sick.

The column struggles on, moving north. German and Turkish troops are retreating north ahead of them, trying to reach the city of Damascus first where they hope to continue the fight. The Light Horse follows, nearly four hundred miles of dusty road behind them since they left Galilee; ahead of them looms the shadow of a bitter battle and they are already very weary men.

*   *   *

The light of the lamps shone gently on the heads bent around the long table. Now, at the end of the day at school, long brown plaits, once tidy and firm, dangled tousled and wispy over the shoulders of the three big girls as they sat at the table reading, or carefully hemming the handkerchief the teacher's wife had set them to sew. Carrie would sit for her Qualifying Certificate in two months, the end of primary education for her. 'I would love to train to be a teacher, like you, Mother,' she said, but Grace found the thought of planning for her daughter's future almost impossible. The boys were coughing again, the harsh sound rasping, and Grace thought with anxiety of the neighbours' children with whooping cough. One by one the children put away their things, took their candles and went to bed, and Grace went from room to room to say goodnight and hear their prayers. She sat on each child's bed as each child prayed, 'God bless Mother, and Uncle Harry, and Carrie and Mary and Connie, and God bless the boys, and the babies, and the new chickens, and the pet lamb. . .' and each one said, in the trustful voice of children, 'And God bless Father, wherever he is, and bring him home safely.'

Grace blew out one candle after another, leaving peaceful children to sleep in the security of their home. Back in the breakfast room, Minnie was finishing a letter to a boy she had met on a holiday, and Harry sat dozing with his newspaper unread in his lap.

'Harry, Harry, go to bed! You look so uncomfortable like that.'

Harry snuffled a little, blinked, then gathered his paper and set off for bed with his daughter Minnie following soon after. At last the house was quiet. It had been a long tiring day, and Grace's body cried out for sleep, but her spirit was unsettled, restless. She took out her red leather writing case and opened the ink bottle. She had a letter partly written to Jim and tomorrow the mailman would come to collect mail. The words on the page were calm and reasonable. There was mention of the weather – fairly dry still – and the shearing – all finished now – and the children at school. The local news, the Sunday School anniversary, the sick minister, the spread of whooping cough in the area, the poor harvest they were expecting. She dipped her pen in the ink, but the words did not come. Where was Jim? What was he doing? Was he even thinking about her and the children? The sense of distance, of utter separation was so intense. The ink dried on the nib and she still had written nothing. She tried again, and this time her confusion and loneliness trickled down with the ink, trailing disjointed sentences, uncertain phrases across the paper. When she blotted the page, it occurred to her that some of it made less sense than her usual letter, but she didn't care to revise it.

The woman put the pen aside and carried the lamp into the dining room. She opened the lid of the big organ and set her hymn book on the music stand. Often she had sat here, playing and singing with joy, teaching the children songs, playing hymns for her own delight. Now she opened the book, turning the pages aimlessly, trying out a line of two of music, putting it aside, moving on. Music had lost its savour; and the only songs she felt like playing were the sad songs, songs played in a minor key. Even her hands refused to move easily on the keyboard and she stared resentfully at thickened knuckles, the pretty hands of which she had once been so proud, but now awkward with arthritis. Her wedding ring gleamed from her hand, and she turned it in the light. She was glad now that Jim had brought her the ring to replace the one she had lost. In her mind she could hear him saying, 'For better, for worse, for richer, for poorer, in sickness and in health till death us do part...'

'Is this how it feels to be a widow?' she wondered. 'So terribly alone – that empty chair at the table – the missing voice in family conversations – the cold space in my bed. God, where are you? What are you doing with my husband?'

She pushed the organ stool aside and paced around the room. It was time to go to bed, she knew it, but the dark hall lay beyond the closed door, and an empty bed, and hours of sleepless blackness. Grace knew that she was trying to fend off that moment when she would have to blow out her lamp and be left in the dark with her fears. Her Bible lay on the table and she went back to look at it, returning as she had often done to the Psalms. Others had walked this way of fear and sleeplessness before her; she read 'My God; in him will I trust... Thou shalt not be afraid of the terror by night... Nor for the pestilence that walks in darkness...', 'Weeping may endure for a night, but joy cometh in the morning...', 'The Lord is my light and my salvation; whom shall I fear? The Lord is the strength of my life; of whom shall I be afraid?' The pages turned and her eye fell on a simple word in an early psalm and she murmured the words aloud. 'I will both lay me down in peace and sleep; for thou, Lord, only makest me dwell in safety.'

Still she could not make herself go to bed. Over the mantelpiece hung the great Illuminated Address, with its small photograph of Jim wreathed in the artist's fantasies of laurel leaves and wild flowers.

'Is that all I have left of my husband?' she demanded. 'Photographs? His shirts and suits hanging in my wardrobe? His tools in the blacksmith's shop? His books and papers in the study?

I need *him*, the man himself, the real Jim with all his funny ways. Not photos and letters. Not war news in the paper. Not admiring speeches about "our brave boys at the front". I want Jim.'

The elegant script of the Address blurred before her eyes as the tears streamed down. 'Your sacrifice appeals to all,' it read. 'Your name will adorn that great roll of membership which shall remain an imperishable record of Australia's patriotic sons. This thought, we trust, will tend to mitigate the pain of loss and anxiety which must be borne by your devoted wife and family in the years to come.'

'I don't want his name on a roll of honour, even in gold letters. I just want Jim, alive and home.'

At last she lifted the lamp and opened the door into the silent hall. Walking to her bed she whispered her urgent plea, 'I will lay me down in peace. . . and sleep. . . for you, Lord, make me dwell in safety.'

*　　　*　　　*

The long columns of squadrons of the 12th Light Horse trot briskly between steeply rising rock faces which edge the road. They ride past Syrian villages, beside creeks, on towards Damascus. The line of slouch hats with their distinctive emu feather ornament – 'our kangaroo feathers' the men call them – bob up and down, rising and falling with the motion of the horses. The horses are too thin, the men tired and sick, but they go on.

The order comes to attack a position south of Damascus. Other Light Horse regiments – British and New Zealand troops – are also converging on the city, each with their own objective. The city lies before them, cubes of ancient stone and brick heaped together. Jim sees the illustrations in his pictorial Bible come to life before his eyes, but this is not an illustrated Sunday School lesson. This is war.

Sounds of battle, machine-gun rattle, shock of shell, gleaming bayonet, ruffle of dust, smell of fear. Retreating troops, arms raised in surrender, dejected prisoners pitching army tents by city walls, watering weary horses, standing guard over thousands of Turkish and German prisoners: sleepless soldiers, sick men struggling to play their part. Troops enter the city of Damascus, expecting resistance, but the enemy has flown. Beyond the city, troops follow the retreat, hurrying, forcing the enemy further and further north. It is the first day of October, 1918.

Men from the conquering regiments gather to join a triumphal procession through the city two days later. Jim and Paddy have both been feeling very ill with dysentery, but this is something special — 'We don't want to miss this, mate!'

'I'm hanged if I can even get up on my horse. . .'

'Come on, I'll get behind you and give you a shove — you'll be right!'

Jim and Paddy ride, albeit tenderly, with the troops through the ancient city streets, and women shower flowers from upstairs windows, people cry a greeting and an interpreter shouts, 'They say, "a thousand welcomes"!'

The troops stay in Damascus, some working with Colonel Lawrence and his Arab Hedjez army, while many are on guard duty. Thousands of prisoners wait despondently. Daily more and more men of the 12th Light Horse are reporting ill — malaria, cholera, dysentery. Rations are very short. Two officers and several men die of disease, though they have lived through battles.

A new order sends the weakened regiment back on the road to ride for Homs. For five days they press north, one hundred weary miles, moving painfully on after the retreating armies. For many, the journey is a nightmare and nearly a quarter of their ranks are forced to fall out as they travel, to be evacuated to hospital. Jim battles on; it is his boast that, despite his age, he is one of very few men who have stayed out of hospital, and he is determined to tough it out to the end.

They straggle exhausted into Homs on the last day in October, fearing that another battle will be the end of them. But the final shot has already been fired. On the morning after their arrival, the news speeds around the lines. An armistice has just been signed by Turkey.

*　　　*　　　*

The tall white November lilies were in bloom near the back door, waxy white bells swinging in the breeze, the yearly sign that it was time for Willie's birthday. Grace was in the kitchen beating a cake mixture for a fifth birthday cake for her son when the phone rang, a message from the telephone exchange at the Springwood Hotel.

'It's over! Germany signed an armistice agreement yesterday.' The neighbour at the hotel talked excitedly of the sudden outburst of churchbells and the town fire bell the previous evening, the public meeting which had been interrupted by a messenger with the cable from Sydney with the news, the single voice which had begun to sing 'Praise God from whom all blessings flow. . .' and the swelling of other voices joining to sing the doxology with every ounce of thankfulness they had.

'Everyone was pretty well behaved, they say,' the woman said. 'People reckoned that it was because they had a practice a few weeks ago, when we all got the wrong end of the stick and thought that a war cable meant that the armistice had been signed already! They shut all the shops and rang all the bells and carried on – and found out that it was a mistake. At least we weren't the only ones – quite a few towns out this way passed the news on to each other and we were all fooled together! But this time it is the real thing. We didn't get the news till late, though – they found out in Sydney about the middle of the day and all the cable and telegraph operators rushed out into the streets to celebrate and didn't get around to letting the people in the bush know until it was practically bed-time. Oh, well, I'd better get on and let the other people out this way know the good news.'

Grace found it hard to believe. Was it really over? Might the embattled enemy rise again? Where was Jim now? Somewhere safe, or sick or in danger? Mail had been so slow that she was still not sure what to think.

'When will Father be home?' demanded the children. 'Will he be home for Christmas? Will he be back for harvest?'

She had no idea. The great gulf still existed between them, only bridged by her prayers for him and his prayers for her. Friends and neighbours arrived to see her, dear friends who had supported her and her children through the past years, and they cried together, tears of relief and joy. But the uncertainty remained.

Harry went with her and all the children to join the crowds in Coolamon on the Wednesday for the celebration of the end of the Great War, that significant moment of signing at the eleventh hour on the eleventh day of the eleventh month, 1918.

'This can be your best birthday party, Willie,' she said, hugging the little boy. 'Five years old today and the whole town is having a procession and a concert and everything!'

The day was hot and the people of the district crowded into their churches, every church overflowing. The Methodists and Presbyterians of Coolamon gathered in the Presbyterian church and, as Grace squeezed her family into a pew and the three little girls gathered on welcoming knees, she looked around at her neighbours.

Many women wore mourning and there was a deep current of grief flowing under the surface of celebration. The loss of sons, brothers, husbands and beloved friends was too painful to be lightly overlooked. The men and women in the church were her friends, and the war years had left none of them untouched.

Later, the congregations of the churches blended to become the town and district community, lining the wide main street to watch the procession go by. All the shops were shut, and the people cheered the passing of the mounted police, the town band, returned soldiers, the women of the Red Cross groups and the War Chest effort. Ranks of school children marched with their teachers, there were children on decorated ponies and the town comics playing the fool for the entertainment of the crowd. Far behind could be heard the clangour of a children's tincan band, beating out a rhythm with shouts of laughter following them up the street. The long, long tail of the procession moved along from railway crossing past the shops and businesses; decorated lorries and buggies and no less than thirty motor cars, each embellished with flowers and streamers and demonstrating how very up-to-date their community was. The great crowd made their way to Kindra Park for the speechmaking and the vicar began his speech by saying, with obvious sincerity, 'Thank God for this happy and glorious day!'

The children wanted to stay in town for the evening concert, but Grace decided that they had had quite enough excitement for one day. 'We need to be home before dark. There's the milking, and the fowls to feed. And, don't forget there is Willie's birthday cake for tea. What a lovely day for a birthday you've had, Will!'

As the sun tipped towards the western horizon and the shadows of roadside gums reached across the red road, the buggy full of children sped for home. The sounds of their singing trailed banners of joy behind them, floating on the quiet air. But the woman holding the reins knew that, though the war was over and it was right to be thankful, their world could never be quite the same again.

17
New green shoots
1919-1929

GRACE WRAPPED HER LONG COAT more firmly around her and thrust cold fingers into pockets. Behind her was the door leading into the warm railway dining room of Junee Junction, but she stayed outside, staring at the gleam of railway lines narrowing into the distance, blending and parting. The sun had begun to set on that April evening, striking fire from the metal of lines, glowing on autumn leaves in Junee backyards. Soon the lights would be lit on the railway platform. Soon the train would come. Soon the waiting would be over.

The first months of 1919 had been very hard. The war was over, but the men had not yet come home. There had been no rain for many months and the harvest had been very poor indeed. At the little bush school, teacher and boys had tilted the corrugated iron water tank to pour off the last of the water and after that the children had to carry their own water to school. Sheep were dying and even the public government tank was dry. Harry had taken his horse teams away to adjistment on the distant Murrumbidgee River, driving off through paddocks adrift with dust. Then there had been rumours of an epidemic of pneumonic influenza which had swept Europe and was now wreaking havoc in Sydney. So far the disease had not reached Coolamon or Rannock, but most of Grace's children had been very ill with whooping cough. She was very tired indeed.

Questions had been with her all day, plucking at her mind as she drove from Caldwell, so that she scarcely saw the paddocks undulating by. It had rained at last and farmers were sowing wheat, puffs of red dust rising behind teams of horses, but she ignored them, her mind on the coming of her husband. She passed the gate leading up the slope to The Hill; it stood empty, forlornly waiting to be sold. At every curve in the road she had asked herself: Will he see changes? Will he be content to be at home after so long away? Will the children seem very changed to him after two years? In her mind's eye she saw a tall man, broad-shouldered, his familiar eyes under the heavy eyelids, thick dark hair waving above a high forehead, his Lord Kitchener moustache. Did he still look like that? Or was her mental picture a fantasy built from a small photograph? Would he still look at her with the love that had always been there? What if the unthinkable could have happened and he returned to her in body, but two years absence had separated him from her in mind and heart? But at least he was coming, sooner than many of his mates, having been given compassionate leave to travel home to his large family while many of his friends remained in the Suez.

Now she waited for the train to come in. Her heart pounded, almost shaking her small frame. 'I'm as nervous as a bride!' she thought. The lights of Junee town were being lit and the pink and gold of a sunset sky shone across her face. A brilliant curve of rosellas rainbowed their way across the burnished sky, an unexpected reminder of the promises of a loving God.

A knot of people further down the platform unravelled and moved forward. 'The train's coming!' A distant vibration, a growing rhythm, a crescendo of sound as the engine roared into the station in a rush of steam, flying soot and power. The waiting people stepped back, then pressed forward, peering along the carriages. Grace moved forward, almost on tiptoe to see beyond the crowding shoulders, the jostling suitcases, the eager reunions. Had he not come?

'Grace.'

A tall man, unexpectedly clean-shaven, much greyer, older, thinner and with a face full of weariness, stood before her. And out of his face, unfamiliar because she had never seen him without his whiskers, shone his eyes brimming with love and thankfulness, the eyes she trusted. Clinging to the roughness of his army coat, she moved beside him through the crowd, speechless with relief. Jim was with her again.

Driving home the next morning from Coolamon, Jim stopped the horse as they came over the crest of the hill just beyond the little town. A wide patchwork quilt of paddocks was flung in a gentle ripple to a fringe of trees on the horizon. Squares of pale gold stubble glittered beside pintucked squares of rich red loam fresh from sowing and green patches. They were featherstitched with the fine lines of fences and embroidered with scattered farmhouses, high thatched haystacks, bush and lines of tree-plantings. Fourteen miles further down the road Caldwell was waiting, shining roof among the trees, smoke rising from chimneys.

Grace watched the man beside her. She still felt shy with him. The profile was almost that of a stranger with deep lines she had never seen before. The battered khaki uniform with the feathered hat was not his working clothes, or his Sunday suit. Yet the strong hands holding the reins were Jim's, and the deep voice.

'This is the most beautiful country in the whole world,' he said. 'I've seen nothing to beat it anywhere. And it's home. . .'

She took his hand and held it tightly. This was no stranger. This was her Jim, the man who loved this land so deeply and who perhaps had feared that he would never see it again. He held her fiercely.

'If I'd known,' he said, 'how hard it was going to be, I could never had gone.'

Man and woman smiled at each other. Harry was there, and Minnie, and the Pearces had come across to welcome him home. They sat with blue rimmed wedding teacups in their hands, three kinds of cake on the best china. 'We are treating him like an honoured visitor, not as Father,' Grace thought.

The little ones had given the tall stranger a cursory inspection and a polite kiss on the cheek as commanded, then disappeared about their own affairs. Small Jean was always afraid of strange men, in any case. Even Willie didn't really remember the father who had become a family legend – he had only been a three-year-old when Father left.

'It will be different when the older children come,' Grace said, sensing Jim's disappointment. 'They've been looking forward to seeing you so much – they can't talk about anything else. Mr Dennis is going to give them an early mark.'

She poured more tea and listened eagerly to the stories of those last months following the Armistice – the onset of a wet and bitterly cold winter spent in Beirut and Tripoli and the sea of mud which surrounded the camp, turning the horse lines into an impassable quagmire.

'They called the main road through the camp the Chocolate Road, and it got so bad that they even cancelled our church services. They handed out a rum ration – but that didn't do *me* much good! While we were in Tripoli in November, nearly a hundred men had to be evacuated out, sick — none of us felt too good. Then Christmas — they killed six bullocks for our Christmas dinner and issued potatoes and cabbage, which was better than the usual food, but I tell you, we all just wanted to go home!'

Running footsteps raced along the verandah, the children arriving home breathlessly to greet Father. The door flew open and five eager faces crowded into the doorway. And hesitated, confused. They stared, puzzled, at the whiskerless man in uniform drinking tea with Mother.

'Come and kiss Father,' Grace said, and only then did they move forward, offering polite cheeks, then scuttled off, disappearing into the kitchen to the sound of embarrassed giggles.

Jim's face was stricken. 'They didn't even know me...'

When the evening meal was over, the stranger in uniform leaned his kitbag beside his chair. The three tiny girls stood back a little, shy and hesitant, while the three small boys leaned forward eagerly, ready to help him unpack and to see whatever treasures he might bring out. Grace sat watching, still needing to believe that the man with the kitbag was not another fantasy, just a dream person come in place of the real husband she had needed so desperately.

Jim stretched an arm into the kitbag and withdrew some neatly folded clothing, then his metal food pannikin and army issue cutlery. The boys examined them minutely, then the little metal container for matches, and his mug. He had bought some new books in Sydney, mostly Australian writers, and pulled them out of the bag with his old zest for a good book.

'I brought home a few little curios,' he said, laying a small cloth bundle on the table. A collection of small pieces of rock, odds and ends of cloth and metal spilled onto the table.

'This is a bit of granite and plaster from the Great Pyramid in Egypt. Do you remember I sent you a postcard of it? And these are stones from the Jordan Valley... a scrap of alabaster from another pyramid... some fabric from the wing of an Italian plane shot down over the desert... a little bit of an aeroplane propeller. And in the Holy Land, I walked in some of the places where Jesus walked! So many stories to tell you — the Bible has come to life in a whole new way. Here is a little stone from King Solomon's quarries and from the Mount of Temptation... some bark from an olive tree on the Mount of Olives...'

Grace watched the little collection of curios grow, as her husband spread out each object and spoke of the place where he had found it. The Jordan Valley, Cairo where he had bought a pair of candlesticks in a bazaar, the pyramids, Jerusalem, the Sea of Galilee – he had been in all these faroff and fabled places, had walked there, had seen, touched, listened – and now a little pile of alien rock and fibre and metal lay on her kitchen table. For Jim, they conjured up images and memories which he would never forget – the lands of the Bible, the paths trodden by Christ himself. And images of war.

For Grace, the objects spoke of separation. While she had been living with drought, grief and death, struggling with farm management and the care of nine children under twelve, Jim had been living in another world which she would never enter. Sometimes they would speak of things which had happened during those two years of separation, sharing fragments of time, little lumps of the substance of what had been whole and immediate. But the sharing could never be more than fragmentary, splinters of time like the splinters of rock spread on her table.

Jim unwrapped the last objects from his cloth. Two metal shell cases rolled among the other things.

'This one is British, and this one is from a Turkish gun,' he said.

The small boys were fascinated, wanting to touch, intensely interested in all their father's trophies. The girls had come forward to ask questions, to begin to make contact with the man with the kitbag.

Grace sat staring at the gleaming metal. The small and malevolent shapes made suddenly visible and concrete what she had known for two years. Jim had not just been absent from home, living a life she could not share. He had been living in a war zone, a soldier of the 1st Australian Infantry Force, sent there to fight, perhaps to kill or be killed.

Abruptly, she abandoned the wriggling toddler on her lap and moved to stand by her husband, to feel his strong shoulders under her arm, his arm around her waist, to know that he was real, at home, with her again.

Some weeks later, the people of the district gathered for Jim's welcome home. Over four years the families had farewelled so many of their friends and the close-knit community was always ready to gather back those who came home. The families all knew each other well; Grinters, Downies, Allens and Moncrieffs, Stinsons, Swanns and Pearces, Chants, Cadys and Cords, Dennises and Denyers, Furnells and Englishs and the others. The welcome home was delayed because Jim's arrival had coincided with the arrival in the district of the influenza epidemic and people were busy with sick relatives or setting up a Red Cross isolation ward at the Showground. When at last they met, Grace listened as men spoke warmly of her husband.

One speaker said, 'There was a lot of criticism, you know, when we heard that you had decided to enlist. But we've had to eat our words. You were too generous to expect someone else to defend your wife and children. You have our admiration.'

Someone else added, 'It's Mrs Higman we take our hats off to – the women at home have had a battle.'

Jim rose to speak. 'If I had known how hard it was going to be, I probably would never have had the courage to go,' he began. He spoke of the loneliness and fear, illness and weariness, the disorientation for a middle-aged man in a totally foreign situation and the threat to normal standards of morality. He spoke his next words with special care.

'War,' he said slowly, 'is a terrible thing. It destroys so much – health, friends, marriages. One thing it often does is to lower a man's ideals. It's no wonder – the chaps are a long way from home and everything that once gave them a clear direction has gone. The girls from home are a long way away. For nine months I didn't hear a woman speaking English, and when I did, it startled me! It's hard on the boys. . .'

Grace watched him as he searched for the words, and thought of some of the things he had shared with her in the privacy of their room about the problems faced by the boys. The things he had seen had shocked him deeply.

'One of the best gifts God has given us,' he went on, 'is to make us man and woman. It is not for us to criticise other people – we must accept the boys coming home with compassionate understanding. For me, the best thing about coming home is to come home safely to my very dear wife and the children.'

The soldier's uniform was aired out on the back fence, then hung out of sight in the wardrobe. The stones from the desert were attached to cardboard, labelled and used for lectures on the Holy Land. Events of the war were stripped of immediate pain and told as tales to the children. The Illuminated Address retained its place above the mantelpiece in the dining room, but its sting had been drawn. A rosemary bush – for remembrance – was planted by the back gate, and Jim planted olive tree seedlings north of the house. Olivewood offering plates arrived from the Holy Land for the Rannock Church, ordered by Jim from his Armenian friend. Grace and the children gradually became accustomed again to Jim at the head of the table, Jim as part of their plans for each day.

Jim threw himself back into public life as if he had never been away. The comfortable and familiar garments of his land, his church and local affairs were donned and within weeks of coming home he was re-elected President of Rannock Farmers and Settlers, voted onto the Shire Council, back in local pulpits, once more Superintendant of the Sunday School and on the committee searching for solutions to the pestilence of skeleton weed destroying wheat land. Charlie Pearce and Harry Playford were sharefarming on Caldwell which allowed Jim the freedom from some of the farm work to follow his interests in public life.

He came home from Coolamon one afternoon, quite excited.

'They had their elections today,' he said, 'and the men have elected me as the new Shire President for 1920!'

Grace was pleased for Jim, and proud of him, but with a certain caution. It would mean that Jim would have more outside responsibilities than ever, and be more tired, though it was true that his chest troubles seemed to have gone since the war.

The Hill was to be sold. Will's executors arranged a sale, with the money to be invested for the two little girls' future. On the day of the sale, friends and strangers tramped through the house, wandered in and out of the bedrooms along the verandahs, poked critical heads into the old kitchen with its rough adzed timbers and wide fireplace, picked over the furniture with its mix of fine pieces and homebuilt from kerosene cases. Jim walked abstractedly among the people, thinking his own thoughts of the past. Grace felt her heart reaching out to him as he saw the fabric of his family home torn apart. She paused in the kitchen, where she had so often shared tasks with Evelyn, and the best dining room where long ago she had first sat with the Higman family at a meal, in the days when she had been shy of Jim. This was the place where they had shared Christmas dinners with old Richard Higman and Evelyn, and where Evelyn and Will had spoken their marriage vows. . .

Some special and personal things had already been put aside for the little girls — Evelyn's opal ring, her lovely amethyst necklace and bracelet, some handwork and books, precious things to pass on. Now other things came under the auctioneer's hammer, and Grace watched Jim bid and buy a large collection of blacksmith's tools and handcrafted metalwork.

'I watched Uncle Jim make these,' he muttered as he piled them in the back of the buggy. 'I'll be using them all, of course – anyway, I wasn't letting them go to someone who didn't care about my Uncle Jim!'

At home later that afternoon, Grace found Jim slumped in their bedroom, head in his hands.

'I remember that hill when my father first pitched a tent on it – when there were no fences – I remember how hard Father worked to clear it, and the great bonfires – and Father harvesting our first crop with a scythe – battling against kangaroos and cockatoos and rabbits – making a good farm of it. I remember my mother cooking in the camp oven over the fire in the great fireplace. It was *our* place for forty years. And now it's not. . .'

He was closer to tears than Grace had ever known him. She held him gently for a while, then left him alone to face his loss in quietness. 'Play on the other side of the house this afternoon,' she told the children. 'Father has a headache.' And the children went on tiptoe because their father never ever had headaches.

Grace was tired, tired to the bone. Even though Jim was home again, the responsibilities and pressures of her own life continued without pause. With nine children, one or more always seemed to be ill and needing special care. There were always workmen to feed, and the yard work. She always had her Sunday School class to prepare for, and her work as Secretary of the local Parents and Citizens' group at the school. People spoke of recent inventions to help with housework, but they all seemed to depend on electricity, which she didn't have, and she was just thankful to have Minnie's help with the endless cooking, cleaning, washing, buttermaking, sewing, mending. Lonely workmen in the neighbourhood, often migrants, found in her a mother, and gladly accepted her invitations home to Sunday tea after church. There were new families in the area, too, with young wives trying to understand their husbands returned from the war, somehow more wounded in their spirit than in their body; these, too, came to visit.

Holidays at Caldwell meant the arrival of assorted nieces and nephews, and the children of her old friends from Sydney, come for a lovely farm holiday – and multiplying the numbers at the table, the numbers of sheets and socks to be washed. Even though she knew that her oldest child Carrie had dreamed of training to be a teacher like herself, when Jim suggested that Carrie must come home to help her mother as soon as she turned fourteen, Grace was too tired to argue.

'You must get away for a real holiday, my dear,' Jim said. 'Take some of the young ones and go to Sydney.'

The mother leaned wearily back against the high back of the long railway seat. The constant rush and roar of the steam engine had assailed her ears for many hours as they had travelled from Coolamon. The patterns of suburban streets with the almost forgotten designs of terrace houses, church steeples, industrial chimneystacks and factories were only visible as glimpses past the crowding heads of the children. There were six little heads, all concentrating, all awestruck, at their first sight of Sydney. The three older girls had not come. Now Carrie and Mary had both left the Rannock school to help their mother at home, and Connie, nervously, had gone to high school in Wagga, boarding with Rootes relatives. So the six children pressing noses against the grimy train window were her three boys, Legh, Richie and Willie, and 'the little girls', Jean, Grace and Evie.

'Are we nearly there?'

Grace looked, and a sign on a platform flew by reading 'Ashfield'.

'Watch out for a school any minute, right near the line, with big fig trees and jacarandas in the yard, and a weathervane on top of a spire — that's where I started teaching when I was our Mary's age...'

Around her, the children were arguing about what a jacaranda looked like — they'd never been able to get one to grow at home — and the school at Petersham swam in and out of her vision so quickly that it almost felt like a fantasy. Yet it was still there. She could almost see the young figure under the fig trees, long hair insecurely pinned on top of her head, long skirts demurely around her ankles, ready to be a teacher...

The brief picture faded. They were nearly into the city now, nearly to Central Station which had still been under construction when she and Jim had honeymooned in Sydney. Her children were ready, hats on heads, assorted bags in hand. Their travelling companions in their compartment were also country people off to Sydney for a summer holiday at the beach. Grace's children had been open-mouthed at the audacity of the family who had stowed half their children in luggage racks or under the seats when the ticket-collector had come for their tickets — 'it costs too much for us all to go to Sydney otherwise,' their parent said complacently as ticketless offspring emerged.

The tight backyards and spaceless factories, palled in grey, squeezed more and more closely around the railway lines and then, suddenly, the journey was over and they were all spilling out onto the long platforms of Central Station, drowning in noise and bustle and strangers. In the vast concourse, a high domed roof soared above them, the last daylight gleaming through glassed fan lights of proportions the children had never imagined. Everything around them seemed larger, grander, higher, richer and louder than home, the elaborately decorated sandstone walls echoing the thunder of many engines, many conversations, many footsteps. The little ones were overwhelmed, clutching their mother's skirt. If ever Grace had doubted it over recent years, she now knew for certain that Sydney was a place of girlhood memories, but it was no longer home. Home was a sheltering house with many chimneys at the heart of Jim's paddocks newly harvested and full of people she loved.

With the help of her brother Legh and his wife Florrie, Grace and the children were settled in a holiday cottage on the beach at Dee Why just north of the city. Every day was full of magic for the children. It was their first visit to Sydney and their first sight of the ocean.

Grace watched the faces of the children on that first day at the beach, walking together down the great crescent of sand with the blue of ocean spreading out to the horizon. For these children, the ocean had only been the stuff of stories, illustrations in picture books, background to Sunday book readings. The sea had been reduced to the size of a page, often flat and lifeless, bordered by narrow strips of pebbly British seaside where British children searched for shrimps with nets. Today, as their feet sank for the first time into the hot grainy sand, glaringly golden in the sun, and they stepped along among gaudy beach umbrellas and lightly clad swimmers, the family was bedazzled, awestruck at the way the tame sea of imported picturebooks had exploded into life. It had colour, and surge of sound and taste of salt, and feel of sudden cold dashing against their skin, and the special smell of the sea.

Clinging to Grace's hand, the little girls danced around the waves, darting back as water curled towards them. The young boys plunged in with Uncle Legh, exulting in the feel of water rushing around them, lifting and tossing them. At home, their teacher had begun teaching some of the boys to swim in the dam, a small mudbrown sheet of water between its heaped banks of earth, but here the thrust of water left them breathless and ecstatic.

'Come out with me, climb on my shoulders and we'll wade out a bit deeper,' Uncle Legh invited, and one of the little girls clambered up, laughing.

Grace's skirt hem was damp with salty water and the child beside her was starting to talk of being tired when she heard a shriek. Her brother waded out with Muriel Grace and a wave had just washed over them. For a moment the mother froze. The little girl had vanished. Then an arm broke through the water and Uncle Legh scooped up the sobbing, trembling child and carried her back through the surf to her mother. The boys came running out, dripping and frightened. Grace held her child, cuddling her close and drying the pale face with a towel, talking gently till she was calm again. Young Legh said anxiously, 'Father said I had to look after the others – I'm the biggest, I'm eleven – and I wasn't even looking. . .'

'The dam will do me, for swimming,' one boy muttered.

'Home will do me,' said another.

A special pleasure of the Sydney holiday for Grace was the chance to visit old friends and relatives she hadn't seen for years. Her friend Gertie had gone, but old Auntie Lydia and Uncle Richard Playford had celebrated their sixtieth wedding anniversary and showed every sign of going on for more years, and her cousins were delighted to see her. One day she took the little girls into the city while she shopped and the three boys had a day of exploring Sydney with their Uncle Legh. There was so much about the city which she found strange. Women wore dresses so fashionably short as to be almost indecent, with tight hats like felt tea-cosies dragged over their ears instead of the froths of feathers and flowers of her own youth. The streets were full of motor vehicles and people took for granted electric lights and household appliances. Except for her time in Young, she had never lived in a house with electricity and she stared in wonder at machines for washing clothes and cleaning floors, stoves that needed no firewood, irons which heated themselves, iceboxes and refrigerators.

Uncle Legh and the boys also had a memorable day out, with a ferry ride across the harbour, a visit to the botanical gardens, exploring city buildings and shops, riding trams and tramping pavements till their feet were sore.

'I thought I'd give them a treat and take them out to lunch at a restaurant,' Uncle Legh said. 'We all had a look at the menu and we thought we'd have fish —'

'And when the fish came on the plates, it had tails and fins still on, and Willie said it wasn't fish at all —'

'Willie says real fish is the kind in tins, and he wouldn't eat it!' The lad was unabashed by the teasing. 'Well, I like what Mother cooks best, anyway.'

Cousins said to Grace, 'My dear, how can you live so far out in the country? Don't you often long to come home to Sydney?'

'But I am at home there!' she had said firmly. And sitting in the train on her way back to Caldwell, surrounded by six sleeping children and thinking of Jim and the three big girls and Harry and Minnie and all her friends, she knew where she belonged.

Winter sun was streaming into the bedroom, lighting the mirror where Grace stood combing her hair into its accustomed tidiness, when she saw the reflection which made her heart jolt. In the shine of the mirror stood a man in the uniform of the Light Horse, a tall man with thick wavy hair. For the space of a moment she was overcome with panic, memories of separation flooding in at the sight of the tall soldier reflected. Then she turned quickly, to see the real man, hair turning white, wearing the old uniform she had so carefully sponged and brushed. It was winter 1921 and the uniform no longer held its threat. Along with many other returned servicemen of the Coolamon district, Jim had dressed in uniform today for the ceremonial unveiling of the town war memorial.

Driving through a winter landscape drenched in sunshine, the family sang and chattered, entertained by the idea of Father in his smart uniform having lunch with a major-general. The town had an air of dignity and confidence, the wide street crowded with people of the district. After the formal luncheon, where Jim proposed the toast to Major-General Cox, townspeople merged with returned servicemen in uniform, schoolchildren, women of the Red Cross, mounted police and the Wagga Brass Band for the procession to the central place in the street where the tall stone column of the war memorial stood, swathed in flags. Grace could see her Jim in his feathered hat of the Light Horse high on a platform beside the war memorial, enclosed in a hollow square of uniformed men. After the glory of the procession, the speechmaking became a little tedious for the young children, but her own children were in awe of Father on the platform.

The moment came for the unveiling. The hundreds of witnesses stood very still, remembering. The names were read out, first 'men who have returned', name upon name. Every name was a character, a part of the story of the small town; sons of the pioneers, sons of the shopkeepers, men of the farms, the banks, the stock and station agents, each a known face in Cowabbie Street, Coolamon. She stared with eyes scalding with unshed tears at the man on the platform, feathered slouch hat under his arm, who had come home to her and her children.

The stillness of the crowd intensified.

'The Fallen,' intoned the reader, and again the names fell, dropping heavily into the silence. Of 214 men who had left the community to fight on foreign soil, forty-six were dead. Again the names were the names of friends, schoolmates, boys on the cricket team, workmen whose main problem at the beginning of 1914 had been the chaffcutters' strike. Family names recurred, one son home safe, another son dead. Girls stood in the crowd, some with heads buried in the shoulders of their mothers, sobbing when the name of their fiance or bridegroom was spoken. Other girls stood staring stonily, alone in the pity of what might have been, if only forty-six men had come home. 'Pearce A.E., Pearce W.E . . .' and Charlie Pearce and his wife stood with heads bowed, remembering his brothers.

The draped flags fell away from the polished stone of the austere column while the notes of the last post wavered in the air. Under bronze wreaths circling the battlefields of the 1st A.I.F. – Gallipoli, Flanders, France, Palestine – were the names, graven in stone, men made memories.

There was going to be a wedding in the family. Minnie Playford, Harry's girl who had been part of their family for so long, was marrying a tall and handsome young man called Keith Evans, a relative of her Auntie Fanny on the north coast. The last time Grace had helped to prepare for a wedding had been ten years earlier, for Evelyn and Will, and the years since 1913 had been often filled with shadows. Caldwell had witnessed its share of grief and now it was time for joy.

Grace found herself at the heart of delightful preparations; dressmaking, texture of laces and sheeny white fabrics, girls giggling over flowered veils, perfume of roses filling rooms, furniture highly polished, lino floors so slippery shiny as to be a danger, silver gleaming, table linen starched and ironed to smooth perfection, aroma of roasting chickens and home-cured hams, cake tins filled with sponges, shortbreads, wedding cake. The house seemed full of sunshine.

On the day of the wedding, the front door was flung open, flooding light down the long hall. Grace walked along the path of light carrying two little baskets she had filled with rose petals freshly picked from the autumn garden, pinks, reds and palest rose mingling. From one door came the three little girls, dancing out in their new dresses, hair gleaming, the older two ready to carry the rose petals as flower girls for the bride. From another door came the excited sounds of daughters and nieces adding the finishing touches to the bridal finery. The girls all swept out into the hall, Minnie a lovely bride with her sister Maude, followed by a train of cousins. Grace watched them walk towards the open door on a wave of orange blossom, tulle, laughter and rose petals. Her eyes misted, remembering a tiny motherless girl who had slept on her lap the day Jim had asked her to marry him by the waterfall.

Outside the front gate in the sunshine, Jim was dressed in his best suit with a dustcoat covering it for motoring. He was bent over the crank handle of his new motor car, his smart green Willys Overland, toiling to bring the engine to life. Harry sat cheerfully behind his mare Mona, laughing and making patronising remarks about the superiority of a good animal over the vagaries of a lump of machinery if his daughter the bride were to get to church on time.

'What this house needs is a happy wedding,' Grace said to herself as she followed the laughing, beautiful party from the house. The fears that had once haunted that hall in times of darkness had disappeared and she remembered the words of Isaiah with his promises to his people to give them '. . . beauty for ashes, oil of joy for mourning, the garment of praise for the spirit of heaviness; that they might be called the trees of righteousness, the planting of the Lord, that he might be glorified.'

Like ribbon of shot silk, the years unwound, threading light and shadows. For most of those years of the growing-up of the children, the nineteen-twenties, the colours which unravelled from their skein of time were bright, vivid. The house with its creamy ochre concrete blocks and many chimneys was full – full of children, full of activity, full of laughter. Everything seemed to be growing. The children were growing, outgrowing their clothes, some growing beyond the scope of the little school. The garden was growing around the house: bulbs were multiplying, banksia roses scaling the verandah posts, the grapevine along the back verandah softening the working area with its milk separator and cool safe with the opulence of summer grapes. The orchard was developing, with Jim bringing piped water to it from the dam, and his olive trees were well established. Behind the house, row upon row of beds of vegetables and grapevines flourished and general hand Charlie Brumfield and young Legh had dug a deep well near the back door. Near the olive trees, Jim was building a tennis court for his growing children.

Jim's farm was doing well, too. He was having finer harvests than he had ever done; at the end of his 1921-1922 harvest he had proudly calculated that his 600 acres under crop had yielded an average of eight bags an acre, with some of his best Federation wheat yielding ten bags to the acre. His seed wheat was his pride. By the harvest of 1924-25, Coolamon district topped the whole state of New South Wales for the acreage of wheat harvested. More farmers began running sheep and both wheat and wool prices were high, with wheat bringing at least five or six shillings a bushel. In the euphoria of a prosperity they had not known in the earlier hard years of pioneering, drought and war, the community set about rebuilding Coolamon with offices, a picture theatre, the Coolamon Co-operative Society and new brick churches. The White Train steamed across New South Wales, stopping in Coolamon for a procession of townspeople and schoolchildren to explore the many carriages carrying Australian products and bearing the proud message: 'Buy Australian Made'. The Shire Council invited a touring Chamber Orchestra from the Sydney Conservatorium of Music to play in their town, and the latest Methodist minister, Mr Skinner, inspired the community to produce an ambitious eisteddfod.

The village of Rannock still consisted of two small churches and a school, but Grace worked hard with the Parents and Citizens' group to see a new school building with better equipment opened beside the tiny old schoolhouse, and Jim was part of the group adding a Sunday School room at the back of the Methodist church. The new schoolteacher, Mr Haug, was full of energy and ideas and Grace was glad for her children. The old dream of a railway through Rannock was being revived.

With fine harvests and good prices, Jim was able to buy things for their home and farm. Grace would watch him, deep in his own thoughts or the pages of a book or newspaper while the life of the household flowed around him, and then he would suggest some new investment. Those were the years when he bought their first car, then a second car, a small truck and his first tractor. (Harry was horrified; nothing could replace the sweep of a dozen fine Clydesdales, each with a name and a personality.) For the home there was a good secondhand piano and a piano teacher for the older girls, a wireless set, a petrol-fuelled lighting system for the main rooms, an Icy Pole petrol refrigerator, a machine with a hand-turned paddle for washing clothes and a big Coolgardie safe to hold half a sheep, made with Jim's considerable welding skills. The bookshelves were filled with new encyclopedias, many Australian works and British classics. Grace knew that his dreaming was partly because he loved to explore new inventions and partly just because he loved her and wanted to give her everything she needed to make her home comfortable.

Then Jim thought of another new role for Grace. 'They are looking for a new location for the Rannock Post Office — somewhere where it's possible for the telephone exchange to be attended twelve hours a day. With Carrie and Mary working at home, I think we should take the job on here at Caldwell. You'd be very good at doing the official book-work and the girls will have a paying job.'

'Jim, you must learn to say no sometimes,' Grace said. 'I don't expect you to give up your interests, but surely there are times when someone else could do the work.'

Whenever Jim saw an issue as a righteous cause in community, church, school or farming life, there he was in the thick of it. Grace saw many things debated vigorously over her table and sometimes added her own gentler wisdom. In politics there was the debate between country Progressives and city Nationalists. In religion there were the differences between the Protestant Loyal Orange Lodge and the Roman Catholic community. Among the farmers the burning question was mechanisation versus horsepower; in the Shire Council whether the town's greater need was for piped water or for an electricity plant; and in the community generally, everyone had an opinion on pubs versus Prohibition. Jim was also involved with trying to find solutions to the skeleton weed infestation and the dreadful state of their rural roads.

'Well, I'm planning to stand down as Shire Council President at the end of the year – if they can find someone else to take on that thankless task. . . I couldn't do it without our sharefarmers.' His latest combination of sharefarmers was Harry Playford and Harry's older daughter and her husband Charlie Rollins.

Grace looked unconvinced.

'I've been meaning to mention it,' Jim went on, almost apologetically. 'A number of people have been urging me to stand in the next elections – they say I'd be a strong candidate for the country cause in parliament. You know how many things I'd like to see done. . .' His voice trailed away as he saw the expression on her face.

'No,' said Grace.

Grace was ironing when the invitation came. A neat timber post office building now stood in the backyard of Caldwell with a counter for official business, the entanglement of cords of the telephone exchange and the smell of hot sealing wax. She had heard Mr Cartwright the mailman arrive and Mary had carried in the clothes basket piled with their order of fourteen loaves from the town bakery. Carrie and Mary helped the mailman sort mail for families further out then brought in their own.

The mother lifted the heavy flat iron back onto the stove top to reheat before she sat down to open her letter. It was an official letter from the shire council. Would Mrs Higman, as wife of their Shire Council President, kindly consent to cut the ribbon at the official ceremony to bring electric power to the town of Coolamon on Wednesday, 20 May 1925?

'That's an honour!' all the family assured her that evening. The small electricity plant which the Shire Council had debated for years was ready at last.

'The problem is going to be convincing people to use the power,' Jim said. 'A lot of people think that it is just as easy to fill the kerosene lamp, and probably cheaper than being linked to the power, and they haven't even thought about buying any modern appliances. A pity, really, that the plant will only be able to service the town. I'd love to be able to buy you some of those things, my dear.'

On a cool May evening, Grace Higman joined her husband on the porch of the shire hall, along with other notables. The citizens' band played the National Anthem and Jim Higman presided, while townspeople gathered for speechmaking.

Jim spoke. 'I remember when I first went on my own land. It was nothing but wild scrub then, and I wondered what kind of jackass I was to try to clear it. But now, twenty-five and more years later, it is a valuable property and supports as many as twenty people at once. This electric plant is a bit like my farm in the early days — we still need people to see the possibilities of it, and get the best out of it.'

The consulting engineer handed Grace the scissors, one of a set in a handsome crocodile-skin case. In the half-dark, she sliced through a blue ribbon attached to a switchboard. As the power came on, the porch was illuminated with strings of coloured light bulbs, festoons of bulbs up the flagpole, lights in the shire hall and streetlights along the main street. People cheered and clapped. The roads were still dreadful and they had to rely on tanks for their water, but at least their town now had electricity.

Later that evening, the family drove home through the dark to the farm. As they lit the lamps and stirred hot coals in the stove into a blaze to boil the kettle, Grace wondered whether she would ever see electricity come to the farm. At least, she thought, she now had a good set of scissors in a crocodile case.

Her guest paused in telling Grace her story to wipe her eyes. Grace quietly waited for her to go on. Among the people of the community, people who had become her dear friends over the years, there was sometimes hidden pain. People liked to mind their own business and not express private feelings, but somehow many of them felt that they could talk to Grace. There were bereavements, broken romances, uneasy marriages, disappointments, troubles related to alcoholism, rebellious youth — the warp and weft of living.

As the woman began again to unburden herself, Grace listened carefully. Absently her finger traced the design of a crochet mat under her hand, a single thread reaching out from a tiny central circle of chain stitches in a complex design, each motif interlocked with the rest so that if one section were damaged other parts could unravel. Since the telephone exchange had come to their home, she was more aware than ever of the relatedness of their community. Through the phone, her family was always the first to know of emergencies, cries for the doctor, bushfire, happy news. Her home was the centre circle, linking people with each other, uniquely positioned to help their neighbours in times of crisis. Sometimes people came to her home for their pension cheque — and a private talk. Sometimes Carrie drove her to visit people in trouble.

Her fingers plucked at the fine chains of the crochet as she listened. Soon her guest would be ready to go. They would pray together, and she would embrace her neighbour before she drove away. Then there would be the family and her house guests to feed and care for. The lines of the design of mutual dependence stretched wider than the local community. There always seemed to be extra people at her table and more and more people to pray for — church dignitaries, missionaries on furlough, troubled youth, convalescents, friends of friends suffering from breakdowns. Long ago she had written in her book of 'Gleanings' the Kipling lines about 'helping lame dogs over stiles', and Caldwell had become a place where that was a natural part of living.

Soon she would have her fiftieth birthday. There had been the time when she thought she would not live to see her fortieth, yet God had allowed her to stay with her family, to create a home that was open, and she was thankful.

Frost whitened the earth, turning the last pale dried grass of last summer into icicles, freezing the water in the sheep-dogs' water tins, blackening the last limp leaves of autumn vegetables. On the back verandah under the bare bones of the grapevine hung the carcase of the pig Jim and the boys had slaughtered and prepared yesterday.

'Today,' Grace thought, 'there won't be time for anything but the pig.' She balanced another slice of bread on the toasting fork, glad to be sitting briefly by the glowing coals of the firebox. The kettle was singing and the big black water fountain on the stove had begun to steam. She had been so very busy lately with end-of-the-month post office bookwork, training children for the Sunday School anniversary, helping devise programs for the winter youth groups, ordering the new world maps for the school, counselling specially demanding house guests, writing to the children away at school. And the household work never stopped.

As soon as breakfast was over, Jim sharpened his butcher's knives to a keen edge and one of the girls scrubbed the wide kitchen table till it was spotless. The pig was cut up and Grace worked carefully to select the portions to be salt-cured, pickled, smoked or eaten fresh, the trotters to be transformed into brawn, nothing to be wasted. Hams, shoulders and rolls were rubbed with a mixture of coarse salt, saltpetre and sugar and carried out to the wooden meat box in a cold outside shed and laid side by side between layers of clean hessian. Tomorrow and the next day and for three or four weeks after that, she and girls would turn each piece and re-salt it till their hands were cracked and chapped with cold and salt and at last the hams could be hung in bags on the verandah to drip and dry out for another week or so. There was no time to lose, because all the salt meat must be finished and packed into its calico and hessian bags in layers of charcoal before spring came with warmer weather, when any meat not properly treated would spoil in the heat.

Jim stood back, his own part completed, and watched Grace and the girls at work.

'You should enter some of your hams and pickled pork in the Coolamon Show,' he urged. 'And not just the hams, my love, but you should go in the new category we've introduced at this 1925 Show – "What a Capable Woman Can Do." Women are to enter thirty items, all made with their own hands – you should go in it!'

'Thirty items!' Grace laughed. 'When would I have time to make thirty things? And what kind of things, anyway?'

Jim was enthusiastic but vague. 'Oh, all the kinds of things our ladies can do. The men on the committee are very proud of their wives and thought it was time to recognise all their skills – you know the sort of things. . .'

Grace's quick hands went on pressing salt into meat, skimming the froth on the surface of pork simmering in the big boiler, preparing the hot pickle, setting out earthenware crocks to hold the pickled pork, melting the fat that would seal it. She knew that she was busy enough, certainly. Then she pictured some of the fine needlework some women did, their wonderful skills in cookery, and the way some farmers' wives were so good at helping their men with the outside work as well as keeping the home. She had never been an expert outside the house and she still hated to kill a fowl, resorting to egg-and-bacon pie if they were out of meat.

'The girls and I always work together, like today, on our work. I'll leave the thirty handmade things for other women!' she said firmly.

The annual show of the Coolamon Agricultural and Pastoral Association was a great success that year. The season had been superb and, as Grace walked among animals and modern machinery, grains and fleeces, sideshows and displays, she felt the exuberance of the community. In the industrial hall, her children hurried to see whether blue ribbons for first prize, or red for second, or even the smaller comfort of 'highly commended' decorated any of their entries; school drawings, woodwork, Carrie's smoked ham, Mary's biscuits, Legh's boot repair job, her own citrus marmalade, Father's fleece or Rannock School's flowers and vegetables.

The biggest crowd stood around the display of 'What a Capable Woman Can Do.' Four women had arranged their thirty items, each setting out her work with pride and care.

'Just look at it all!' a neighbour said to Grace. 'How clever they all are!'

'They are — it's good that the judges have given them *all* a prize. They all certainly deserve it.' She joined her friends in gazing in admiration at rows of homemade jams, pickles and sauces, bottled and dried fruits from farm orchards, cured meats, honey from their own bees, cakes, scones, breads and biscuits, pats of yellow butter, embroidery, dressmaking, knitted garments, crochet edging and doilies, woollen rugs patchworked from scraps, aprons created from sugarbags, samples of perfect laundry work with starching and ironing, flower arrangements and even examples of one woman's interest in sketching and painting in oils.

She felt her husband's presence beside her. He inspected the display with pleasure then turned to her.

'*You* can do all those things.'

'Oh, no, not everything — and some things not nearly so well...'

His voice was quiet and others did not hear his words. 'Thirty items made by the woman's own hands... thirty... nine children, fourteen nieces and nephews, Harry and me, the procession of people who stay in our home, your years of Sunday School classes, your work for the school, Christian Endeavour, setting up activities for our young people, women who come to you for counsel... am I over thirty yet?'

'Hush!' Grace was embarrassed. Any moment she feared her husband would make a public announcement demanding a prize for his wife! 'That's not anything special — all women do things like that.'

'Perhaps that's why it seems easier to give prizes for the things a man does. How can you give a blue ribbon for raising a child who grows into a good person, or a championship cup for a beautiful marriage where love never gives up over a lifetime?'

The news filtered home to Caldwell that some children had begun to take sides in the Catholic versus Protestant debate. Neighbours remained civil, but everyone knew which side everyone else was on. For a time it was limited to some mild name-calling among the children and some sharp conversations between the adults. The two groups had coexisted peacefully for years, though they made no claims to agree with each other.

Jim, as always, had very strong opinions on the subject. 'Their doctrine is not sound,' he'd say firmly. 'Things like praying to the Virgin Mary and purgatory, and transubstantiation, and saints, and the infallibility of the Pope – I can't agree with any of those things.' Jim was always reading and Grace left weightier matters of doctrine to his judgment. She found she had very little time to read these days and regretted it.

The occasional rumblings of ill feeling between the churches had been going on for years, usually heightened by politics, or questions like conscription or Prohibition. Religious partisanship came to a head that year when a young nun ran away from the convent in Wagga and was taken in by a Protestant family. Suddenly everyone had an unshakeable opinion on whether it was a tragedy or an escape. The story was told, with ornaments, for miles around, reaching the quiet paddocks of Rannock.

A public meeting was called about the conflict, held in another part of the district with Jim as Shire President in the chair. 'It turned into a riot,' Jim told Grace wearily when at last he arrived home from the meeting. 'I've never seen anything like it in this district, not since the violence at the chaffcutters' strike ten years back. And even then it was local men against travelling chaffcutters. Tonight was bad. Tonight was neighbour against neighbour.'

Grace watched him from the bed as he dragged off his boots.

'People were making speeches,' he said slowly, 'but nobody was listening to them. Any time a man started to speak someone would be shouting, and any Protestant speaker was drowned out by very loud singing of Irish songs. Then someone started throwing rocks on the roof, to add to the noise. I don't mind telling you, I was afraid of what might happen next. I sent one of the fellows off to ring up for the policeman from Coolamon to come over. Then someone said something that stirred the possum in the opposition and next thing a crowd of men had rushed onto the little stage. And the hall we were in was used by the Baptists and the platform covered their baptistry. At any moment I thought the flooring would collapse and we'd all fall through into the baptistry! When the policeman arrived, he found a hall full of angry men, all local people of the district and all yelling at each other. The policeman was in the middle with his firearm, shaking all over and in danger of shooting someone by mistake! He's probably never had to handle anything worse than a drunk-and-disorderly, or moved on a vagrant through town.'

Jim dropped onto his knees by the bed for his evening prayers as he always did. Before he buried his face in his hands, he looked at her with deep lines of weariness and anxiety on his face. 'There's too much division these days. We're having the best seasons we've had for years, but we are all arguing about too many things – Prohibition, religion, politics, who to blame for the roads. I'd much rather we didn't mix up our opinions with our good friendships with our neighbours.'

Then he was silent and, watching his bowed white head, Grace knew how much she loved this man.

The telephone shrilled beside her as Grace worked in the post office. The voice was gasping, distraught, a recently widowed woman struggling to keep her farm going for her children, sobbing from her farmhouse some miles away.

'An accident – it was an accident – call the doctor quick – but it's too late, tell him it's too late. She's dead.'

From the incoherence, Grace learned that three of the widow's children had been walking together to bring in the cows, two little girls and her oldest son. The boy had his father's rifle, in case he saw a rabbit, but the rifle had slipped in his hand, struck the ground and fired, killing his sister instantly. Grace wound the handle of the telephone in haste to call the doctor and the policeman, then alerted several neighbours before asking Carrie to get out the car.

All the way along the quiet country road, Grace thought of the widow and the poor child who'd carried the gun. The dead girl was Evie's age and in her class at school. The sun shone across paddocks of ripening grain and it seemed impossible that there could be such pain in such a peaceful setting. Yet pain was part of the community and always had been. She remembered deaths, accidents, sometimes shame or conflict. They too had lived in this lovely setting, but peace needed to be deeper than landscape.

They drove into the widow's yard to the yapping of dogs. The doctor and policeman had not arrived yet, as they had some fourteen more miles to travel, but another near neighbour, a Catholic woman, drove in soon after Grace. The two women went together to the house, together gathered the weeping woman and her little ones in their arms, together gently talked with the stunned lad — 'but we were friends,' he said, puzzled. They made tea and sandwiches for the doctor and policeman when they arrived. The two guests, Catholic and Methodist, had had mutual respect and friendship for each other since both had arrived in the area twenty years earlier. Before they at last set off for their homes, Grace put an arm around the shoulders of the widow and prayed a prayer for peace in their home, the peace of God in the middle of pain.

As they walked to their cars, the Catholic woman turned to Carrie. 'If I were ever in bad trouble, your mother would be one of the first people I would want to be with me,' she said.

'Come for a walk, my dear, and look at the orchard with me.'
It was Sunday morning, and Sundays were special. Every week had its own rhythm of work days, Saturdays had work and sport — and Sunday. Sunday was truly a 'day of rest'. It was the one day in the week when Jim didn't go out to work around the farm, nor did his sons or workmen. The cows had to be milked, of course, and the animals fed, but nothing else was urgent enough to break into the rare peace of Sunday. For Grace, it was a day of freedom, too. On Saturday she and the girls had worked to prepare Sunday clothes, Sunday meals, Sunday special atmosphere and today she was free to ignore all those mundane household things which never ever could be completely finished. Now she would walk quietly with Jim through the garden. Often she liked to attend the Anglican Morning Prayer, but today was not a Sunday when the vicar came to Rannock. Today there would be time to sit in the sunshine on the verandah and read for a little while, or write some letters. Then this afternoon they would all go up to the little church. Jim was not preaching today, as he often did, and they would both teach their Sunday School classes before the afternoon service. The cake tins were full and she would probably invite a few of her children's friends home to tea.

As she and Jim walked from the house, she could hear the children preparing for Sunday School. The young ones were busy learning their verses of scripture, memorising questions and answers of catechism. A chorus of voices prompted each other, correcting, repeating the words, sometimes arguing. The older ones were reading, or learning a new song at the piano. Jim and Grace walked slowly into the spring sunshine through the garden, heaped beds of spring bulbs bursting up, a butterfly dancing in the lilac blossom.

In the orchard, stumbling a little over the loose clods of ploughed soil, they walked up the cathedral nave of colour — pink, cerise, white, red — with the high vault of blue soaring overhead. Fig and apricot, apple and peach, plum and nectarine, mulberry, almond and quince; a choir of colour sang a Sunday song.

Each of their children was precious to them, and it seemed to Grace in the orchard that their family was in its own springtime. Carrie was almost a woman, nearly twenty-one and, though she had admirers, she had not chosen a special friend yet. Sometimes Grace wondered whether her capable oldest child ever regretted that her dreams of training to be a teacher or a nurse had come to nothing. At the time there had seemed to be no choice and now, with the post office, no-one ever suggested that the girls might go away for further training. Mary had no ambitions to study further. She was very serious, a perfectionist in everything she did, but not so quick as the others. Connie was home too: she had completed her high school studies in Wagga, with the prestige of being a prefect in her final year, but Connie was so often ill that for now further training for a profession seemed out of the question.

'The boys all need a chance. Young Legh has been working on the farm since he turned fourteen and next year I want him to go to Wagga to the experiment farm — he's turning into a good farmer and he's smart. And Richard is doing so well at Wagga High School, even though he seems to miss home so much: he tends to be a very sensitive and introspective lad.' They both had private dreams that perhaps one day their second son might become a doctor or a minister. 'Will finishes at Rannock soon, and probably Yanco Agricultural High is best for him — he's never wanted to do anything but be on the land.'

They walked on, looking up through branches embroidered with blossom, gold threadwork of sunshine edging petals. The beauty of spring was around them, but one day soon the petals would float away and the fruit would follow.

'The little girls. . .' Grace said. 'Will's executors are already saying that Jean and Evie should go to a good private school when they are old enough — perhaps the new Annesley School at Bowral. We'll need to find a way to give Gracie something similar. Perhaps Minnie and Keith would let her stay with them and go to school in Manly. They've always done everything together, ever since they were babies.'

They walked on, talking and thinking, Jim looking at his fruit trees and thinking about their irrigation during the dry weather and Grace picturing the fruit which summer would bring into her kitchen. Ideas began to flow between them about family and farm as they walked. A gust of wind tossed a handful of blossom into the air, floating away from the branch, and Grace knew that the springtime for her family could not last forever.

That afternoon, Jim brought the car around for church. The little girls sat in the back, bouncing and chanting 'German Sausage! German Sausage!' as instructed until Jim's cranking finally brought the engine to life. They drove to church through wattle blossom and sunshine. Spring was the time for Sunday School anniversaries and new dresses, concerts and picnics, school holidays and shearing, the show and the finals of winter sports competitions. Soon the shorter working days of winter, with evening activities, would be over and the whole community would be committed to long working days and harvest.

There was a feeling of happy anticipation as they drove, and Grace knew that it was not only because her children would be meeting friends. During winter their minister, Mr Skinner, and his musical wife had invited the community to come to the little church every evening for a week. They taught Christian music, prayed together and urged everyone to examine their own understanding of faith. It had been an important time in the spiritual journey of several of her children, and Grace was thankful.

The timber church was full that afternoon with farm families and their workmen, people who knew each other very well after many years of building a community together. There was a feeling of purpose and hope as they stood to sing their first hymn. Even though this season wasn't as good as some recent ones had been, they were all well-established now, the days of pioneering were long past and they all saw their sons and daughters growing up around them, ready to take over their family land when the time came.

Later, when they all gathered outside in the sun, men on one side of the building and women on the other, Grace moved from friend to friend, gathering the strands of their shared lives. It was good to see them face to face, women whose voices had often come to her on the telephone through the week. She moved to a few of the young migrant workmen, inviting them to come back to Caldwell for tea. It was getting a little more difficult, she decided, to feel free about inviting these boys home now that the three big girls were old enough to be looking for life partners. 'They might think that I'm looking for husbands for my daughters!' she thought. 'And some of these lads are *not* the ones I'd choose. Yet they probably just want some company and cake for tea.'

With family and guests gathered, they went home through the late afternoon, home for a shared meal, laughter, singing around the piano, tea and cake. The house felt very contented.

The extra guest almost wasn't invited. Most of the young people of the district had already been invited to Carrie's twenty-first birthday party, to be held on an evening of full moon in March 1927. It was only after church on the previous Sunday that Grace realised that there was a new young man who had been left out.

'Jim, who is that tall fair-haired fellow?' she murmured.

'That's young Hector, the Crawford's son from Berry Jerry – he's a brother of our girls' piano teacher. His dad bought their Berry Jerry place from my Uncle John Swann some twenty years ago and now Hector is buying his own place here in Rannock. I've met him before.'

On impulse, Grace went to the young man. 'Would you like to join us for our daughter's birthday party this week? Have you met Carrie yet? Once or twice. . . We'd be glad to have you, specially as you are going to be a neighbour.'

Carrie's party was great fun. Through the telephone exchange, the church, her tennis, the Lodge and other community activities, Carrie had many friends and there was a happy crowd filling Caldwell. There were games outdoors in the moonlight, puzzles and brain-teasers indoors by lamplight, music and good food. Grace went around the guests making them welcome. She knew that to some of their neighbours, the Higman pattern of living seemed very Spartan and joyless; no dancing, no alcohol, no playing cards, no sport on Sundays. For her daughter she had tried to think of the happiest and most joyous of party games, the most beautiful songs, the most delicious party food, the most loving atmosphere. Shouts of laughter and song wove a crown of joy around the moonlit verandahs with the banksia roses in bloom. Jim was heard to mutter, 'The only spirits this lot seems to need to have a good time is high spirits!'

The new young neighbour was part of the crowd. Grace made him welcome and decided to invite him back for Sunday tea some time soon – he seemed an intelligent young man with a lively sense of humour. She was not to know that her last-minute invitation would be remembered later, along with 'the first time Carrie wore her birthday pearls' as 'the first time Hector came to Caldwell', or that Hector Crawford would one day be part of the family.

Sunday evenings had often been times when guests had sat at their table, or times when there had been special family times. When the children were little, Grace had read Sunday evening serial stories to them and, now they were bigger, it became a time for courtships.

Usually the boys of the family had no part in household duties, as men's work and women's work were clearly divided. But on Sunday evenings, Grace sometimes suggested, 'Would you boys like to help the girls with the washing up?' and would then busy herself with the little ones, allowing the older young people to make a social occasion of plying mop and tea-towels around the tin bowl of washing-up water and dripping cups and plates on the draining tray. When everything was tidy, they would all go for a walk – 'just down through the bush paddock till nearly sunset, and then come back for a sing'.

Grace would watch them go, first all clustered in a group and then spreading out so that a boy and a girl would have a rare chance to talk to each other as they strolled through the wattles. Her sons were at an age when the romances of their sisters were viewed with amusement, and she knew that the boys sometimes thought it was riotously funny to creep up behind trees ready to leap out on a couple as they walked. As the evening darkened, Grace would light the lamps in the dining room, set out fresh cakes and the cups and saucers for supper and look through a hymn book at the organ, peacefully choosing some of her favourite hymns to sing when the young ones came in. As months of Sunday evenings went by, she knew that, for two of her daughters, friendships were blossoming into something deeper.

It was no surprise when one evening in 1929, Carrie and her friend Hector Crawford came together to ask Grace and Jim for their blessing on their love for each other. And some months later, Jim came home from a trip to preach at another country centre as he often did, a very bemused expression on his face.

'He must have been trying to get up the courage all the way home in the car!' he said. 'You know that I took young Stan Grinter with me to the service? Well, he sat there in silence all the way home till we got to the last gate, got out and opened it and closed it after me.

Then, in sight of the house, he just leaned over and switched off the car engine and suddenly asked my permission to marry our Connie!'

Two weddings were to take place in the family, probably each after the usual two years of engagement to prepare a glory box and trousseau. Grace was very happy for her daughters: both girls would be marrying very good young men who loved them. However, there were early signs that, at the end of the nineteen-twenties, things could not remain as they were for much longer.

18
Hope for harvest
1930-1931

THE CRACKLE AND STATIC of the big wireless set wove in and out of the breakfast conversation, but Grace was paying no attention to it. As she poured a second cup of tea for Jim, she was thinking about the day's work ahead of her. Jim suddenly lifted his hand, commanding silence. Even in the obedient quietness, she could only hear odd phrases from the fractured voice of the newsreader, and they meant nothing to her — 'Wall Street... financial crisis... serious implications...'

Jim shook his head. 'Missed it!' he muttered. 'He said something about a serious financial crash in America — something important in Wall Street. I don't suppose it will affect us, though.'

He reached out his hand for the worn Bible on the bookshelf beside him and turned to the reading for the day. Grace sat listening to his steady voice as he read the familiar words of Psalm 89, a psalm of confidence: 'I will sing of the mercies of the Lord for ever, with my mouth will I make known thy faithfulness to all generations...'

'Let us pray,' he said and, as they bowed their heads in prayer, he placed his family into the keeping of their loving God for the day.

With a scrape of chairs, the three boys moved away from the table and disappeared out through the back door to their work. Grace heard their voices, eager, argumentative, three strong-minded boys who had always shared everything and who all spoke their minds loudly and all at once if necessary. The back gate clanged shut after them and they were gone for the day. As she gathered up breakfast dishes, she found herself smiling about those three. Each boy was growing up strong and good-looking aged sixteen, seventeen and eighteen. Both Richard and Willie (now calling themselves Dick and Bill) had wanted more than anything else to come home to work on Caldwell.

In recent months things had changed on the farm. Since before the war, sharefarmers had worked on Caldwell with Jim – Charlie Pearce, then Ted Cochrane, Harry Playford, Charlie Rollins. Shearers and harvest workers had come and gone, as well as other farm workers, and their good friend and general hand Charlie Brumfield had only recently bought himself a place near Temora and moved away. Now that the boys were old enough, Jim's dream was coming true: he and his sons could manage the work and keep the farm in the family. One day, of course, the place would be theirs. 'It's going to help us – not having to pay labour or divide our income with the sharefarmers,' Jim confided. 'Last season we had a very poor harvest and money is tight. We'll all be working for our keep this year, but if things go well we'll be able to pay for a good holiday and some new equipment.'

The first phone call of the day was calling one of the girls to the post office and the other girls were already moving into their own work. Grace carried the empty teapot back to the kitchen, tidying away the latest *Sydney Morning Herald* as she went. If she had paused to read it, she would have seen words of foreboding, stories of financial ruin threatening some people in England and America, fears of a worldwide depression, of increased tariffs and dwindling prices, of steep decline in the value of wool, wheat and hides, of rising unemployment. But Grace had no time today to read the paper, and the day went on.

Grace unhooked the cotton lace curtains that hung behind her bed and bundled them into her arms. It was Monday, washing day, and the dust of summer had reddened the curtains again, tingeing the once white bobbled fringe with the colour of rust. It had been a very dry year and dust filtered through everything in the house. Her sheets were already boiling in the copper in the corner of the kitchen and she decided to wash her bed-drapes as well.

In the kitchen, one of the girls hoisted sheets from the boiling suds in the copper. They were draped over the end of a thick copper stick, steaming and dripping as they were dragged up and over into tubs of rinse water and blue water. Another girl pushed the handle of the washing machine to and fro, while another washed the best silk shirts and blouses in a tin dish. Another dish of boiled starch was ready for pillowslips and tablecloths, shirt collars, embroidered linen and aprons. In the graded piles of washing still to be done lay the accumulation of a family of eleven, usually swelled by visitors, with soiled work clothes of four men to be done last of all.

Grace lay her dusty curtains aside and went outside to the watertanks by the back verandah. She had seen many dry years, and this one promised to be another. Her knuckles rapped sharply against the corrugation of the iron tank. There was an ominous hollow ring and she beat an anxious rhythm further down, listening for the tone which would tell her the water level. Both big tanks were getting low. From now on, every wash copperful, every bucketful, every kettleful was going to need to be carefully hoarded.

Overhead, the sky was cerulean blue. There had been no sign of rain for weeks. She thought of baths for the family over the next weeks, even when everyone only used a dipperful each, and washdays with the men's clothes stiff with mud and grease, work socks thick with grass seeds and burrs. For a moment she dreamed of her brother Legh's house in Sydney, where the turn of a tap released the resources of a city water supply. Still, summer was summer and soon, with autumn, the rains would come.

'Jim will be counting on it this year, specially,' she thought, 'with his great plans for growing more wheat.'

Jim's latest enthusiasm had stemmed from a government campaign aimed at Australian wheat growers. With international financial problems, the government challenged wheat growers to come to the aid of the nation by growing more wheat in 1930 to provide a rapid increase in export production. They promised that in return for the extra outlay and effort of the farmers, they would guarantee a minimum price of four shillings a bushel delivered to the railway, a price not as high as previous years, but reasonable in the circumstances. There was talk of a compulsory wheat pool to be organised around Australia. For weeks Jim had been planning it with the boys; the extra paddocks to be sown, the soil preparation to be done. Listening to them talk, Grace had the feeling that they hoped to rescue the economy of Australia almost single-handed. 'But if he sows all that extra land, he'll have to have the rain,' she thought, 'or the whole farm will be in trouble.'

Washing day went on. Basket after basket of clean damp clothes was carried out to the clothes lines beyond the woodheap, filling the lines with a dancing company of disembodied garments leaping and galloping in the hot wind, hoisted high above the dirt by forked clothesprops. Monday midday dinner was prepared, cold meat for washday simplicity, and soon Jim and the boys would be coming in from their morning work repairing fences. The last of the workclothes had been scrubbed, the rinsing water carried in buckets to soak into thirsty earth around the vegetables, and the hot suds from the copper emptied out by dippers to scrub the kitchen floor.

The cottonlace curtains remained unwashed. 'We won't wash them this week – they are such dust-catchers – maybe I'll leave them down altogether. The room might look more modern without...'

The boys were called home to dinner with the clang of metal plough discs hanging on the fence. They came in hot and thirsty, glad to rinse face and hands in the dish of cool water on the washstand under the window.

'At least it is beautiful drying weather,' Grace said.

The sky of late summer spread brilliantly blue from one tree-fringed horizon to the other with not a smudge of cloud to soften it. The sheep had eaten their paddocks down to the dirt and the boys were cutting branches of kurrajong or the suckers of the grey box trees for them to eat. Sometimes the strange diet killed the sheep, but they were dying of hunger anyway.

Hot dry winds made chaffcutting a misery as the dust particles flew around, getting in eyes and hair. The dams were very low; the boys would find dead and dying sheep bogged, trapped in the damp silt with its deceptive surface skin which had lured them across it to try to reach the last of the water. The big tank for watering stock had dried out so that the base of it was hard-caked mud, set like cement, which the boys struggled to clear out. The paddocks were too dry to harrow easily, yet the time for autumn sowing of the new crop was fast approaching. For weeks after harvest, Jim and his sons worked on repairing fences; there had been no thought of a holiday this year.

As the weather cooled and the days shortened, the family watched with growing anxiety for rain, but the sky remained unrelentingly clear. It was nearly April, the autumn sowing season.

Grace saw the shadow in her husband's eyes. The boys were working beside him every day, taking on more and more of the heavy work as their father aged and they matured, but even so they were still only lads. The responsibility of decision-making remained Jim's.

'What do you think, Father?' the boys were asking. 'Should we go ahead and sow dry, and hope for rain soon?'

'We'll wait a little longer,' he replied, 'and then perhaps we'll risk it. But it is hard to know. If we do sow and it doesn't rain, we lose our seed, but if we don't sow soon, we'll miss the season altogether.'

April came. They had disced and harrowed the paddocks, but knew that under the conditions it had not been possible to prepare the ground as well as it should have been. Every day, the sowing season was passing. Finally they began sowing their oats, and then their wheat, in faith that in the end the rain must come. Even as they began sowing for a hoped-for harvest, they were feeding their sheep in an effort to keep them alive.

For several weeks during the time of sowing, the boys' places at the family table remained empty. The old house was empty now and the boys camped there in order to use every daylight hour. Grace missed their noise and conversation, the never-ending discussions of cricket or football, Dick's violin, their energy and friendships. Once or twice, Grace drove with one of the girls to visit the old house, now looking dilapidated with the mud walls crumbling after thirty years of weather, and took meals out to the boys. She watched the two teams of eight Clydesdales, four abreast, as they trod steadily across the ridged earth pulling the cultivator and the seed drill behind them. Invisible through the dust was the precious seed, flowing into the soil and carrying with it the hopes of the family for a harvest.

Rain came, at last, but not as they'd hoped. Jim had gone out to an evening meeting and came home late and disappointed. 'Our guests for the meeting didn't turn up,' he said. 'They rang to say that they were held up by *rain*, further east, but not a drop fell around here.'

Next morning, Jim came back into the house to report that the creek was up, water flooding down from heavy rain miles away to the north, overflowing its creekbed and spreading away across the creek paddock. 'It's enough to make a man jump on his hat!' he fumed. 'The weight of floodwater has knocked down a lot of our fencing. The boys will have to knock off sowing to work on the fences again!'

And still no rain fell on the sown paddocks and the seed lay dormant under red dust. The house water tanks rang more and more hollowly and the dams sank lower, small muddy pools between cracked mosaics of dried mud. The autumn was passing and soon winter would come.

Then, one day in late April, Grace woke to the sound of rain beating on the iron roof. It was Legh's nineteenth birthday, and the boys were coming home that night for a special birthday tea. She beat the eggs for a birthday cake to the rhythm of falling rain, rain flowing into the tanks. Across the farm, water was running into the dams, soaking steadily into the soil, bringing the crops to life. There would be a harvest after all.

The wheat crop was standing vividly green and hopeful, refreshed by good autumn and winter rains and promising a good harvest. Winter tasks had filled the short days; ploughing, fencing, rabbitting and fox-hunting, mending deep potholes in dirt roads. Wet days were spent mending and patching used wheat bags and working in the blacksmith's shop doing up ploughshares. Long winter evenings again made time for community meetings and social events. Pigs were killed and cured on the coldest days – 'ready for the weddings, after harvest,' Grace said. The orchard was ploughed and the fruit trees pruned with the promise of blossom when spring came and a summer harvest of fruit. The big new ten foot H.S. Taylor header had been ordered from Sydney and, as the family looked at the spread of young green across the paddocks, they looked forward to seeing the green crop turn gold and the new machinery sweeping through it.

In July, the news came. The Wheat Marketing Bill had been defeated in parliament and the promise of a guaranteed price had vanished.

'They said "Grow More Wheat"!' Jim was outraged. 'They promised a guaranteed price of four shillings a bushel – not as much as the last few seasons when we have been getting five and six shillings a bushel, but still quite fair. Now, goodness only knows what price we are likely to get. We've sown a much larger crop, we've done the work, we're committed to pay for the new header – we really need a good price.'

In the privacy of their bedroom, Jim confided in Grace. 'I haven't told the boys how committed we are financially. But I've had to take out a mortgage on the property. I hate to have that hanging over my head. Still,' he went on, his natural optimism reasserting itself, 'you never know, even if they can't *promise* four shillings a bushel, we might still get it anyway and the mortgage will only be temporary.'

The weeks passed, winter blending into the softer days of spring. The gold of wattle in bloom merged into a wash of pinks and white as the fruit trees blossomed. The white lilac perfumed the garden. The Coolamon Show came and went, church concert rehearsals and winter meetings of various societies came to an end and football gave place to cricket at the weekends. The shearing shed burst into life through October.

It was also in spring that world wheat and wool prices plunged, and went on falling. Men in the district shook heads in disbelief and shock as they met in town or at the saleyards or outside rural churches before service. Even the oldest farmers couldn't remember such prices. Grace found Jim doing sums in the margin of his newspaper, matching his expenses with the probable prices, and even his natural confidence seemed to waver just a little. Somehow it seemed unbelievable that all their work and the fine crop now standing in the paddocks would not bring a good return.

The weather was perfect for harvest, hot and dry, when Grace saw her husband and sons begin cutting oats in November 1930. All day, a dust cloud rose around the binder as it cut a swathe through the oat crop. Standing grain was transformed into rows of sheaves, propped together into stooks marching across the paddock. In the house, Grace worked with the three big girls, matching the long hours of the men with harvest meals, housework, yard work and the post office.

Haycarting began and Grace saw the wagon swaying slowly along behind the team of Clydesdales, top-heavy with its precious load of hay. The boys were building the haystacks, and once she took out their midday dinners packed into the wooden lunch box. In the shade of the stack, in the sweetness of new hay, she unpacked their mugs and plates, hot dinners steaming, and watched the health and energy of her men, Jim and Richard standing high on the stack laying the sheaves in place, while Legh and Bill pitched them up from the ground. The sun burned down on the rhythmic swing and pitch, sunlight reflecting off sunbrowned and sweaty shoulders and on crisp sheaves in flight against a sky of polished blue. When both stacks were finished they would be skilfully architected, higher than houses with neat thatched roofs, storing seventy to seventy-five tons of hay for stockfeed for the year.

The new header arrived and Grace and the girls were urged out to see the glory of it. Paddock after paddock of wheat stood ripe for harvest, the climax of the year's work. The wheat harvest had begun. Daily the litany of varieties of wheat was recited: Federation,

Bomen, Nabawa, Canberra, Union, Yandella King, Baringa. Wide expanses of grain rippled in hot winds, gold against the red soil, more grain to harvest than ever, a wonderful season. Grace watched Jim go off each day into the heat and flies and dust, into the bounty of a great harvest. Yet she knew that under his optimism he was asking himself what they would get for this crop.

In December dusk, waiting at the kitchen table for Jim and the boys to come home for their tea, she felt that the long day had gone on forever. The harsh sun seemed unwilling to let go its grip on the men working by its light, men and boys who wouldn't stop till it was too dark to see, would eat and sleep briefly then be drawn back to the tractor and team by the pull of first light. They would come in coated in dust, throats parched, eyes reddened, almost too tired to eat. Out in the darkening paddocks stood long lines of wheat bags, propped one against the other, neatly sewn up with a curved bag needle, each bag with two ears on the top corners for her sons to grab as they swung bags from the bag kicker onto their strong young backs to load them onto the bed of the truck.

The slices of bread for their tea were beginning to curl with dryness and the dish of butter, so hard-won by the girls after long turning of the handle of the butter-churn, was turning back to oil in the heat. At least the dish of sun-ripe apricots and early peaches looked cool and filled with juice. The kitchen stove had at last been allowed to die down after a long day of cooking and ironing, and a row of bottles of red tomato relish stood cooling, fruit of her garden and her preserving pan.

While she waited, Grace idly turned the pages of the newspaper. There had been no time to look at it earlier in the day. There were articles on the troubles of men on the land with collapsing prices of wheat and wool, of farmers who could not afford to pay for labour, of thousands of men out of work searching for a job – any job. She had begun to see them, tired men calling at the house looking for work on the farm, yet she knew that Jim had no money to pay for extra hands these days. The newspaper wrote of the Labor government insisting on maintaining award rates at earlier levels, even though this made Australian products uncompetitive in world markets. It commented on the recent ruling by the Federal Arbitration Court that wages were to be reduced by 10% from February 1931 and suggested that the unions might demand a general strike if that happened.

At last she heard the voices of Jim and the boys coming up from the stable. Grace folded the paper away. 'Wages up or wages down — it will make no difference to my boys,' she thought. 'They are well-fed and clothed and share everything we have, but they've never been paid a penny for their labour! They do it for the love of it . . .'

On Christmas Eve, rain fell during the night, bringing relief from the heat and refreshment for the garden. Grace went to bed very late, leaving everything ready for the morning. With the sound of rain on the roof, the house had seemed intensely alive with an energy of its own as doors had opened and shut secretly, footsteps running up the hall trailing laughter behind them, paper rustling and voices calling, 'You can't come in!' The wireless had been turned on and the music of Handel's *Messiah* filled the rooms. Family members came and went through the wave of music, coming to stand together in the breakfast room for the glory of the 'Hallelujah Chorus'. Grace heard the music, filtered through static, and remembered; it seemed a lifetime away, and another world, when she had stood in the crowds in Sydney Town Hall for the same music.

The Christmas hams had been unearthed from their bed of charcoal and soaked free of salt. Chickens and goose had been chased around the woodheap, captured, and 'had gone to their reward', as Jim said, at the hands of one of the boys. The remains of a snowfall of feathers still drifted here and there outside the backdoor where the girls had plucked them. They lay ready on their dishes, replete with herb stuffing, pinioned with skewers, skin crisp and browned to perfection, cloaked in gauze covers to protect them from flies. Hanging in the pantry encased in their flourbag pudding cloths were the puddings, rich with fruit and tiny pudding favours Grace had added to the sticky, sweet-smelling mixture. The perfume of mince pies, hinting at raisins and sultanas, apple and lemon, still hung in the air in the kitchen.

Grace went at last from bedroom to bedroom, saying goodnight to each one. The boys had recorded details of the numbers of bags harvested or carted in their diaries and were already nearly asleep.

'Don't forget our stockings, Muzzie,' Bill said sleepily and Grace laughed. Her little boys were men now and it seemed a long time since they had come climbing into her bed before dawn on bright Christmas mornings. They all delighted in showing how much taller they were by tucking her under a loving arm for a hug.

The 'little girls' Grace, Jean and Evie were young teenagers, Grace and Jean revelling in the joy of being back home from boarding

school for the holidays and Ev ready to go away in the new year to
Annesley. Once these three had been the babies, but they were
growing up very quickly and she kissed them goodnight with love.

The three big girls were still awake, finishing little tasks before
the morning. Grace sat on Connie's bed for a few moments, relishing
the pleasure of being with her beloved older girls, all three of them
women. Carrie and Connie had wrapped gifts for their fiances and
were suffering the Christmas Eve pangs of wondering whether
Hector and Stan would like their gifts. Grace knew that their hearts
were already divided between wanting to share Christmas with their
family and wanting to share it with the special men in their lives.

In the study later, Grace and Jim wrapped the family gifts and
sorted them into clean pillowslips. When most of the children were
asleep, or pretending to be asleep, she would take each pillowslip
and leave it at the foot of each bed. For each one, the family formula
had been followed: an item of needed clothing, something personal
and a book. The books were mostly such classics as Dickens,
George Eliot, R.L. Stevenson, Victor Hugo, ordered from Sydney,
and Grace knew that the bill for Christmas gifts still needed to be
paid. She touched each gift gently, thinking of each deeply-loved
member of her family.

'Do you think we'll have another Christmas together, just like this,
Jim?' Grace spoke wistfully, thinking of her daughters and one day
her sons who would year by year find partners and move away from
the family home to begin homes of their own.

Jim looked up at her sharply. His thoughts had been on something
else. 'I don't know,' he said, his voice unexpectedly gruff.

'When Hector and Stan come to join us for Christmas dinner, I'm
going to ask if one of them would take a family photo for us – the
children and Harry and us. I know you hate having photos taken,
and I always look so extremely solemn, but it's years since we had
a photo of us all together.'

On Christmas morning, she woke to a gentle tap on the bedroom
door. 'Are we too early, Mother?'

Christmas morning was the one day of the year when her family
invaded the privacy and quiet of her bedroom. Now all nine filed
in, clutching their knobbly pillowslips, and found places on rocking
chair and couch or perched on the side of the bed. When they were
little, they had climbed in beside her, the youngest always snuggled
at her side, but now they were so big, so grown-up. . . Later they
would go to a Christmas service together, and Hector and Stan would

come over for Christmas dinner. They would enjoy the finest meal of the year, most of it grown and prepared on Caldwell and there would be laughter over the pudding. Who would find the ring for romance, or the thimble or the coins in their slices this year? Jim would disappear into his Christmas book and the boys would probably take the cricket bat and ball out for a game. There would be Christmas music on the wireless and carols around the piano. . .

Now her children crowded around her, bringing Christmas morning hugs and kisses. Jim was beside her, tousle-haired and blinking, still half awake. The sunlit room sparkled with light on crystal, brass bedknobs and on raindrops still clinging to the roses outside the window.

'Christmas,' she thought, enfolded in the love of her family. 'Immanuel – God with us!'

It was still pitch dark when Grace woke. Jim had left her side. She felt for her bedside candle and lit it. It was four o'clock in the morning.

In the kitchen she found Jim sitting in a pool of light from the hurricane lantern, hat beside him and cup of tea in hand. 'I don't know when you can expect me home,' he said. 'I hope to be in the queue at the railway siding fairly early. It will depend on how many others beat me to it.'

He stood up, gathering his parcel of lunch and his hat, and moved to the door. Grace walked with him out into the warm darkness, carrying the lantern as they walked out to the loaded truck waiting beyond the gate. 'My love,' he said slowly, 'what if the stories about give-away prices for wheat are true?'

She put her arms around him, a small woman holding a big man, trying to give him her strength. They both knew that the wealth of grain towering beside them on the back of the truck might prove to be almost worthless. There were no easy words of comfort to be said.

After the sound of the truck had faded into the distance, she returned to her room and, when the first pale streaks of dawn lightened the eastern horizon, she was still on her knees putting her family and their needs into the hands of her heavenly Father.

Hours later, Jim came home, the empty truck bouncing up the road to the house. He marched into the house looking wretched.

'Wouldn't it haunt you?' he said, tilting his hat onto the back of his head and giving a characteristic scratch to his thick hair. 'They're only paying one and ninepence a bushel! So much for all the talk about a guaranteed minimum price of four shillings... The rumours of bad prices were true, all right. It cost us just on four shillings a bushel to produce, and that's without allowing any costs for our labour. We might just as well *give* the wheat away...'

Jim pulled a piece of paper from his pocket and inspected it. 'This is only the first of many wheat scripts we'll be collecting this season,' he said. 'We have thousands of bushels of wheat still to cart – three bushels to every bag. But we are not going to sell it at one and ninepence a bushel. I've told the agent to hold it and let us know when prices improve. We might as well stack a lot of it on the farm and cart it in later when things get better. *If* they get better!'

He lifted down a spike file from the top of the bookcase in the breakfast room and stabbed the paper onto it, impaling the wheat script through the middle, then departed, muttering his own colourful imprecations against the Labor government, the Nationalists, the Commonwealth Bank, the entire national and international economy.

Jim was not alone in his disappointment. For nearly two years, Carrie had been preparing for her marriage: hemming sheets, preparing household linens, gathering and making everything for her home, sewing her own trousseau. The wedding had been planned for 'after harvest', the time when farmers were free to relax.

Early in 1931, when farmers around the country were reeling under the crippling fall in prices for their crops, Carrie and Hector came one Sunday evening to talk to Grace and Jim. They had been encouraged to have some time together, to talk about their plans in the privacy of Jim's study, and emerged with downcast faces. Looking at her daughter, Grace suspected that Carrie had been crying.

'Mrs Higman, we've decided that we can't get married in March after all,' Hector said. 'No – no, I don't mean we are breaking the engagement! But I don't see how I can go ahead now, when my farm is in such trouble. It's taken everything I've got to put in this crop, and with the terrible wheat prices the only thing I can do is stack the wheat on the farm for the year and just hope that prices improve. And the old house on the place is practically falling down, and it wouldn't be fair to Carrie to get married till I've the money to fix it up a bit. So we've decided to wait till I'm not in such debt.'

Grace put her arms around Carrie to comfort the girl. She had a very good man in Hector and there was no risk that the farmer, just starting out on his own with all the problems of beginning a new place, would let her daughter down. As she embraced her firstborn, she felt Carrie's strength, yet in her heart wept for the disappointment of the girl, now in her mid-twenties and denied the beginning of her married life for at least another year.

High summer, and heatwave pressed down on the land. The countryside lay, parched, gasping for water. The paddocks lay under a burden of heat, their red-brown, stone, straw and ochre tones reflecting up into the heavy air, shimmering and vibrating in a haze. Leaves of the kurrajong and box trees, pepper and quince, apple and pine trees around the house hung listlessly under a patina of red dust. Rows of summer vegetables wilted, waiting for an evening kerosene tin of water. The narrow shade of the back verandah barely contained the drip safe and even there the shade was weighted. Bleached grasses drooped against the hot red dust of the bare earth. A canvas waterbag hung under the verandah eaves, beaded with moisture, every drop of cool water precious. Even the old dog lay spread under the shade of the rosemary hedge, tongue hanging out and panting.

There was little relief in the kitchen. Grace and the girls had been bottling fruit and making jam for several weeks, capturing the fruit of each tree at its most perfect, not daring to leave it till the weather was cooler. Nothing could be allowed to go to waste, even if Grace was hot and tired. These fruits and vegetables would feed her family through the winter and, with money so short, there was no thought of buying anything the family could produce. Now the rows of bottles of jams, preserved fruits, sauces, relishes, pickles and chutneys lengthened in the pantry. Translucent jewels of grainy orange-brown fig, palest green of grape, rose-pink of quince, bright red of tomato and purple-red of plum with tones of peach and apricot gleamed through the glass. But it was so hot, and Grace stood stirring the seething pan full of apricot jam and longed for a cool breeze.

As the afternoon wore on, a cloud of dust was seen trailing along the main road behind the old truck. One more load of the wheat harvest had been unloaded at the silos and one of the boys was coming back to load up yet again. Somewhere beyond the trees in the bush paddock the other men were still harvesting, working in a permanent aura of dust, sweat trickling down from under their hatbands, armies of flies assembled on the backs of their singlets.

A fiery wind sprang up, breathing threat, and came gusting across the paddocks, swirling dust in spirals and thrusting trees impatiently to one side as it passed over the land.

The jarring sound of the telephone bell shrilled from the post office and Mary went to answer it. She came running back. 'There's a fire on a neighbour's place — they need the boys with the water truck! They said it's getting close to the house.'

She turned and hurried back into the post office to alert other help while one of the younger girls ran to wheel out a bicycle to ride for the boys. Grace went to the door and stared across the countryside. Far away, a grey pall was growing behind the line of trees on the horizon and she knew that the terror of summer was loose again. She walked down the path into the little post office and stood by Carrie and Mary as they systematically alerted one neighbour after another, pushing the connecting cords into their sockets in the telephone exchange. In every farmhouse a woman or a child would be responding to the emergency phone call, going to find husband or sons or father, and soon men would be on the road with their water tanks on the back of trucks, ready to share in the battle against the common enemy.

Soon the little truck roared past the house on its way to the fire, joining others on the road. For every family there was the reality that this fire could touch *them*, that the cruel wind would sweep it in any direction. Every farm was vulnerable. Every household could lose everything they possessed in one hideous afternoon.

On the neighbour's farm, parties of men gathered in the rising dust, beating running flames in the dry stubble with damp bags, thrashing sparks with green branches. Trucks bearing the tanks of dam water rushed to spray their precious cargo across the fire. Men who had spent their day working in the heat of the sun stood against the deeper, fiercer heat of fire. Flames were outrunning them, sweeping toward an old house, the first home of the man who pioneered the place.

'The old place is going to go — get the wife and kids away from the new house, just in case!' Bushfire brigade leaders yelled directions. A woman and children, with a miscellany of hastily snatched possessions, were retreating away down the road out to the gate and the comfort of the neighbourly arms.

Timber fence posts burst into flame, trailing useless wire between them. Dry tree trunks erupted, spraying sparks like firecrackers on Empire Night, and the wind carried the burning sparks on to catch in more dry grass. The fighters struggled again and again into the choking smoke, beating, beating. The old house blazed up and collapsed into a blackened skeleton, the posts that had once been felled and erected by a hopeful young settler now a ruin. Timbers lay awkwardly, still glowing with live coals having the power to ignite new fires, and the firefighters worked on into the dusk checking the hot timbers and pouring on water.

Beyond the firebreak which had been ploughed, a nearby farmhouse had its doors open to receive weary firefighters and the distraught family whose home had come close to being gutted. Mugs of sweet tea and scones, and honest kindness, were shared with those who needed it.

Across the stricken farm, the land lay black. Fence posts of charcoal still glowed with hot coals and spirals of smoke twirled up from scattered heaps of ash. Under a few trees, a pool of pale grey ash lay like a shadow marking where thicker grass had once grown and where leaves and fallen bark had ignited. The sun went down in a fiery ball beyond the western horizon, but the people stayed on till late. The wind had dropped at last and the fires appeared to have been extinguished, but the heat of the day still lay heavily in the summer darkness.

Grace waited at home, listening for the truck. When at last she heard it coming, it was very late. Her sons came in wearily out of the darkness, filthy with dust, soot and sweat, and dragged off their heavy boots. Each boy took his turn with a dipper full of water and soap, washing away the stains of the day in the grateful coolness.

'The whole district is as dry as chips,' they said. 'Any of us could go up in smoke. . .'

She fed them slices of cold mutton with fresh tomatoes and lettuce at the kitchen table, listening to their tired talk of the fire and filling their cups with tea. After they had gone to bed she walked outside. Even now the air was thick with heat, only slightly cooler than the still air inside the house. She looked up into the wide dark sky, full of stars. Not a cloud obscured that brilliance, not a sign of rain.

The boys burst into the kitchen one evening, streaks of soot striping their dusty faces. 'Mother, we had a fire – nearly lost the haystacks!'

Grace sat down abruptly, her legs suddenly weak, and listened with pounding heart to their story.

They had been working with the deiselpowered chaffcutter. It shuddered and roared as it devoured hay and spat it out as chaff. Tiny flecks of chaff and dust flew around, coating father and sons as the father fed the machine with hay and the boys collected the full bags of chopped chaff. The noise of the machinery clanking and chewing made conversation impossible. Suddenly Father waved urgent arms and shouted something inaudible. Legh and Bill looked up. The expression on his face alerted them before they heard his words.

'Fire!'

A sinister wisp of smoke was rising. Sparks from the engine of the chaffcutter had caught in dry kindling of straw. A gust of wind urged the low flames into a sudden blaze, chasing it into dead saffron thistles and on, running before the wind.

'The chaff bags – pick up the bags, son! Watch the haystacks. . .'

Bill threw himself at the engine to turn it off and Legh snatched up empty chaff bags. Close by stood their haystacks, higher than houses, enough hay to feed the horses well for a year or more. Each stack was precious, the fruit of a year's work of ploughing and sowing oats, harvesting, stack building, and each stood ready to explode into an enormous bonfire if the flames reached it. Beyond the stack yard lay a wide paddock of stubble, crisp and dry, glittering pale straw left after the harvester had stripped away the heads of grain, ripe for fire.

The boys swung chaff bags, ready to beat the flames, but their father yelled, 'No!'

'Don't beat the fire,' he commanded. 'You'll send it racing away! Smother it – like this. . .'

The wind scorched their faces, throwing the flames to and fro, teasing them as they moved in with their bags, each trying to lay his bag over a line of flame, coughing and choking as thick smoke enveloped them. In a nearby paddock where he was harrowing with the team, Richard had seen the column of smoke. It seemed to be rising directly from a haystack, and he was appalled. Unhitching the horses, he came running, running for his life across the ridged earth towards the spectre of smoke and flame which threatened them all.

The hot wind came from the direction which would chase the fire straight through the farm. They all knew that if an uncontrolled fire ran through that stubble paddock it would take fences, run on into the next stubble, race across patches of dried grass and thistles, engulf sheep, reach across the farm to the shearing sheds, the thatched stable, the rough timbered machinery shed, the house. . .

Jim's imagination saw his whole property blackened, desolate, the bones of livestock bleaching on charcoal paddocks.

'Dear Lord, help. . . help us catch it before the haystacks go. . . Lord, please. . . not fire, too,' he prayed, as he fought to smother the treacherous lines of flame.

Then it was over. It had seemed to last for hours, but by the time Richard had run the width of the paddock, the fire was out. Father and sons stood staring at the charred remnants of thistles and grass, frighteningly close to the base of a haystack. The haystacks still stood, and the stubble paddock still lay glittering in the sun. . .

'Don't worry, Muzzie, we beat it,' the boys said. They hugged her, soot and all, and went off to wash.

Jim followed them into the kitchen, his feet slow. He met her eyes and shook his head. He looked very tired indeed.

Great sheaves of wheat and oats fanned out their golden heads in whiskered tassels of grain, lightening the usually austere interior of the little church for the harvest festival. Jewels of ripe fruit — peach and apricot, plum and nectarine — glowed against the grey-green ridges of pumpkins, green of leafy vegetables and fat melons, with the opulence of cascades of grapes, purple velvet, spilling across. The sheen and aroma of a fat loaf, intricately plaited, lay at the centre of the display, speaking of plenty, of the fulfilment of harvest.

Grace stood with the congregation to sing the harvest hymn.

> We plough the fields and scatter
>   The good seed on the land,
> But it is fed and watered
>   By God's almighty hand. . .
> We thank Thee then, O Father,
>   For all things bright and good,
> The seedtime and the harvest,
>   Our life, our health, our food. . .
> Then thank the Lord, O thank the Lord,
>   For all His love.

She sang with mixed feelings. The richness of the harvest was all there in front of them — the heavy crop of oats, the fine harvest of wheat, the fruit. It had been a wonderful year and the harvest had been completed.

And yet there was a sense of bitterness underneath. Was the

display of the fruit of a good harvest just a mockery? What of the families in their church, and their Catholic neighbours who had attended Mass earlier in the day, whose good harvest was stacked on their farms, waiting without much hope for prices to improve? How were the men feeling who had sold their wheat at a loss, and were staring bleakly at longterm imprisonment to the banks? Surely many of the families were struggling with anger and confusion as they sang their thanks to God for a fine harvest this hot February day. Not anger at God. The Almighty had provided conditions which produced enough grain to feed the world. Their anger and bitterness was against the faceless forces of economic disaster, political unwisdom, financial machinery which seemed far removed from the natural rhythms of seedtime and harvest, rain and sunshine.

'We can't blame God,' she thought. 'We have nowhere else to turn, no-one we can trust, if we don't cling to him in our trouble.'

The weeks and months of harvest and wheat carting dragged on and on. No holiday was planned for after harvest, nor would there be a wedding. Most years after harvest they could look forward to a good wheat cheque, a time to clear debts and buy what was needed for family and farm. This year was different. Prices were bad and everyone knew it.

In the middle stack yards, near the great haystacks, the boys built a mountain of full wheat bags, nine bags high, laid on a base of timber poles. Armed with bag needles, they stitched together a wall of protective chaff bags and roofed it with old sheets of corrugated iron, but a storm knocked away the iron, mice gnawed holes in the bags and some bags had to be replaced with the boys handling every weighty bag again.

When the silos at the railway siding were open, the men of the family took in loads of wheat, stacked neatly on the back of the little truck or a hundred bags on the wide wagon pulled by a team of eight horses. The wheat was fine, and plenty of it, but in the evenings they shared their anxieties.

'The agent says the prices are still down to one shilling and ninepence a bushel, and the best they've been was two shillings and twopence.'

'And according to my calculations it has cost us at least four shillings a bushel to produce, not counting any labour costs for us! If the past few seasons had been better we'd be in better shape, but this, after a few very poor years. . .'

'We keep waiting for the phone to ring with better news of prices, and then we'll sell, but when will that be?'

'Mrs Downie was telling me that when the phone rings with the latest wheat price, she ties a note to the dog's collar and sends it off to find Mr Downie, but it still hasn't been worth bringing Mr Downie back to the house,' Grace added.

'At least we won't be going hungry,' Jim said. 'I've been taking our wheat to Pyke's Flour Mill for our flour and porridge, and bran and pollard. And we've got our own cows and poultry, and a good vegetable garden. We're better off than plenty of families.'

Jim flicked through the papers impaled on his spike file. The wheat dockets collected at the weighbridge had been replaced by the formal paper from the wheat agent with the total number of bushels of wheat waiting to be sold on their behalf. The new sowing had begun and the days were getting cooler and shorter. They had waited in vain for an improvement in wheat prices.

When at last the call came from the agent, Grace called Jim to the phone. 'Wheat is at two shillings and threepence a bushel. What do you think? It's been worse and doesn't look much like getting better.'

Jim gripped the phone tightly and made the cruel choice. 'Sell the lot,' he said.

As Grace sat beside Jim at the long table that evening, he seemed somehow diminished, his bulky frame slumped in dejection.

'Things are not good,' he said. 'We all put in a hard year's work and we had a good harvest. But we might as well not have bothered. We could have taken a trip around the world – the cruise to England that we've dreamed about doing one day – and been better off at the bank than we are today.' He pushed his chair back suddenly and moved away from the table, leaving his family staring at each other in shock as he disappeared through the door to retreat to his study.

Grace moved automatically through the familiar motions of clearing the table, filling a dipper of boiling water from the hot water fountain and pouring it carefully into the metal washing-up bowl. She watched the water steaming and splashing up, turning the block of soap into creamy foam. The dishes passed through her hands without thought, steam fogging her spectacles as she worked without words, a weight of anxiety pressing on her, almost immobilising her.

Around her the family was moving about their tasks, their murmurings of conversation strangely subdued. One of the boys said, 'It's really crook!' and one of the girls was using the broom with more than ordinary passion. She scrubbed vigorously at the sticky remains of the rich jam roly-poly pudding she had served, a tangible thing of ordinary living. The boys had enjoyed their pudding, and had asked for second helpings with the healthy appetites of working men. She wept for them, that their year of hard work had been for nothing. The last of the things were put away and the washing-up water tossed outside on the garden. She watched her children move away to do some evening sewing or reading. They looked healthy enough, safe in their home, yet Grace knew a strong sense of fear for them, something felt, not reasoned.

Jim had shut himself in his study for the evening and she decided to carry him a cup of tea. She walked slowly, moving as if she could avoid what was coming if she moved slowly enough. Her husband was sitting at his desk in the study, a bank statement in front of him.

'My dear. . . If we have another year like this, we could lose Caldwell. . .'

19
Threat of loss
1932-1933

'WE COULD LOSE the farm.'

Jim's voice was so quiet that she almost missed his words. His head was bent over his papers and his spike files with their papery layers of bills, bank statements and farm notes. Columns of figures crept down a page, inky little marks on paper trailing a cryptic message. Grace put down the cup of tea very slowly. He seemed to find it hard to look at her.

'It's not impossible. . . With the price we got today for the wheat our position at the Bank is worse than ever. This year we only got back about half what we laid out on machinery, fencing, superphosphate, seed and everything else – I couldn't even give the boys a holiday for their work, let alone pay any of us any pocket-money! It wouldn't happen immediately, but if next season is as bad as this one, the Bank will nearly own Caldwell. We might even lose it. . . It's happening to other men.'

He began to explain the calculations he had been making: the size of their overdraft, the problems of the international economy and the heartbreaking depression which was crippling their nation. 'Of course, the Bank probably wouldn't sell the place from us. Who'd buy a wheat property these days, with these prices? Though I've heard of men just packing up and walking off their places when things had got impossible for them.' Grace was barely listening. Her mind had halted at his phrase – 'we might lose the farm. . .'

Hours later, sleepless, Grace wrapped a gown around her and crept from her bed to walk along the moonlit verandah. Jim had been sleeping heavily, but her own imagination had been painting vivid and painful pictures in her mind.

Lose Caldwell. . . In her mind, she saw a small eight-year-old boy, perched on a dray among household furniture fifty years earlier, and his father telling him, 'This will be your land one day, son.' She remembered his hands when she first met him in the days when his hair was brown and his beard long. His hands had been marked with fresh scars of timber-felling, the virgin bush having been cleared tree by tree, stump by stump, yard by yard, to make way for wheat. She could still see in her mind's eye the work he had put into building their first home of wattle and daub, and his pride in the lovely house they called 'Caldwell' which had been home for seventeen years. The smallest detail had been thought out by Jim, even the timber lace ornaments on the verandah posts, silhouetted against the garden and the paddocks beyond. From the verandah she could see the orchard and the olive trees, now established firmly on the far side of the tennis court and a reminder of his years away in Palestine and the desert, the years when she had struggled to keep his beloved farm going so that he could come home to Caldwell.

Lose Caldwell. . . She remembered the pain of her own father. She was a young woman at the time when he had to admit defeat and the loss of his business. She had never forgotten the strain and humiliation of the sale. Would the day come when all the farm plant would come under the auctioneer's hammer? The new ten-foot header and tractor, the ploughs new and old, the truck, the six-ton wagon and the eight-ton wagon, the shearing machinery and equipment, even the Clydesdales – Diamond, Joker, Blossom and the rest – would they all be sold? It had happened to her father. It was happening to other farmers around the state. Why not to them?

Lose Caldwell. . . What about their children? Some of the girls, maybe all of the girls, would marry. But how would a young husband on the land be able to survive drought and depression any better than his father? What would become of the girls if they lost their home? How could they pay for the girls to be trained for some sort of employment? And the three boys. All three had wanted nothing else except to come home to Caldwell to work on the land – their land, their livelihood, their home, their future. With thousands and thousands of unemployed young men tramping the roads of Australia, who would employ them elsewhere?

What of herself? As she looked across her garden, she realised that everything in it – the roses, the fruit trees, the bulbs, the flowering shrubs – had been planted by her mother, her husband, her children or by herself.

I have taken root here, she thought. This has become my soil, my place, my home. When I came here first, I felt like a visitor, almost an intruder among those who had been the pioneers twenty or more years earlier. But now I belong here and to tear me out of this soil would perhaps destroy me.

She thought of the faces of people she had seen camped on the outskirts of Coolamon, waiting for their 'susso', or sustenance chits, which allowed them to receive rations of groceries. Amongst them were women torn away from their homes and the stability of their previous life by a Depression which had swept them up and set them adrift, whether they understood what was happening to them or not.

'Dear Lord, what is happening to us all?' she prayed. 'What can we do? Where are *you*? Will you give us strength to hang on for as long as it takes to survive? Or will our family join those who are forced to abandon the work of a lifetime, of generations, to despair of a future for our young? Are you listening to us, Lord?'

On a bleak afternoon when spring still thought it was winter, the gate squeaked unexpectedly and Grace looked up. A stranger came walking up the back path. He walked with hesitation and Grace knew, from other strangers who had come to her door over the past year, that he was unsure what sort of reception he would receive. They had all come like that: battered hat pulled over their brows and the tell-tale black overcoat which told the world that here was a man down on his luck, out of work and forced into the protection of an army surplus overcoat, dyed black for the unemployed. They would come to her door, trying to size up her home. Would it be a place where they'd give a bloke a feed? Might there be a job or two? Sometimes Jim had work for a few days, sometimes not, but always she would offer something to eat and the man would go on.

It was nearly dusk, wintry and cold outside. Soon her own men would come in, take their bucket of hot water from the stove and disappear into the bathroom for their evening bath. They would come back into the warmth of the kitchen to tell her about their day, or go into the bright breakfast room to stand in front of the blaze of an open fire, collecting a book from the bookshelves or picking up the newspaper till the meal was ready. In the dining room she could hear Jean practising the piano and the other girls were setting the table for tea.

The stranger stood outside the door and knocked. As she opened the door, a gust of wind carried rain under the eaves, chilling them both.

'Would you have any work, missus?' His voice was humble and undemanding. He had asked the question so often and been refused so many times, that it seemed he was without expectation. She saw his boots standing on her doormat, broken-down boots which had walked many miles.

'Come into the kitchen. My husband will be home soon and you can ask him.'

He sat awkwardly on a kitchen chair, gripping his hat in his hands, and she felt his eyes watching her hands as she finished mixing her scone dough and patted it out ready to cut into neat rounds. In the morning they'd make more bread, but tonight she was making hot scones for tea. Jim had decreed that they could no longer afford baker's bread so they'd been baking their own from their own flour.

'Would you like a cup of tea?' She dusted flour from her hands and slid the tray of scones into the oven, adding more wood to the fire. Her guest thanked her as she handed him a mug of hot tea. As he drank, he seemed to be listening to the tones of the piano in the next room.

Jim and the boys came in as darkness fell. It had begun to rain heavily. Jim talked with the traveller. He had little work to offer, but invited the man to stay till the weather improved – 'You can eat with us and sleep in the shearers' quarters.'

The family gathered around the table for the evening meal and Jim asked a blessing over the food. There were fresh vegetables from the garden and Grace brought in plates piled high with scones, golden and hot from the oven, with dishes of jam and cream. The stranger ate one scone after another, as well as the other food, with the young ones watching him discreetly. She had trained them that it was not polite to stop eating long before a guest was satisfied, and they all toyed with the last crumbs of scones as another plateful was brought.

'Excuse me asking,' Grace whispered, 'but when did you last have a proper meal?'

'Two or three days ago; I'm not sure. . .' and the family looked aghast.

The talk turned to music. Their guest asked about the music that the girls were learning and spoke knowledgeably of composers and instruments. Grace suggested that after the meal had been cleared away, they light the lamps in the dining room and the girls would play for them.

Outside, the rain fell steadily, cold and bleak. Inside, the family toasted their faces around the fire, the girls playing the piano and Grace knitting in her rocking chair. Their guest asked permission to play, and brought from the piano the sounds of classical music for their pleasure. Somewhere, in another time and another place, this man must have lived in a gracious home where music was appreciated. Now he was travelling through the countryside jobless, homeless, cold and hungry.

Grace watched him with compassion, and thought of other travellers. There was the man who had stayed for long enough to repair the old mattresses in the shearers' quarters with his upholstery skills, the man who had begged for ends of binder twine which he fashioned into strong doormats and the man who came trying to sell the tinware he had produced with his metalwork. For him she had lined up all the tinware from her own pantry – trays, biscuit tins, washing-up dishes – to help him think of new lines to produce. Then there was the whole family who had stayed a few days, searching for work with everything they owned piled into their old buggy, moving from one country town to the next to collect their 'susso'. She had seen many families like them camped outside Coolamon. She also remembered a man who had assured Jim that he was a good mechanic and had been set to fixing the old car. He had tinkered with it for days, with Legh doing as much work as he did, and had departed with thirty shillings for his efforts, though the old car still wasn't fully repaired.

Looking around the security of her warm room and hearing the rain on the roof, Grace pictured her home as an island in a stormy sea – not very large, itself lashed by the storm, yet a place of safety for her family, a refuge for the many family visitors who clambered onto its shores, a temporary haven for some in the community in danger of drowning.

'At least we still have our land and our home,' she thought, 'and, however hard it is, we must hold on to it.'

Fogs settled over the countryside, obscuring, disorientating. Sometimes the grey cloud hung over the paddocks all day. The rain drizzled on, leaving paddocks too wet to work, floods flowing down dry creekbeds, and deep bog and potholes defying anyone trying to drive to town. If only the rain would stop, they might have a wonderful harvest, but as things stood, the rain just added to the depression of the community.

Outside the little church, Grace stood with the women, chatting before the service between showers of rain. Each one had her own tale of family members bogged on the roads, or broken machinery and no funds to repair it, or flooding on their property. They rarely talked about their financial troubles – it was too private – but Grace knew that if Jim was worried, then many of his neighbours must also be very anxious indeed. Some men had no sons to help them with family labour, while others had a number of sons and wondered how their boys would all survive with little money to buy more land. A few had made major outlays on new equipment just before the prices for their crop collapsed, and others were bringing home children from boarding schools they could no longer afford.

Women spoke more of family illness, or the difficulties of getting the washing dry after weeks of wet weather, or joked about having full water tanks so there was plenty of water to wash off everyone's muddy feet. Yet there was a feeling of discouragement and downheartedness among them which was deeper than the trials of a grey winter.

'Sometimes you feel like giving it away, farming I mean,' a woman said.

'Our fellows work so hard, and these days you wonder just what for. Nothing seems to work out any more on the land, what with prices and that, and if we're not having a drought it's a flood or skeleton weed or disease or bushfire!'

'My husband reckons he'd get off the land tomorrow if there was anywhere to go – but there *is* nowhere to go. . .'

On the far side of the little church porch, the men talked of fat lambs and weed control, prices and problems. As they all moved into church, Grace felt the weight of communal discouragement and depression – not only the burden of an economic condition, but the defeating despondency of human spirits who see no end to their troubles.

Jim walked into the pulpit and invited them together to worship God. Later, when Jim opened his Bible to read, Grace turned the pages of her own Bible to read Psalm 11 with him.

In the Lord put I my trust: how say ye to my soul, Flee as a bird to your mountain? For lo, the wicked bend their bow, they make ready their arrow upon the string, that they may privily shoot at the upright in heart. If the foundations be destroyed, what can the righteous do? The Lord is in his holy temple, the Lord's throne is in heaven. . .'

'My text,' said Jim, 'is: if the foundations be destroyed what can the righteous do?'

Speaking as one of the community, one who felt the fear of failure and loss, the sense of powerlessness when the very foundations of their world were being shaken, Jim spoke of hope. He pictured men and women trembling at the rumblings of earthquake in the world, losing all that ought to be stable and secure, bringing homes and businesses and farms crashing in ruins.

'What can the righteous do? Do we let it terrify us? Do we run from the enemy? Do we ask: "Why doesn't God *do* something?" Or do we say, "We are God's children", and when everything is falling around us, we can say with the Psalmist: "In the Lord put I my trust. . . The Lord is in his holy temple. . ." He knows our needs. What can we do? The only thing we *can* do is trust him.'

Under the pressure of attack from beyond the community – prices, difficult seasons, the strangling skeleton weed, stress of mortgages and overdrafts, with fear of Bank foreclosure hanging over the heads of some – the people of the district became more closely knitted together than they had ever been. If they were going to survive, they knew they must support each other. During the winter months, Grace watched her family going out in the evenings to their many interests – the boys to their health and physical fitness club, Farmers and Settlers, Mutual Improvement Society, Bible study, Loyal Orange Lodge, concert practices and tennis and Australian Rules football competitions each Saturday. With so many young people growing up in the district, all the meetings and sports provided social contact, a chance for romances to develop and strong community solidarity. Some of the themes which had divided people in the past seemed to be less important now that there was a common foe.

Neighbour stood by neighbour. A story did the rounds of the district of a farmer who had reached the end of the road financially at the Bank. A sale was arranged to sell off all his farming plant, machinery, tools, sheds, stock: a lifetime of effort to fall into the impersonal hands of the Bank. His neighbours turned up for the sale and, as the auctioneer called for bids, with one accord they bid a shilling for everything – one shilling for a tractor, one shilling for a harvester, one shilling for a good team. The auctioneer and the Bank officials, confused, decided to cancel the sale and leave the farmer where he was while they tried to work out an alternative, and his friends went home grinning.

Outsiders from beyond the district were viewed with suspicion. The Mutual Improvement Society organised a debate in mid-winter which caused a lot of lively discussion in the family. 'We have to debate: That the unemployed should be placed on the land,' Legh told his mother. 'I'm dead against it, so it's just as well Dick and I are on the opposition!' The subject was loudly debated at mealtimes. Grace's sons, in common with other farm families, were not paid for their labour, yet they had the shelter of their home and the capacity to grow most of their own food. Jim had his own strong opinions; he read widely on politics, economic theory and justice. 'I could write a book myself on how this country could get out of its economic difficulties,' he assured them, and Grace knew that he was collecting ideas. 'Social honesty and cooperation, that's the answer,' he said.

On the evening of the debate, Grace watched her family drive away, armed with their notes and their opinions, with some trepidation. When it came to a good debate on any substantial theme, it had been said of some of her family that they were strong-minded, determined, even pig-headed, that 'you couldn't knock them off with a stick'! They came home late, just as she was ready for bed, some enthusiastic and some enraged by the outcome of the judging. Those who spoke in favour of placing the unemployed on the land had won. Grace heard upraised voices still talking about it as she went to bed. She knew that this question of work and land was not simply an academic issue for them.

Jim was half asleep as she joined him. 'Our children are better off then most,' he said. 'Better off than all those poor souls out on the roads, or wearing out their bootleather around the cities. That'd break anyone's heart. A demoralised man is no good to himself or anyone else. I don't like the way things are for our boys, but I reckon they're much better off with work and no pay than if they were collecting susso and had no work.'

During that long wet winter, religious arguments seemed to lose their sharpness. The rains sent waters flooding across roads, turning them into bogs, and Jim offered his Catholic neighbours the right to come through the Caldwell property instead of struggling through the quagmires of roads on their way to Mass. Then more rain flooded right through the farm, spreading from the normally dry creekbed and lying in a shallow lake across the farm road.

On a bleak Saturday afternoon, Grace heard the sound of a car engine in the distance. Saturday tennis had been washed out and she and the girls sat by the fire with their knitting and sewing. The older girls were embroidering flowers on table linen for their future homes, Carrie and Connie both planning hopefully for weddings, despite financial worries for them both. One of the boys came to the door.

'The priest was coming through the farm, to try to keep away from the bogs on the road, but his car has stopped in the middle of the creek. We are harnessing up a team to drag him out. Father says can you please put the kettle on for when we get in.'

Grace went to the door. Rain was falling across a grey world and the girls had come in cold and wet from the milking and feeding the fowls. Poor thing, she thought, going by himself to sleep in the Presbytery room at the back of their church, ready for early Mass in the morning – he'll be wet and miserable.

It seemed a long time before she heard the chug of the car coming to the house, and the sound of voices. The voices of Jim and the boys mingled with the less familiar voice of the Catholic priest. Many ministers had visited their home through the years – Methodists, Presbyterians, Anglicans, with missionaries and a variety of church officials – but there had always been a clear line dividing Roman Catholic from Protestant. Priests and ministers knew and visited their own people.

A very miserable figure limped into the kitchen, clerical collar sitting awkwardly between limply wet hat and dripping clothing. The first thing Grace saw was his woeful face and then his bare feet, below rolled-up trouser legs, trickling blood and muddy water onto the floor.

'You poor man! Girls, bring me some towels and a blanket. Here, sit down – let me get some antiseptic and clean your foot.'

She knelt beside the priest, gently washing away the mud and cleaning the wound where he had gashed his foot on a jagged stick under the water. The man was shivering, apologising for causing trouble to the family, embarrassed about his foot. 'I just wanted to save my shoes, so I took them off when I got out of the car to push. . .' Grace bound up Father Gahan's foot carefully. He may be a priest, she thought, but he's also a cold wet man with a hurt foot who needs someone to care for him a little bit.

At the table, with bowls of vegetable soup steaming in front of them and a great log blazing in the whitewashed hearth, Grace sat beside Jim and waited for him to say a grace before the meal. From the corner of her eye she watched her children, all of them trying not to stare at their guest. Jim bowed his head for the prayer and, as she opened her eyes at the end, Grace saw the priest, now warm and dry, make a sign, a sign which was at once a foreign gesture in a Methodist house and yet a deeply known symbol. It was the sign of the cross.

The shearing shed, which had stood silent for many months, sprang to life again in September. The shudder and roar of shearing machines and the layered sound of the bleating of sheep, deep voices mixing with treble, filled the building. The three young men worked their way through their flock, stooping over each animal as it was dragged protesting from the holding pen and guiding the comb through the fleece till their animal was thrust, naked and afraid, out through the little doorway. The strong pungency of the shearing shed, of sheep and fleece and sweat, lay over the workers, penetrating their clothing. In the old days, when the boys were small or away at school, Jim had hired shearers to work with him at shearing time, but now his boys were grown and they took the full responsibility of yarding, shearing, woolclassing and trucking the woolbales.

When the nine hundred Caldwell merinos had all been shorn, neighbours came asking for the boys to shear their flocks. The boys worked on, struggling with machinery breakdowns and broken combs, with rain and sheep too wet to shear, with constant noise and tiredness, aching backs and irritability. The women of the family faced more heavy washing than usual as the odour and staining of sheep on work clothing meant the men needed to change more often. As well as shearing meals, the dressmaker was staying at Caldwell and the house was full of wedding sewing. Grace never seemed to have daylight enough for everything she needed to do. Because the younger girl's fiance's family had more resources and were building them a new house on their property with their own cypress pine, Connie's wedding was to come before her older sister Carrie's. Carrie and Hector planned to be married in March 1932 and on Sundays after church they would walk around his fine crop, translating the ripening wheat into money for a wedding and furniture and to pay the workman who was renovating the old house.

The shearing at last came to an end, with the final bales of wool carted to the railway stencilled with the family markings on the bales. The skins of foxes, sheep, cows and rabbits were also sent for pocket money for the boys. Prices were still poor, but the family had confidence that somehow God would look after them.

Jim came to the boys some weeks later with money in his hands. 'Boys, here's the money from our neighbours whose sheep you shore. Divide it up between you.'

There was silence. The three boys looked at each other. Between the three was a strong bond of understanding which had grown through a lifetime of sharing everything, and which was more powerful than the differences in personality and interests. When one of them finally spoke, it did not matter which boy said the words. The intention had been understood. 'You keep the money, Father. We don't really need it so much. Use it to try to improve things at the Bank.'

The father stared at his sons. Grace watched his face, dropping her sewing unheeded into her lap. They had worked for that money, they deserved it. And yet . . . Jim tried to speak, found no words and turned away. As he walked quickly from the room, Grace saw the gleam of tears.

In the spring, when the white lilac was in bloom, Grace saw the first of her children married. She sat in her usual pew near the front before the service began, this time as mother of the bride, her hands clasped in her lap and her heart praying for her daughter. Carrie was sitting at the organ, watching the open door of the little church, ready to play the Bridal March. Overhead hung the ribboned bridal bell with all the joy of flowers and streamers waiting to welcome the bride.

Grace watched her older daughter's face behind the organ. Carrie was still waiting for her own wedding day and they all hoped it would be in March, after harvest. There was a stir from the doorway behind her, the organ burst into the Bridal March and Grace turned to see Connie walking under the wedding bell on Jim's arm. Under the film of veil, her young face was glowing with happiness as she walked past her mother to stand beside her darkhaired bridegroom, Stan Grinter.

Tears misted the mother's eyes as she heard the two young voices make their promises to each other. This young woman, lovely in her bridal white, was the child she had borne, the tiny one she had cuddled, the anxious adolescent she had taken to Wagga to spend years away at school. This was the girl she had loved and cared for through many illnesses and for whom mother and Caldwell had been a place of security. A tear, warm and salty, ran silently down

Grace's cheek, a tear of relinquishment. She liked Stan very much. He was a good young man and she knew she could trust her daughter to him. But that didn't take away the pain of letting her go.

After the service was over, they would all go back to Caldwell for the wedding breakfast. The sixty guests would enjoy the vast meal she had left prepared at home, sitting under the tarpaulins the boys had erected to form a large open-air room beside the verandahs. There would be speeches and laughter and at last the bride and groom would drive away from the house, probably chased down the road by a crowd of young friends, to go away on their honeymoon and then to return to their own little house, so new it all still smelled of fresh pine, back in time for haycutting.

'My daughter is leaving home,' she thought. Then, as she watched the bride take her hand from her father's arm and place her hand in her bridgegroom's, she knew that Connie had left already.

The two strangers appeared at the house one morning in November while the men were out harvesting oats. They were dusty and rather bedraggled but courteous.

'We'd like to speak to the boss, please,' they said. 'Could you tell us where we would find him?'

Grace offered them something to drink, then pointed them in the direction of the paddock where Jim was working with the boys at stooking oats.

'Do you have bicycles, or horses?' she asked. 'I didn't hear a car coming.'

'Well, we walked out, that's why you didn't hear us.'

'You walked all the way from Coolamon — fourteen miles?'

'The two of us have walked all the way from Melbourne, missus! We just keep going till we find some work — and that is pretty hard to find. We're mates, so we're on the road together.'

Grace watched them set off across the farm to find Jim, and shook her head. All the way from Melbourne! She tried to picture her own boys walking hundreds of miles across country, searching for work.

'Our boys are very well off indeed,' she thought. 'Even though we are still struggling to pay back the bank overdraft, we still have the farm, and a house, and plenty to eat. This harvest looks very promising, too. And we have the security of each other. Surely we'll survive.'

Later, when Jim and the boys came in for midday dinner, she was not surprised to learn that he had told the two men that, if they really wanted work, they could come back in two weeks for the beginning of the wheat harvest.

'If they seriously want work, they'll be back,' he said. 'And it is going to be a huge harvest so we'll be able to use all the help we can get.'

'After harvest...'

Always, year after year, the promises had been made. 'After harvest we'll have time...', 'after harvest we'll be able to afford it...', 'after harvest we'll be able to rest for a while and take a holiday,' but for several years now the promises had remained unfulfilled. Harvests had brought grain, endless bags of it, but not the freedom to spend without counting every coin, or the freedom to take comfortable holidays. Even Jim's annual pilgrimage to the Methodist Conference early in the year was not an easy thing to plan, and he spoke of expecting to see many empty seats at the meetings where country people would once have sat, but could no longer afford the time or the fare to travel.

This year would be different, Grace hoped. It was not that things were good on the land though the harvest had again been excellent. It was certainly not that things had improved in the economy of the country at large, and the paper spoke of increasing numbers of unemployed people searching in vain for work. She thought of the two men Jim had employed for harvest, who had walked all the hundreds of miles from Melbourne. For people on the land, the feeling was strong that a family simply had to battle things out; that, like drought and flood, bushfire and grasshopper plague, it was part of a long life and that the main thing was not to give up. If you stuck it out and helped your neighbour to survive, one day things would be good again.

But this year when Jim went to Conference he had promised that the three boys, Legh, Dick and Bill, should go with him. The first step was the re-painting and varnishing of the Willys Overland, ready for sale in Sydney. Jim and Legh set off one day in February, the car disappearing bravely down the road on the long and difficult drive to the city. A few days later, Dick and Bill caught the train to Sydney, full of the excitement and importance of their own first adult, unsupervised trip to the city. After they had gone, the women of the family settled into the uninterrupted feminine fun of preparing for Carrie's wedding.

The week and a half without the boys took on the feeling of holiday for Grace and the girls. With their men away, meals could be simple and washday less of a burden. The dressmaker came from Ariah Park and stayed for several weeks, and the big table disappeared under the white softness of bridal fabric, paper patterns and pins. Carrie stood very still as the bridal gown was fitted, not daring to move within the treachery of pins, and around her they chattered of her glory box, of wedding breakfast foods, and of their mother's lists of jobs to be done.

The telephone bell shrilled often on the back verandah, summoning someone to attend to the exchange in the little post office, but Carrie would call, 'Mary! Can you look after the phone, please? I'm all pinned up.' After the wedding, Carrie would be resigning from her job as postmistress and Mary would take over. Sister Grace would be able to help, now that she, too, was part of the family-at-home. The presence of the post office beside the house had provided jobs for the girls, official and unofficial, with responsibility, management skills and an interesting place at the heart of the community network of telephone lines. For Carrie in particular, as the oldest child in the family and the oldest daughter, the post office had been an outlet for her competence and gifts of leadership, though Grace wondered whether perhaps her strong, reliable and intelligent daughter still grieved for the teaching role or the nursing training of which she had dreamed.

Connie came for the day several times while they were preparing for Carrie's wedding. On one occasion she drew her mother away from the others.

'Mother, come out into the garden for a minute, please. I want to talk to you . . .'

They walked together along the earth pathways dividing flower beds, and Grace learned that she was to become a grandmother later in the year.

Everything is changing, Grace thought later when she retired to the quietness of her own room. The tight braid of our family life is loosening, unravelling. Little by little we will be separated, detached, no longer totally interlocked with every moment of each other's lives. Connie and Stan now come to Caldwell as visitors, and when the child is born their new family unit will be whole, connected by love to us here, but also independent of us. Carrie's wedding gown is taking shape and soon she, too, will have her own home. The boys are grown men, gone to Sydney to buy a car. Soon they, too, will be thinking of looking for wives and homes of their own. The love between us is as strong as ever, but in a way we are beginning to unwind from each other, releasing each other little by little. Many years ago, this is what I prayed to see, she thought. But there are still those things which are unfinished. . .

The boys arrived home with a flourish and a great tooting of the car horn in the middle of Saturday morning. When Grace and the girls hurried out to greet them, they climbed out of a strange new black car, rumpled and unshaven and full of their adventures. As they all surged into the house, balancing bundles and suitcases, the wonders of their trip spilled around them, torrents of words and images.

'It is a Hudson Super Six sedan, a 1927 model. . . very good value. . .'

'We slept last night by the road at Binalong. . .'

'And the night before halfway up Razorback Mountain. . .'

'With a bull, by accident!'

'And a flat battery, and had to walk for miles to find someone to fix it − a terrible night!'

'. . .a wonderful concert at the Lyceum Theatre in Sydney. . .'

'. . .and saw a film, "Ben Hur" there, too. . .'

'Legh went out to the cricket at the Sydney Cricket Ground before Bill and I arrived. . .'

'We all took a ferry across the harbour − the new bridge is nearly finished, and by the time Carrie and Hector go on their honeymoon, it will be open.'

'We walked around Circular Quay and the docks and saw the *Strathnaver* and the *Mariposa* liners in their berths − and we thought about the world trip we didn't have.'

'Wait till you see our new suits for the wedding − and our photos. . .'

'We left Father at the Methodist Conference, of course. We all went to the big opening service at the Lyceum − it's a bit different from Sunday afternoon services in the Rannock church! There were *hundreds* of people there, from all over New South Wales!'

Grace could picture it. It was many years now since she had been in Sydney at the time of the Conference meetings, but the intensity of her memories brought images of rich singing, of crowds of people of one mind worshipping God and the delight of reunions with loved friends. One of the unfinished things she had in her heart for her family was to see them experience a wider world, a wider vision, than the beloved world of the farm and the district.

The talk went on as the boys were refreshed with cups of tea, stories of tram rides, the theatre, the Botanic Gardens, the war museum where their father had pointed out items from his own war years. They had shopped, been to the photographers and visited Sydney relatives. 'Sydney is a good place to visit,' one of them said, 'but I wouldn't want to live there. Too crowded, too busy. It's good to get home again.'

Another commented soberly, 'And it would be rotten to be unemployed and be in Sydney these days. Everywhere we went we saw a funny mixture. Some people seemed to be really rich. But at the Quay and the railway stations there were always people playing banjos or old violins, waiting for someone to throw some coins in their hats. And we saw people queuing up for their 'susso', lines and lines of them, all looking so – so discouraged. And men sleeping on park benches, or making a place to sleep behind broken boxes down in the Domain. I'd hate to be them...'

Some of the suitcases and bundles were opened and the new suits, shirts and collars were displayed. The formal photograph of the three brothers was passed eagerly from hand to hand. It was a fine picture of three good-looking young men, handsome in their new suits, but... 'You look about as comfortable as if you were sitting on a barbed wire fence,' someone said.

They urged their mother and the girls outside to come for a ride in the new car, and dazzled them with technical information. The new car carried them along behind the house to the applause of yapping dogs around the wheels and the scattering of poultry. Soon the boys hurried to change into their cricket flannels and rushed off to play their Saturday afternoon match.

Grace sat at the kitchen table and looked again at the portrait of her three sons. Yes, they did look rather stiff in that alien setting of a photographer's studio. But all three looked such fine boys, so good to look at, so healthy. She had no illusions about their human frailties. She knew better than anyone those things about each one which was a weakness, the things which irritated or disturbed other members of the family, the disappointing traits. But she loved them deeply, and gave thanks for their many strengths.

Grace was glad that Jim had taken them to Sydney. She could see that it had been a magical time for them, a gift of time and new ideas, new experiences. It was not a formal pay-packet for their work, but a gift from their father in appreciation for work shared. The man from the Bureau, with his strong views on labour and wages, would probably be angry to think that the boys had not been paid regular wage packets. And yet, she suddenly saw, it was very like the story in the Bible of the Prodigal Son. The elder brother in the story was complaining about his father's welcome to the runaway son and said: 'But you don't give *me* things like that.' And the father had replied, in astonishment at his lack of insight, 'Everything I have is yours!'

That is how Jim is with his family, she thought. We work together, we go without together, we celebrate and buy new things together — and the land is *ours*.

'Mrs Higman, please,' the dressmaker pleaded. 'When will you be free to have your new dress fitted? There isn't much time left.'

The young woman had nearly finished making all the wedding garments, but somehow Grace had been putting off the moment of pausing in her busy round to worry about her own new dress; it had not seemed sufficiently important. The dressmaker was looking so anxious and had been asking for her time so patiently that at last Grace relented and submitted to the indignities of being draped in a partly made garment while someone crawled around the hem with a mouthful of pins. Even as she stood still, trying to be patient, she kept thinking of jobs still to be done. The cousins were beginning to arrive, representing the tribe of Harry, Sarah, Robert and Will's children, for whom Caldwell was a second home. With the multiplying of folding beds and hammocks on the verandah, it was like having everyone home at once for school holidays. Trapped inside the coils of the dressmaker's art, Grace mentally rehearsed the details of wedding tasks. There were the hams to be resurrected from their winter layers of calico, hessian and charcoal, the fowls to be killed, trestles and benches to be brought from the school, cakes to be collected from the railway, tarpaulins to be erected around the verandahs, gardens to be tidied, deciding whether the weather was too hot to try to set jellies. . .

'You can get down off the chair, Mrs Higman, I'm finished.'

Grace stepped to the floor, brought back abruptly to the present. It suddenly occurred to her that her focus on her lists was only a defence against other thoughts. Within days, her firstborn would have left home and she didn't want to think about it.

The light of the lamps hanging from the verandah fell gently on the tables, illuminating laughing faces, shining hair, new clothes.

Crowded along the trestle tables, elbow to elbow, were the guests, her sons and daughters, the nieces and nephews, the friends and neighbours, people from town and people from the farms. The bridegroom Hector's large family were all there with a brother and sister as part of the bridal party. Mary was happily busy in her role as bridesmaid and Legh splendid in his new suit as groomsman. The soft warm light shone on the bride, illuminating the halo of filmy veil and delicate circlet of flowers wreathing her brown hair, framing a face alive with happiness.

'She has waited a long time for today,' Grace whispered to Jim. 'She looks very lovely — and very happy. I pray they will have as long and happy a marriage as we have had.'

'We waited, too,' Jim murmured. His eyes were on his wife and, as she looked at him with love, she saw that this whitehaired man beside her truly still loved her 'from the top of your head to the soles of your feet' as he had said long ago.

With part of her mind, Grace observed the neighbourhood ladies going about their task of serving the wedding meal. At another level, she was thinking about Carrie. Since Carrie was a newborn baby, she had always lived at home. Carrie's room, Carrie's bed, Carrie's place at the table were woven inextricably into the fabric of their family life. Of course, Carrie and Mary had gone on holidays on many occasions, travelling to spend happy times with relations and friends, but that had always been temporary. All the others had gone away from home to school, for a year, three years, five years, with the thread of their presence in the home weaving in and out with the design of school holidays. But Carrie's thread had always been there, always significant. 'Carrie, you're the oldest, please help me with . . . Carrie will be able to do that . . . Carrie's a sensible girl, I'll teach her to drive the car — to handle the shotgun — to cure hams . . . Carrie is always responsible for that job. . .' Now the strong bright thread of Carrie's personality was to disappear from the design of their everyday family life. It was not ripped out, not leaving dangling threads, but completed, to begin a new tapestry with her husband. Grace tried to comfort herself with the thought, 'At least we'll still be neighbours.'

The wedding feast went on till at last the time came for the bride and groom to leave. The night was late; Carrie and Hector were to be driven to Junee to meet the special train taking sightseers to Sydney for the opening of the Sydney Harbour Bridge, and the train was due in Junee at one o'clock in the morning. Their two bridesmaids, best man and groomsman were driving over to Junee with them. When it was time to go, all the guests surged out through the front gate to the car, hugging, laughing, throwing rice and confetti, waving them on their way. Grace watched the headlights of the car piercing the darkness and lighting up the gate out onto the main road. Her head was aching and her eyes full of unshed tears. She turned back towards the house. Against the blackness of the starry night sky the house stood, solid and secure. Now that the car had gone, there was not a pinprick of light anywhere else to be seen across the surrounding countryside, but the house itself glowed with the light of many lamps, hung outside in the garden and in the main rooms, a nimbus of light in a darkened world. She took her husband's arm and slowly walked back inside.

Within a week of Carrie's wedding, when the family had scarcely had time to return to normal, Legh asked his mother to go for a drive with him. Grace nearly brushed off the invitation. She was still feeling the weariness of anticlimax after the wedding and, though she hadn't mentioned it to Jim, she had had a few more brief encounters with pain. Then she saw Legh's face. Never before had he asked her 'to go for a drive'. She drove to take hot dinners to the paddocks, to go to town or to church, always with a purpose. She was sure that this was not without purpose.

She sat beside her son in the sulky as they drove across the farm, enjoying a slight breeze which cooled her aching head. She often had time to talk intimately with the girls as they worked together, but it was harder to find privacy to talk with the boys. Many of the boys' interests were outside her sphere – how many bags of wheat they carted, the inside mysteries of an engine, cricket scores, weight-lifting prowess. They came across the farm to the old house, now looking very dilapidated with the mud walls weathering away. Jim's timber kitchen was now used only as a camp for the boys, but she remembered the room when it was full of tiny children.

'Do you remember when you were little and you'd kneel up on a chair beside me while I was cooking? Here in the kitchen?'

'I remember you boiling sheep knucklebones with red and blue cloth, to make us coloured jacks to play with, and teaching us games. Maybe it's the girls getting married, but I've been remembering things that I haven't thought about for years. Like the Chinese market gardener visiting, and those Indian hawkers with their cart full of things, who always asked *my* permission to stay if Father wasn't there — even though I was only a young lad, because they thought that the oldest boy was senior to any of the women in the house.'

'And the chillies! Do you remember when you boys ate the red chillies they offered you . . . ?'

'And we came yelling to you with our mouths burning out?'

Legh laughed ruefully and she remembered the three little boys rushing to her for comfort.

'Something else I remember is when I was twelve, and I sat beside you in church the first time I took Holy Communion, and you gave me a little New Testament.'

She reached out and took his hand. The bonding of mother and son was strong and always had been.

'Mother, I wanted to have a private talk to you,' he began, shy and hesitating. 'I'll be twenty-one next month and I wanted to talk to you first about something important. I haven't said anything to her yet, but I really care about Daisy Downie and one day I want to ask her to marry me.'

Grace knew Daisy well, and loved her. Daisy's parents had been close friends since they arrived as young selectors in 1907 and Legh and Daisy Downie had grown up together. Daisy was a charming and gifted girl who would be a lovely wife for her son.

As she offered some careful wisdom to her son about the best ways to show real love, her eyes fell on the old house, the place where once she had come as a bride, leaving her own family to begin a new home. The house itself had served its purpose, had its time of life and joy, but the family had grown and moved on.

The ancient words of scripture come into her mind: 'To everything there is a season, and a time for every purpose under heaven . . .'

Carrie and Hector came from their honeymoon with new furniture, bought within the limits of Hector's bank overdraft, and a great sense of contentment. Their holiday had been full of delights — sitting on the rocks at Lady Macquarie's Chair with the crowds on the day the Sydney Harbour Bridge was officially opened, watching fireworks over the harbour, buying cheap meals at city cafes, sharing a pineapple sitting on the floor in their beach holiday flat, swimming in the surf and riding trams to the theatre. They saw the plight of people with no jobs and no home, and came home to farm and house with great thankfulness. Hector said apologetically to Grace and Jim, 'I wish the house was in better condition. I had a man rip out some of the inside walls to make bigger rooms, and replace the hessian walls with ply.'

Jim said, 'It's a better house than I took my bride to, anyway,' and the bridegroom was comforted.

Several weeks after Carrie and Hector came home from their honeymoon, Grace went with Jim late one evening to visit them. They were not alone. When Jim parked the car well beyond the Crawford outside gate, they were joined by a whispering crowd of young well-wishers, all armed with cake tins filled with cakes and biscuits and a motley assortment of noise makers. With subdued laughter, they marshalled their strange weapons and went stealthily off through the gate, disappearing into the gloom on the road down to the darkened house.

The parents waited, bracing themselves. A dog barked – and a cacophony of sound erupted: metal on metal, cowbell, spoon on pan, pebbles in tin, shouting, giggling, every farm dog awake and yapping. In a window, the glow of lamplight flared, and a door opened. Jim started the car and they moved through the gate to join the party for the traditional tin-kettling, to find the young couple slightly shy and laughing, but welcoming their friends into their home. Although the essence of the tin-kettling was surprise, Carrie and Hector were not astonished to find their friends appearing out of the dark – they had done the same to other newlyweds many times – recently, in fact, at the new home of Connie and Stan. The kitchen fire was re-lighted and the kettle put on, cake was set out on new wedding cake plates and friends were offered seats on the new furniture smelling of paint and varnish.

Grace heard a guest who owned a wireless set say, 'Did you hear what happened today? Premier Jack Lang was sacked! Such a thing is unheard of. . .' and the men were away on the theme of the NSW Premier and their opinions of him and his policies. The complications of NSW politics interested Jim greatly, but Grace cared more about the establishment of a new home. The newlyweds had a great capacity for enjoying life, for exploring places and ideas, for extracting the best from their world and compensating with energy and warmheartedness for the fact that they probably would have to battle financially for years. She imagined their home as a place where people would like to go, where their friendliness and humour would make people feel at home.

Connie and Stan were there, too, and their friends were teasing them about the night, only months ago, when they, too, had been tin-kettled. Grace loved to visit their home and to be served a dainty afternoon tea from their new china, laid on an embroidered cloth Connie had stitched so beautifully by the fire at Caldwell. This, too, was going to be a home of faith, a setting for two young people who were thinkers and carers. Now that Connie was expecting a baby, there were the special private conversations between mother and daughter as they looked ahead to the coming of the child. Connie was often not well, and her mother found that gifts of mothering were still needed even with married daughters.

One Sunday evening later that year, Grace set the table for the evening meal. When Jim came to the table, the two of them sat alone at the head of the table built for fourteen.

'Where is everyone?' Jim asked.

'Some of the children have gone to have Sunday tea with Carrie and Hector, and the others have gone to Connie and Stan's. Legh has gone to visit Daisy — and of course the "little" girls are away at training and school.'

'Just for tonight, we seem to be back where we started, just the two of us,' Jim said smiling at her, and bowed to ask a blessing on their food.

Her first grandchild was born in the spring when the orchard was a wash of pinks and white. Grace sat in the hospital corridor with the young husband during the hours of waiting, remembering other births, other new babies. This time the woman in labour was her own daughter, and all she could do was be nearby, waiting and praying.

Later, when there was time to reflect, she realised that for hours and days a psalm had been running through her mind, words to cling to, words of hope. These words had strengthened her at many times of stress through many years. 'My help cometh from the Lord. . . He that keepeth thee will not slumber. . . The Lord shall preserve thee from all evil. . .' After the child was born, Connie was very ill. For Grace, sitting for hours by her daughter's bed, there was a sense in which she was anchored to her chair, eyes watching the very ill young woman lying there. In another way her spirit was stretching out to God, pleading with him for her child. She needed desperately to feel God's peace and comfort, to keep at bay the monsters of fear and panic which tried to attack and destroy her. As she watched her daughter, her beloved sister Sarah's face came into her mind, Sarah who had died within a week of childbirth, and her dear sister-in-law Evelyn who had died in this town after the birth of her second baby. 'The Lord is thy keeper,' she breathed, struggling to hold the loving care of God as a shield against the temptation to let her imagination carry her away in an assault of fear. For days her daughter was very ill, and then less ill, but still very weak. Through that time, the prayers of her mother surrounded her.

The baby was a little boy. Holding the tiny child wrapped in his little blanket, Grace held him tenderly, studying the baby face for likenesses to the family. 'We'll take him home to Caldwell, dear, and look after him until you are well enough to come home from hospital. Between us all, we'll take good care of him for you. He's a lovely little boy!' she told Connie. 'When you are well enough, you must come and stay at Caldwell till you are really strong again – you and the baby – and Stan must spend as much time with you as he is able.'

The spring blossom was long gone and flowers of late spring filled the dining room at Caldwell when the family gathered one Sunday evening in November to celebrate the baptism of baby Kenneth Stanley Grinter. At last Connie was well enough to attend the baptismal service in the church where she had herself been the first Methodist baby to be baptised. Back at the house, with all her children, her sons-in-law and her new grandchild safely under her roof, Grace brought out the fruit cake which had been the top layer of the wedding cake, rich and spicy with age.

While the girls passed slices of wedding cake to the family, Grace cuddled her grandson. 'Look at him, Jim. He's the first of our grandchildren. What will this little boy be like, I wonder?' She paused, looking from infant to white-haired man. 'If he has something of his grandfather in him, I think he'll be a good man.'

The pain gripped her suddenly, tightening around her chest. Grace sat down abruptly. Jim looked up from his book and saw her white face. 'I don't feel well. I've been having some chest pains – perhaps I'm just tired...'

Jim was on his feet, helping her to her bed, finding something for the pain, lines of anxiety on his face. She was his anchor, his beloved, his bridge to communication with his family, his dear wife who accepted him with all his good and bad points, the centre of his life.

'A holiday – you must have a break – go to see Dr Buchanan –

spend some time in Sydney with Grace McDowell – you've been too busy – oh, my dear!'

It was true that she had been under a lot of pressure over several years. Fears of losing the farm had almost left her, though prices of wheat and wool remained painfully low. But there had been the weddings, and caring for the baby and Connie, and one after the other the family had been ill – tonsilitis, appendicitis, dental problems, as well as the usual house guests and daily work. Jim was always heavily committed to everything he undertook, so much so that sometimes the family thought that he didn't observe what was happening under his nose at home. Her own hands had been troubling her, too, with a loss of mobility through arthritis, and it concerned her that she was becoming less able to do the many tasks she set herself.

'Yes, I must talk to the doctor,' she admitted. 'And, yes, it would be good to have a holiday with Grace McDowell.' Grace McDowell was single and putting all her energies into her work as an officer with the Salvation Army, while the other McDowell children were married.

Yes, she knew that her health was deteriorating and she well remembered symptoms her own mother experienced when she was suffering from a heart condition. But in her heart she pleaded, 'Not yet, please not just yet; there are too many things unfinished.'

20
Harvest
1934-1935

THE YEAR REVOLVED to summer again. Harvest, Christmas, New Year and the release of after-harvest. The familiar colours of rust-red soil, gilt of grain, luminous pale straw, ochres; dry, thick colours painted by a wide brush against harsh blue of sky, powdered over with fine red dust. The scene had been painted year after year, only the details changing little by little – power machinery instead of horses, a big new truck carting wheat as well as the wide wagon and team, hired workmen replaced by the men of the family. The smells of summer were as always – the fragrance of pine, eucalypt and box trees in hot sun, the sweetness of abundance of peaches and plums in the house, the heavy smell of overripe apricots fallen under the trees and the smell of dust.

This year, the pressures of harvest were not those of a drought year, when farmers broke their hearts over failed crops, nor of impossible prices, because things were improving. The strain this time was that this crop of 1933-34 was going to be bigger than they had ever known, every paddock still waiting to be harvested bearing a richer reward then ever before.

'It's not only us,' Jim explained. 'The whole district is having a great year! A wonderful harvest for us all. The only problem is getting the harvest safely into the silos at the railway and sold.'

The boys, with the help of the two men from Melbourne who had returned again in hope of more harvest work, were out in the paddocks from dawn till it was too dark to see. Bill was the main carter: the rest of the family only saw him fleetingly. Every day he was gone well before dawn to join the queue of trucks, horse wagons and even bullock wagons, waiting for the gates to the silos to open. Each day he tried to take three loads, but spent many hot weary hours in the queue, edging forward little by little in the jostling procession, bringing the wealth of the district. For the men in the paddocks there was always the urgency of harvest, the knowledge that the grain was ripe *now* and that delay would bring the risk of damage, deterioration and loss.

Under the surface of the familiar harvest scene, other elements circled around, creating their own ripples. Though Grace was not well at times, it was Connie that took most of the attention.

Connie was ill again, this time so very ill that she had been sent to hospital in Sydney. Little Ken had been cared for through much of his first year by his grandmother and aunties because his mother had spent so much time in hospitals in Coolamon and Wagga, or convalescing at Caldwell. There was talk of the need for an operation, and great anxiety over where money to pay for such a thing was to be found.

As Grace mixed scones for the harvest morning teas, six cups of flour at a time, her thoughts moved in prayer for her sick child. For years, Connie's poor health had disappointed and frustrated the girl herself, mystified the doctors and left her family dismayed and helpless. Her fine mind and capacity for hard work and concern for people was being limited and, as Grace pictured the girl in the distant hospital, she imagined her loneliness and depression. The more she thought of her daughter, the more she became convinced that Connie needed her now, even in the middle of harvest.

'I'm going to Sydney, to Connie,' she announced, 'even though it's harvest. I think she needs me. Stan is going soon and I'm booked on the train for Thursday.'

The train rattled and roared across the countryside, spitting sparks and cinders into the hot December air. From her window, Grace watched the land unfurling beside her, mile after mile of land under harvest, distant shapes of anonymous men on their harvesters and dust clouds following faraway trucks on the roads to railways, sidings and silos. The train flickered past tiny stations, paused at such larger ones as Cootamundra, Yass, Goulburn and Moss Vale and moved from flat country to hills, from wheat and sheep through dairy cattle, from wide open plains to thickly timbered slopes, from tones of gold and ochre to cooler blues and greens. She watched the first of the red-roofed houses of Sydney slip by, multiplying till the open country was swallowed in suburbs, and she knew that her long and weary journey would soon bring her to the vast bustle of Central Station.

Even though she had made the train journey many times, she still felt a clutch of anxiety at the thought of the crowds of strangers she must pass through, the stress of finding her way to the right suburban train and bus to get to Wahroonga without getting lost, and even the wilderness of blank corridors in a strange hospital before she found her child. Stiff from sitting for hours, she stood up to inspect with distaste her once neat dark suit which now looked rumpled and smelled of coal smoke. A black cinder had smudged her blouse. Even her hat, when she replaced it after tidying her hair, looked a bit the worse for wear after the journey and the little mirror reflected dark, weary rings under her eyes.

'I do hope I am doing the right thing in coming,' she thought, as the train made its final run through the tight inner web of the city. 'It would be awful if Connie thought that I was being a bit silly, and I've left everyone in the middle of harvest for nothing.'

Some time later, having safely negotiated the wilds of Sydney, she found herself standing in an open hospital doorway, looking at the pale face of her daughter lying against a pillow.

'Connie.'

The girl looked up. A look of incredulous delight transformed her face. 'Mother!'

When at last they released each other and sat quietly talking together, the young wife looked at her mother with eyes which shone with tears.

'Mother, I wasn't expecting you – I was lying here feeling so alone and so useless. And I looked up, and you were standing there, smiling at me. No-one has ever looked so beautiful . . .'

When Grace arrived home from Sydney, Christmas was very close and harvest continued. A new element had entered dinnertable conversation. A youth camp was to be held over the New Year holiday at Young for the Methodist young people of New South Wales. Though a few earlier camps had been held, the Crusader camp for New Year 1934 was the first to be held in a country centre.

'We never had anything like that in *my* day,' said Jim. His friend Andrew Downie had announced that he planned to take his daughters to the camp, and would judge for himself whether it was a helpful program.

'We four girls would love to go with the Downie girls, but we can't unless one of the boys can drive us to Young.'

'Sleeping on straw mattresses at Young showground doesn't appeal to me,' Dick said. Grace knew that the thought of being with a hundred total strangers for several days was even less appealing.

'There's too much to do at home — if it's any good I'll go next year,' said Bill. 'If we've finished harvest, let Legh go.'

Of all of them, Legh was the one who most wanted to go to the camp. The others teased him that it was just because Daisy Downie would be there, but Grace guessed that it went deeper than that. She remembered well her own growing-up years in the eighteen-nineties. The stability and influence of Christian faith in her own home had been very important, and her own children had that. They also were part of their local church, as she had been, and open to Christian teaching. Yet she remembered the stimulation of a wider world, of hearing strong preachers, the fun of doing things with large combined groups of youth, the chance to study together with new friends, the influence of seeing a range of young people around Sydney who dared to take the Christian faith seriously. Those people had modelled for her the possibilities of being the people of God. She wanted God's Spirit to be alive in her children, beyond the habits of home, more powerful than religious patterns copied without thought from parents. She hoped it would be possible for them to go to Young.

'Well, if harvest is finished. . .' said Jim.

Christmas came and went in intense heat and pressure of hard work. 'I'll work flat out!' Legh had said, but the year was running out and still acres waited for the harvester. Everyone was tired and sometimes irritable as the beckoning mirage of the New Year's camp seemed more and more impossible to reach. In the end Dick and Bill said, 'Take the girls and go to Young, Legh. It'll only be three days — the silos will be shut over New Year, anyway. We'll keep going till you get back.'

On New Years Eve, in a smother of luggage and excitement, Legh with Mary, Jean, Grace and Evie set off to drive to Young. Legh said to his mother, 'I'm dog-tired, and now that we're really going, I just hope it is worth it!' Grace watched them go with many unspoken hopes. 'Lord, let them meet you. Please help them walk with you further than they have dreamed,' she prayed.

At the table on New Years Day, strangely sparse with only the two boys at home, Jim was full of hope for the future.

'I think 1934 is going to be the year of the record harvest,' he said.

They had never had a harvest like it. Even though Legh had been away for three days, it made little difference in the end and Jim and his sons harvested and carted 5,900 bags of wheat off 284 acres on Caldwell for the 1933-34 harvest. That year was a record for the whole district, with more wheat passing through the silos at Coolamon than anywhere else in the state. Wheat prices were still poor, but neighbours came to Jim to buy his excellent seed wheat and the boys selected several bags of their best Yandella King and Baringa seed wheat to set aside for the Coolamon Show later in the year. There was an air of great pride in achievement among the men of the family. Caldwell had never produced so bountifully, and Grace found Jim gazing abstractedly across the paddocks, seeing again in his mind's eye the acres of bush and scrub, the fires of heaped-up dead trees, the ravages of kangaroos, rabbits and cockatoos on bared earth and a lone young man fighting to turn it into a farm.

For Grace there was a second harvest that January. Five of her children came home from Young and their Crusader camp with the greatest excitement. They couldn't stop talking about the new friends they had made from all over the state, the speakers who had inspired them, the hard straw-filled mattresses they had slept on, the jokes that had been told and pranks played, the campfire and concert, the midnight watchnight service on New Years Eve, the singing and times of prayer. Each had been very impressed with the young leaders of their study groups and young Grace in particular told her mother all about the young schoolteacher, Ida, who had been her leader and whose studies had meant a lot to the girl.

For Legh, it had been a very profound experience at a number of levels. 'If you offered me thousands of pounds,' he declared, 'or the chance to go to that camp at Young, I'd rather go to the camp!' His brothers, knowing that his financial position was as uncertain as their own, decided that he couldn't say fairer than that.

Before January was out, Legh stood in the pulpit at Rannock, having his first tentative attempt at leading worship and preaching. Grace remembered another young man many years earlier. Jim had been nervous too! There were tears in Grace's eyes as she listened to her son. It was clear that her prayers for Legh were being answered and his faith was something which was deepening and maturing to the point that he needed to share it.

Though neither Grace nor any of the others could know it, the camp at Young was to produce another result for the family. But that was in the future.

'I want to do something for the boys,' Jim said. The door of their room was shut and Grace was ready for bed.

'They are growing up – both Legh and Dick are over twenty-one and Bill will be twenty-one this year. And they'll be wanting to marry one day.'

Grace laughed. 'Well, Legh certainly has his heart set on Daisy – he's talked to her father and I think Daisy feels as he does, so it will be only a matter of time now – and money!'

'That's the point, of course. We can build them houses on the place when the time comes, but they'll all need something in the Bank, too. If prices had been good this year, or even just fair, we'd all be rich after last harvest, but even as things are I want to make a financial arrangement with the boys. I've talked it over with them and we'll make a start by putting aside a regular percentage of the harvest and wool cheque in a separate bank account for them to share, while I'll still be responsible for all the farm expenses.'

Grace was glad. She lay back on her pillow, tired at the end of a busy day, and pictured her boys growing up into strong and responsible men and establishing homes of their own. Though Dick or Bill had no particular girlfriends at the moment, she felt that that would come.

'That's very good, Jim,' she said sleepily. 'They will be glad to have their own bank account. "Higman Brothers" – yes, it sounds well.'

He climbed into bed beside her and she leaned against his warmth. Jim was a good man and she loved him. In fact, she loved him a great deal more, even twenty-nine years more, than she had when they were first married.

With a large basket packed with farm eggs, homemade butter, apples from the orchard and cakes, Grace visited her Rootes relations living in Wagga. In the years when Connie and then Richard had been at high school in Wagga, she had often seen her cousins, Sivyer, Jessie and Amy, the family of her uncle James Rootes whose home at Razorback she had often visited as a child. Her family had lost touch with some of the other Rootes relations, but she was very fond of the aging Jessie whose memories went back the furthest of any of them.

They sat together with old family photos spread around them: Jessie herself as a girl, Uncle James and Aunt Mary Ann, Uncle Richard and Auntie Lydia, very old photographs of their grandparents James and Anna Rootes.

'These old pictures came to me,' Jessie said, 'because I was with my father and stepmother till they died, and then cared for Uncle Richard Playford and Auntie Lydia.' Richard and Lydia Playford had lived to a great age, long enough to enjoy their sixty-fifth wedding anniversary together.

'Do you remember our grandparents much?' Grace asked.

'Grandfather James Rootes I remember very well of course, but I remember our grandmother particularly because she cared for us as young children after our mother died. She was wonderful if we were sick and so kind, but she was always sure something dreadful was going to happen next, poor old love! I think she had to survive a lot in her life, so we can't blame her.'

Jessie stared at the battered little photograph of a dour woman with down-turned mouth. 'She didn't always look like that – she liked to sing, too, and she was the first one who taught me that God cared about me. Our family never forgot how God had brought them safely to Australia. Did you ever know that my full name is Augusta Jessie Rootes, after the ship they travelled in? And I wasn't born till twenty-five years after they arrived!'

The two women sat quietly with the pictures, thinking of the old people of their family, unknown to the young generation, gone years ago, only held in faded photographs and fragments of memory, of no importance to historians who looked for fame or achievements.

'They've left us a lot, haven't they?' Grace said quietly. 'Strength, toughness to survive, a grounding in what is right and what isn't – they've brought us to faith in God...'

Easter was beautiful that year. Autumn rains had prepared the land for sowing and the weather was cooling and crisp after the long, hot summer. Legh took his sisters Grace and Jean and his friend Daisy Downie with him to the Easter Crusader camp at Moss Vale, and they again came home alight with everything that they had heard and seen. For them it was an Easter unlike any other they had known, a powerful time of learning at a deeper level about the meaning of the dying and rising of Christ.

On Easter Day, Grace sat in the sunshine on the verandah, her Bible in her lap and a feeling of peace and serenity flowing around

...er. In the afternoon they would all go to the church for the Easter Day service, and they would sing with great joy, 'Christ the Lord is risen today, Hallelujah!' Carrie would be at the organ, and Connie would be there with Stan and her beloved grandson Ken. She had just read again the story of the women who came to the tomb early on the first Easter Day and found it empty. Leaning back in her chair, she closed her eyes and pictured them, confused, tearful, questioning – then seeing the angels and hearing the words, 'He is not here, he is risen!'

In other parts of the world, she knew that Easter came at the time of spring, of new life and new growth. Here at home in Australia, Easter came in autumn, a time when many of the flowers in her garden were dying and the leaves on her fruit trees were beginning to fall. Yet just beyond the edge of the verandah, there was a flash of brilliant iridescent red-gold of nerines. They seemed to spring straight up out of the hard earth, with their summer leaves withered and drooped on the ground around their stems, glowing in autumn beauty, shouting to the world, 'You thought we were dead, didn't you!'

In the distance she could see ploughed paddocks where wheat had been sown during the past week. Autumn was not only a time of dying, but a time of sowing the seed for a future harvest, a time of promise and hope, a time of burying in the earth in the sure knowledge that in due time the buried seed would be transformed into something new, something greater, more beautiful, multiplied. She turned the pages of the book in her lap to the fifteenth chapter of Paul's first letter to the Corinthians, and she read, 'When you sow a seed it does not sprout to life unless it dies. And what you sow is a bare seed, perhaps a grain of wheat or some other grain, not the full-bodied plant that will later grow up. . . That is how it will be when the dead are raised to life. When the body is buried it is mortal; when raised it will be immortal. When buried it is ugly and weak; when raised it will be beautiful and strong. When buried it is a physical body; when raised it will be a spiritual body. . . Just as we wear the likeness of the man made of earth, so we will wear the likeness of the man from heaven. . . Where, Death, is your victory? Where, Death, is your power to hurt?. . . Thanks be to God who gives us the victory through our Lord Jesus Christ!'

When the autumn sowing was complete, Jim took Grace away for a week of holiday, touring around NSW in the car to visit old friends.

They had never had a holiday like that before. Always in the past, Jim had travelled on one kind of business or another — Farmers and Settlers conferences, annual Methodist conferences, with work as Chairman of the Coolamon Cooperative Society or farm affairs. Occasionally Grace travelled with him, but often there was too much to do at home. Jim had taken the boys on holidays to visit Yarrangobilly Caves in the Snowy Mountains, and to Sydney, but 'holidays' always meant visitors to Caldwell with the hope that family would have the chance to take time off to enjoy their company. Holidays meant games of chess in the evenings, quoits across the big kitchen, singsongs, noisy discussions, tennis on their court and more players for afternoon games of cricket.

Though sometimes the family thought that Jim was so immersed in his books that he noticed little around him, Grace knew that he was always conscious of what concerned her. Since she had confided that sometimes she wasn't feeling as well as she might, Jim was making a special effort to care for her. The holiday was planned with her pleasure in mind and was a great success. For a week she had no responsibilities, no meals to prepare, just being with Jim and sharing his enthusiasm and delight in everything they saw and every old friend they met. As they drove, he talked of his ideas for a book, thoughts he had been gathering since the beginning of the Depression on possible solutions for their nation's economic ills. Jim's mind ranged widely and as well as his reading in economics he was involved in a correspondence with the controversial Professor Angus over the theological question of the Virgin Birth, searching for answers to the curse of skeleton weed in the crops of his district, pondering scriptures for a new sermon or the young people's bible class, or studying the latest methods of fodder conservation.

As they drove they were free to talk to each other at length in a way which had not been possible for many years.

'Wasn't that a surprise to have an article about you in the *Methodist* a couple of months ago!' she commented.

Jim looked across at her with a twinkle in his eye. 'You mean an article about us,' he corrected. 'Both our photos, and glowing words about you — "gentle wisdom", "sanity of counsel", "full consecration to the cause of our Saviour" — those were the quotes, were they not?'

Grace brushed his words aside. Jim was the public figure in their family and she had been embarrassed when their young minister, Russell Gibson, had written of her in such warm terms. But Mr

Gibson, like many other ministers before him, had sat at her table and they had talked deeply and widely: she felt that they were friends.

As they passed through country she had not seen before, visiting the new capital city of Canberra and enjoying fresh vistas each day, he talked with special excitement of the Coolamon Agricultural and Pastoral Association's plan for 1934.

'The Show has been losing money over the past few years, with the Depression. A lot of people haven't wanted to travel to the Show or take the trouble to enter exhibits. But this year is going to be excellent. We are sending invitations all over the place and calling it "Back to Coolamon Week". The committee is planning a souvenir book and I've been asked to write some articles on the early days.'

He talked on as they drove, drawing from his memory old bush stories, details of the early settlements at Berry Jerry and Rannock, his childhood. Some of the stories Grace had heard before, but as he talked, he dug deeper and deeper into his memory, relishing the tales of striving and effort, chuckling over the humour of many situations. 'I'll put in the story about the Berry Jerry postmaster who played a trick on a mate by advertising for a wife in his name — and leaving him to deal with the replies!' he said. He produced names of families who had been there in the earliest, toughest days, and painted word pictures of a hardy, inventive, closeknit and humorous people.

'You should write those stories down, Jim,' she urged him. 'It would be so sad if they were forgotten, and so many of the people who were there then have gone already, or wouldn't be comfortable about writing the stories. You should write of the mistakes, too — things you wish had been done differently.'

As he enthused about the project, she knew that there was no risk that Jim would write anything slanderous about any of his neighbours of the past. Their minister had said of Jim, 'Is it just that Mr Higman doesn't ever see the flaws in people? Or does he see them perfectly well, but chooses only to talk about the good in people?' Her Jim always thought the best of everyone, and they tended to try to live up to his expectations; that was one of the things she loved about him.

They came home from their holiday with a good feeling of having spent important time together. Their love for each other was as strong as ever and Grace found herself thinking of how her life would have been deprived if she had listened to those cautious relatives long ago who thought that this Jim from the bush must be some sort of hayseed. The family was all delighted to have them safely home.

Yet in one thing Grace was disappointed. She had hoped that the holiday would ease her continual tiredness and the pain which was becoming more common. 'Perhaps a week wasn't quite long enough – or maybe sleeping in strange beds meant that I didn't sleep as well as I might,' she thought. 'Now I'm home it will be better.'

In May, the whole family appeared in church for Mother's Day with white chrysanthemums pinned to suits and dresses. They had all cherished her specially that morning, coming for Mother's Day hugs and surrounding her with love. Little Ken came toddling to her outside the church with a big kiss. Next Mother's Day, Carrie hoped to be a mother, too, and a new intimacy was growing between mother and married daughters. Sitting in the pew with Jim, Grace was intensely aware of her children. Almost all were taller than she was; stronger, more energetic. Once each of these young people had been her baby, her toddler staggering along beside her, clinging to a finger. Each of them had been cuddled and disciplined, comforted and warned, advised and listened to, washed and fed. They were men and women now, nearly all of them, but she had prayed by their beds, taught them songs, spanked them on occasion, and listened to endless tales of tennis, cricket and football. For each one she felt a depth of understanding, of compassion and love that was almost shaking in its fierceness. 'Who else cares as much as I do for these young ones?' she asked herself.

The minister was reading from scripture. Suddenly she saw a picture she had never recognised before. He read, 'For thus saith the Lord, as one whom his mother comforteth, so will I comfort you.'

She shut her eyes to see it better. If she, an ordinary human mother, felt as she did about her children, how much more. . . It was as if she felt herself enveloped in the warmth and safety of a loving hug, and even though there were things which disturbed and frightened her, uncertain things about the future for herself and her children, she could hear the voice of God whispering in her ear, 'Don't be afraid, you are all safe in my arms.'

It did not come as a great surprise to her when she found that she was forced to stay in bed one day. And then the next. Through the early days of winter she was ill and, after trying to struggle against it, she accepted that she was very tired and needed to rest. The girls lit a fire in her bedroom fireplace, making the room warm and comforting, and she lay for days, half-awake and half-asleep, taking her medicine as instructed and drifting in and out of conscious thought. Vaguely she remembered the bad winters, before the War, when Jim had been ill every winter, and their room had always been cold. Different family members came to sit by her, quietly stitching or reading, and in a confused way she thought of the many times they had been the ones in bed and she had sat beside them.

During the weeks she was ill, some of the family went to Wagga for a youth rally, this time including Bill, and they came home to tell her all about it. They brought home a young teacher teaching in a small school just beyond their immediate district who had been at the camps at Young and Moss Vale, Jack Jordan by name, and she was delighted to see Legh, Dick and Jack working together to set up a Crusader band. The three young men committed themselves to leading church services together in various country churches, and the mother rejoiced in their growing maturity and desire to share their Christian faith. As she began to recover, they often came into her room to talk to her about the concert practices at the church, to rehearse their lines and recite their poems, or to discuss how many sweets they needed to make or buy to stock the sweet stall for the evening.

By the time she was feeling stronger, the smell of fresh paint was all through the house. Jim had decided to paint all the main rooms and her bedroom and when she came out to sit by the breakfast room fire, the fireplace was newly whitewashed and the room was sparkling bright. 'I thought you'd like it,' Jim said happily.

When she was well enough to join the family again in the evenings, she found the three boys sitting around the kitchen table night after night, preparing a sample of their best wheat for the Coolamon Show. On sheets of newspaper they spread tins full of seed, pushing the seed this way and that searching for anything which was not perfect. With quick fingers and critical eyes, they culled out stray black oats, or any other foreign seeds, and searched out any grain that was discoloured or imperfect.

'I can't even see some of the things you can see!' she said, peering through her spectacles into the mosaic of grain.

'We have to keep on looking – if we miss anything that shouldn't be in the sample, we'll lose points.' Sometimes the girls bent over the spread of grain, adding their eyes to the search, but this was the boys' exhibit, their responsibility, and they took it very seriously.

There was a crop competition, too, and they were preparing one paddock to be judged for that competition.

Grace sat in the kitchen rocking chair by them. There was growing confidence in the boys. Now they were Higman Brothers, not just Father's lads giving him a hand on the farm. Legh had done very well at the Wagga Farm School years earlier, coming second in his year, Dick had achieved a fine result in his Intermediate Certificate and, while Bill preferred the practical to the academic, he was intelligent. The three of them were doing everything they could to study, learn and apply good methods to their farming, and were taking great pride in their work.

'Last year,' one of them said, 'we got a ribbon at the Show for one of our bushels of wheat, but this year they are offering a championship cup. Do you reckon we could win it?'

'Don't know, but we'll have a good try!'

The violets were in flower again. Whenever the purple fragrance appeared again between the smother of leaves, Grace always thought of her mother who had planted those violets in her garden. Her mother had told her that the violets had first come from the garden of *her* mother, Anna Rootes. She often thought of her mother, not in a sad way, but as if Mary Playford were still a significant part of her family life. Her mother's knotted old hawthorn stick had been relegated to the back of a cupboard and other people sat in her rocking chair, but the vigorous personality was a presence in her mind and, when the violets came again in the early spring, she knew that the old lady was alive with God.

Grace picked a handful of the violets, each flower nodding on its fragile stem, wrapped them in broad leaves and held them to her face. The perfume was very beautiful. In that sheltered corner of the garden she was free to feel the warmth of the spring breezes, to be unhurried and at rest. Since she had been ill during winter, her family had taken much of the work load from her, and her friend, Sarah's daughter Grace McDowell, had come to visit.

She valued the quietness. The house had been very busy lately. There had been all the preparations for the church concert and tea meeting, with her own family helping to decorate the stage, hang stage curtains, erect a booth for a sweet stall and transport a piano to the church. The concert had been a great success, with the audience very willing to applaud every act and to laugh long and hard at the dialogues and the jokes. They had even made some money from it to paint the church. As well, Jim had been working very hard on his articles for the 'Back-to-Coolamon' souvenir book, filling pages with anecdotes, pioneer tales and detailed descriptions of early farming methods. His writing about the early days of his district was lively, entertaining and very readable, less solemn than his more serious work on the problems of the economy, and certainly Jim was enjoying writing very much.

There was also a lot of excitement and anticipation in the family as they prepared for the special 1934 Back-to-Coolamon Show. One of the girls planned to enter a sponge cake and another some handwork, while Legh's Daisy spoke of entering cut flowers from her garden. For the boys, everything centred on their wheat entries and, night after night, they sat at the kitchen table sifting and sorting their bags of Baringa and Yandella King. They wanted to find a perfect bushel weight of excellent grain for each, about a third of a full wheat bag. Everyone expected that a lot of one-time residents would come back to Coolamon for the show and competition in all sections was sure to be keen. Grace had encouraged everyone else in the family to participate, but this year she didn't take part herself. 'I'll go and see it all, of course,' she assured them, 'and I'll be so proud if any of you win a ribbon.'

For now she was content to pick violets in the spring sunshine.

Grace lay sleepless. The wind was brushing through the trees beyond the gate and beside her Jim was gently snoring. There was a noise in the distance, at the end of the hall. Someone was still in the kitchen. Wrapping herself in a warm gown, she left her bed and walked down the hall towards the light.

In the kitchen the boys were still bent over a table spread with wheat.

'It's so late! You boys should go to bed – you have to be up early for shearing in the morning.'

'But Mother, Father will be taking our entry to town in the morning, for judging at the show, and we just want to be sure that it is right.'

Grain by grain they were checking, sifting over and over, lifting wheat in their palms, rolling it to and fro so that nothing imperfect would be missed. She walked to each one, leaving a kiss and an embrace with each son.

'Then try not to be too long – you've been working on this for weeks and weeks, so I'm sure you've done the best you can.'

She left them to finish and return to the warmth of her bed, to pray a brief prayer of thanks for her boys, and to dream of acres of wheat, grain multiplying from grain.

In the morning before they went down to the shearing shed, they presented their father with the precious bags, their chosen bushels of Yandella King and Baringa wheat. The girls had their own entries ready to send in and Grace admired each carefully presented article before it was packed into the car. Today was for displaying entries for judging in all categories and tomorrow they would all go in to see the glory of everything their whole district could produce.

'There'll be plenty of entries for the wheat – don't know how we'll go – hope we get a ribbon, at least.' Now that the time had come, the boys were unsure and a little anxious. The girls were beginning to wonder whether they should even send their own entries, and Grace encouraged them to try – 'this year everyone will be in it and that will make it good fun, even if you win nothing.'

Jim departed in a cloud of dust on his way to town and the boys headed off to the shearing shed. Through the bright September day, Grace could hear the endless bleating of sheep and the roar of the machine in the shearing shed. When she walked down to the shed with the girls with morning tea, all they could talk about was their wheat entry.

The boys were still working in the shed when Jim returned. He poked his head briefly through the kitchen door, said, 'Something to tell the boys. . .', and disappeared in the direction of the shearing shed. Grace didn't have long to wait.

'Mother – mother, we won!'

'Won?' She was breathless with being hugged. 'A blue ribbon?'

'No, the cup, the championship cup!'

It was true. Next day, when Grace went with the rest of the family to the Coolamon Show, they all had a wonderful day. The showground was more crowded with visitors than it had been for years, the standard of entries was high, and the district seemed to be saying with its fine display, 'Despite international prices and a Depression, our land and our people are very productive and skilful.' Old friends came to talk to Grace. She was taken to see Daisy's flowers and the wonderful range of cakes and needlework entered by family and friends. Many people came to congratulate Jim on his excellent article 'Pioneering Experiences' with its humour and insights into the past which had been published in the

Back-to-Coolamon book, complete with a photo of Jim.

But the crown of the Show was the championship cup, a large silver rose bowl, set beside the bag of Baringa grain bearing the card 'Higman Bros'. Family pride in the boys overflowed. Now they could be truly described as successful farmers in their own names.

The cup came home to Caldwell later, after an official presentation. With a flourish, Legh produced a bottle of lemonade.

'We all have to drink a toast out of the cup,' he announced, pouring lemonade in a fizzing fountain into the inscribed silver bowl. 'And Mother, we all want you to have the first drink!'

Across the farm, the young greens of spring crops slowly transmuted from bright young shoots into the gold of crops heavy with grain. The year was coming to its climax, the time of harvest. In the wider community, many people continued to struggle against bitter poverty and the heartbreak of long unemployment and Jim sometimes shook his head over news of the world, particularly ominous rumours of affairs in Germany. On the farm the family lived simply, able to feed their large family with their own produce, wasting nothing, putting aside anything at all which 'might come in for something one day', doing without anything which was not necessary.

More and more, Grace found herself concerned with the interior life of the family, all her close friends and relations, and less interested in the affairs of the world. The important things were Carrie's health as she waited for her baby in the New Year, Mary's conscientious work as postmistress, Connie and the improvement in her health, Legh, Dick and Bill and the new confidence they had all gained and the way each was developing as a young Christian. Then there was young Grace with her shyness and her affectionate nature, Jean who had come home after a year of training in child care and Evie who was about to do her end-of-year exams at Annesley School. Beyond her own family, there were the interests of her brothers and their families and she continued to write loving letters to her nieces and nephews, thinking of them in times of personal ups and downs, exams, romances.

For Jim there was yet another honour offered in a year of honours. The publishers of a large volume to be called *Pioneers of Australia* wrote to say they would like to include him and his father Richard Higman in their work, among many other established Australian pastoralists, stud owners and farmers. Jim was overwhelmed to be invited to be part of it, discounting his own achievements as perfectly ordinary, but searching out an old photo of his parents, Richard and Caroline Higman, and portraits of himself and Grace with photographs of their home and property to illustrate the chapter on the Higman family.

In November, just as they began haycutting, they celebrated Bill's twenty-first birthday. At the family party when they honoured Bill, Grace sat quietly watching her athletic son. It was when Bill was born that she had been so very ill. At that time she had not expected to see her baby grow up. She was very thankful. Yet she knew that once more things were not as they should be in her body – not just her heart or the arthritis, either. 'Perhaps if I rest, it will clear up,' she thought. 'In any case, I don't want to mention it till after Carrie has had her baby safely. If I'm still worried then, I'll ask the doctor about it. . .'

On New Year's Day 1935 the house seemed very empty indeed. Those of her family who had attended the Crusader camp in Young the previous year had persuaded the others to go this time – 'and it is only in Wagga, this time, practically at home!' She and Jim ate a solitary breakfast and a quiet dinner at the long table.

'It will be very strange when they are all grown up and gone, won't it?' she said. 'It's a very long time since you and I had a quiet day alone in our own home.'

'Probably about twenty-nine years ago,' muttered Jim. 'Since Carrie was born and your mother came to live with us, the house has never been empty. The next month is our thirtieth anniversary. . .'

In the quietness of the day, she opened her drawer where she kept old photos, old letters, treasures from the past. There were the faded pages of notes her grandfather James Rootes had written in his old age, telling the story of migration with Anna and the children, tantalising references to long gone events, floods, illnesses, deaths. She had kept letters from Gertie, her friend long gone, her notifications of transfer to schools with her teaching certificates, and her book of cuttings of poems gathered as a girl. The pages of her oldest Bible were loosening and she turned the pages carefully. All through were her markings and notations: preachers' texts noted in the eighteen-eighties and eighteen-nineties, special verses she had underlined, marginal notes against passages saying 'Coonong' and 'Gwynne'. Then there was a later Bible and between the pages she found the papery remains of a pressed frond of maidenhair fern; she smiled at it, remembering herself plucking that frond, green and delicate, from near the foot of a waterfall as she walked hand in hand with the man who was to become her husband.

The turning of pages revealed other memories of her parents, photographs, memorial notices, and a small bookmark imprinted with 'For God, King, Country and Our Boys, 1/6/17'. She touched the bookmark with a pang; that was the time when Jim was ready to sail with the 1st AIF. Tied together were the letters from that terrible time, the letters that had linked Jim and herself. A loose clipping slipped from a Bible, a poem she had liked: 'I have to live with myself and so, I want to be fit for myself to know. . .'

Very gently she replaced the papers and photographs. 'I have a lot to be thankful for,' she thought.

When the family came home from the camp at Wagga, they didn't come alone. As they all burst through the back door, struggling with bags and blankets, sunburnt and noisy, they brought in with them some extra guests, the boys' friend Jack the teacher, and Jack's sister Ida, also a teacher. The girls introduced Ida happily. 'Do you remember how much we appreciated our leader last year, the teacher? Well, this is Ida!'

Grace had been long accustomed to having extra guests at her table, and welcomed the slender young woman warmly with her brother who was already a frequent guest. The girls were happy to have her in their home for a few days on her way home from camp and showed her around the house and the farm, enjoying her pleasure in it all. They took pride in her gifts as a study leader and whispered with some awe, 'Mother, she's an accredited lay preacher! I didn't know girls could be. . .'

Again the effects of the time with other young Christians had been very powerful, this time for all her single young people. As they pored over their camp photograph, describing the influence of one and another, or the challenges they had met, Grace was very thankful. Nor was that all.

There came the time some weeks later when they heard that Ida Jordan had been transferred from a small school near Dungog to teach at South Wagga Primary. And then the evening when Mary came to tell her mother something very interesting. 'You'd never guess who is busy writing a letter to Ida, armed with the dictionary. . . Bill!'

The long table was full for Grace and Jim's thirtieth wedding anniversary. The girls insisted that she should sit and be waited on while they brought in a festive meal.

'Happy anniversary, Mother and Father!'

Grace looked around the table, from face to face. Carrie and Hector were there, glowing with pride in their new baby daughter Ruth. Mary presided over the tea-pot, solemn and contented. Connie was better, for the moment, and Stan had little Ken wriggling on his knee. Legh had Daisy beside him and, though Dick and Bill were alone, she knew that Bill had asked if he could invite Ida for a weekend soon. The three younger girls, Jean, Grace and Evie, were growing up as distinct individuals, happy, capable and secure, each with a faith of her own.

Beside her at the head of the table sat Jim. This was the man whom she had walked to meet thirty years before, the one who had waited seven years for her to love him, the one she had vowed to love and honour there in the little school at Cullinga under the draping gum branches. This was her husband who had sheltered and cherished her, respected her judgment and asked for her advice, built a home for her so that she could build a home for him. This was the godly man who had shared her life for thirty years, a man who commanded respect for the way he lived out his Christian faith, the father of these children who were her pride.

He was talking farm-talk again, tracing with the boys the work of recent months and planning for the future.

She caught his last words: '. . . been another good harvest.'

Grace laid her small hand over his large and work-roughened fingers.

'Yes,' she said. 'We have had a good harvest.'

Epilogue

MORE THAN FIFTY YEARS later, they recalled Easter 1935. It wasn't until after Carrie's baby was born safely in January that Grace admitted to her family that the reason she had not been well over some months, and had gradually been forced to spend much time resting, was not only because of general tiredness or heart troubles. She feared that the cancer had returned. The Coolamon doctor sent her to Wagga, and Wagga hospital arranged for her to travel to Sydney for surgery.

In her last weeks at home, the family came to sit with her when they could, sharing their thoughts, the little details of their day. Old friends came to see her, wanting to return to her a little of the care she had given them when they had needed it. The family gathered at Caldwell to see her off to Sydney for surgery, travelling with Jim and daughter Grace on the train. They sent her off with love and concern, but all spoke of 'when you come home again . . .' Perhaps Grace knew then that it was not to be.

The family was just finishing breakfast around the big table on Saturday 13 April 1935, speaking of their mother and listening to autumn rain. The phone rang and their father asked to speak to Legh. Legh returned to the table stunned. Their mother had just died in hospital, of heart failure, before she had gone to surgery. She was fifty-nine years old.

Years later, the memories of that Easter were shared. They recalled their good friend Mr Downie offering to drive Legh through mud and bogs to Junee to meet a brokenhearted Jim Higman from the train. They spoke of the funeral service in Coolamon Methodist Church on the Monday of Holy Week, when the Rev. Russell Gibson preached on 1 Corinthians 15, 'Thanks be to God, who giveth us

431

ry through our Lord Jesus Christ.' They travelled along
ry road running north to Rannock. As they passed along,
gnbours waiting at farm gates and crossroads joined them, and
the schoolchildren stood at attention outside Rannock school as they
passed.

Grace Higman was buried in the beautiful peace of the Rannock
cemetery, among the pines, very near the grave of her mother Mary
Playford. Her sons and daughters were there, and sons-in-law, with
her brothers and several nieces, and a great many neighbours and
friends from further afield who shared their grief. As well as gifts
of flowers from families and friends, the graveside was heaped with
flowers from organisations – councils and committees, sporting
groups and lodges, churches and schools, subscribers to the
telephone party line. Clergy of other churches brought tributes and
the family was particularly touched when Father Gahan, the priest,
called at their home with the sympathy and care of himself and their
Catholic neighbours. That week it rained, rain soaking into the
paddocks from grey skies, somehow in keeping with the grief and
pain of the family. Yet the rain was a healing thing, and when the
boys went back to work after Good Friday and Easter Day, they
were able to begin the sowing for the year in perfect conditions,
knowing that the seed flowing into the moist soil would grow and
flourish, and that was a comfort.

Each one had private memories of conversations and treasured
letters. Cousin Grace McDowell shared how she had visited her
Auntie Grace in Scottish Hospital, Paddington on the evening she
had arrived in hospital after a terrible train journey to Sydney. Her
aunt was too ill to speak, but when Grace said, 'I've been thinking
of your favourite psalm, Auntie, Psalm 121 – "The Lord shall
preserve thee from all evil; he shall preserve thy soul . . . My help
cometh from the Lord . . .,"' then the eyes of the sick woman
responded.

Carrie told the others of her last conversation with her mother with
tears. 'She said that before her first operation, twenty-one years
ago, she couldn't sleep on the night before going to hospital. She
got up and went and knelt beside each one of us, praying for us
individually, and that included her baby, Bill – and then she asked
God to spare her, until we were older. God had answered her prayer
and she felt she had so much to be thankful for.'

Several very glowing tributes were written to honour the memory
of Grace Higman at the time of her death. Carved on the stone on

her grave are the words: 'Greatly beloved'. It would have been equally true to have carved 'She loved greatly'.

With the death of his beloved wife, Jim Higman lost the central person of his world. He lived on, cared for by his daughters, absorbed in his books and writing, continuing with his committees and church work. To his disappointment, he was unable to find a publisher for the book he had been researching and thinking about for twelve years, but had it printed himself under the title 'For Peace'. After a lifetime of work for local, regional and state church committees, his highest honour was to be chosen as a representative to the national General Conference of the Methodist Church, held in Brisbane in 1942. During World War II, when many ministers were serving as chaplains, Jim wrote offering his services to the church, to act as a temporary lay pastor in any parish needing help. Before this offer could be taken up, Jim preached what was to be his last service at Rannock. He had been working as a lay preacher for forty-seven years. The following week, 6 July 1944, he died in his sleep at home at Caldwell, aged seventy-three.

For the rest of the family, the years brought changes. Carrie and Hector lived and worked on their Rannock farm till retirement and now live in Coolamon. Mary married Fred Eyles in 1948 and lived in Corrowa and Temora till her death in 1965. Connie and Stan Grinter worked on their own farm at Rannock for many years till ill health forced Stan to pass the farm on to his son Ken who is there still. Though Connie has always suffered from poor health, she has lived to see some of her grandchildren married and a great-grandchild born. In 1937, Bill married Ida Jordan, the teacher he had met at a Crusader camp. Significantly for the rest of the family, Ida invited her best friend Daisy James to be a bridesmaid. When the bride and her maids joined Bill and his groomsmen for the marriage ceremony, Daisy was partnered with Dick Higman; the two were married several years later. Legh and Daisy Downie were married in March 1938. The three boys worked the property of Caldwell as Higman Brothers for a number of years, broken by the years of war when all three were prepared to enlist. The decision was made that Bill, the youngest with a wife and child, should be the one to stay and run the farm while the other two were away in the army and air force. This he did through drought years with the help of aging father and uncle, till Dick and Legh were free to return. Grace met a young farmer, Sam Stanyer from Illabo, when he and his family attended Crusader camps and they were married in the Rannock church in 1941. The Thomas sisters, Jean and Ev, remained single and kept the family home and the telephone exchange till 1970, when they moved to Coolamon.

Grace and Jim Higman saw few of their grandchildren and none of their great-grandchildren. As with most Australian families, the younger generations have had much greater opportunities for education, vocational choices and travel than their forebears ever did. Among the grandchildren are farmers and nurses, teachers and a medical doctor, business people, homemakers, a professor of history, secretaries, a missionary. Appearing among the generations are gifts of music, art and inventiveness and many homes where love and faith are found.

On a fine Sunday in February 1988, cars came from all directions to gather at the little church in Rannock. They came to celebrate the eightieth anniversary of that congregation, once Methodist and now Uniting Church. Families came who felt a kinship with that district and that church. Among them was a handful of people who had been there as children, eighty years ago, and others who remembered World War I and the impact on their families. There were the men and women who had grown up and married there during the Depression, and children, grandchildren and great-grandchildren of the pioneers. We wore name tags and such family names as Grinter, Moncrieff, Allen, Higman recurred.

One of Jim and Grace Higman's grandsons had made a large map of the area, showing land ownership since selections were first taken up in the eighteen-seventies. Small children were shown with pride how their farm had been in their family since the long-ago days when their great-great-grandfather had cleared the land with an axe and bare hands.

A local farmer welcomed the crowd who filled the church and sat outside in a large marquee. There is only a small population at Rannock these days as current farm technology means that one man can do what once took a team of men in his grandfather's generation. The trio which have always affected the district — national economy, farming technology and the weather — were as evident as ever. In his welcoming speech, the farmer said that, though it was good to have a fine day for the celebration, '. . . we could do with an inch of rain.'

There was a sense of celebration as we honoured those men and women who had planted their family, community and spiritual lives so surely in that Australian soil. Even those family members who had lived in other districts and other states for many years were grateful for a sense of rootedness, of belonging, of an inheritance of worth.

Of Grace and Jim Higman's family, five of their nine children were present at the anniversary: Carrie, Legh, Dick, Jean and Ev. Connie in Sydney, and Grace in Illabo sent greetings, but were unable to be there because of ill health. Mary died in 1965 and Bill died in 1977, weeks after celebrating forty happy years of marriage with Ida. Recently both Dick and Grace lost their partners, each after marriages which lasted over forty years. Carrie and Hector have celebrated fifty-six years of marriage and Legh and Daisy fifty years. Jean and Ev Thomas have kept their home a place of special hospitality and Christian caring. In each family home, Christian faith has been central.

At the anniversary, daughters, daughters-in-law and granddaughters chose to wear treasures they had inherited from women of the Higman family. There was Mary Playford's gold wedding ring, fashioned into a brooch. There was the brooch William Playford had given Mary near the end of his life, a gold nugget set on gold bars and engraved 'Hillend 1860 Cullinga 1904'. There was Daisy's wedding ring of Cullinga gold and the beautiful amethyst necklace and bracelet which had been worn by Evelyn Higman. And there was the lidded gold brooch which Jim Higman gave his wife Grace, with the hidden message under its lid, 'I love thee'.

Anna, Mary and Grace, the mothers, are not forgotten.

There is a dilapidated empty house standing on Caldwell where once a large family flourished. It has been empty since 1970. The banksia roses have grown into a thicket around the verandahs, blocking the way to the front door and forcing the front gate shut. The back gate has disappeared under an impenetrable hedge of rosemary and sage and the ancient plough discs still hang on the fence to call in to dinner men who left long ago. The metal plough seat still swings under the kurrajong tree, but no child comes to swing there. A weathered post marks the place where once young people played tennis and a graveyard of obsolete farm implements lie around the spot where the blacksmith's shop once stood. On the far side of the farm, the original old house has vanished completely after years of standing in ruin with fragments of red clay still holding together its skeletal remains. Many miles away at Cobbitty, a stone floor remains the only reminder of the overseer's cottage which once stood on the Matavai property, and cottages on Marshdale Farm, St Peters and Petersham have long been demolished.

Jim would be happy to know that the Caldwell property, after some years of being divided with parts sold off, has been restored to the original block of 1800 acres which Jim knew. It's in the hands of another Jim Higman, Legh's son, and the cycle of sowing and harvest goes on, using methods, technology and equipment of which the earlier Jim never dreamed.

The flowers and the bulbs remain. In the red earth the bulbs go on multiplying, bulbs that were planted long ago by Mary Playford and Grace Higman, some inherited from the garden of Anna Rootes. In their season, the abandoned garden is sweet with crocus and daffodil, nerine and hippeastrum, iris and white-belled November lilies, violets and quince blossom. In a way it is sad. Yet it says again, as the ancient writer of Ecclesiastes wrote: 'To everything there is a season, and a time for every purpose under heaven. . . God has made everything beautiful in his time. . .' The house which sheltered one family and all those who needed the haven of its walls for fifty-six years is empty and the earlier houses have gone. Yet none of the houses made the true home. The home was always the people: Grace and Jim, Mary and William, Anna and James, those they loved and those who needed them. That home has been recreated in other homes, other households of other generations. The bulbs multiply and flower again where they are planted.

Acknowledgements

Piecing together the elements which combine to tell this story of three generations has been very like stitching a complex patchwork quilt. The varied fabrics have been gathered over a long period, examined, sorted and some pieces discarded. From the fabric of each life, portions have been chosen and laid together to use their colour and texture in the new design. Small embroideries have been added – imagined conversations, scenes which may have happened, but probably did not. In the end one has what is a novel, a new design, yet the whole is created from real pieces of the lives of real people: gathered memories, family artifacts, photographs, old houses and gardens.

Many descendants of Anna Rootes, Mary Playford and Grace Higman have been very generous with their own collections of family treasures, opening their drawers of photographs and memorabilia, sharing memories and insights. The richness of oral history in a family which has remained stable and close till the present day has been a delight, producing such things as stories passed from generation to generation of how their great-grandmother Anna had tended the wounds of convicts after floggings, the girlhood stories of grandmother Mary. One lady of over eighty told a story which had been told by her grandmother of her mother Anna losing her bonnet overboard on the voyage from England and refusing to leave the ship till another could be bought, taking the memory back to 1837. Very sincere thanks and love go the children of Grace Higman for their help over many visits and letters: Carrie and Hector Crawford, Connie Grinter, Legh and Daisy Higman, Dick and Daisy Higman, Grace Stanyer, Jean and Ev Thomas. Appreciation also goes to other descendants and people who remember who have contributed over a number of years through letters, conversations, and family papers: my late parents Bill and Ida Higman, Grace McDowell, Faye, Margaret and Rosemary Playford, David Playford, Frank Playford, Adeline Harnett, Edna Brownrigg, Doreen Playford, Sandra Rootes, Ken Grinter, Bruce Edwards, Gertrude Tonkin, Ned and Beryl Ingold.

It has been important to visit most of the sites mentioned in the story. At each point, people were very helpful and their kindness has been appreciated: Brian Walsh for a video of Northiam, Sussex, Barry and Gloria Marsh of the Rectory, Cobbitty, the Papi family of the former 'Matavai' and Mr and Mrs Jim Macintosh of 'Denbigh', Frank Playford who took me to Cullinga mine, Mervyn Holden of what was once 'The Hill'.

Appreciation also goes to the staff of NSW State Library, the Mitchell Library, Australian War Memorial Archives, National Library, Canberra, and in particular to good friends the Rev. Eric Clancy of Uniting Church Archives at North Parramatta and the late Rev. Dr Alan Tippett of St Mark's Library Canberra.

My love and thanks go to my own extended family, dear relatives who have been great encouragers, my former church family at Central Belconnen Uniting Church and friends across Uniting Church, Canberra Presbytery. Particular thanks goes to my own special people – Ron, Jenni, David, Ruth and Glen – whose love assures me that being part of a family is very precious indeed.

Chapter notes

In addition to the sources listed below, most sites described in the work were visited, photographs from a number of family collections were examined and oral history was gathered from family members through interviews and correspondence over a two year period.

Anna's story
Chapter 1: Native soil
Eric Clancy, *A Giant for Jesus*, Link Printing, 1972

C.M.H. Clark, *Select Documents of Australian History, 1788-1850*, Angus and Robertson, 1950

Frank Crowley, *Colonial Australia, Vol.1*, 1788-1840, Thomas Nelson, 1980

Winifred L. Davis, *O Rare Norgam: An East Sussex Village and its story*, 1965

T.W. Horsfield, *History and Antiquities of Sussex*, 1834

Dorothy Marshall, *Industrial England 1776-1851*, Routledge and Kegan Paul, 1973

Genealogical Society Shipping Records, Vol.X

The Christian Advocate, 11 September 1875, notice of death of Silas Gill

Wesleyan Methodist Magazine: issues from 1832-35; stationing of Methodist ministers; effect of cholera

Death Certificate of James Rootes, died 5.9.1898, registered in Camden No. 9026

James Rootes, autobiographical notes written for family on 31 December 1888, 2 January 1893, 14 December 1894. Privately held.

Video of village of Northiam, Sussex, UK, filmed 1987 by Rev. Brian Walsh.

Chapter 2: Uprooted

Alan Atkinson and Marian Aveling, *Australians: A Historical Library*. *Australians 1838*, Fairfax, Syme and Weldon Associates, 1987
Eric Clancy, op.cit.
Jonathan Binns Were, C.M.G., *A Voyage from Plymouth to Melbourne in 1839. The Shipboard and Early Melbourne Diary*. Issued to clients of J.B. Were and Son, 1964.

Guide to Convict Records in the Archives Office of NSW, Mitchell Library.
Index for Immigrant Ships arriving in NSW 1837-96, Mitchell Library.
Augusta Jessie, Journal of Superintendent P.R.O. Reel, 3213 Mitchell Library.
Extract from *Historical Records of Australia Vol.XXI*, Sir Richard Bourke to Lord Glenelg on arrival of the ship *Augusta Jessie* 21 October 1837; Enclosure to Lord Glenelg's Despatch from Colonial Office 10 July 1837 with reference to *Augusta Jessie*, signed T.F. Elliot, Emigration Agent; records of loss of life on migrant ships in 1838-40.
Family trees of Sussex families migrating together to Australia in 1837-1840, prepared by B.A. Edwards, Feb. 1982.

Chapter 3: Transplanted

W.W. Burton, *Religion and Education in NSW*, J. Cross, 1840
C.M.W. Clark, *Select Documents, 1788-1850*, Angus and Robertson, 1950
Frank Crowley, *Colonial Australia Vol.1, 1788-1840*, Thomas Nelson, 1980
Lloyd Evans and Paul Nichols (eds), *Convicts and Colonial Society 1788-1868*, MacMillan, 1984
D.N. Jeans, *An Historical Geography of NSW to 1901*, Reed Education, 1972
John Dunmore Lang, *A Historical and Statistical Account of NSW*, Vol. 11, 1837
Rachel Roxburgh, *Early Colonial Houses of New South Wales*, Lansdowne Press, 1974

The *Australian*, August – December 1838, 11 February 1841

Maps of Parish of Camden indicating original landholdings, National

Library of Australia
Account of subscriptions paid towards the building of St Paul's
Church, Cobbitty: June 1839-March 1840 (manuscript at St Paul's,
Cobbitty)
James Rootes, notes, op.cit.

Chapter 4: Withering winds
C.M.H. Clark, *A History of Australia, III, The beginning of an
Australian Civilisation: 1824-1851*, Melbourne University Press, 1973
James Colwell, *The Illustrated History of Methodism*, William Brooks
and Co., 1904
Frank Crowley (ed.), *A New History of Australia*, William Heinemann,
1974
Frank Crowley, *Colonial Australia, Vol.2 1841-1874*, Thomas Nelson,
1980
Robert Hughes, *The Fatal Shore: A History of the Transportation of
Convicts to Australia, 1787-1868*, Collins Harvill, 1987
John Watsford, *Glorious Gospel Triumphs*, Charles H. Kelly, 1900

Australian Church Record, 15 June 1967, 'Some Links with the Past;
St Paul's Cobbitty'
The Methodist, James Colwell, article on Thomas (Tom) Brown,
1806-1871, 21 October, 1911
The Christian Advocate, 4 January 1876, obituary of Silas Gill.
*Journal and Proceedings of the Australian Methodist Historical
Society*, September 1971, Dennis Towner, 'Cobbitty, Cradle of Country
Methodism'
The Weekly Advocate, 6 October 1888, obituary of Anna Rootes.
Sydney Morning Herald, 26 November 1842, references to failing
fortunes and final insolvency of James Hassall between February 1843
and January 1845; depression in colony of NSW

Baptismal, Marriage and Funeral Register, St Paul's Anglican Church,
Cobbitty, NSW for period 1840-1870.
Family letters from migrants to Australia on ship *Juliana*, written from
Capetown after ship was grounded, sent to families in Northiam,
Sussex; from H. Perigoe, Samuel and Ann Ranger, R.B. and C. Cook,
October 1838, February 1839. Original letters in possession of Perigoe
descendents, Northiam, Sussex. Family letters of Thomas Hassall,
James Hassall, Fanny Dixon (Hassall), Eliza Hassall; Hassall
correspondence, Mitchell Library.
James Rootes, op.cit.

Chapter 5: Root and branch

W.J.M. Campbell, *Old Tom Brown of Wesley Vale*, Dalton, 1938
James Hassall, *In Old Australia*. R.S. Huws and Co., 1902

Australian Methodist Historical Society, Journal and Proceedings:
No.72 May 1957, Methodism in Camden and Cawdor
Christian Advocate and Wesleyan Record, Sermon by Rev. Thomas
Binney, 'The Wife, or A Mirror of Maidenhood', September 1859.
Family letters from Thomas Hassall and Eliza Hassall, 1847, 1850;
Hassall correspondence, Mitchell Library.
James Rootes, op.cit.

Mary's story
Chapter 6: Gold in the rock

Geoffrey Blainey, *The Rush that Never Ended: A History of Australian
Mining*, Melbourne University Press, 1963
W.L. Blamires and John B. Smith, *The Early Story of the Wesleyan
Methodist Church in Victoria* (A Jubilee Volume), Wesleyan Book
Depot, 1886
C.M.H. Clark, *Select Documents in Australian History 1851-1900*,
Angus and Robertson, 1955
C.M.H. Clark, *A History of Australia, IV: The Earth Abideth Forever,
1851-1888*, Melbourne University Press, 1978
James Flett, *A Pictorial History of the Victorian Goldfields*, Rigby,
1977
Harry Hodge, *The Hill End Story: History of the Hill End-Tambaroora
Goldfield, Book 1*, Harry Hodge, 1964
Historical Studies, Australia and New Zealand, Eureka Supplement,
Melbourne University Press, 1954
D.N. Jeans, op.cit.
Geoffrey Serle, *The Golden Age: A History of the Colony of Victoria
1851-1861*, Melbourne University Press, 1977

The Christian Advocate and Wesleyan Record, 12 May 1859, account
of combined Sunday School Picnic; 5 October 1859, a report of Camden
Quarterly Meeting
Methodist Magazine, 1852, Part II re goldfields
*Australian Wesleyan Methodist Missionary Society Annual Reports
1859-64*; lists of collectors and amounts collected
Death Certificate of Sarah Playford, 28 March 1856. Privately held.
Marriage Certificate of Richard Playford and Lydia Rootes, 26
December 1860. Privately held.

William Playford, diary notes on life. Privately held.
Family history recorded by Grace McDowell during 1970s. Privately held.

Chapter 7: Foundations

Australia, the First Hundred Years, being a facsimile of Vol.I and Vol.II, picturesque Atlas of Australasia 1888, Andres Garran (ed.), Summit Books, 1978

Michael Cannon, *Life in the Cities: Australia in the Victorian Age: 3*, Thomas Nelson, 1975

J.E. Carruthers, *Lights in the Southern Sky*, Methodist Book Depot, 1924

James Colwell, *Illustrated History*, op.cit.

Halford E. Luccock and Paul Hutchinson, *The Story of Methodism*, Abingdon-Cokesbury Press, 1926

Richard Piper, *Illustrated History of Ashfield Methodism (1840-1936)*, published for the 96th anniversary of Ashfield Methodism and Jubilee of the Model Wesleyan Methodist Sunday School building, 1936

Alan Sharpe, *Colonial NSW 1853-1894, from pages of Illustrated Sydney News*, Harper and Rowe, 1979

The Border Post (Albury), 31 September 1873, 'A Disastrous Occurrence on the Mitta Mitta'
The Christian Advocate and Wesleyan Record, March 1860, May & July 1865

William Playford, diary notes. Privately held.
Birth Certificate of James Caldwell, 25 February 1871
Death Certificate of Richard and Mary Caldwell, accidentally drowned 12 September 1872
Family Bible of William and Mary Playford, with record of births and deaths
Marriage certificate of William Playford and Mary Rootes, 2 May 1862.
Marriage certificate of Richard Higman and Caroline Swann, 4 April 1867
Minutes of Meeting in Schoolroom, St Paul's Cobbitty, planning for new parsonage, 27 July 1868 (manuscript held at St Paul's)
Our Babes in Heaven. Lines written on the Death of Mr and Mrs Playford's two children, James and Anna, by their friend, Joseph Kelley (c. 1864).
Private letter from John Gregson to Richard Higman, 10 October 1873
Sunday School Committee Minute Book, Newtown Methodist Church,

1855-1872. Ms with Uniting Church Archives.

Chapter 8: Stone upon stone
A Century of Journalism: The Sydney Morning Herald and its record of Australian life, 1831-1931, John Fairfax and Sons Ltd, 1931
David Moore & Rodney Hall, *Australia: Image of a Nation 1850-1950*, Collins, 1983
Souvenir of Coolamon 1881-1934, Back-to-Coolamon Week September 3-9, 1934

Australian Methodist Historical Society, Jubilee of Granville Methodism, October 1956
Weekly Advocate, Obituary of Anna Rootes, October 1888
The Methodist, Obituary of Mrs Caroline Higman, 27 August 1904
The Weekly Advocate, 1879. Various entries, particularly P.109, 'Women's Affairs No.1. Women's Work.'
The Weekly Advocate, August-September 1888

Birth certificate of Grace Playford, 12 September 1875
Notes on family history by Richard H. Higman, 1984. Privately held.
Legal papers regarding original selection by Richard Higman of Block 39, Parish of Robertson, County of Bourke, 26 February 1880 with partner Henry Bryant: Conditional Purchase Certificate 29 March 1884; Deed of Grant October 1884; partnership dissolved 26 February 1890. Privately held.

Chapter 9: Cracks in the brickwork
Alan Barcan, *A History of Australian Education*, Oxford University Press, 1980
G.L. Buxton, *The Riverina 1861-1891, an Australian Regional Study*, Melbourne University Press, 1967
J.E. Carruthers, *Memories of an Australian Ministry*, The Epworth Press, 1922
James Colwell, op.cit.
Frank Crowley, op.cit.
Eric Russell, *Victorian and Edwardian Sydney from Old Photographs*, John Ferguson, 1975

Souvenir of Coolamon, op.cit.
The Methodist, 1895-1896, particularly 13 and 28 December 1895, January 1896 Lewisham Methodist Quarterly Meeting Minutes, 1895 (ms in Uniting Church Archives, North Parramatta)

James Rootes, letters written to Mary Playford 1892-1894. Privately held.

Various official papers from New South Wales Education Department concerning appointment of Grace Playford as pupil-teacher; May 1889-June 1891. Privately held.

Bible presented to Grace Playford with inscribed flyleaf from The Boulevarde Wesleyan Sunday School 13 December 1895; annotations and dates in margins from 1896-1903. Privately held.

Grace's story
Chapter 10: A barren land

Australians: A Historical Atlas, J.C.R. Camm and John McQuilton (eds), Fairfax, Syme and Weldon Associates, 1987

Martin Dyson, Australasian Methodist Ministerial General Index, third edition, E. Whitehead and Co., 1903

Hilda M. Freeman, Murrumbidgee Memories and Riverina Reminiscences: A Collection of old bush history

Methodist Ministerial Index for Australasia, Horton and Williams, sixth edition, revised to 1926, published by authority of General Conference, 1926

Pioneers of Australian Education: A Study of the Development of Education in the Nineteenth Century, J. Turney (ed.), Sydney University Press, 1969

Bible given to Grace Playford in 1883, with marginal annotations and dates from 1888-1900. Privately held.

Notification of transfer by NSW Education Department; Grace Playford, 31 August 1897, 3 January 1898, 1 October 1898. Privately held.

The Methodist, obituary of James Rootes, 5 November 1898

Maps of western NSW, 1910, National Library of Australia, Canberra

Chapter 11: The colour of gold

James Colwell, op.cit.

Camden News, obituary of James Rootes, 8.9.1898 and 17.10.1898

Grace Playford, diary notes kept in 'Blessings Book', 12 September 1899-1901, at Gwynne and Young. Privately held.

Certificate of Classification and Inspector's Report, New South Wales Department of Education; Grace Playford, 24 October 1899

Manager's Certificate of Service, Mines Inspection Act, for William

Playford, Cullinga, NSW, 12 March 1902. Privately held.

Chapter 12: A land chosen
William A. Bayley, *Rich Earth, History of Young and the Shire of Burrandong, New South Wales*, Young Municipal Council, 1956
Michael Cannon, *Australia, Spirit of a Nation: A Bicentenary Album*, Currey O'Neill, 1987
James Colwell, *The Methodist Jubilee Conference Album 1855-1905*, containing photographs of all the ministerial and lay representatives to Conference of 1905 with historical sketch, Mark Blow, 1905

The Methodist, 14 January 1905, 18 February, 18 March 1905

Collection of cuttings and hand-copied verses collected by Grace Higman between 1896-1904. Privately held.
Marriage Certificate of James Caldwell-Higman and Grace Playford, 15 February 1905
James Caldwell-Higman, a private letter to brother Will Caldwell, 25 September 1900
Henry Playford, diary kept during journey to Richmond River, March-April 1901

Chapter 13: Spring growth
Souvenir of Coolamon, op.cit.

Coolamon Echo, 1900-1905, particularly 5 May, 2 June, 16 August, 13 October 1905, NSW State Library
The Methodist, obituary of William Playford, 31 March 1906
The Coolamon-Ganmain Review, Report of North Berry Jerry and Rannock Progress Association, 6 September 1907, 31 January 1908, 21 February 1908, National Library of Australia
J.R.C. Higman, notebook of sermons, written 1905-1910

Chapter 14: Drought
Patsy Adam-Smith, *The Anzacs*, Thomas Nelson, 1978
Souvenir of Coolamon, op.cit.

Coolamon Farmers' Review, 1914-1917, National Library of Australia

Chapter 15: Storm-clouds
C.E.W. Bean and H.S. Gullett, *Photographic Record of the War: Reproductions of Pictures Taken by the Australian Official*

Photographers, Angus and Robertson, 1938
Australia in Palestine, Gullett and Barrett (eds), Angus and Robertson, 1919
Ion Idriess, *The Desert Column*, Angus and Robertson, 1932

The Methodist, 6 January 1971, 30 June 1917
Coolamon Farmers' Review, 1917-1918

Illuminated Address, text signed 2 April 1917
Embarkation lists of 44th Infantry, A.I.F., 1917; microfiche at Australian War Memorial, Canberra
War Diaries of 12th Light Horse, manuscript recorded on location August 1917-December 1918 in Sinai and Palestine, War Memorial Archives, Canberra

Chapter 16: Blackened land
Leslie Weatherhead, *It Happened in Palestine*, Hodder and Stoughton, 1936

Coolamon Farmers Review, 1918

War Diaries of 12th Light Horse
Various postcards sent by J.R.C. Higman to children from Egypt and Palestine

Chapter 17: New green shoots
Moore and Hall, op.cit.

Coolamon Farmers Review, 1918
Wagga Wagga Express, 1925

Chapter 18: Hope for harvest
A Century of Journalism: The Sydney Morning Herald and its record of Australian Life, 1831-1931, John Fairfax and Sons Ltd, 1931
L.J. Louis and Ian Turner, *Problems of Australian History: The Depression of the 1930s*, Cassell, 1968
C.B. Schedvin, *Australia and the Great Depression: A Study of Economic Development and Policy in the 1920s and 1930s*, Sydney University Press, 1970

Legh Higman, personal diaries 1930-1934. Privately held.

Chapter 19: Threat of loss
Souvenir of Coolamon op.cit.
'Back to Coolamon Week' Souvenir, August 25-September 1, 1956
Matthew Williams, *Australia in the 1930s*, Trocadero Publishing, 1985

Legh Higman, op.cit.

Chapter 20: Harvest
J.R.C. Higman, *For Peace*, Epworth Printing and Publishing House, Sydney, 1942
Pioneers of Australia: A. Historical Review, Robert Jeffery (ed.), 1935

The Methodist, January 20 1934, April, July, September 1934

Legh Higman, op.cit.

Epilogue
Coolamon Review, 15 April, 1935, obituary of Grace Higman
The Methodist, 27 April 1935, 6 July 1935, obituary of Grace Higman
The Methodist, 22 July 1944, 2 September 1944, obituary of J.R.C. Higman

Funeral address by Rev. Russell Gibson on death of J.R.C. Higman, 7 July, 1944. Privately held.